PARADISE LOST
AND THE
ROMANTIC READER

Paradise Lost
and the
Romantic Reader

LUCY NEWLYN

CLARENDON PRESS · OXFORD
1993

Oxford University Press, Walton Street, Oxford OX2 6DP
Oxford   New York   Toronto
Delhi   Bombay   Calcutta   Madras   Karachi
Kuala Lumpur   Singapore   Hong Kong   Tokyo
Nairobi   Dar es Salaam   Cape Town
Melbourne   Auckland
and associated companies in
Berlin   Ibadan

Oxford is a trade mark of Oxford University Press

Published in the United States
by Oxford University Press Inc., New York

British Library Cataloguing in Publication Data
Data available

Library of Congress Cataloging in Publication Data
Newlyn, Lucy.
Paradise lost and the romantic reader / Lucy Newlyn.
Includes bibliographical references and index.
1. Milton, John, 1608–1674. Paradise lost. 2. Milton, John,
1608–1674—Criticism and interpretation—History—19th century.
3. English literature—19th century—History and criticism.
4. English literature—18th century—History and criticism.
5. Influence (Literary, artistic, etc.). 6. Milton, John, 1608–1674—
Influence. 7. Romanticism—Great Britain. 8. Fall of man in
literature. I. Title.
PR3562.N49   1993
821'.4—dc20   92–463
ISBN 0–19–811277–7

F 25831659

Typeset by BP Integraphics Ltd, Bath, Avon
Printed in Great Britain
on acid-free paper by
Biddles Ltd,
Guildford and King's Lynn

To Martin

'What shocks the virtuous philosopher
delights the camelion Poet'

Acknowledgements

Many of the ideas in this book have been tried out in lectures, or have come into sharper focus as the result of tutorial discussions: I would like to thank my students for everything they have contributed to its making.

I was fortunate enough to receive comments from John Carey and John Creaser on an embryonic version of Chapter 2, which subsequently grew into a lecture I delivered to the International Wordsworth Summer Conference in 1986. (Part of its argument was published the same year in *The Times Literary Supplement*.) I read a version of Chapter 5 to a graduate seminar at Cambridge, and I hope that it has benefited from the helpful criticism of those present, including John Beer. I am grateful to Jonathan Wordsworth for encouragement during the early stages of writing; to Tony Brinkley and Eve Stoddard for commenting on portions of my argument; and to Blair Worden for letting me read an article of his before its publication. The reports provided by the readers at Oxford University Press have been invaluable to me during the process of revision; and Martin Slater's questions (the more unsettling for coming from outside the discipline) have caused me to rethink some shaky ideas and assumptions. My biggest debt, though, is to Nicky Trott, who gave up valuable time to read the book in its first draft, and whose observations were wonderfully shrewd and detailed. Sarah Barrett has patiently and scrupulously copy-edited the text: any errors that remain are of course entirely of my own making.

A term's sabbatical leave enabled me to complete the book: I am grateful to the Principal and Fellows of St Edmund Hall for granting me this, and to Duncan Wu for taking over my teaching. I owe a special debt to Kate Ward-Perkins, who generously performed my pastoral and administrative duties during that time.

Martin, Paul, and Fiona have experienced the book at close quarters, and have coped with my distraction in the final stages of writing. Their companionship has been immensely helpful in seeing it (and me) through.

L.N.

St Edmund Hall, Oxford, 1991

Contents

Editions and Abbreviations Used

Listed below are the editions and individual works on which this book most heavily depends, and to which all references are made, unless it is otherwise stated. Shortened titles which appear in italics are used as abbreviations in the Notes.

Biographia	*Biographia Literaria; Collected Coleridge*, vii, ed. J. Engell and W. J. Bate (2 vols., Princeton, NJ, 1983).
Blake Poems	*Blake: The Complete Poems*, ed. W. H. Stevenson, text by D. V. Erdman (London, 1971).
Burke Enquiry	Edmund Burke, *A Philosophical Enquiry into the Origin of Our Ideas of the Sublime and Beautiful*, ed. with introd. and notes, J. T. Boulton (Oxford, 1958; repr. 1990).
Byron Poems	Lord Byron, *The Complete Poetical Works*, ed. J. McGann (6 vols., Oxford, 1980–91).
Caleb Williams	William Godwin, *Caleb Williams*, ed. D. McCracken (Oxford, 1970).
Coleridge Lectures	*Lectures 1795 on Politics and Religion; Collected Coleridge*, i, ed. L. Patton and P. Mann (Princeton, NJ, 1971).
Coleridge Letters	*The Collected Letters of Samuel Taylor Coleridge*, ed. E. L. Griggs (6 vols., Oxford, 1956–71).
Coleridge Poems	Samuel Taylor Coleridge, *Poems*, selected and ed. J. Beer (Everyman edn., London, 1974).
Collected Coleridge	*The Collected Works of Samuel Taylor Coleridge*, gen. ed. K. Coburn (Princeton, NJ, 1971–)
CPW	*The Complete Poetical Works of Samuel Taylor Coleridge*, ed. E. H. Coleridge (2 vols., Oxford, 1912): used sporadically to refer to materials (such as prefaces and plays) that do not appear in Beer's selection.
Gray, Collins, Goldsmith	*The Poems of Thomas Gray, William Collins, and Oliver Goldsmith*, ed. R. Lonsdale (London, 1969).
Hayley Life	William Hayley, *The Life of Milton* (2nd edn., 1796); fac. reprod., with introd. by J. A. Wittreich, Jr. (Gainesville, Fla., 1970).
Johnson Life	Samuel Johnson, 'Life of Milton', in *Lives of the English Poets*, ed. G. B. Hill (3 vols., Oxford, 1905), i.

Keats Letters	*Letters of John Keats*, a selection, ed. R. Gittings (Oxford, 1970).
Keats Poems	*The Poems of John Keats*, ed. M. Allott (London, 1970).
Lamb Letters	*The Letters of Charles and Mary Lamb*, ed. E. W. Marrs, Jr. (3 vols., Ithaca, NY, 1975).
Lowth Lectures	Bishop Lowth, *Lectures on the Sacred Poetry of the Hebrews* (2 vols., London, 1787.)
MHH	William Blake, *The Marriage of Heaven and Hell.*
Milton Poems	John Milton, *Complete Shorter Poems*, ed. J. Carey (London, 1968).
Milton Prose	*The Complete Prose Works of John Milton*, gen. ed. D. Wolfe (8 vols. in 10, New Haven, Conn., 1953–82).
PL	John Milton, *Paradise Lost*, ed. A. Fowler (London, 1968).
Political Justice	William Godwin, *Political Justice*, ed. I. Kramnick (Harmondsworth, Middx., 1976).
Pope Poems	*The Poems of Alexander Pope*, a 1–vol. edn. of the Twickenham Pope, ed. J. Butt (Bungay, Suffolk, 1963; repr. 1980).
Prelude	William Wordsworth, *The Prelude, 1799, 1805, 1850*, ed. J. Wordsworth, M. H. Abrams, and S. Gill (New York, 1979). All references are to the 1805 version.
Romantics on Milton	J. A. Wittreich, Jr. (ed.), *The Romantics on Milton: Formal Essays and Critical Asides* (Cleveland, OH, 1970).
Shelley	*Shelley's Poetry and Prose*, selected and ed. D. H. Reiman and S. B. Powers (New York, 1977).
Table Talk	Samuel Taylor Coleridge, *Table Talk; Collected Coleridge*, xiv, ed. C. Woodring (2 vols., Princeton, NJ, 1990).
Thomas Paine Reader	*The Thomas Paine Reader*, ed. M. Foot and I. Kramnick (Harmondsworth, Middx., 1987).
Urizen	William Blake, *The Book of Urizen.*
Vindication	Mary Wollstonecraft, *A Vindication of the Rights of Woman.*
Wollstonecraft Works	*The Works of Mary Wollstonecraft*, ed. J. Todd and M. Butler (7 vols., London, 1989).
Wordsworth	*William Wordsworth*, selected and ed. S. Gill (Oxford, 1984).
Young, *Conjectures*	Edward Young, *Conjectures on Original Composition in a Letter to the Author of Sir Charles Grandison* (London, 1759).

Introduction

> The first rule I have observed in notes on Milton and others is to take for granted that no man had ever a thought originate in his own mind; in consequence of which, if there is anything in a book like it before, it was certainly taken from that. And you may go on, particularly by their like-nesses, to the time of the deluge, and at last it amounts to this: that no man had a thought but some one found it, and it has gone down as an heirloom which one man is lucky enough to get and then another.[1]

In its contempt for the activity of source-hunting, Coleridge's rule might stand as a sort of 'anti-advertisement' for the central preoccupation, if not method, of this book. My justification for seeking out Miltonic allusions in Romantic writing is twofold: I would argue that a picture of Milton's influence on those who came after him is vital to an understanding of what Romanticism is; and I would claim that one method for building up such a picture is to analyse the verbal intricacies of Milton's presence in Romantic texts—to analyse them, moreover, with the same degree of scholarly attention that Milton's eighteenth-century editors and commentators accorded to the classical resonances of *Paradise Lost*. The limitations of such an approach do however become apparent, as soon as one realizes that Milton's influence is a much larger, more complex, and more pervasive phenomenon than any of its kind. There are aspects of poetic influence which no amount of source-hunting can adequately explain, and which would appear to support Harold Bloom's claim that 'criticism is the art of knowing the *hidden* roads that go from poem to poem'.[2]

This can be readily demonstrated by examining, for instance, the aesthetic assumptions which are encoded in Coleridge's comment quoted above. In its use of Milton as a test case for literary-critical methodology, the comment is a typical product of Enlightenment debate, and might have been made at any point in the eighteenth century. But the ends to which it appropriates Milton are heavily accented and historically specific: Coleridge's open rejection of neo-classical values (learnedness, imitation) and his implicit avowal of their op-posites (originality, imagination, creative genius) announce him to be a 'Romantic reader', whose tastes would not have been thus a century earlier—indeed, would probably not have been thus before the publication of Young's *Conjectures on Original Composition* in 1759. His comment inserts itself into a debate whose inflections are well established by the time he writes it, and whose evolution has already been highly influential for the changing character of

---

[1] Coleridge, 'Philosophical Lectures at the Crown and Anchor', Lecture 10 (1 Mar. 1819); in *Romantics on Milton*, 238–9.

[2] *The Anxiety of Influence: A Theory of Poetry* (Oxford, 1973), 96.

English poetry. Crucially—and this is a point I shall later develop in full—it is a debate in which the reception of *Paradise Lost* has played a persistent and significant role. The formation of Romantic aesthetics is bound up with Miltonic influence in ways that are indirect, and possibly incalculable: certainly it would not be easy to chart them through quotations and allusions alone.

At the level of individual poetic utterances, the importance of Milton's influence is well known, and has spawned whole libraries of theses, monographs, articles, and notes. Its extent cannot be overstated, nor has it yet been exhausted as a worthwhile subject of study. Every one of the writers belonging to the tradition of English Romanticism could be said to have engaged with what Milton had to say, as well as with his poetic reputation (and by 'engaged' I mean something less antagonistic than combat, but more argumentative than imitation or assimilation). Without a doubt, *Paradise Lost* represented a challenge to the poetic ambition of those who came after Milton; but it also voiced certain theological and political ideas, and stood for certain moral and aesthetic values, more powerfully than any other poem in the language. These ideas and values were confronted, by Romantic writers, as part of the process whereby their own poetic, moral, and philosophical projects came to be defined. The Romantic dialogue with Milton amounts to something more, therefore, than passive homage or servile imitation: it has intellectual content, and is involved with the expression of identity.

Following through the implications of Coleridge's comment, it can be seen that Miltonic allusions are not just coincidental borrowings, made by writers who passively receive the ideas and words of others, like impressions on the *tabula rasa* of the mind. (Here Coleridge's epistemological assumptions become apparent: he rejects the 'heirloom' theory of echo because it makes the mind lazily receptive, as in the models purveyed by Locke and Hartley, which he came to reject.[3]) These allusions are, rather, a meaningful register of the extent to which Milton's ideas are actively refuted, approved, or discarded, by each of the many writers concerned. An informed understanding of *The Prelude*, for instance, is not possible without seeing the extent of the author's conscious and detailed reliance on *Paradise Lost*. In declaring independence from its central values, Wordsworth was not simply, in some generalized sense, adapting the epic tradition to his own needs; he was appropriating Milton's specifically *Christianized* epic in order to make his own personal and secular claims. Equally, one cannot begin to understand Blake's visionary iconoclasm without first placing him in a prophetic tradition and next grasping the extent to which his undermining of authority depended on the massively ambitious project of rewriting the Bible and *Paradise Lost*.

Milton played a crucial role, then, in the process of self-definition which each of the Romantics separately underwent; but he is also bound up in the

---

[3] For Coleridge's rejection of Locke, see *Coleridge Letters*, ii. 708–9, iv. 575; for his refutation of materialism, including associationism, see *Biographia*, i. 89–140.

macrocosmic evolution of what is called 'Romanticism'. Analysing the reception of *Paradise Lost* by writers of the eighteenth and early nineteenth centuries is not just a question of tracing the intricate verbal connections that exist, as though in a vacuum, between different texts, written by different writers, in different centuries; it involves examining the part Milton played in the most important political, aesthetic, and philosophical changes that were taking place during those years. Ideas about revolution, for instance, were given direction by Milton's support of regicide and the liberty of the press (both of these emerging from his political pamphlets). They were also shaped by the more ambivalent and problematic 'republicanism' of *Paradise Lost* itself. The concept of the sublime is inseparable from Milton's influence on eighteenth-century theorists: Addison, Johnson, Burke, Blair all turn to *Paradise Lost* for their prime examples of sublimity of language; so that by the end of the eighteenth century, Milton and the sublime have come to be regarded as practically synonymous. (Indeed, certain passages of *Paradise Lost* have by then emerged as touchstones for the poetic sublime.) Most important of all, though, is the part played by Milton in the formation of Romantic attitudes toward the 'imagination': that creative aspect of the human mind which is seen sometimes as transgressive, and sometimes as celestial. Milton stands as the prime example of imagination to those who come after him, and at the same time *Paradise Lost* demonstrates the moral ambivalence—the angelic heights and Satanic depths—of this 'Vision and ... faculty divine'.[4]

AIMS AND INTENTIONS

As my discussion so far has suggested, there are two aspects of the Romantics' relationship with Milton, which would seem to invite two quite different critical approaches. There is the matter of individual writers, engaging with a particular text in order to define their own creative identities, which asks for the detection and interpretation of quotations, echoes, and allusions, in accordance with a preconceived theory of influence. There is also the matter of reception, as an aspect of intellectual history: this requires an account of the transformation of political, religious, philosophical, and aesthetic ideas to which Milton contributed, and by which he was himself constructed and reconstructed in the minds of generations of readers. Recent studies of poetic influence (notably those of Harold Bloom and Leslie Brisman) have rightly emphasized both the excitement and the anxiety generated in Romantic writers by Milton's overshadowing presence. But in presenting the emergence of individual creative identities, purely as a matter of canonical or 'family' relations, such studies have inadequately explained Milton's influence as a historical phenomenon. Equally, in stressing the extent to which Romantic tradition was shaped by the assimilation, reformulation, and rejection of values embodied in *Paradise Lost*, the

[4] Wordsworth, *The Excursion*, i. 79.

'revisionary' nature of Romantic allusions has emerged as of prime importance, whereas the continuity between Milton's own habits of allusion and those of his followers has tended to be overlooked. Only by placing Romanticism in its eighteenth-century context can one hope to restore the balance, thereby per-ceiving change in its proper relation to continuity—individuals in relation to larger trends. And only through close analysis of a wide range of texts will the implications of 'continuity' (by which I mean something very different from the passive transmission of echoes as 'heirlooms') become fully apparent.

Broadly speaking, my book is intended to mediate between the two approaches to Milton's influence which I have outlined above, so as to correct their respec-tive deficiencies, and show the interrelatedness of cultural reception and textual allusion. As the thematic organization of my material suggests, I am not pri-marily concerned with intertextuality as an aspect of what Harold Bloom calls the 'family romance'—that is, the struggle made by separate authorial per-sonalities, or psyches, for creative identity. Rather, I wish to draw attention to practices of allusion shared by different Romantic writers, which when inter-preted comparatively might be said to constitute a 'Romantic reading' of *Para-dise Lost*. For this purpose, my study of intertextual references has necessarily to be mapped onto a broader understanding of reception.

In my first chapter, I examine the history of Milton's reputation, in the eighteenth and early nineteenth centuries, as a cultural phenomenon. I am concerned here to establish the ingredients that went to the making of the 'Milton cult', and to trace the origin of appropriations which become con-solidated as Romantic traditions: Milton as political, moral, and spiritual guide; Milton as exemplar of sublimity and imagination; Milton as sublime phenom-enon; Milton as God. My central focus is on the factors in Milton's reception which were responsible for merging his authorial identity with the theological tenor of *Paradise Lost*, thus producing a model of 'deified' authority which is unparalleled in English literary history. This I see as having important reper-cussions: ideas about originality and imagination changed rapidly in the mid-eighteenth century; and this occurred (at least in part) as a response to Milton's reception. The phenomenon of 'Romanticism' is itself bound up with the nature of those changing ideas.

Since much of my argument in this first chapter depends on analysing the ways in which Milton as authority figure was seen, transformed, and distorted, my method involves for the most part the study of critical observations, invo-cations, and quotations. Only occasionally do I make use of the less overt (and more ambiguous) kinds of intertextuality with which the remainder of the book is concerned. In thus separating invocation and intertextual reference, I wish to underline one of the central findings of my research: namely, the apparent contradiction between the 'Milton' who is constructed through conscious and explicit acts of appropriation and the Milton who emerges from carefully recep-tive and imitative habits of allusion. The first is a model of authority, intentionality, and religious certainty—a caricature of the deified imagination, which Romantic readers frequently contrast with the 'negative capability' of Shakespeare.[5] The second is a collocation of ambiguities and indeterminacies, gathered from the Romantics' close reading (and rereading) of *Paradise Lost*.

I hope it will become evident, from the ways in which Romantic writers replicate Milton's open-ended textual procedures, that they were alert to a quality in *Paradise Lost* which they would themselves have labelled 'Shakespearian'. That they chose not to foreground this, in their invocations and critical observations, is itself an interesting phenomenon. The reception of Milton is thus historically implicated in the polarization of two kinds of poetic activity—intentional and closed on the one hand (Milton), ambiguous and open-ended on the other (Shakespeare); a division which we can still see reflected in our own critical practices and assumptions, especially where the interpretative choices of *Paradise Lost* are concerned. It is the aim of this book to reintegrate the 'negatively capable' Milton who has been suppressed, not only by Romantic caricature, but by all those replicas of Romantic caricature that are perpetuated in the critical debate surrounding *Paradise Lost*. To this end, I turn from the reception of an author to the reception of a text; and my method hereafter involves close intertextual analysis, of a kind devised to highlight the continuities between Milton's own allusive habits and those of the writers who came after him.

I establish the grounds for claiming continuity firstly by defining allusion as a focus for indeterminacy and secondly by offering an analysis of Milton's ambiguous poetic modes. I argue that, from opposite sides of the Milton debate, it has been customary to acknowledge the presence of ambiguities in *Paradise Lost*, but none the less to underestimate their importance—thereby perpetuating the Romantic caricature which I have described above. Thus, Miltonists (most notably Stanley Fish) have gone along with the myth of Milton as a repressive authority figure, to the detriment of the text's open-endedness; while Romanticists (headed by Harold Bloom) have overemphasized the revisionary nature of Romantic allusions, in the belief that Milton (as the same authority figure) demanded to be overthrown by his misreaders. By restoring the 'subtext' of *Paradise Lost*, it is possible to adjust the perspective from which Romantic developments can be viewed, replacing a revisionary model of allusion with one that is open-ended.

The theory of allusion established in my second chapter therefore discards the 'one-way system' of Bloom's revisionary ratios, and suggests an alternative which works both ways, thereby stressing reader interpretation, as opposed to authorial intention. Allusion, I claim, countering both Bloom and Hollander, is a crossing-over from one conceptual frame into another. It involves not so much the 'revision' of an original context as the ambiguous conjunction of two

---

[5] *Keats Letters*, 43. Negative capability is discussed at various points in this book: see esp. Chs. 2 and 7.

different contexts, each modifying the other. Wittgenstein's discussion of Gombrich's 'duck-rabbit' provides a model of indeterminacy which prompts my central argument, and this in turn establishes a method for analysing the allusive procedures of *Paradise Lost*. Instances of classical and Shakespearian allusion, of dramatic and verbal anticipation, of cross-reference and self-echo, are used to demonstrate the sustained formal ambiguities of a poem which is traditionally thought of as authoritarian and closed. My central claim is that the incremental effect on the reader of these ambiguous poetic modes is such as to qualify any moral 'message' that it is supposed Milton intends to convey. The text (as distinct from its author) stands as one kind of evidence for Northrop Frye's claim that 'Poetry is a *disinterested* use of words';[6] and furthermore, it appears to invite a response on the part of the reader which is itself 'negatively capable'.

The remainder of the book is concerned with the ways in which Romantic writing reproduces, amplifies, and prolongs the ambiguities of *Paradise Lost*. Since, as I have suggested, it is important to perceive the interconnectedness of cultural reception and textual allusion, I have adopted a thematic approach throughout. Instead of analysing Milton's 'influence', author by author, as though it were solely a matter of individual talent struggling for self-definition, I examine 'allusion' as both the product and the expression of larger cultural concerns. To this end, I have grouped commentaries on a range of texts by different authors under appropriate headings: Politics, Religion, Sex, Subjectivity, and Imagination. (Two further topics, 'the Sublime' and 'Language', are not given separate chapter-length treatment, but are addressed at various points in the book—most notably in Chapters 1, 6 and 7.)

There is no particular reason for the order in which topics appear, except in the instance of 'Politics', which comes first because the beginnings of Romanticism, as it is traditionally defined, coincide with the French Revolution. These topics are not by any means supposed to offer an exhaustive account of the spheres in which Miltonic allusion is significant; nor do I intend to imply that they existed as separate categories in the minds of each of the writers involved. They are meant, rather, to provide a convenient means of organizing disparate material, which none the less meaningfully interconnects. In my discussion of Blake's *Milton*, most of these separate themes will be reassembled in the analysis of a single poem: this text receives chapter-length analysis, for reasons which I discuss below.

My third chapter focuses on the political debate which is provoked in and by *Paradise Lost*. Ever since Blake appropriated Satan as republican hero of the poem, and made him the mouthpiece for Milton's own political ideals, there has ensued a misunderstanding of the ways in which the Romantics, generally, read the poem's political meaning. By tracing some of the ambiguous trends discern-

---

[6] *Anatomy of Criticism: Four Essays* (Princeton, NJ, 1957; repr. Harmondsworth, Middx., 1990), 4.

ible in their allusive language, it is possible to undo the assumption that they made a straightforward alignment between Milton and Satan (thereby reading the text as political allegory), and so to perceive the underlying concerns they had in common with their precursor. The writing of Wordsworth and Coleridge pre-1800 provides a detailed focus for analysis, and is used to demonstrate that Satanic allusion is not the register of ideological certitude, but of moral and political *angst*: the Romantics turn to Milton when they are themselves preoccupied, as he had been, by the problematic relation of earthly politics to religious or moral truth. A doubleness of historical perspective thus provides a useful context for reassessing the ambivalent and changing responses to Revolution which are registered through Miltonic allusion.

Under the heading of 'Religion', I examine the problem of the origin of evil, and the linked concern of responsibility, both of which are reflected in Romantic literature's many and various rewritings of the Fall. A range of procedures is examined, from Coleridge's conservative use of theodicy in 'The Ancient Mariner' to the radical myth-making of Blake, and each is discussed in relation to the unresolved problems which arise from God's status in *Paradise Lost*. The connection between political tyranny and religious oppression (which radicals such as Godwin make the basis of their atheist claims) is shown to have a parallel in Milton's depiction of God, and in some of the political theory which is propounded as the word of God by His archangels. Furthermore, the questioning of religion which is achieved in Romantic versions of the Fall is shown to be an expansion of Milton's own procedures for dramatizing the Almighty—procedures which inevitably involve giving Him human characteristics and human foibles. Thus, the deeply troubled and divided attitude of Romantic writers toward religious authority can be seen to emerge as much through the amplification of Miltonic ambiguity as through revisionary misreading. Milton as monolithic authority figure is deconstructed by the indeterminacies of his text.

Just so with Milton as patriarch. My fifth chapter offers a reading of Eve's fall, in the light of post-Miltonic treatments of female sexuality, which brings to the fore the latent feminist implications of *Paradise Lost*. The parallels Milton suggests between Satan and Eve are sufficient, I argue, to enlist the reader's sympathy for their shared plight of subjection, and so to read 'falling' as liberation. Milton's followers extend this pattern by internalizing Satan as an aspect of the female psyche, and by presenting the fall into experience as a necessary and beneficial stage of growth. Their use of Miltonic habits of anticipation and conflation has the further effect of dissolving the distinction between fallen and unfallen states, thus complicating the moral issues. My argument depends on the close and detailed exposition of five Romantic texts, all of them composed by male writers. Comparative analysis demonstrates that *Paradise Lost* is not used as a model of rigid morality and patriarchal repression, but as a vehicle for expressing sympathy with the female lot, and for presenting sex as growth.

Furthermore, the open-ended textual procedures which are here adopted can be seen to anticipate later writing, by women such as Charlotte and Emily Brontë, who have formerly been identified as revisionary 'misreaders' of Milton. It is hoped that an awareness of the continuity of such textual procedures might clear a path for the 'feminizing' of *Paradise Lost*.

My study of 'Subjectivity' sustains an equation between the expansion of human consciousness and the fortunate fall, but takes the further step of linking this with Romantic aesthetics. Subjectivity is seen by Romantic writers as the price of experience—a pattern they emphasize in their use of Miltonic allusions to frame imaginative activity as a mode of transgression, and to suggest an intimate connection between loss and gain. The formal indeterminacies of *Paradise Lost* themselves become models for the loss/gain paradigm on which Romantic aesthetics depend. Thus, the confusion which Milton allows between fallen and unfallen language (or between innocent and experienced perspectives) can be understood in terms of the gain of human subjectivity which is consequent on falling; and it can be celebrated as such, even while there is an apparent lamenting of the loss of Adamic language, the disappearance of original plenitude and pre-lapsarian truth. Linguistic indeterminacy is thereby made a function of imaginative activity: a pattern which accommodates it to Burkean and Kantian notions of the sublime. This loss/gain paradigm is replicated in the ambiguous games with perspective which are played by Gray, Wordsworth, Blake, and De Quincey, all of whom appear to be calling Milton to mind; but it is also perceptible in the (less verbally allusive) ambiguities of Lamb, whose concepts of stage illusion and irony have a useful part to play in defining the role of the reader, and indeed subjectivity itself.

My study of the release of subjectivity is complemented by an account of more sober Romantic attitudes to imagination. In Chapter 7, I am concerned to trace the preoccupation with responsibility and control which (in differing degrees, according to the strength and nature of their political and religious affiliations) caused the Romantics to perceive in imagination a threateningly disruptive and antisocial force. In the first part of this chapter, I concentrate specifically on the ways in which this manifests itself, in treatments of the *poetic* imagination. Here I provide close commentary on Collins's 'Ode on the Poetical Character', on 'Kubla Khan', and on passages from *The Prelude*. As these poems demonstrate, the readiness with which a given Romantic writer is prepared to align himself with a Satanic perspective suggests the extent of his willingness to usurp divinity: *Paradise Lost* is seen to acquire the status of a sacred text, while competition with Milton is felt to be analogous to the dangerous and potentially blasphemous activity of competing with God.

My attention turns in the chapter's second half to a wider contextualizing of imagination and to its moral, social and political responsibilities. Here I focus less on the implications of a struggle for poetic power, in which verbal allusions are used knowingly by the poets concerned, than on something akin to the idea of 'conscience', as it emerges in Miltonic patterns (and sometimes allusions). My study of De Quincey's *Confessions of an English Opium Eater* establishes this notion of conscience in an openly Christian context; while a range of poems by Keats illustrate its undoctrinal presence as a counter to the escapist imagination. Two poems of Shelley's, 'Julian and Maddalo' and 'Alastor', demonstrate the sense in which even atheist formulations of the imagination and of the self are haunted by the Satanic threats of egoism, irresponsibility, and over-idealization.

In offering this bipartite treatment of imagination, my exploration of the Milton phenomenon is designedly different from Harold Bloom's. I shift my focus away from the anxiety of influence by placing discussion of Miltonic allusion in two contexts that are wider than the psychological (though they do not therefore exclude psychological concerns): the first of these is a context of eighteenth-century poetic tradition and debate, the second that of social morality. I have the further intention, in this extended treatment of the imagination, of stressing a cautionary aspect to Romanticism, which I see as importantly qualifying the celebratory confidence of High Romantic Argument. In my discussion particularly of Keats and Shelley, I join a growing consensus of opinion which acknowledges the duality of Romanticism, its tendency towards ambivalence, irony, and self-critique.

In my final chapter I turn to Blake's *Milton*, which has a special claim on my attention for a number of reasons. First, it is the single most detailed and extensive treament of Milton (as cultural symbol, as authority figure, and as exemplar of creativity) produced by any Romantic writer. Its somewhat anomalous position in this respect can be realized very quickly by glancing at Joseph Wittreich's anthology, *The Romantics on Milton*, where it occupies sixty-three uninterrupted and unignorable pages, making a curious contrast with the fragmentary observations, sometimes only a sentence or so in length, of other Romantic writers. Its range and scope are indeed such that it might appropriately stand as the centre-piece for any of the chapters in this book: in it, Blake confronts the issue of Milton's reception as a matter of general concern, holding *Paradise Lost* responsible for ideas about politics, religion, sexuality, and the imagination which in his view need to be revised. In its ambitious engagement with all these ideas, Blake's prophecy underlines Milton's important cultural and historical status, thus highlighting the insufficiency of a purely psychological approach to the study of influence. And in its diversity, it incidentally offers the opportunity of bringing together the various themes which I shall be treating separately in other chapters: a reintegration that is necessary, if one is to realize 'Milton' as more than the sum of these various parts.

My most important reason for giving *Milton* extended treatment, however, is that it stands in a unique position in relation to other Romantic texts: in self-consciously crossing the border-line between 'critical' and 'creative', it belongs neither solely to the category of 'invocation' and 'reception' explored in

Chapter 1 nor to the category of 'allusion' discussed throughout the remainder of my book. In this respect, it offers a special challenge to the division I am proposing, between acts of critical appropriation in which Milton becomes a figure of authority, and acts of creative assimilation in which *Paradise Lost* is plundered for textual ambiguities. I hope to meet this challenge by arguing that Blake perceives and exploits such a disjunction, as a means of restoring the open-ended Milton who has become obscured in the process of reception, and whom Blake sees as a more salutary role model for his own beliefs and creative practices than the authoritarian alternative. Blake makes powerful and sustained use in *Milton* of allusive techniques which I shall be examining throughout this book: techniques which have their origin in *Paradise Lost*, and which could be said to reveal evidence of 'negative capability' in Milton himself. Furthermore, Blake appears to do this more consistently, and with more consideration of the implications, than do any of the other writers with whom I shall be concerned. For these reasons, I not only give *Milton* the extended treatment of an entire chapter but offer it as a model for the critical procedures which I shall myself be adopting throughout this book.

CRITICAL BEARINGS

My concern with the reception of *Paradise Lost*, as opposed to its authorial intention, might at first sight suggest that this book will be of limited significance to Milton specialists. I have, however, engaged (particularly in Chapter 2) with what I see as a consolidated tradition of Milton criticism, deriving from Stanley Fish, and I have attempted to counter its authoritarian reading of *Paradise Lost* with a closely argued and illustrated alternative. It is of particular interest that Fish's book, *Surprised By Sin: The Reader in Paradise Lost* (1967), should depend on reader-response theory, since this makes it readily available to critique through my own procedures. That Fish's programmatic application of method is brilliantly persuasive is no doubt borne out by the continuing influence of his argument on Miltonists of every conceivable kind. Its repression of ambiguity, however, makes it uncongenial to the approach I have here formulated. Fish himself provides a good antidote to the conclusions he reached in 1967, in an essay called 'Interpreting the *Variorum*', first published in *Critical Inquiry* in 1976. Here, the closed procedures for interpretation which he had earlier outlined are replaced with an open-ended model similar to the one that I have adopted:

> In a sequence where a reader first structures the field he inhabits and then is asked to restructure it (by changing an assignment of speaker and realigning attitudes and positions) there is no question of priority among his structurings; no one of them, even if it is the last, has privilege; each is equally legitimate, each equally the proper object of analysis, because each is equally an event in his experience.[7]

---

[7] 'Interpreting the *Variorum*', in D. Lodge (ed.), *Modern Criticism and Theory: A Reader* (London, 1988), 319.

In following and amplifying this argument, the conceptual framework I rely on is confessedly eclectic. By and large, my concern is with reading practices rather than with reception theory: in so far as my method has a theoretical analogue, however, it is to be found in Iser's phenomenological approach to reader response. The point at which this becomes most apparent is in my discussion of the *Gestalt* of allusion (see Chapter 2): here I consider 'allusion' as it relates to acts of recognition and interpretation, taking as my model Wittgenstein's discussion of 'seeing as' (*Philosophical Investigations*[7]). In the application of *Gestalt* theory to a literary text, I owe a debt to Iser's argument in *The Reading Process: A Phenomenological Approach*.[9] The adaptation of this argument, both to the practice of alluding and to the reader's role in interpreting allusion, is my own—though I have recently encountered something similar, in the introduction to *Intertextuality: Theories and Practices*, edited by Michael Worton and Judith Still. What these authors call a 'tropological' reading of quotation is one that '"sees it as" something other than it is/was in its original context, sees it as metaphor'. They point to an analogy between this 'act of reading' and Ricœur's description of 'the iconic moment' in metaphor:

The reader passively receives the vehicle and actively tries to understand not only the tenor but also the Gestalt, the figure in which similarity or analogy coheres. The tenor of the quotation-as-metaphor encompasses its first meaning and its interpretation by the quoting author, but the Gestalt, formed or determined by the reader, is ambiguous (like Wittgenstein's duck-rabbit). . . . In each encounter with a quotation, the reader perceives that, while there is an obvious conflict between sameness or identity and difference, there is also a covert fusion of differences *within* the single textual utterance.[10]

Worton and Still go on to suggest that 'every quotation is a metaphor which speaks of that which is absent and which engages the reader in a speculative activity'. My own analysis (see particularly Chapters 2 and 6) bears this out; but I lay particular emphasis on the refusal of closure which such 'speculative activity' involves. My interest in *Gestalt* is thus closely linked to my wider concern with the aesthetics of indeterminacy.

Throughout this book, my use of the word 'indeterminacy' evokes a configuration of ideas—of ambiguity, of impartiality, of open-endedness, and of unrepresentability—which are valued for the interpretative freedom they give to the reader, and for their creation of an aesthetic space that *appears to be* separate from 'doctrine' or 'ideology'. (Only 'appears to be', for reasons which will become apparent below.) In emphasizing the role of the reader, I examine the increased subjectivity which is invited by, as well as involved in, Romantic writing; and I have a particular interest in tracing the relationship between sublimity as a

[8] Trans. G. E. M. Anscombe (Oxford, 1958; repr. 1963), 194.
[9] Included in Lodge (ed.), *Modern Criticism and Theory*, 211–28.
[10] M. Worton and J. Still (eds.), *Intertextuality: Theories and Practices* (Manchester, 1990), 11–12.

Romantic aesthetic and indeterminacy as a function of reader response. I focus
on Kant's definition of the sublime, in which the displeasure entailed by the
failure of representation is converted into the pleasure of imaginative deferral—
what Wordsworth calls the 'something evermore about to be'.[11] This provides a
model for indeterminacy as an aesthetic which (either explicitly or implicitly)
foregrounds reader response, thus converting the 'loss' or 'failure' of coherent
meaning into the 'gain' or 'success' of interpretative potential.

In my concern with indeterminacy, I am doubtless in danger of betraying what
Jerome McGann would call 'an uncritical absorption in Romanticism's own
self-representations'.[12] That is to say, I read Romantic texts in the light of
Burkean and Kantian theories of the sublime, and I freely borrow my terminology from the poetry and the literary criticism of Romantic writers: notably
'imagination' from Wordsworth and Coleridge, 'contraries' from Blake, 'negative capability' from Keats, 'irony' from Lamb, and the concept of 'Romantic
irony' from Schlegel. Furthermore, I extend the aesthetic of indeterminacy not
only backwards—to pre-Romantic texts such as Collins's 'Ode on the Poetical
Character' and Pope's *The Rape of the Lock* and, even further, to my consideration of *Paradise Lost* itself—but also forwards, to the concerns of twentieth-
century critical theory. In my sporadic use of terms such as 'subtext' and
'deconstruction', and in my borrowing of Barthes's distinction between
'readerly' and 'writerly', I may appear to be doing no more than translating
Romantic assumptions into more recently articulated critical vocabulary, while
leaving those assumptions essentially unchanged. Moreover, it may seem at
times that I dissolve historical distinctions in order to assert, not 'continuity' as
such, but permanence, thus conniving in the perpetuation and ossification of
Romantic ideas—or, as McGann would put it, transforming 'the critical illu-
sions of poetry into the worshipped truths of culture'.[13]

My defence against this charge can, I think, be made in McGann's own terms.
I have a *historical* interest in explaining the emergence of the aesthetic of indeterminacy *as a Romantic phenomenon*. I am in agreement with his view that 'the
polemic of Romantic poetry . . . is that it will not be polemical; its doctrine, that
it is non-doctrinal; and its ideology, that it transcends ideology'.[14] Therefore,
in using the ambiguities of *Paradise Lost* as 'one kind of evidence' for Northrop
Frye's claim that 'Poetry is a disinterested use of words' (see p. 6 above) I am
fully aware that they are being pressed in to the service of an argument whose
origins are Romantic. However, I share with Clifford Siskin a mistrust of
'criticism with a mission': McGann's desire to expose as anachronistic all those
Romantic ideas which have survived into the late twentieth century seems to me
to ignore what Siskin calls the 'ongoing power of the discourse' to which those

---

[11] *Prelude* vi. 542. For strategies of interruption and deferral in definitions of sublimity, see
Ch. 6.
[12] *The Romantic Ideology: A Critical Investigation* (Chicago, 1983), 1.   [13] Ibid. 135.
[14] Ibid. 70.

ideas belong.[15] My critical purchase on Romanticism must come from the historical contextualization which I offer, rather than from the uprooting of Romantic ideology which McGann proposes. I examine the indeterminacies of *Paradise Lost*, then, not as formal properties of a text which floats free of history, but as a function of that text's reception, by time-bound individuals. I have no particular investment in undoing any one stage in the evolutionary process which that reception involves.

In respect of indeterminacy, my reading of Romantic texts has been deeply influenced, and persuaded, by two very powerful books: Anne Mellor's *English Romantic Irony* and Tilottama Rajan's *Dark Interpreter: The Discourse of Romanticism*. The first offers a coherent account of Schlegelian theory, skilfully applying it to a range of major Romantic texts, and suggesting the presence within them of 'Philosophical irony, the inevitable and all-important consciousness of the limitations of human knowledge and of human language', which is 'the necessary prerequisite and counterforce to love and imagination'.[16] The second examines in Romanticism 'the peculiar coexistence of one discourse with another that radically contradicts it', stressing that 'the text cannot simply be replaced by a subtext', and that 'the official content of a work does not cease to exist because it is undermined from within'.[17] This emphasis on Romanticism's doubleness I have found particularly illuminating for the link it suggests with the ambiguities inherent in *Paradise Lost*. Indeed, if I have an important difference with Rajan, it is that she overlooks continuity:

Where previous periods saw literature as not permanently subject to temporality, as the unmediated or (in the case of Milton) mediated expression of a transcendent language, the Romantic period recognises that the discourse of innocence is spoken from within experience.

My own work, therefore, seeks to discover the sense in which, for Milton too, 'the discourse of innocence is spoken from within experience', establishing *Paradise Lost* as the type and model of an ambivalence which is amplified by the Romantic reader.[18]

METHODOLOGY

The theory of literary influence with which this book most evidently engages is Harold Bloom's. However, I resolutely side-step the question frequently asked in the wake of *The Anxiety of Influence* —namely, 'did Milton really make his followers that anxious?'—for the simple reason that I think it the wrong ques-

---

[15] *The Historicity of Romantic Discourse* (New York, 1988), 57, 60.
[16] A. K. Mellor, *English Romantic Irony* (Cambridge, Mass., 1980), 11.
[17] T. Rajan, *Dark Interpreter: The Discourse of Romanticism* (Ithaca, NY, 1980), 22.
[18] Ibid. 261.

tion. As my discussion of the 'Milton cult' shows (see Chapter 1), there were many and various reasons for the extraordinary reception of *Paradise Lost,* and for the deification of its author. The Freudian explanation of anxiety offered first by Walter Jackson Bate[19] and later by Bloom deals powerfully and persuasively with the psychological dimensions of a phenomenon whose implications are also religious, philosophical, and aesthetic. To be drawn into anti-Bloomian replies, of the kind that have recently become the norm, is to remain within the psychological parameters laid down by the Bloomian system, and so to ignore these macrocosmic concerns. Dustin Griffin's book, *Regaining Paradise* (1986) is a case in point: a great deal of anxious energy is here wasted in fending off the suggestion that Milton caused Oedipal anxiety in his followers. In at least one of the cases addressed (Cowper), such anxiety is highly plausible, and at the same time there are a number of larger (but by no means incompatible) issues that might usefully be examined. The fact that what is being termed 'anxiety' is a widespread phenomenon, and that this can be explained by considering the contested status of the imagination at a time when God was still very much alive, is something that Griffin allows to escape from view. He does so because his adoption of an anti-Bloomian position prevents the larger concerns from being perceived.[20]

There is, moreover, a tendency for anti-Bloomians to move the discussion of influence further into the arena of psycho-biography than Bloom himself takes it: Jonathan Bate's *Shakespeare and the English Romantic Imagination* (1986) and Edwin Stein's *Wordsworth's Art of Allusion* (1988) replace Bloom's pugnaciously attractive system of revisionary ratios with value judgements and personal testimonials, designed to prove that influence is not anxiety but creative stimulus. This does nothing effectual to contest Bloom's proposition, since he himself believes influence to be both: believes it, crucially, to be the one *because* the other. A vulgarized version of the 'anxiety of influence' tends to forget how powerfully coherent Bloom's explanation is, at the figurative level on which it is intended to operate. To read his analysis of the troping functions of language as though it were purely a matter of the clash between personalities is at once to reduce the subtlety of what he has to say and to leave unchallenged the position from which he says it. Studies such as Paul Sherwin's *Precious Bane* (1977) or, more recently, Robin Jarvis's *Wordsworth, Milton and the Theory of Poetic Relations* (1991) are more persuasive, because written from a perspective that is sympathetically and knowledgeably Bloomian.

Within its own terms, then, the Freudian model offered by Bloom remains more compelling than the replies it has engendered, most of which are forced into positions of defensiveness which involve a misreading of those terms. There is, indeed, nothing more supportive of the argument which *The Anxiety of Influence* offers than the reception of *The Anxiety of Influence*: it has established

---

[19] *The Burden of the Past and the English Poet* (London, 1971).
[20] Cowper's anxiety in relation to Milton is discussed in Ch. 1.

itself as a text analogous to *Paradise Lost*, in the degree of 'revisionary' creativity it has made possible; and this, in its turn, has caused some of its central assumptions to become distorted and misconceived. In offering a reply to Bloom, I have attempted to keep these distortions in view, and to avoid repeating them. My intention is to *supplement* his analysis of individual creativity with a larger historical understanding of intra-poetic relations, rather than to replace (or reverse the direction of) his psychological model for intertextual language.

Bloom's use of Freudian theory pushes the phenomenon of influence-as-anxiety firmly into the unconscious, where it happens behind the screen of verbal borrowings easily discernible to the reader. This makes his method unhelpful as a model for discussion of echoes and allusions themselves, which we might think of as the audible traces of other writers, as opposed to 'the hidden roads that go from poem to poem'. Leslie Brisman, on the other hand, makes more attempt to engage with the phenomenon of intertextuality, as empirical proof of literary influence. His book, *Milton's Poetry of Choice and its Romantic Heirs* (1973) offers the nearest critical analogue I can find for the combination of close commentary with wider ranging thematic discussion, which I have myself employed. Some of Brisman's concerns are further pursued in my own treatment of choice, but with an altogether different focus (see Chapter 2); and whereas his analysis extends to the whole of Milton, mine concentrates exclusively on *Paradise Lost*.

Three further discussions, more theoretical than Brisman's, have been useful in clarifying my ideas on allusion. An article published by Carmela Perri in *Poetics*, 7 (1978) draws attention to the acts of 'recognising, remembering, realizing, connecting' which are necessary for allusion to work; and discusses the pleasure these acts involve, by way of analogy with the 'rediscovery of something familiar' which Freud sees as an important ingredient in jokes. (I focus on such pleasurable acts myself, in the discussions of allusion and reader response which are to be found in Chapters 2 and 6.) John Hollander, in *The Figure of Echo: A Mode of Allusion in Milton and After* (1981), offers a diachronic definition of echo which is in some respects close to mine; but he follows Bloom in placing undue emphasis on revision, in what he terms 'echo metaleptic'. More recently, Michael Worton and Judith Still, in their Introduction to *Intertextuality: Theories and Practices*, give a full historical account of approaches to intertextuality, from Plato to Kristeva (including the account of allusion as a species of metaphor, discussed above), and offer an extremely useful general bibliography.

My account of methodology would not be complete without a full acknowledgement of the contribution made by Joseph Wittreich to the study of Milton's tradition and legacy (though, significantly, not to the study of allusion itself). *The Romantics on Milton* (1970) provides an anthology of observations, arranged author by author, through which one is enabled to build up a picture of the (conscious and critical) reception of Milton by his Romantic readers. *Milton and the Line of Vision* (1975) places Milton in a tradition of prophecy going back, through Spenser, to the Bible: this 'line of vision' is seen by Wittreich as running counter to the 'line of wit'. *Angel of Apocalypse: Blake's Idea of Milton* (1975) analyses the critical reception of Milton by his misguided eighteenth-century commentators, and traces Blake's reclamation of his true prophetic voice; and *Visionary Poetics: Milton's Tradition and his Legacy* (1979) pursues the inheritance of the prophetic tradition, more generally amongst Milton's followers. More recently, Wittreich has departed from the canonized representatives of a male tradition, to research the reception of Milton by eighteenth-century women, not all of them established writers. *Feminist Milton* (1987) may well be his finest contribution in this field, conveying as it does the unexpected picture of a Milton who was very far from being vilified by women readers for his misogyny, and who, on the contrary, was hailed by them as a political and moral hero.

Some of the disagreements I have with Wittreich are of a detailed kind, and can emerge meaningfully only in their proper context. (I refer the reader, in particular, to my discussion of Blake's *Milton* in Chapter 8, where my own argument is in close dialogue with *Angel of Apocalypse*.) In general terms, however, my reservations are methodological, and can be summarized here. Wittreich joins the large body of critics who see it as their mission to refute Bloom, and the effect of his resistance is damaging, on two different levels: first, it produces a monochrome picture of the prophetic tradition; secondly, it replaces an active (writerly) model of reading practices with one that is submissive (readerly). There is no room in such a picture for the articulation of poetic relationships between individual writers, nor for the close analysis of verbal echoes and allusions. The role of the reader is more or less overlooked.

Wittreich's intention, in repudiating the 'revisionary' model of reading which Bloom presents, is clearly a valid one: that is, to stress the continuity of tradition which the Romantics inherit from Milton. But his concentration on the tradition of prophecy, to the exclusion of more varied intra-poetic relationships, seems to me to produce a serious distortion in the history of Milton's reception: it offers an inflexibly sublime Milton, a Milton for whom there is no such thing as ambiguity or indeterminacy, and who is therefore a model of univocal authority. This picture may be in keeping with Romantic critical myth, but it is untrue, as I shall demonstrate, to the alternative Milton, who emerges through allusion and imitation.

Furthermore, Wittreich's stress on the *continuity* of prophetic tradition produces a passive model for the reception of Milton's ideas. Each contributor to the line of vision is seen, not as an individual struggling for self-definition, but as a vehicle for the transcendent truth, to which prophecy as a genre has access. Influence is not anxious, but beneficent and fruitful, because what is being transmitted is a body of values which are communally shared: there is no struggle, in Wittreich's view, for ownership of those values. This model of creativity is in some respects inviting, but it seriously misrepresents the cultural climate which fostered Romanticism, and which made the ownership of ideas—'originality'—a matter for concern. (One has only to turn to the 'Preface' to Blake's *Milton* to see how pressing this concern was.[21]) If Bloom's analysis is insufficient, this is partly because it examines anxiety at the purely psychic level, ignoring the social and cultural constraints which might also explain such a phenomenon. To contradict Bloom in the way that Wittreich does is merely to continue ignoring those constraints, and to offer a communal ideal of creativity which is historically inaccurate—even for poets such as Blake, who are centrally placed in the tradition of Prophecy as Wittreich defines it.

In addition to Wittreich's works, there are a number of scholarly studies which have proved invaluable tools in my research. Although outdated and cumbersome in its critical method, R. D. Havens's *The Influence of Milton on English Poetry* (1922) provides a survey from which I have culled some useful facts and figures. I owe a great deal of my understanding of Collins to Paul Sherwin's argument in *Precious Bane: Collins and the Miltonic Legacy* (1977)—a rare book, in that it judiciously extends and enriches Bloom's theory, avoiding the alternate traps of slavish dependence and defensive reaction. Dustin Griffin's *Regaining Paradise*, for all its caution, has suggested a coherent way of reading Milton's influence on eighteenth-century poetry, and is particularly useful in its account of Milton's puritan reputation. Finally, Max Schulz, in *Paradise Preserved: Recreations of Eden in Eighteenth and Nineteenth Century England* (Cambridge, 1985) has provided a wide-ranging and detailed study of the 'Edenic', as it achieved expression during the Romantic era—not only in literature but in other forms, such as visual art and landscape gardening. Further details of my reliance on and disagreement with these works are provided in the notes to each chapter. With reference to these last two studies, however, I take the opportunity here to point out that my own work is 'revisionary' in the humanist reading it offers of the Fall and the loss of innocence. Where Griffin and Schulz are keen to stress a preoccupation in eighteenth- and nineteenth-century culture with the 'preserving' and the 'regaining' of paradise, I concentrate on the positive implications for Romanticism of a non-nostalgic, non-regressive attitude to the Fall. That the particular brand of 'humanism' which I explore in *Paradise Lost* and its sequels takes on a sceptical colouring is due to the sense I have that irony and self-critique are constitutive of Romanticism.

CHOICE OF TEXTS

I have argued that, to be useful, the study of allusive language must involve close and detailed analysis of verbal resonances; but to be convincing, my own argument has to demonstrate that these allusions are not only of local interest, in clarifying and enriching textual interpretation, but of wider significance, both

---

[21] See Ch. 1, n. 117.

to the writer's own preoccupations and to the concerns reflected in his or her writing. A problematic division therefore exists, between the empirical proving of allusiveness and the extrapolation of meaning, which it is extremely difficult to overcome. My strategy has involved ruthless selectivity where the choice of texts is concerned. Thus, rather than attempting to keep track of sporadic borrowings which crop up, often in unexpected places, I have for the most part selected cases of dense and sustained Miltonic allusion. One advantage of this method is that it allows for the demonstration of my argument across the whole (or a large part) of the text concerned, thus avoiding superficiality, and allowing for a proper placing of Milton's importance in the process of interpretation.

One obvious disadvantage, however, is that a great deal of interesting and relevant material has been put to one side: I am particularly conscious that Shelley and Byron are treated less extensively than they deserve; and that my neglect of women writers (other than Mary Shelley) may convey a lopsided view of English literature during this period. I must stress, therefore, that those who begin this book in the hope that it will provide a comprehensive taxonomy of Miltonic borrowings in post-Miltonic literature are likely to be disappointed. It does not and cannot aim at inclusiveness in its account of what Romanticism shows itself to be in the act of responding to Milton. Rather, it studies what certain Romantic texts suggest about Romanticism; its aims and methods are exploratory rather than definitive.

With regard to the eighteenth-century components of the discussion, my intention has been to highlight the continuity between Miltonic and Romantic habits of allusion, thus softening the conventional distinction between Augustanism and Romanticism: I hope that Chapter 7 will offer a coherent way of understanding those ingredients of the distinction which I believe to be worth preserving. In the choice of texts to demonstrate my argument, I have taken into account not just density of allusion and adaptability to detailed commentary but the likely requirements of undergraduates approaching Romanticism for the first time, as well as the familiarity of specialists and more experienced readers with material which I hope to be presenting in a new light. If there is a tendency to focus rather too exclusively on obvious canonized texts, I hope that this will be compensated for, on the one hand, by the approachability of the material and, on the other, by the detailed application of method. The justification for close commentary of this kind, as opposed to a wider-ranging and more general discussion, is that it does successfully draw attention to the detail with which Milton's followers respond to his textual ambiguities, and to the extent to which they build ambiguity into their own procedures. It is hoped that, if awareness of indeterminacy is heightened, both *Paradise Lost* and its Romantic sequels might be reassessed.

I

Reception

THE MILTON CULT

'I am sick of hearing of the sublimity of Milton', complains Mary Wollstone-craft, in the chapter on reading in her *Education of Daughters* (1787).[1] Even without entering into the question of Milton's patriarchal reputation (which, according to Joseph Wittreich's research,[2] was less widespread in the eighteenth century than we might assume), it is not difficult to imagine the causes of her impatience. Between 1705 and 1800, *Paradise Lost* alone was published over a hundred times: along with *The Pilgrim's Progress* and the Bible, it was the most widely read book of the century.[3] Passages from it were excerpted and anthologized for the moral edification of the young and the female, not least by Wollstonecraft herself.[4] Children, familiarized with it during the early stages of their education, were encouraged to read it as a kind of primer; and in the popular imagination it acquired the status of a biblical text.[5] Novelists, male and female alike, turned to it as a model for the structure of their narratives and for the delineation of their characters. They knew they could rely on the immediacy and effectiveness of its popular appeal to bring home any moral point they themselves wished to convey.[6]

Absorbing *Paradise Lost* into the arena of public debate, politicians of different persuasions used it (and, alongside it, Milton's prose pamphlets—or sometimes

[1] *Wollstonecraft Works*, iv. 21. Despite her antipathy to Milton's sublimity, Wollstonecraft includes the 'Conversation between Adam and Eve on going to rest' in her anthology of edifying literature, *The Female Reader* (London, 1789); see ibid. 262–4.

[2] *Feminist Milton* (Ithaca, NY, 1987), esp. ch. 3.

[3] The estimate of 'over a hundred' is taken from R. D. Havens, *The Influence of Milton on English Poetry* (Cambridge, Mass., 1922), 4. Havens does not include 'translations, prose versions, adaptations, or issues containing only part of the poem'.

[4] As Wittreich points out, 'Milton was recommended reading for young children' and 'a particularly important part of the educational system for women' (*Feminist Milton*, 4). For Milton editions especially designed for female readers and children, see Havens, *Influence of Milton*, 25–6.

[5] Ibid. 25; Wittreich, *Feminist Milton*, 39.

[6] W. Massey comments that '*Paradise Lost* . . . is read with pleasure and Admiration, by Persons of every Degree and Condition'; *Remarks on Milton's Paradise Lost* (London, 1761), p. iii. Its popularity is exploited by Fielding, who calls Squire Allworthy's estate 'Paradise Hall' and, when his hero is expelled from home, quotes the obvious lines from Milton: 'The world, as Milton phrases it, lay all before him' (*Tom Jones*, bk. vii. ch. 2).

just his name) for sectarian purposes;[7] while poets and essayists frequently exploited its libertarian appeal (with or without Satanic overtones) to advocate or to condemn republicanism, civil and religious liberty, and the freedom of the press.[8] Passages from *Paradise Lost* emerged as touchstones in discussions about education, private and public morality, innate goodness, and the equality of men and women. Sometimes the same passages were appropriated and reappropriated on different sides of a moral, political, or philosophical debate.[9]

Milton's conception of Eden provided the focus for sustained attempts to rebuild Paradise in the fallen world—as a political actuality, a linguistic possibility, or a millenarian ideal.[10] The eighteenth century was indeed nostalgically haunted by Eden as pastoral metaphor—a metaphor which seemed in *Paradise Lost* itself to establish the state of perfection both as an absolute that had been lost and as a recoverable possibility. In the face of encroaching industrialism, the old rural values became doubly precious: writers turned to *Paradise Lost* for inspiration, because Milton's ambiguity with regard to the preserving of paradise reflected their own anxieties and hopes. Everywhere, in topographical writing, essays on the picturesque, and poetry, Milton's descriptive phrases are echoed by writers of the eighteenth and nineteenth centuries.[11] These writings evoke the tranquillity, the potential for contemplation, but also the Edenic fragility of rural enclaves. Conversely, Milton's portrayal of hell is used repeatedly, and with extraordinary consistency, as metaphorical shorthand for the invasive noise and confusion created by industrial excess in England's expanding cities.[12] The familiarity of this trope can be judged by Shelley's comment in 'Peter Bell the Third'—'Hell is a city much like London'—which comes trippingly off the tongue, after a century of clichés working the other way round.[13]

[7] Wittreich argues that, during the Civil War, the Royalists were known as 'the devils' party', whereas after 1660 it was a phrase deployed against the revolutionaries; he claims that by 1764 it was a cliché to refer to the Whigs, or to the Republicans, as belonging to the party of the devils. See *Angel of Apocalypse: Blake's Idea of Milton* (Madison, Wis., 1975), 214. For further historical details, see C. Hill, *Antichrist in Seventeenth-Century England* (Oxford, 1971).

[8] Burke, for instance, used Milton's account of the fall of the angels to uphold the monarchy and to warn against revolution (see Ch. 3); while Paine saw the revolution as a re-establishment of man's Adamic rights: see 'The Rights of Man' in *Thomas Paine Reader*, 215, 227.

[9] Wollstonecraft, for instance, is in dialogue with Milton, and with passages in Rousseau and Burke which underwrite Milton's prejudices; see the opening of Ch. 5 (and its n. 12).

[10] When Edward Young refers to Milton's blank verse as 'verse unfallen, uncurst' (see n. 26 below), he draws on universal language theory. The classless languages of Adam is discussed by many writers in the 18th c. (see O. Smith, *The Politics of Language, 1791–1819* (Oxford, 1984)), and provides a wider political context in which allusions to *Paradise Lost* should be understood. Equally political in resonance, and Miltonic in accent, is the stress on 'Domestic Happiness' which Cowper claims to be 'the only bliss | Of Paradise that has survived the Fall' (*The Task*, iii. 41–2).

[11] See M. F. Schulz, *Paradise Preserved: Recreations of Eden in Eighteenth- and Nineteenth-Century England* (Cambridge, 1985).

[12] Among those who liken London to hell are Thomson, Young, Cowper, Wordsworth, and Coleridge. See my '"In City Pent": Echo and Allusion in Wordsworth, Coleridge and Lamb, 1797–1801', *Review of English Studies*, n.s. 32 (Nov. 1981), 408–28.

[13] 'Peter Bell the Third', pt. iii, l. 147.

Eden as a 'happy rural seat of various view' (*PL* iv. 247) shaped and directed the taste for the picturesque which dominates eighteenth- and nineteenth-century aesthetics; and its impact on landscape gardening reflects a practical implementation of the paradisal ideal. Max Schulz cites examples of direct reference to *Paradise Lost*, in comments on the layout of specific gardens, and establishes a number of witnesses to Milton's share in creating a model for the 'new natural taste'. Joseph Warton, for instance, commented that Milton is at least partly responsible for 'this enchanting art of modern gardening'; while Anna Seward referred to Lancelot Brown as embodying 'the rational spirit of improvement' which is exemplified in Milton's description of 'the primeval garden'. Walpole said that Milton's ideas corresponded 'so minutely ... with the present standard' that it could hardly be doubted that modern gardening is 'but the execution of his imagined celestial design'.[14]

The central ingredients of this 'new natural taste' in gardening were variety and informality of appearance, both of them exemplified in Book IV of *Paradise Lost*; but Schulz draws attention, also, to the crucial role played by hard-working gardeners in Milton's Eden, and to the influence their example exerted in economic terms. The attentive husbandry of Adam and Eve provided a model that 'the Whig lords emerging after the Glorious Revolution of 1688–89 could emulate with good Christian consciences', while at the same time materially improving their fortunes by the better management of their estates.[15] Indeed, the Edenic pattern of 'responsible stewardship' was readily appropriable in different directions: not only is it implicated in the rising momentum of bourgeois entrepreneurialism, which turns to the Puritan roots of the work ethic to provide its *raison d'être*; it also offers legitimization for retreating from the demands of the real world—so long as this retreat is accompanied (as, for instance, in the case of William and Dorothy Wordsworth) by economic self-sufficiency, along Edenic lines.[16]

In literary salons, as in rural retreats, Milton's name was pre-eminent throughout the eighteenth and early nineteenth centuries. From the publication of Addison's *Spectator* essays onwards, *Paradise Lost* became a byword for the sublime, providing a fashionable topic of conversation in educated circles and an interesting new subject for essayists and critics. Aspiring poets emulated its awesome seriousness, and made slavish imitations of its style, to put alongside their Virgilian or Ovidian apprentice-pieces. Established poets paid tribute to it in echoes and allusions. It was plagiarized by Sir Richard Blackmore, John

---

[14] Cited by Schulz, *Paradise Preserved*, 12–13.   [15] Ibid. 14.

[16] For Wordsworth's fictionalization of the paradisal hopes embodied in his retirement with Dorothy to Dove Cottage, see *Home at Grasmere* (1800); and for extensive critical discussion of the poem's Miltonic parallels and implications, see J. Wordsworth, *William Wordsworth: The Borders of Vision* (Oxford, 1982), 98–148.

Dennis, and Matthew Smith;[17] successfully parodied in John Philips's *The Splendid Shilling* (1701) and John Gay's *Wine* (1709);[18] used as a stylistic model in William Thompson's *A Poetical Paraphrase on part of the Book of Job* (1726);[19] imitated in distinguished classical translations (by Alexander Pope and Joseph Trapp); and itself translated into Virgilian Latin.[20] Dryden set it to music in 1667 in his opera 'The State of Innocence and the Fall of Man'; and Fuseli made paintings to illustrate it, which were on public show in his 'Milton Gallery' during 1799 and 1800.[21]

The prosody and diction of *Paradise Lost* were gradually absorbed into literary language (Havens suggests he contributed to an increase in the 'connotative, imaginative and poetic values of words');[22] and it was responsible for major generic and stylistic developments, dramatically registered by changes in public taste. Not least of these was the gradual acceptance of blank verse. Initially so disliked that five rhymed paraphrases of *Paradise Lost* were published in the first quarter of the century,[23] blank verse grew in modishness as time wore on: Thomson's *The Seasons*, Cowper's *The Task*, Young's *The Complaint, or Night Thoughts*, and Akenside's *The Pleasures of Imagination* became widely read, and increasingly rhyme was condemned. When Wordsworth began *The Prelude*, in 1799, he turned to Milton as a model; but in using blank verse he was not conscious, as he would have been a century earlier, of doing something outlandish or even new. The kind of blank verse he wrote is itself evidence of the extent to which this form has become domesticated through familiarity (and particularly through the conversational transformations it receives from Cowper and Coleridge), so that it moves readily and comfortably through a range of registers, subjects, and moods.[24]

Issuing his challenge to rhyme in the late seventeenth century, Milton had claimed that blank verse was a means whereby heroic poetry could recover its

---

[17] R. Blackmore's *King Arthur, an Heroick Poem*, (London, 1697) and *Eliza, an Epick Poem* (London, 1705), make extensive use of Miltonic features borrowed from *Paradise Lost*; as do J. Dennis's *The Battle of Ramillia: or, The Power of Union* (London, 1706) and M. Smith's *The Vision, or a Prospect of Death, Heav'n and Hell* (London, 1702). See Havens, *Influence of Milton*, 95–6.

[18] For a full account of these burlesques, see ibid. 96–9.

[19] W. Thompson's *Poetical Paraphrase on Part of the Book of Job, In Imitation of the Style of Milton* (Dublin, 1726) 'not only makes use of the language and style of *Paradise Lost*, but borrows many phrases from it', see Havens, *Influence of Milton*, 112. Pope's use of Miltonisms is less easily separable from his use of archaisms in general, as Havens shows (ibid. 117).

[20] Ibid. 17.   [21] Ibid. 29.

[22] Milton is here only one of several influences, according to Havens: 'English poetry from Pope to Keats shows a steadily increasing attention to the connotative, the imaginative and poetic, value of words, that is due largely to the influence of Spenser, Shakespeare, and Milton' (ibid. 66).

[23] Ibid. 46

[24] H. Lindenberger offers a full account of Wordsworth's handling of register, and in particular discusses the 'touchy balance between formality and matter-of-factness' in his blank verse; see *On Wordsworth's 'Prelude'* (Princeton, NJ, 1963), 303.

'ancient liberty'.[25] Seen against the background of widespread and sustained attempts to establish the nature of Edenic language, its rise as a reputable literary mode is to be understood as clearing the way for Romanticism: showing the triumph of affectiveness, primitivism, and egalitarianism over the cultivation and restraint of élitist neo-classical forms. Edward Young's view that 'blank verse is verse unfallen, uncurst'[25] is representative of the second half of the eighteenth century and onward, conveying not just how pervasive Milton's influence has been but how inseparable are the style and content of *Paradise Lost* from the 'unfallen' myth of its author.

It is the phenomenon of this 'unfallen' myth of Milton (which consolidates itself through the various manifestations of influence I have outlined) that will be of central concern in the discussion that follows. Many factors contributed to its making: some of them, as I shall show, have a specific bearing on Romanticism, whilst others can be seen as consistent features of Milton's eighteenth- and nineteenth-century reception. I intend to examine the ways in which Milton (pre-eminently as the author of *Paradise Lost*) was 'deified' in the minds of his readers. Having first demonstrated his status as moral and spiritual guide for writers who turned him into a personal role model, I shall show how this conception of Milton is rooted in the biographical tradition which establishes him as an exemplar of private and public virtue. In my analysis of Milton's political reputation, I shall go on to explore the Christian resonances which accrue to him, as he acquires the dimensions of republican saviour to those awaiting the millennium in late eighteenth-century England. My focus will then shift to the wider literary repercussions of Milton's influence. I shall discuss the expansion of possibilities for the vernacular which came about through the acceptance of *Paradise Lost* as a worthy exemplar of the epic form. Placing its reception at the centre of a debate which focused on the relative merits of Ancient and Modern literature, I shall suggest that the significance of Milton's epic for the evolution of a new concept of originality lies in its merging of sublime manner and religious tenor with authorial identity. This, I will argue, establishes it as a unique—and in some senses inimitable—object of idolization. In my discussions of sublimity and divinity I shall pay special attention to the appropriation of sacred material, by means of which Milton lays claim to divine status.

The method adopted in later chapters will involve close intertextual analysis, of a kind that will qualify, complicate, and (in some important respects) contradict the claims made here. By contrast, this chapter will pay considerably less attention to verbal nuance, and will make wider-ranging reference to critical opinions. For a full and careful analysis of the successive stages of Milton's

---

[25] See the note to the 2nd edn. of *Paradise Lost*: 'This neglect . . . of rime . . . is to be esteemed an example set, the first in English, of ancient liberty recovered to heroic poem from the troublesome and modern bondage of rhyming' (*PL*, p. 39).

[26] Young, *Conjectures*, 60.

reception during the second half of the eighteenth century, readers are advised to consult the Introduction to John T. Shawcross's volume in the Critical Heritage series, *Milton 1732–1801*. My account will no doubt appear slanted by comparison, since I am covering a longer period of time, more selectively, and with a view to tracing the evolution of Romantic ideas. My concern is, indeed, quite specifically with the Milton who is constructed by the cultural needs of his readers, being invoked or named by them, frequently in a kind of symbolic shorthand for the concepts with which he comes to be associated. The chapter is subdivided for convenient presentation, but I hope it will become obvious that 'Milton' is part of a complex system of signification, and that all the aspects I have examined interconnect. Thus, when Wollstonecraft grumbles about 'the sublimity of Milton', she refers as much to the phenomenon of a poet deified through his subject-matter as to the style for which he is renowned: in this single word, she dismisses the century of adulation which had turned Milton into a household name.

MORALITY

In the third book of *The Prelude*, Wordsworth remembers a visit during his Cambridge days to a fellow student who lived in rooms once occupied by Milton. Here, 'seated with others in a festive ring', the young poet proceeded to get drunk on the memory of his great (and, importantly, 'innocent' and 'temperate') precursor. Having 'poured out libations' to Milton in his private thoughts 'till [his] brain reeled', he recalls running awkwardly to chapel, overcome by the 'fumes of wine'. Summing up the episode, his adult persona dismisses it with shame, and asks forgiveness from both Milton and Coleridge for the moral weakness he then displayed:

> Empty thoughts!
> I am ashamed of them; and that great Bard,
> And thou, O Friend! who in thy ample mind
> Hast stationed me for reverence and love,
> Ye will forgive the weakness of that hour
> In some of its unworthy vanities,
> Brother of many more.[27]

Clearly, the central point of the anecdote is Wordsworth's sense of his own unworthiness—as a role model for Coleridge but also, and more importantly, as the rightful successor to Milton. Haunted by doubts and self-questionings (how vain, in both senses, is his ambition to write an epic that might equal *Paradise Lost*?), he broods over the contrast between himself and Milton which his Cambridge memory offers. It is a humiliating and bathetic contrast: Milton, on

---

[27] *Prelude*, iii. 322–8 (for the episode in its entirety, read ll. 284–328).

the one hand, a stripling youth, with his 'rosy cheeks | Angelical, keen eye, courageous look | And conscious step of purity and pride', and himself on the other: a drunken adolescent, his gown upshouldered 'in a dislocated lump | with shallow ostentatious carelessness', rushing like an ungainly 'ostrich' out of Milton's lodgings, to reach the chapel door.

The complex of emotions which this episode displays is at once specific to Wordsworth's (semi-fictionalized) autobiography and typical of eighteenth-century habits of reverential and self-reproachful mythologizing. Pope, for instance, claimed that he kept the pictures of Dryden, Milton, and Shakespeare in his chamber around him, 'that the constant remembrance of 'em [might] keep [him] always humble';[28] while Cowper, who 'danced for joy' over his discovery of *Paradise Lost*, and later went on to know Milton by heart, records a dream in which he met Milton, and felt towards him as an 'affectionate child' does towards his 'beloved father'.[29] It is perhaps not surprising that Milton should have inspired in his followers various forms of respect, reverence, and awe, some of them as much to do with his godliness—Cowper called it his 'masculine piety'[30]—as with his poetic reputation. What is remarkable in these anecdotes is the strength of their adulation, the extremity of their self-abasement, and the consistency with which they internalize Milton as a figure of conscience, wisdom, and restraint. The pictures which decorate Pope's chamber are there to 'keep him always humble'—not to inspire in him a sense of his own potential, or to give him a realistic role model, but to remind him of his own littleness by comparison. In Cowper's dream, which Dustin Griffin (in a characteristically anti-Bloomian manœuvre) contrives to read as unanxious, the very fact of projecting onto Milton a paternal role reveals Cowper's dependency, his need for a moral guide.[31] And in Wordsworth's anecdote, Milton is used to voice a message of temperance and modesty, which acts as a reminder of the moral weakness to which Wordsworth himself is prey, and of the 'unworthy vanities' which are involved in poetic ambition.

In these extreme forms of admiration, which amount almost to hero-worship, one might readily (and despite Griffin's assertions to the contrary) find evidence to support the claims of critics such as Walter Jackson Bate and Harold Bloom, who see Milton as occupying the role of surrogate father, dominating his poetic

[28] *Correspondence of Pope*, ed. G. Sherburn (5 vols., Oxford, 1956), i. 120; cited by Havens, *Influence of Milton*, 114; and discussed by D. Griffin, *Regaining Paradise: Milton and the Eighteenth Century* (Cambridge, 1986), 115.

[29] The dream took place in 1793, toward the end of Cowper's life, and was reported to Hayley. See *Correspondence of Cowper*, ed. T. Wright (4 vols., London, 1904), iv. 373.

[30] Cowper claims that 'the unaffected and masculine piety, which was [Milton's] true inspirer, and is the very soul of his poem' will not be accessible to other than a Christian reader; see his *Milton* (4 vols., Chichester, 1810), ii. 428.

[31] 'Far from being stern and intimidating', Griffin argues, the Milton of Cowper's dream is 'mild, accessible, and reassuring. Relations with fathers then, even imaginative and dream fathers, need not be dominated by oedipal rivalries and fears' (*Regaining Paradise*, 219).

heirs and exerting excessive influence over them.[32] Ascribing this anxiety to a moral and religious origin need not necessarily entail discountenancing its literary effects: indeed, in Cowper's case, the evidence for anxiety is given particularly strong support by the publication in 1810 of his four-volume edition of Milton. This contains his 'The Fragment of an Intended Commentary on Paradise Lost', along with Hayley's 'Life of Milton'. Appended is an account by Hayley of Cowper's 'fruitless endeavour' to complete the Commentary, including an excerpt from a letter written on 2 October 1792, in which he acknowledges Milton's power to induce in him a sense of impotent guilt: 'The consciousness that there is much to do, and nothing done, is a burthen, I am not able to bear. Milton especially is my grievance; and I might almost as well be haunted by his ghost, as goaded with continual reproaches for neglecting him.'[33] Accentuated as it is by the pathos of Hayley's account, this comment provides a psychological insight into Cowper's private mental state, while publicly according to his precursor the status of a resented father, or of a conscience that troubles and thwarts the creative mind. It is a high-profile acknowledgement of Milton's daunting power, which must have influenced numerous readers, and which was the more readily consumed by them because it was offered as justification for the unfinishedness of the Commentary itself.

As a title, 'The Fragment of an Intended Commentary on Paradise Lost' was, furthermore, extremely well judged for its potential readership, since the 'Fragment' was establishing itself at this period as a modish form, around which were assembling a set of sophisticated generic expectations.[34] Seen as an offshoot of sublimity, incompleteness had already become a trope for the intensity and ambition of creative power—a power which is indeed truncated *because of* its potentially hubristic scope, and not because of any failure of vision. I shall be returning, at several points in this book, to the interconnectedness of ideas of fragmentation, sublimity, and indeterminacy:[35] here I need point out only the sense in which Bloom's 'anxiety of influence' might provide a cogent psychological explanation for their presence as a 'Miltonic' phenomenon in Cowper's edition. Cowper's anxiety in relation to Milton is offered as a justification for the unfinished state of his Commentary; and in the compliment that is thereby paid to Milton's paramount status, Cowper claims the credit for modesty and imaginative intensity, at one and the same time.

The attitude of self-abasement, which characterizes a great many of Milton's followers, can be only partially explained as a residue of Augustan habits of imitation I shall discuss later in this chapter, which involve moderate deference

---

[32] See W. J. Bate, *The Burden of the Past and the English Poet* (London, 1971), and H. Bloom, *The Anxiety of Influence: A Theory of Poetry* (Oxford, 1973). Their views are strongly contested by Griffin: see esp. the 'Afterword' to *Regaining Paradise* (229–38).

[33] See Cowper's *Milton*, iv. 392–3.

[34] For the most substantial account to date of the formation of this new genre, see M. Levinson, *The Romantic Fragment Poem: A Critique of a Form* (Chapel Hill, NC, 1986).

[35] See esp. my discussion of 'Indeterminacy and the Sublime' in Ch. 6.

to established authority, but not adulation. It is more plausibly to be seen as the product of that imaginative confusion between authorial identity and creative artefact which characterizes the reception of Milton more than of any other poet in the literary canon. This is by no means an exclusively 'eighteenth-century' phenomenon: one only has to glance at the poem Keats wrote after Leigh Hunt showed him a lock of Milton's hair to see how thoroughly the awesome sublimity of *Paradise Lost* has become absorbed into Keats's conception of Milton the man:

> For many years my offering must be hushed.
>   When I do speak, I'll think upon this hour,
> Because I feel my forehead hot and flushed,
>   Even at the simplest vassal of thy power—
>   A lock of thy bright hair.
>   Sudden it came,
> And I was startled, when I caught thy name
>   Coupled so unaware,
> Yet, at that moment, temperate was my blood.
> Methought I had beheld it from the Flood.[36]

After composing this embarrassingly fetishistic poem, Keats went on to have a burst of creative activity, during which he seemed committed to merging his identity with those of his great precursors: 'Shakspeare and the paradise Lost [*sic*] every day become greater wonders to me', he wrote in August 1819; 'I look upon fine Phrases like a Lover.'[37] This phase ended when he failed to complete *Hyperion*, in his own account because of the oppressive power of Miltonic influence: 'I have but lately stood on my guard against Milton', he wrote, by way of explanation; 'Life to him would be death to me'.[38] The burden of the past is in this case openly acknowledged, by a poet whose ambitions for himself were unusually intense: aside from Cowper, Keats is perhaps the most straight-forward example we have of the anxiety of influence.

A convincing context in which to place this phenomenon of anxiety (which, as we have seen, has a peculiarly *moral* dimension) is the eighteenth-century biographical tradition which was responsible for purveying the saintly image of Milton that was familiar to Cowper, Wordsworth, and Keats. This tradition is carefully reconstructed by Dustin Griffin, in the second chapter of *Regaining Paradise*, and need be only briefly characterized here. It is one, importantly, of *defensiveness*, whose roots are to be found in Milton's own autobiographical writings: sections, that is to say, of three pamphlets published in the 1650s: *A Defence of the People of England* (24 February 1651), *A Second Defence of the English People* (30 May 1654), and *Pro se Defensio* (8 August 1655). Designed

[36] 'On seeing a Lock of Milton's Hair', ll. 33–42. According to J. Bate, Keats's response to the lock of hair as a surviving 'relic' epitomizes the difference between his view of 'Milton the man' and his view of Shakespeare as an artist 'subsumed in his works'; see *Shakespeare and the English Romantic Imagination* (Oxford, 1986), 190.

[37] Keats to B. Bailey, 14 Aug. 1819; *Keats Letters*, 277.

[38] Keats to G. and G. Keats, 24 Sept. 1819; ibid. 325.

partly to fend off attacks on his character (the contingent products of his engagement in political controversy), these defences are written in what Griffin calls a tone of 'offended righteousness'.[39] In them, Milton constructs a water-tight self-image—an image, indeed, of immaculate purity and goodness—claiming credit for honourable conduct, and for a life 'free and untouched by the slightest sin or reproach', devoted to the service of God. He uses the cause of liberty as unquestionable justification for his own polemical invective and, by reference to his blindness, strengthens the idea that he was a martyr in the cause of freedom, who never received sufficient acknowledgement for his contribution to the public good.[40] The central emphasis of this image of self is its internal coherence: public and private are seamlessly joined, in an exemplary life which is designed to be read, in Milton's terms, as 'a true Poem, that is, a composition and patterne of the best and honourablest things'.[41]

This image of Milton survives into the eighteenth century and beyond, not just in its unmediated form (the *Defences* were widely available to readers, in Toland's and Birch's editions)[42] but in the sequence of biographies which were themselves written as part of a long-drawn-out polemic debate. The attacks on Milton's politics, which had begun in the 1650s and had very early taken the form of personal character assassination, resurfaced at various points in the eighteenth century, most notably in the charges of plagiarism levelled by Lauder in 1747[43] and in the even more shocking and damaging insinuations of hypocrisy made by Johnson in 1779.[44] Responding to these attacks, Milton's defenders turned to the self he had carefully constructed, as a model for the image of him they wished to convey. Indeed, as Griffin points out, it was a 'common practice among the biographers from Toland to Hayley (with the signal exception of Johnson), to let Milton speak for himself, and to insert extracts from the *First* and *Second Defences* into the narrative of his life or the discussion of his character'.[45] Even without such extracts, however, the terms which were adopted

[39] Griffin, *Regaining Paradise*, 23.

[40] See esp. *A Second Defence of the English People* (8 Aug. 1655), preface and notes by K. Svendsen, trans. P. W. Blackford; *Milton Prose* iv/1, ed. D. M. Wolfe (New Haven, Conn., 1966), 611, 620.

[41] Milton writes in 1642 that 'he who would not be frustrate of his hope to write hereafter in laudable things, ought himself to bee a true Poem, that is, a composition and patterne of the best and honourablest things'. See *An Apology against a Pamphlet* (April 1642), preface and notes by F. L. Taft; *Milton Prose*, i, ed. D. M. Wolfe (New Haven, Conn., 1953), 890.

[42] J. Toland published the first collected edition of Milton's prose works in 1698, prefaced by a 'Life of Milton', which praised him for 'those excellent volumes he wrote on the behalf of Civil, Religious and Domestic Liberty'; see *The Early Lives of Milton*, ed. H. Darbishire (London, 1932), 83. T. Birch's edn., *A Complete Collection of the Historical, Political and Miscellaneous Works of John Milton*, was published in London in 1738.

[43] Lauder's notorious accusations of plagiarism in 1747 were followed by the publication of his *An Essay on Milton's Use and Imitation of the Moderns, in his Paradise Lost* (London, 1749).

[44] See *Johnson Life*, 84–94. Johnson is particularly cutting about Milton's treatment of his family: 'It has been observed that they who most loudly clamour for liberty do not most liberally grant it. What we know of Milton's character in domestick relations is, that he was severe and arbitrary' (ibid. 157).

[45] Ibid. 23.

by these biographers, in praising the purity of Milton's thoughts and the right-eousness of his actions, are recognizably Miltonic in origin.

Hayley (whose *Life* comes at the end of the century, and is highly influential for the Romantic image of Milton) brings to a climax the tradition which sees Milton as irreproachable. The personal actions for which Johnson vilifies Milton are reclaimed, in Hayley's polemical defence, as proofs of Milton's 'refined and hallowed probity':[46] indeed, they show the consistent matching of private and public morals, which makes his life exemplary. Thus, his behaviour to-wards his first wife is seen as entirely consistent with his views on divorce—in Hayley's opinion 'as extensive and liberal as his intention was pure and benevolent' (p. 84); his loyalty to Cromwell is vindicated (even while the latter is vilified as a time-server: here a parallel between Milton and Abdiel makes the contrast more strongly apparent);[47] his dedication to the British people is shown to have remained unshaken; and his treatment of his daughters is justified on the grounds that they were ungrateful, and conspired against him (pp. 198–201). Throughout, there is emphasis on Milton's religious temperament as the cohe-sive principle in his life and writings: this, Hayley claims, 'enabled him to ascend the sublimest heights, both of genius and virtue' (p. 28). Although sublimity is 'the predominant characteristic' of *Paradise Lost*, yet (Hayley claims) 'Milton's own personal character is still more sublime' (p. 225). Indeed, 'sublimity in composition may be expected only from the man, who has attained the sublime in the steady practice of virtue' (p. 74). We have here, then, a defence of Milton that remains very firmly within the terms established by Milton's own *Defences*, and that is based on a strongly Renaissance conception of the self: there can be no division between the public and the private, or between life and art, when both are sustained by the unshakeable morality that comes from true religious faith. Milton's biography, according to this view, is indeed 'a composition and patterne of the best and honourablest things'.

If it is true, as Dustin Griffin remarks, that 'to an extent we have perhaps not properly recognized, eighteenth-century readers were accustomed to read poetry biographically' (p. 5), then we should take into account, in understanding his reception, not only the impact of Milton's explicitly autobiographical contri-butions but also the constructions of self-image which are to be inferred from his poetry. An example which occurs very early in the Milton *œuvre*—and which might therefore be assumed to have had a pervasive effect on the Milton myth—is the 'Ode on Christ's Nativity'. As Richard Halpern has argued, there was nothing random in Milton's decision to open his first published volume of verse (*Poems* 1645) with this Ode, since 'by so doing he appropriates the occasion of Christ's birth to announce his own poetic nativity and to anticipate the matur-

---

[46] *Hayley Life*, 23.

[47] 'In praising Cromwell, he praised a personage, whose matchless hypocrisy assumed before him a mask that the arch apostate of the poet could not wear in the presence of Abdiel, the mask of affectionate zeal towards man, and devout attachment to God' (ibid. 131).

ation of his own powers'.[48] Halpern goes on to suggest that 'Christ enables
Milton to mediate his own relationship with literary history by providing a
model for that history and for his place within it'; and he offers a reading of the
poem as 'a narrative of anticipation'.[49]

   The detailed ramifications of Halpern's (Lacanian) thesis need not concern
us here. It is, however, worth adapting his central idea, so as to observe that a
close identification between Christ and Milton is made almost inevitable when
the Nativity Ode is read in the light of Milton's subsequent poetic output, and
especially *Paradise Lost*. The role which Christ adopts in the Ode—that of
disrupting human history and dispelling pagan religion ('the oracles are
dumb')[50]—parallels Milton's later literary-historical role in displacing the
classical tradition by Christianizing epic. In other words, when read with
hindsight, Christ's mission in the Ode serves as a kind of poetic figure (as well
as a self-fulfilling prophecy) of the poet's own. The significance of the Ode's
position, at the beginning of Milton's first published collection, is enhanced
by the reader's retrospective awareness of the ways in which Milton's literary
career will develop, culminating in the revisionary Christianity of *Paradise
Lost*.

   In the light of this self-identification, it is perhaps unsurprising to find that
Milton is repeatedly associated with Christ by his eighteenth- and nineteenth-
century readers. As I shall be showing later in this chapter, metaphors of
incarnation and resurrection recur frequently in Miltonic invocations: the first
as a convenient paradigm for the dualism of Milton's genius (divinity of spirit,
accommodated within human form) and the second as an appropriate figura-
tion of Milton's status as saviour: 'O raise us up, return to us again'.[51] In
Milton, Blake exploits both literary conventions, having Milton descend to
earth as fulfilment of the prophecy of Christ's second coming: Milton is thus
made central to the millenarian hopes of Romantic writers.[52] In addition, it is
worth noting the presence (within Romantic allusion particularly) of an
identification between Christ's mission and the poet's, which is given a peculiarly Miltonic resonance by those who make it.[53] Coleridge subtitles his
consciously Miltonic poem, 'Religious Musings', 'a desultory poem, written
on the Christmas eve of 1794'—thereby making a parallel with Milton's
Nativity Ode, while claiming for himself some of the Christian associations
which had been the prerogative of his precursor.[54] Wordsworth, at a similarly

---

   [48] R. Halpern, 'The Great Instauration: Imaginary Narratives in Milton's "Nativity Ode"', in
M. Nyquist and M. W. Ferguson (eds.), *Re-Membering Milton: Essays on the Texts and Traditions*
(New York, 1988), 6.
   [49] Ibid.   [50] 'Ode on the Morning of Christ's Nativity', ll. 173–220.
   [51] See Wordsworth's sonnet, 'London', l. 7.
   [52] See my discussion of Blake's *Milton* in Ch. 8.
   [53] See M. H. Abrams, *Natural Supernaturalism: Tradition and Revolution in Romantic Literature*
(New York, 1971), 119; and Wordsworth, *Borders of Vision*, 327.
   [54] For Coleridge's millenarianism in 'Religious Musings', see ibid. 49–51.

pivotal moment in his poetic career, makes a clear parallel between himself and the Christ of *Paradise Regained*.[55]

The redemptive and sacrificial overtones which Milton's life-story acquires, and which he himself appears to have been at pains to accentuate, are provoked by the sonnets on his blindness, but perhaps even more famously by the proems of *Paradise Lost* Books III and VII. In these heroic digressions, Milton consolidates the idea of martyrdom which he had constructed in his *Defence*. He emerges as one who, despite his blindness, despite the collapse of his political hopes through the unworthiness of the British people, and despite being under direct threat from his enemies, remains none the less cheerfully dedicated to the cause of freedom:

> More safe I sing with mortal voice, unchanged
> To hoarse or mute, though fallen on evil days,
> On evil days though fallen, and evil tongues;
> In darkness and with dangers compassed round,
> And solitude;
>
> (*PL* vii. 24–8)

The potency of such passages for the eighteenth-century reader is to be judged by the frequency with which they are quoted in biographies and alluded to in poems: Richardson wonders at Milton's extraordinary 'courage in understanding and resolution in persisting' with *Paradise Lost*, when he had 'the load of Such Difficulties upon his Shoulders! Ill health, Blindness; Uneasy in his mind, no doubt, on occasion of the Publick Affairs, and his own'.[56] Newton elaborates on the poet's cheerful disposition in the face of calamity and his own wretched condition;[57] and Hayley (quoting the lines above) offers a portrait of the poet, in hiding from his enemies, which considerably heightens the Christian overtones of martyrdom suggested by Milton himself. A decade later, Wordsworth's evocation of 'our blind poet', as one who 'Stood single, uttering odious truth, | Darkness before, and danger's voice behind'[58] is characteristically moulded by the terms of Milton's own discourse. Even the archly knowing tones of Byron, in the 'Dedication' to *Don Juan*, leave intact the Miltonic myth—even if its prime function is a contrast with Wordsworth which must have caused the latter to squirm:

[55] In 'The Discharged Soldier' (1798), the line 'While thus I wandered, step by step led on' (l. 36) clearly recalls Christ as he goes out into the wilderness, in *Paradise Regained*: 'Thought following thought, and step by step led on' (i. 192). The Christian association is intriguing, given that Wordsworth saw himself at this time as having a mission to begin his millenarian poem, *The Recluse*.

[56] J. Richardson, *Explanatory Notes and Remarks on Milton's Paradise Lost* (1734), in *Early Lives*, ed. Darbishire, 289.

[57] *Paradise Lost*, ed. T. Newton (2 vols., London, 1749), vol. i, p. xlix.

[58] *Prelude* iii. 285–6. Compare Coleridge's comment: 'My mind is not capable of forming a more august conception, that arises from the contemplation of this great man in his latter days: poor, sick, old, blind, slandered, persecuted, "Darkness before, and danger's voice behind"' (*Biographia*, i. 37).

If fallen in evil days on evil tongues,
Milton appealed to the revenger, Time,
If Time, the avenger, execrates his wrongs
And makes the word *Miltonic* mean *sublime*,
He deigned not to belie his soul in songs,
Nor turn his very talent to a crime.[59]

The importance of Milton's role, then, in directing and controlling the reception of his authorial image, should not be underestimated. As Richard Halpern has argued, 'More than any English poet who preceded him—and, for that matter, more than any who followed him—he was able to fashion a coherent poetic *career* ... the narrative he constructs for himself comes to display an astonishing durability, absorbing immense historical and personal shocks without seeming to fragment.'[60] I have examined the contribution made by Milton's own construction of self to future reconstructions of his character, with a view to understanding his extraordinary resilience, as a symbol of purity and probity, in the face of his detractors. The Renaissance notion of self that he stands for (a seamless coherence of morals and manners, words and deeds) survives the Enlightenment, and remains intact, as a kind of nostalgic or unattainable ideal, long after the self is reconceived along lines that include duality, fragmentation, and discontinuity. (Indeed, as we have seen, this ideal conception of self endures, for writers such as Cowper and Wordsworth, as an internalized reminder of their own deficiencies—a conscience that rebukes them, and calls them to account.) That this durability should persist at the level of invocation, and with specific reference to the author as a biographical entity, is a measure of the primacy of what Foucault calls the 'author function' in reception mechanisms.[61] Later chapters in this book will deal with ways in which the author function is challenged and eroded by a quite different kind of reading practice.

POLITICS

It has already become clear that Milton's status as political hero is closely bound up with his moral character; indeed, that the two are inseparable, since, as Dustin Griffin puts it, 'what Milton offered above all was the ideal of public virtue'.[62] Griffin convincingly demonstrates that, although absent from the parliamentary arena in the eighteenth century, Milton was 'lodged as an exemplary political figure in the minds of thousands of readers';[63] and that this broadly liberal reputation has more to do with the biographical image which

---

[59] st. 10.   [60] 'The Great Instauration', 3.
[61] M. Foucault, 'What is an Author?' in D. Lodge (ed.), *Modern Criticism and Theory: A Reader* (London, 1988), 196–210.
[62] *Regaining Paradise*, 20. Griffin defines what Milton stood for as 'a personal example of individual integrity and purity of motive, divorced from circumstances', and 'an essentially moral standard by which men might be encouraged to measure their public behaviour' (ibid. 21).
[63] Ibid.

emerges from Toland, Richardson, Newton, and Hayley than with the appropriation by partisan interpreters of a distinctly perceived ideological perspective.

Granted, there were those at both ends of the political spectrum who chose to denounce or acclaim Milton, on purely political grounds. In 1718, he features in *The History of King-Killers*; and he is later attacked in the *Critical Review* for defending the murder of the King, and for acting as secretary to 'the usurper and tyrant Cromwell, who destroyed the liberties, and trampled on the constitution, of his country'.[64] He appears in the *Biographia Britannica* (1760) as a hypocrite and a time-server;[65] and he is repudiated by Johnson in 1779 as an 'acrimonious and surly republican', whose political actions were fired by envy, the 'sullen desire of independance' and 'pride disdainful of superiority'.[66] At the other extreme, Toland hails him as a lover of Liberty.[67] His prose works were edited by Birch in 1738, by Baron in 1753, and by Blackburne in 1780—this latter as a conscious attempt to 'apprise the men of England of their danger'.[68] He was toasted by the Revolution Society, at their centennial anniversary meeting on 4 November 1788;[69] and Richard Price points to him as the forerunner of revolutionaries who inspired 'the overthrow of priestcraft and tyranny'.[70] For numerous radicals, in the wake of the French Revolution, he became republican hero and champion of freedom of speech.

But, Griffin argues, these appropriations of Milton are minority and extremist reactions, uncharacteristic of 'the broad middle-range of eighteenth century opinion'.[71] For an understanding of the latter, we must observe Milton's enduring reputation as 'a man of sincerity, self-sacrificing, willing to put his very life on the line, a lover of liberty, and of his country'.[72] This *sentimental* image is the one that weathers disparate political allegiance and religious doctrine, withstanding the test of time. Griffin's analysis is confined mainly to the reception of Milton's prose works, and he does not consider the part played by *Paradise Lost* in tempering and making palatable its author's political views. It is, in fact, quite difficult to arrive at a clear understanding of the extent to which the eighteenth century read *Paradise Lost* as a political text, and this difficulty should alert us to the effectiveness of reception mechanisms, which at an early stage succeeded in aestheticizing potentially subversive material.

---

[64] *Critical Review*, 5 (1758), 321; cited by Griffin, *Regaining Paradise*, 12.

[65] Milton is referred to as 'abjectly crouching to wear the yoke of slavery, and even licking the hand that put it on'; see *Biographia Britannica: or, The Lives of the most Eminent Persons in Great Britain and Ireland* (6 vols., London, 1747–66), v. 3118; cited by Griffin, *Regaining Paradise*, 12.

[66] *Johnson Life*, 156, 157.   [67] See Griffin, *Regaining Paradise*, 16.   [68] Ibid. 17.

[69] Ibid. 16.

[70] Quoted by J. DiSalvo in *War of Titans: Blake's Critique of Milton and the Politics of Religion* (Pittsburgh, Pa., 1983), 36.

[71] *Regaining Paradise*, 11. Griffin claims that Milton's reputation as 'a symbol of republican ideals and resistance to tyranny, even in the French Revolutionary period, has probably been overstated' (p.18).

[72] Ibid. 20.

Milton as spiritual guide was a more suitable product for the consumption of his readers than Milton the radical; and the theological disputes which surrounded *Paradise Lost* at times distracted attention from its political import. Furthermore, as Joseph Wittreich has argued, a concealment of the poem's radical implications was made possible by following Milton's own act of self-division, and disconnecting the 'left hand' of his prose writings from the 'right hand' of his poetry.[73] Whereas his audience engaged directly with the political content of the former, they chose to decontextualize *Paradise Lost*, realigning it with 'the literary and generally conservative tradition of epic'.[74] In the case of Marvell's 'On Paradise Lost' (1674) there is, in Wittreich's view, a deliberate and strategic emptying out of the political status of Milton's ideas. In order to evade censorship, *Paradise Lost* is given a religious and biblical lineage; it becomes, in Marvell's eyes, an exemplar of prophecy.

Wittreich believes that there may have been a tacit agreement—amongst Milton's radical allies, as amongst his enemies and, later, his conservative audience—to overlook the political tenor of *Paradise Lost*, or at least to subordinate it to the poem's overarching religious concerns. But the testimony of H. L. Benthem suggests that readers were accustomed to seeing through the biblical theme, as though it were really nothing more than a thin disguise for Milton's political message. According to Christopher Hill, 'when Milton's friends were told the title of the poem, they feared that it would be a lament for the loss of England's happiness with the downfall of the revolutionary regime. But when they read it they saw that the prudent Milton had dealt only with the fall of Adam: reassured, they withdrew their objections to publication.' Hill goes on to paraphrase Benthem's response on reading *Paradise Lost* in the German translation of Theodore Haak, in 1686–7:

But (so far as I understood what Haak told me and what I read myself) although at first sight the epic's subject was indeed the fall of our first parents, in fact 'this very wily politician ... concealed under this disguise the sort of lament his friends had originally suspected'.[75]

According to Merritt Hughes, there is a tradition that supposes Milton's censors to have objected to certain passages of *Paradise Lost* because they were politically subversive. He quotes Book I, lines 591–9 ('His form had not yet lost | All her original brightness', etc.) as a passage which caused particular anxiety, on grounds that 'it might encourage the superstitious hopes of Charles II's enemies'.[76] It is difficult to gauge the extent to which early reception of the poem involved a fully fledged allegorical interpretation; but we have a clear suggestion in these last-quoted comments that the 'camouflage' reading was current and well understood. It is plausible that, as a consequence of such reading

[73] *Feminist Milton*, 5.   [74] Ibid.
[75] *Milton and the English Revolution* (London, 1977), 391.
[76] *Ten Perspectives on Milton* (New Haven, Conn., 1964), 181.

strategies, *Paradise Lost*'s political resonances were gradually suppressed, and that an understanding of the continuity between Milton's prose pamphlets and his epic was thereby delayed.[77]

There are none the less explicit attempts, throughout the eighteenth century, to engage with the question of Milton's political allegiances as they emerge in *Paradise Lost*. John Toland claimed that the 'chief design' of the poem was 'to display the different Effects of Liberty and Tyranny';[78] and in the *London Chronicle*, during 1763–4 there was a debate over the poem as political allegory, the content of which illustrates its remarkable adaptability to partisan readings. From both sides, Satan is here appropriated as spokesman for the opposition, and as the measure of its unacceptable extremity. The Tory position is voiced truculently and clearly: 'how could [Milton] better refute the good old cause he was such a partisan of and such an advocate for than by making the rebellion in the poem resemble it, and giving the same characteristics to the apostate angels as were applicable to his rebel brethren?' To which the only logical response is a Whig realignment of sympathies, along identical lines: 'The Tory plan, where man assumes a right of dominion over man, was nearer related to Satan's aim of setting himself up over his peers.'[79] This debate foreshadows later, Romantic appropriations of Satan as republican hero; though it is noteworthy that for the moment the moral accent comes uppermost, and identification with the Satanic perspective is a matter of damning one's enemies rather than claiming kinship with one's friends.

In the years after the French Revolution, when republican writers turned for support and authority to the most radical of their literary precursors, Hayley's *Life of Milton* created the standard by which to measure his status, as political, spiritual, and moral guide. The account of Milton's career which Hayley offers is largely framed as personal apologia: Addison and Hume are reprimanded for speaking harshly of Milton's political character 'without paying due acknowledgement to the rectitude of his heart' (*Life*, p. 159); and this faulty emphasis is corrected in Hayley's own approach. If Milton ran into political errors, Hayley argues, this was the result of assuming altruism in others, to match his own;[80] and he seeks to reassure his readers that Milton's 'veneration and esteem for the protector were entirely destroyed by the treacherous despotism of his latter days'.[81] *Paradise Lost* is used to support a sympathetic account of Milton's republican spirit: Cromwell is likened to the 'arch apostate', while Milton himself is given affinities with Abdiel, being vindicated for his loyalty to the protector on grounds that his 'sublime religious enthusiasm' led him to be duped.[82] Despite

---

[77] For the controversial ingredients in Milton's writing that were suppressed by his canonization, see Wittreich, *Feminist Milton*, 29.

[78] Quoted by DiSalvo, *War of Titans*, 29.   [79] Ibid.

[80] *Hayley Life*, 87, refers to Milton's 'generous credulity respecting the virtue of mankind'.

[81] Hayley's discussion of the Milton–Cromwell relationship (ibid. 135–9) makes for suggestive reading, in the light of later responses to Robespierre.

[82] Ibid. 131–2.

the overarching emphasis on morality, however, there is in Hayley's biography a distinctly republican flavour, which distinguishes it from earlier and more broadly liberal Lives. It was published at a moment when the very fact of associating one's name with Milton suggested seditious intent or Jacobin principles; and its timing, as well as its content, had a profound impact on the radical community which fostered the beginnings of Romanticism.

The invocation that follows is from one of Coleridge's lectures of 1795, delivered in Bristol:

Sages and patriots that being dead do yet speak to us, spirits of Milton, Locke, Sidney and Harrington that still wander through your native country, giving wisdom and inspiring zeal! The cauldron of persecution is bubbling against you—the spells of despotism are being muttered.[83]

In it, we can see how intimately the political events of Milton's day are connected in Coleridge's mind with contemporary happenings. The two bills introduced by Pitt's Government in 1795 to curb sedition are denounced by Coleridge, on the grounds that they effectively annihilate freedom of speech and the liberty of the press.[84] Milton, as the author of *Areopagitica*, is a fitting hero to call upon in such despotic times: he stands as the figure-head of that spirit of free-thinking which Coleridge sees as his natural, patriotic inheritance. Wittily, the passage's central metaphor succeeds in exposing Pitt as a wicked sorcerer, whose 'cauldron of persecution' and 'spells of despotism' must, by implication, be ultimately powerless against the godly 'wisdom' and 'zeal' of the republican cause. With Milton as mascot, Coleridge can be certain that he has right, and God, on his side.

Wordsworth's famous invocation of 1802—'Milton, thou shouldst be living at this hour! | England hath need of thee' ('London', ll. 1–2)—shows him to be less confident than Coleridge that the 'ancient English dower | Of inward happiness' (ll. 5–6), once forfeited by Britain's war with France, can be restored.[85] Milton is still relied on as sage and patriot; but his wisdom speaks only to the few, and is ultimately as inaccessible as the 'heroic wealth of hall and bower' whose passing Wordsworth laments. An image of resurrection connects the imagined return of Milton's spirit to the British people with his raising of them from the dead: 'We are selfish men; | Oh! raise us up, return to us again; | And give us manners, virtue, freedom, power.' But this urgent prayer for future salvation quickly gives way to elegy, Milton's heroic qualities taking on the permanent but unreachable dimensions of the elements:

---

[83] 'The Plot Discovered, or An Address to the People against Ministerial Treason', 28 Nov. 1795, in *Coleridge Lectures*, 290–1.

[84] The Treason Bill was designed to assassinate the liberty of the Press, and the Convention Bill to smother the liberty of speech; both were introduced in Nov. 1795.

[85] For Wordsworth's shamed response to the declaration of war with France, see *Prelude* x. 227–74.

Thy soul was like a Star and dwelt apart;
Thou hadst a voice whose sound was like the sea;
Pure as the naked heavens, majestic, free

(ll. 9–11)

Like Toussaint L'Ouverture, for whom air, earth and skies are 'allies', powers that will work on his behalf,[86] Milton is apotheosized as a kind of pantheist deity, absorbed into the elements he animates; and yet he figures simultaneously as a time-bound human being, who travelled 'on life's common way | In cheerful godliness', and 'the lowliest duties on [him]self did lay'. The central paradox of Christianity is reworked, in metaphors which at once abstract Milton from human foibles and bring him vulnerably down to earth.

The Milton who is identifiable as spokesman for the libertarian cause is thus transformed by his followers into hero, prophet, sage, and even, as the figurations of Wordsworth's sonnet show, a sort of Christ figure, whose second coming would mean salvation for the British people. Such transformations play an important part in the mythologizing process which allowed Milton his dual status: firstly as a historical figure, actively involved in politics, and engaged in the setting up and administration of the Commonwealth; and secondly as the oracular vehicle for timeless truths—the voice which, as Coleridge puts it, 'yet speaks to us', across a century of change. These invocations are of particular interest for their handling of the double nature they project onto Milton—the humanity/divinity which is so readily understandable in terms of a Christian paradigm.

In some obvious respects, the authorship of *Paradise Lost* contributes to this process, as my discussions of divinity and sublimity will show: Milton confirms his status as political, moral, and spiritual guide by addressing himself to a sacred theme, and by claiming direct access to the word of God. The message of the early political pamphlets is thus, arguably, given greater weight and credence by its connection with the subject-matter of *Paradise Lost* and, in particular, by the prophetic role the epic narrator adopts. This pattern of confirmation is somewhat complicated, however, by the problematic relation which exists between the political views of the earlier and later Milton, as well as by the perceived discrepancy between non-fiction and fiction. So although Milton's pamphlets are a reliable record of his views up to and during the early days of the Commonwealth, allowing him safely to be called on as champion of the libertarian cause, his position after the Restoration is less clear-cut. Here we have only *Paradise Lost* to go by; and the political stances adopted by characters

---

[86] See Wordsworth's sonnet 'To Toussaint L'Ouverture', ll. 8–14. The son of a black slave, Toussaint L'Ouverture became famous as the governor of Haiti who resisted Napoleon's edict re-establishing slavery, and who died in prison during 1803. The resemblances of theme and imagery between this sonnet and 'London' show a close connection in Wordsworth's mind between Milton as republican hero and Toussaint as political martyr. See also the Miltonic resonances of the lines 'Though fallen thyself, never to rise again, | Live, and take comfort' (ll. 8–9), which call to mind Milton's self-portrait in the proem to *PL* vii.

from an imaginary world form no reliable basis for extrapolating Milton's own position. To read *Paradise Lost* as straightforward political allegory, with Satan as the representative of the republican cause and God as monarchical authority, is to discount the possibly jaundiced perspective of a blind and besieged poet who, at the very moment he was writing his epic, was also witnessing the collapse of the Commonwealth and the return of the monarchy.[87]

There is, then, in *Paradise Lost* a potential rift between Milton as spiritual guide and Milton as political hero, which affects the process of deification I am discussing. Many of the central problems which continue to face Milton criticism have their origin here. Quite frequently, the interpretative choices involved are repetitions of choices made by Milton's Romantic readers: Milton the man is identified either with the character of Satan, as political hero, or with the character of God, as vehicle for spiritual truth. The first position is usually accompanied by a radical rethinking, even sometimes rejection, of Christian assumptions, which itself necessarily involves dividing Milton in two: he can thus be seen to espouse the libertarian cause, even despite its conflict with religious imperatives. The second position involves a much loftier conception of Milton, as a poet sublimely removed from earthly politics, and capable of detaching himself from views he had at one time passionately held. In the opposition of these two interpretations, one might see a reflection of the human/divine duality, which I have discussed in the context of Wordsworth's sonnet.

It was as political allegory that the Romantics read *Paradise Lost*, at least in the first instance, because to do so lent support to their own radical positions; but, as I shall later argue, they tended increasingly to turn to Milton as a way of exploring the moral issues that politics raised, rather than simply appropriating Milton as champion of their cause. Initially seizing on Satan as the poem's hero, they chose not to see the changes in Milton's thinking which had, conceivably, taken place as a result of the Restoration. It was only later, under the impact of their own disillusionment with the French Revolution, that they began to see the opposite point of view, and at this stage they identified with a defeated Milton, who turned to spiritual values as a retreat from and consolation for lost political causes. This aspect of the Romantics' relationship with Milton is, of course, immensely important, not least because it illuminates their own 'retreat' from Revolution into imagination: a subject to which I shall be returning in Chapter 3.

Early Romanticism reads as explicit the connection in Milton's mind between monarchical authority and heavenly power. Satan, according to this reading, is not so much a dramatic rendering of Cromwell as the spokesman of republican views that were Milton's own—and, according to one kind of interpretation, this makes him the hero of the poem. We can see a crude form of political reading in

---

[87] Milton's self-revision, and the difficulties it poses for interpretation of *Paradise Lost*, is fully discussed in Ch. 3.

Burns's comment, 'Give me a spirit like my favourite hero, Milton's Satan'[88]—a comment which does not even stop to consider the anti-Satan viewpoint, but takes it for granted that Burns's hero is Milton's too. The alternative way of reading Satan's republicanism is to see it as the measure of Milton's distance from his former self: in those moments when Satan actually quotes Milton's earlier political statements, one should not be blind to potential irony.

More sophisticated than Burns's comment is the answer given by William Godwin in *Political Justice* (1793) to his own provocative question: 'Why did [Satan] rebel against his maker? It was, as he himself informs us, because he saw no sufficient reason for that extreme inequality of rank and power which the creator assumed.'[89] In Godwin's view, the arbitrary power of God is both intellectually unacceptable and politically unjust. We can see just how elevated a hero Satan becomes, when read in the light of Milton's championing of human liberty: 'He bore his torments with fortitude, because he disdained to be subdued by despotic power. He sought revenge, because he could not think with tameness of the unexpostulating authority that assumed to dispose of him'. Godwin is close, here, to the rhetoric of his admirer, Hazlitt, who wrote: 'Satan is the most heroic subject that ever was chosen for a poem . . . He was the greatest power that was ever overthrown, with the strongest will left to resist or endure.'[90] In this context, 'heroic subject' means more than merely 'epic protagonist'; it implies 'spokesman of Milton's republican views'; hero in moral and political, as well as poetic, terms.

This political/moral dimension is present in the most famous of all Romantic critiques of *Paradise Lost*: Blake's pronouncement, in *The Marriage of Heaven and Hell*, that 'The reason Milton wrote in fetters when he wrote of angels and God, and at liberty when of devils and Hell, is because he was a true poet, and of the Devil's party without knowing it'.[91] Like Godwin and Hazlitt, Blake associates liberty with Satan—but he goes further, in claiming an internalized liberty which is the 'true poet' in Milton, which Milton himself does not consciously acknowledge. According to Blake's psychological hierarchy, angels and God are dramatizations of the repressive super-ego: they stand for Milton's conscious mind, which cannot countenance his own rebellious instincts. In this way, Blake not only splits the psyche in two, producing a struggle for power between the tyrannical conscious and the oppressed unconscious; he also splits *Paradise Lost* in two, producing a subtext and a supertext. This Blakean act of division is of course highly productive, in Blake's own terms, for 'without contraries is no progression'.[92] It is also interesting, in terms of the history of

---

[88] *The Letters of Robert Burns*, ed. G. Ross Roy (2 vols., Oxford, 1985), i. 121.

[89] *Political Justice*, 309.

[90] Hazlitt, *Lectures on the English Poets* (1818), Lecture 3, 'On Shakespeare and Milton'; in *Romantics on Milton*, 384, Cf. Burns's comment, in a letter to W. Nicol (June 1787), on 'the dauntless magnanimity; the intrepid, unyielding independance; the desperate daring, and noble defiance of hardship, in that great Personage, Satan' (*Letters of Burns*, ed. Ross Roy, i. 123).

[91] *MHH*, pl. 5, ll. 52–5.   [92] Ibid. pl. 3, l. 7.

Paradise Lost's reception, because it makes the conflict between different kinds of reading central to the act of interpretation. Milton's poem can be claimed by either party, each of whom would thus produce what Bloom would call a 'strong misreading'; but it is the debate between them that matters.

The reader of *Paradise Lost* is placed in the position of choosing between a Milton who is humanly involved in political concerns and a Milton who divinely abstracts himself from them. I shall be examining the further implications of this choice, both in general terms, as it relates to the critical appropriations of *Paradise Lost* which have their origin in Romantic thinking (Chapter 2) and in more specific terms, for its bearing on the connection between Milton's politics and the ideology of his Romantic readers (Chapter 3). But it should also become apparent, from my argument in the remainder of this chapter, that Milton's oscillation between humanity and divinity is a recurrent feature of Romantic myth-making; and that, in the metaphors with which he is frequently invoked, there is suggested a potential merging between these separate states. Figural language of this kind could indeed be thought to have important political implications: by placing Milton in an intermediate position, it challenges the notion of a rigidly ordered hierarchy, and allows for the possibility of movement both up and down the ladder which leads through the vegetable, animal, and human kingdoms to God.[93] The levelling implications of this possibility will be developed further, as I move from the Romantics' transfigurations of Milton through invocation to Milton's role in Romantic theories of imagination.

IMITATION AND ORIGINALITY

So successful was the Milton cult that, by the time Blake wrote his *Marriage of Heaven and Hell* in 1790, *Paradise Lost* had earned its right to be considered on a par with *The Iliad* and *The Odyssey*. Indeed, it was the view of some eighteenth-century poets that Milton had surpassed his classical forebears: 'This man cuts us all out, and the ancients too', Dryden proclaimed, on first reading *Paradise Lost*.[94] Thomson goes nearly as far in 'Winter' (1726), aptly incorporating an allusion to Adam and Eve's departure from Paradise into his joint tribute to Homer and Milton:

> Great Homer, too, appears, of daring wing!
> Parent of song! and equal, by his side,
> The British Muse, joined hand in hand, they walk
> Darkling, full up the middle steep to fame.[95]

---

[93] I refer to the Platonic world-picture that is conveyed by Raphael to Adam (*PL* v. 468–505).

[94] Reported by J. Richardson in *Explanatory Notes and Remarks on Milton's Paradise Lost* (London, 1734), p. cxx. For a MS variant in Richardson's own annotated copy, see Griffin, *Regaining Paradise*, 273.

[95] James Thomson, 'Winter', ll. 533–6, in *'The Seasons' and 'The Castle of Indolence'*, ed. J. Sambrook (Oxford, 1972), 143.

Even Johnson, whose iconoclasm shocked the British public when his *Life of Milton* first came out ('no-one ever wished [*Paradise Lost*] longer than it is', he had rudely commented, at one point[96]) makes an interesting concession when it comes to putting Milton alongside his classical forebears: *Paradise Lost* 'is not the greatest of heroic poems', he claims, '*only because it is not the first*'[97]—a comment which shows how deeply neo-classicist were his values. To his mind, priority is almost a guarantee of poetic superiority; whereas for his Romantic followers, originality (of which more later) emerges as a separate criterion of success.

In the Postscript to his translation of *The Odyssey*, Pope justifies using Miltonic language 'to dignify and solemnise the plainer parts' of the narrative, and he goes on to explain that 'a just and moderate mixture of old words may have an effect like the working of old Abbey stones into a building ... to give a kind of venerable air'.[98] We might label this an antiquarian attitude to allusion: literary status is here bound up with age, and Miltonic language is distinguished from current language by its saturation in classical allusion. The flavour of classicism can therefore be given to translations of the classics, by the addition of Milton-isms. One of the interesting side-effects of Milton's growing status is that translations of Homer and Virgil begin to look more and more Miltonic: Joseph Trapp translated the whole of Virgil into Miltonic blank verse; and Cowper's Homer is even less Homeric than Pope's—the diction and rhythms are all copied from *Paradise Lost*.[99]

For the average twentieth-century reader, classical allusions seem inaccessible, whereas Miltonic ones are relatively familiar. At the beginning of the eighteenth century, however, classical imitation was not just a literary device used by learned writers but a habit of mind in which all educated readers were trained. It may have been a significant novelty, for such readers, to find recent vernacular poetry being quoted in the same breath as the revered classics: significant, because when echoed in the company of Homer and Virgil, Milton's status was being proclaimed as equal to theirs. There was nothing uneasy, however, in the conjunction. Augustan habits of allusive thinking did not preserve distinctions between a light-hearted topical reference and a weighty Homeric parallel (see, for instance, *The Rape of the Lock*), nor between the frivolity of mock-epic and the seriousness of Miltonic implication. Milton was himself so revered a classicist that Miltonic echoes could be put alongside classical ones without loss of decorum.

Milton's role in relation to the classical authors he imitated had a levelling effect on the canon. His skills in imitation helped establish his right to be

---

[96] *Johnson Life*, 183.   [97] The sentence is the last in ibid. 194.

[98] 'Postscript' to *The Odyssey*, in *The Twickenham Edition of the Poems of Alexander Pope*, gen. ed. J. Butt (11 vols., London, 1961–9); vols. ix–x: *Homer's Iliad and Odyssey*, ed. M. Mack (London, 1967), x. 390.

[99] Havens claims that 'It is hard to see how Homer could be made any more Miltonic' (*Influence of Milton*, 171).

considered as their equal, making way for the juxtapositions of Miltonic and classical language which increasingly characterized eighteenth-century habits of allusion. These in their turn eventually contributed to the promotion of *Paradise Lost* as an honorary (and to some extent substitute) classic. It is indeed an interesting feature of Milton's reception that it can be seen to have made more accessible the process of allusion itself. No longer associated only with learned reference to the ancients (and therefore precluding the understanding of less educated readers), allusion depended more and more on the vernacular. Milton's epic provided literary material which was available to readers of vastly differing classes and educational backgrounds: it levelled hierarchical distinctions, both within the literary canon and within the readership itself.

This process was helped along by the rise of the novel, a genre which was appropriated by figures as diverse in their attitudes to classical allusion as Fielding and Richardson, but who managed none the less to come together on the 'universal' relevance and applicability of *Paradise Lost* to discussions of morality. From an élitist perspective which elevates the Ancients over the Moderns, and which sees ignorance of the classics as an unpardonable crime,[100] Fielding constructs in *Tom Jones* a narrative which follows the biblical (and Miltonic) paradigm: paradisal innocence, followed by expulsion and trial, later to be rewarded by the return to a paradise that is enhanced through experience. This is a 'learned' neo-classical novel, in the sense that it engages *en route* with ancient sources, and depends for its subtlety on playful allusive games; but it succeeds none the less in levelling a hierarchical distinction between classical and vernacular models, by allowing a biblical (Miltonic) paradigm to organize the overall pattern and outcome of its narrative events. Meanwhile, from an utterly different perspective, Richardson challenges the hold which is exerted over his readership by the Ancients—dreaded symbols, for him, of literary exclusiveness and academicism. In *Clarissa*, he offers a consciously bare and original narrative: original, that is, in its repudiation of antiquarianism. *Clarissa* depends, as Gillian Beer has amply and subtly demonstrated,[101] on a Miltonic organization of the pattern of innocence–temptation–fall, which the heroine (Clarissa/Eve) convincingly refuses, but which its anti-hero (Lovelace/Satan) brings frighteningly alive. The strength of its Puritan message derives very largely from its Miltonic scrutiny of morality and psychological motivation.

When Mary Shelley constructs her richly intertextual narrative, *Frankenstein*, in 1818, she can rely on her readers' acceptance of Milton as an honorary classic: the subtitle of her novel is 'The Modern Prometheus', but Greek legend proves less important in this novel than the story of Genesis, as it is transformed

---

[100] For Richardson's ardent support of the Moderns against the Ancients, and for the part he played in sharpening the polemic of Young's *Conjectures on Original Composition*, 'in the direction of a new anti-classical hierarchy of literary values', see I. Watt, *The Rise of the Novel* (Harmondsworth, Middx., 1957), 281–2. Fielding's opposite point of view is also discussed in ibid. 282–6.

[101] 'Richardson, Milton and the Status of Evil', *Review of English Studies*, n.s. 19 (1968), 261–70.

by *Paradise Lost*. Shelley's narrative is constructed along Miltonic lines, and is held together by a dense network of allusions, the meaning of which can emerge only from detailed familiarity with Milton's account of the Fall. In the confidence and ease with which she deploys these allusive methods, Shelley may be regarded as sustaining the neo-classical tradition—indeed, her use of Miltonic quotation is not so very different in kind from the witty and learned practices of Pope and Dryden. Yet this tradition has been transformed by the reception of *Paradise Lost*. In embedding quotations from 'The Ancient Mariner' and 'Tintern Abbey', together with echoes from 'Mont Blanc', into a Miltonic story-line,[102] the author accords to Coleridge, Wordsworth, and Shelley the same elevation of status as Milton had been granted, a century before, when he began to be quoted in the same breath as Homer and Virgil. There has occurred a successful process of democratization, in the habit of allusion itself.

This process was given some of its momentum by the pugnacity with which Milton had issued a challenge to the supremacy of Homer and Virgil,[103] and by the readiness with which his audience received his Christianizing of epic as evidence of his greater claims to genius, sublimity, and seriousness of purpose. Thomas Newton, for instance, whose annotated two-volume edition of *Paradise Lost* went through more reprints than any other in the eighteenth century, had no hesitation in hailing Milton's epic as the consummation of its genre:

for just as Virgil rivaled Homer, so Milton emulated both. He found Homer possessed of the province of *morality*, Virgil of *politics*, and nothing left for him but that of *religion*. This he seised, as aspiring to share with them in the government of the poetic world; and by means of the superior dignity of his subject, got to the head of that triumvirate which took so many ages in forming. ... Here then the grand scene is closed, and all farther improvements are at an end.[104]

Cowper observed that 'Milton's divine subject afforded him opportunities of surpassing in sublime description all the poets his predecessors, and his talents were such as enabled him to use those opportunities for the best advantage'.[105] Comparing Milton's similes for the lost archangel with Homer's likening of Agamemnon to a bull, he observes that 'not only does [Milton] not degrade his subject, but [he] fills the mind of his reader with astonishing conceptions of its grandeur'. Cowper appears to appreciate *Paradise Lost* for precisely those ingredients which challenge established epic rules. So, whereas Aristotle lays down that the voice of the narrator must never, in epic, obtrude itself on the notice of the reader, Cowper claims that it was Milton's *duty* (and presumably he means duty as a Christian) not to suppress his remarks: 'there is more real worth and

---

[102] *Frankenstein* (London, 1976), 77–81, 132.

[103] See esp. the Proem to *PL* ix, where Milton claims his own handling of epic to be 'not less but more heroic' than *The Iliad* and *The Aeneid* (l. 14). He goes on to establish the credentials of his 'higher argument' (l. 42) on the basis of his faith, his internalization of epic themes, and his opposition to war.

[104] *Paradise Lost*, ed. Newton, ii. 127.

[105] In his 'Fragment of an Intended Commentary on Paradise Lost'; see Cowper's *Milton*, ii. 438.

importance in a single reflection of his', he comments decisively, 'than in all those of his heathen predecessors taken together' (p. 449).

Hayley agreed that Milton represented the culmination of the epic tradition, and placed special emphasis on his flouting of the classical rules. The *Essay on Epic Poetry* (1782) refers to him as 'that English, self-dependant soul | Born with such energy as mocks control',[106] and claims that, if he had attended to the rules of Boileau, he would never have written, and there would have been no-one to rival Homer.[107] Similarly, in his 'Conjectures on the Origin of Paradise Lost', Hayley's emphasis falls on Milton's surpassing of his predecessors—specifically, here, through a revision of the concept of the hero:

Milton seems to have given a purer signification than we commonly allow to the word hero, and to have thought it might be assigned to any person eminent and attractive enough to form a principal figure in a great picture.[108]

This revision of Homer is strongly appreciated by Hayley, who argues (from the perspective of Christian pacifism advocated by Milton) that he 'cannot admire the propriety of devoting [the term] to illustrious homicides', and that 'the Grecian bard had too great a tendency to nourish that sanguinary madness in mankind, which has continually made the earth a theatre of carnage' (p. 276).

As these comments of Cowper's and Hayley's suggest, Milton has not only had the effect of democratizing allusion; he has also caused a loosening of the strict rules laid down by academicians for the imitation of classical forms, and has been responsible, in particular, for the transformation of the generic expectations raised by epic, so that they can now include Christian values. Whilst being received as a paragon of neo-classicism by an age of imitation, Milton's challenge to the classical models he imitated has, in effect, put him in a category of his own. For this reason, he becomes implicated in the evolving of a new concept of originality which has important repercussions for Romanticism, and especially for ideas about the creative imagination.

The originality debate, in which Milton's reception played an immensely influential part, was provoked by the publication in 1741 of a short essay by C. Falconer entitled *An Essay upon Milton's Imitations of the Ancients in his Paradise Lost*. Falconer here takes a view that represents the extreme of neo-classicism. His starting-point is the Aristotelian claim that poetry is the pleasure mankind takes in the imitation of a thing by an image, on the basis of which Falconer argues for the double pleasure involved in the imitation of poems by poems. (This double pleasure, he claims, is derived from the fact that the imitating

---

[106] *An Essay on Epic Poetry (1782) by William Hayley*; fac. reprod., with introd. by M. C. Williamson, SSJ (Gainesville, Fla., 1968), 19 (epistle I., ll. 355–6).

[107] 'Could his high spirit, with submissive awe | Have stoop'd to listen to a Gallic law, | His hallow'd subject, by that Law forbid | Might still have laid in silent darkness hid' (ibid. ll. 357–60). Hayley's note draws attention to the fact that Boileau's *Art of Poetry* 'made its first appearance in 1675, six years after the first publication of Paradise Lost' (ibid. 136).

[108] Hayley, 'Conjectures on the Origin of Paradise Lost', in *Hayley Life*, 275–6.

poem is twice removed from the object itself.) He goes on to argue that in imitation, 'a considerable alteration from the original has a very agreeable effect';[109] and that likeness and variation should be combined. He does not approve borrowing parts of a story-line, but he does see the usefulness of allusions. Milton, he claims, is far superior to the Ancients, because his allusions *improve on* their descriptions. 'Vastly less Invention and Judgement', he pithily argues, 'is required to make a good Original than a fine Imitation.'[110]

In 1747, Lauder launched his charges of plagiarism against Milton, and went on in 1750 to publish *An Essay on Milton's Use and Imitation of the Moderns in his Paradise Lost*—a title which mockingly turns Falconer's essay on its head, within the terms of a long-established war between the Ancients and the Moderns. Lauder's intention, as outlined in the 'Preface' to this essay, is to discover if the 'founder' of *Paradise Lost* dug his foundations 'from the quarries of nature', or alternatively 'demolished other buildings to embellish his own'.[111] The essay discloses in Milton's epic a sequence of unacknowleged debts, by ingeniously juxtaposing the forged writings of Masenius, Ramsay, and Du Bartas with passages from *Paradise Lost*. Despite the evidently baroque contortions of his accusations, Lauder manages to maintain a tone of aggrieved superiority in the face of Milton's alleged treachery:

It is no difficult task to reply to *Andrew Marvell*'s *judicious query*, addressed to the author of *Paradise Lost*, in his commendatory verses prefixed to that poem:

> *Where* coulds't thou words of such a compass find?
> *Whence* furnish such a vast expence of mind?

The answer is obvious, namely, *from every author who wrote anything before him, suitable to his purpose, either in prose or verse, sacred or profane.*[112]

Lauder's cheeky onslaught on the nation's literary hero provoked immediate and outraged response from a number of different quarters. Among those who replied, the Revd. John Douglas offered a defence of Milton which is singularly the product of its time, renegotiating Milton's supremacy, not by exposing the forgeries on which Lauder's charges rest, but by claiming the sublimity of imitation, along lines that are reminiscent of Falconer's essay. 'A good Writer', Douglas argues, 'will exercise his Right to Imitation, in such a Manner as to convince everyone, that his having Recourse to it, is not the Effect of Sterility of Fancy, but of Solidity of Judgement.' And he goes on:

He will borrow only to shew his own Talents in heightening, refining and polishing all that is furnished to him by others, and thereby secure his Character as a fine *Writer* from being confounded with that of a *dull Copyer*.[113]

---

[109] *An Essay upon Milton's Imitations of the Ancients, in his Paradise Lost. With some observations on the Paradise Regain'd* (London, 1741), 4.

[110] Ibid. 61.   [111] p.2.   [112] Ibid. 61.

[113] *Milton No Plagiary: or a Detection of the Forgeries Contained in Lauder's Essay on the Imitations of the Moderns in Paradise Lost* (2nd edn., London, 1756), 10.

The debate came to a head with the publication in 1759 of Edward Young's *Conjectures on Original Composition*. The argument of this influential essay is diametrically opposed to the position maintained by Falconer and Douglas, in that it condemns the activity of imitation, and sees originality as imaginative. Importantly, for his Romantic followers, Young makes use of mechanical and organic metaphors to illuminate his central contrast:

> An *Original* may be said to be of a *vegetable* nature, it rises spontaneously from the vital root of Genius; it *grows*, it is not *made*. *Imitations* are often a sort of *Manufacture*, wrought up by those *Mechanics, Art* and *Labour*, out of pre-existent materials not their own.[114]

He goes on to suggest the staleness of imitators, who 'only give us a sort of Duplicates of what we had, possibly much better, before; increasing the mere Drug of books, while all that makes them valuable, *Knowledge* and Genius, are at a stand' (p. 10). Placing himself firmly on the side of the Moderns rather than the Ancients, Young suggests that Milton could have spared some of his learning, and that Pope would have done better to write his own epic than to translate Homer's (p. 69). He declares that the reason there are so few 'Originals' is not that 'the human mind's teeming time is past' but that the effect of great writers on those who follow them is to cause anxiety: 'Illustrious Examples *engross, prejudice*, and *intimidate*' (p. 17). As a result, although 'modern powers are equal to those before them, modern performance in general is deplorably short' (p. 46).

Young sees excitement in the activity of emulating such superior forebears—'What glory to come near, what glory to reach, what glory (presumptuous thought!) to surpass our Predecessors!' (p. 23)—and he sees no reason why later poets should not improve on them, having 'time' and 'nature' on their side. But he warns that the very act of setting up illustrious examples may have an effect that is damaging on creativity itself, since 'too formidable an Idea of their Superiority, like a spectre, would fright us out of the proper use of our Wits' (p. 25). He also warns of the close relation between imitation and passive submission, or even plagiarism, and advises that 'it is by a sort of noble Contagion, from a general familiarity with their writings, and not by any particular sordid Theft, that we can be the better for those who went before us' (pp. 24–5). Importantly, then, Young's stress lies, not on being better *than*, but on being *the better for* an illustrious example: he writes from within a tradition that is painfully conscious of the burden of the past.

The repercussions of this essay can be felt for many years to come, as the debate on imitation versus originality rumbles on. In his *Cursory Remarks on Some of the Ancient English Poets, particularly Milton* (1789), Philip Neve claims that 'Milton's language is so peculiarly his own, that the style of no former, or contemporary writer bears any resemblance to it' (p. 121). He points to 'the constitution of Milton's genius; his creative powers; the excursions of his imagination into regions untraced by human pen, unexplored by human

[114] p. 12.

thought', and concludes, with Young, that these 'were gifts of nature, not effects of learning' (p. 142). He is still sufficiently steeped in classical tradition to draw attention to Milton's allusions, but the distance of his essay from Falconer's can be judged by the sophistication and inventiveness of the metaphors he uses to describe the borrowing process. They suggest an allusive practice which involves first dissolving and dissipating, then re-creating, the finished materials of other writers:

It was his peculiar study to explore the traces of genius, in whatever authors had gone with eminence before him. He read them all. He took the golden ornaments from the hands of the best artists; he considered their fashion, their workmanship, and their weight, their alloy; and, storing and arranging them for occasion, he adapted them, as he saw fit, to the chalice, or the pixis, formed from the sublime patterns of his own mind.   (pp. 145–6)

Hayley, in his 'Conjectures on the Origin of Paradise Lost' (appended to *The Life of Milton* in 1796, and clearly alluding to Young's essay), adopts a similar position to Neve's. He sees the strength of Milton's credentials as classical imitator, but none the less claims the unquestionable originality of *Paradise Lost*:

There is frequent allusion to the works of antiquity in Milton, yet no poet, perhaps, who revered the ancients with such affectionate enthusiasm, has copied them so little. This was partly owing to the creative opulence of his genius, & partly to his having fixed on a subject so different from those of Homer and Virgil, that he may be said to have accomplished a revolution in poetry, and to have purified and extended the empire of the epic muse.[115]

This is a hybrid view of Milton, simultaneously encompassing imitation and originality. It would not have been possible at the beginning of the century (or even before the publication of Young's *Conjectures*); and it sets the scene for Romanticism. Hazlitt later echoes it almost exactly:

Milton has borrowed more than any other writer, and exhausted every source of imitation, sacred and profane; yet he is perfectly distinct from every other writer. He is a writer of centos, yet in originality scarcely inferior to Homer. ... In reading his works, we feel ourselves under the influence of a mighty intellect, that the nearer it approaches to others, becomes more distinct from them.[116]

This observation is fascinating for the convergence it suggests between Milton as a neo-classical model and Milton as original genius. Hazlitt invokes the contrasting values of Augustanism and Romanticism; but in addition he suggests a human/divine duality in Milton, which emerges as a persistent feature of Romantic criticism. Whereas human beings are imitative in their creative acts, God is the great originator: even for the non-religious, Genesis offers the prime account of creation that involves no imitation. In being thought to possess this double nature, Milton is constructed by Hazlitt as a model of the

---

[115] p. 274.   [116] 'On Shakespeare and Milton', in *Romantics on Milton*, 38.

Romantic imagination; he is also placed at an important crossroads, historically speaking, in relation to literary ideas which have been undergoing
rapid change during the eighteenth century, and which have been directly
confronted by Young.

   The importance of Young's essay should certainly not be underestimated. It
makes the century's clearest and loudest claim for originality as the first
requisite of 'genius' and the paramount concern of poetry. It brings into focus,
as an aesthetic issue, the author's claim to 'ownership' of his own ideas; and in
so doing it gives expression to an expanding individualism, itself contingent
on economic pressures, which is representative of the prevailing system of
values in the latter half of the eighteenth century.[117] Its powerful appeal, even
to those who stood outside (or were highly critical of) these values, can be
judged by the 'Preface' to Blake's *Milton*. Like Young, Blake comes down
heavily in favour of originality, genius, and imagination (Hebrew poetry) as
distinct from memory and imitation (Greek poetry); but he sees in Milton too
great a deference to the classical tradition which he ought by rights to have
repudiated. The repercussions of Young's essay may also be discernible
(though less overtly) in the 'anxiety of plagiarism' manifested by writers such
as Coleridge. Indeed, by setting so high a premium on originality, Young
manages to suggest that several species of borrowing could be construed as
'sordid theft'.[118]

   The overriding importance of Young's essay, however, lies in its clearing
the way for an identification of Milton as the monopolist of a certain species of
sacred poetry, who managed to scare his followers out of a proper use of their
wits. 'Illustrious examples engross, prejudice, and intimidate': in Harold
Bloom's view, if not in Young's, Milton was the arch-intimidator. His presence haunted the writers of the eighteenth century, at once commanding and
defying emulation—the more so because, despite being seen as the greatest of
imitators, in a literary climate that fostered imitation, he none the less
managed, as Hazlitt observes, to escape the taint of unoriginality. As a 'writer
of centos ... yet scarcely inferior to Homer', he provided a model of originality thriving on imitation—Romantic genius emerging out of neo-classicism.
He could therefore be used as an 'illustrious example', on both sides of the
originality debate. To generations of writers trained in the art of imitation, this
made him at once more worthy of imitation—'What glory to come near, what

---

[117] Blake's annotations to vol. i of Sir Joshua Reynolds's *Works* contain numerous references to
'Invention' as a prerequisite for genius. The extent to which 'Invention' has by the early 19th c.
become a commercial value is humorously exposed in the following annotation: 'When a Man talks
of Acquiring Invention, & of learning how to produce Original Conceptions, he must expect to be
call'd a Fool by Men of Understanding; but such a Hired Knave cares not for the Few. His Eye is on
the Many, or rather the Money'; *The Complete Writings of William Blake*, ed. G. Keynes (London,
1966), 469.
[118] Coleridge's anxiety with respect to his own borrowing habits is documented in N. Fruman,
Coleridge, the Damaged Archangel (New York, 1971), and can be discerned in the quotation with
which I opened this book.

glory to reach, what glory (presumptuous thought) to surpass our predecessors!'—and, ultimately, more impossible to outdo.

SUBLIMITY AND DIVINITY

Addison's essays in *The Spectator* (1712) are responsible, so far as Milton was concerned, for the beginnings of the sublime cult. Their popularity ensured that *Paradise Lost* was hailed, at the start of the century, under an exciting new heading; and that the name of Milton was from the first connected with discussions of imagination. Milton's 'chief talent' and 'distinguishing Excellence', according to Addison, lay in 'the Sublimity of his Thoughts'. By 'Sublimity' (at this stage in England a relatively untheorized concept), Addison means grandeur of idea and emotion, as distinct from skill of poetic craftsmanship:

There are others of the Moderns who rival him in every other part of Poetry; but in the greatness of his Sentiments he triumphs over all the Poets both Modern and Ancient, *Homer* only excepted. It is impossible for the Imagination of Man to distend it self with greater Ideas, than those which he has laid together in his first, second, and sixth Books.[119]

In Hugh Blair's *Lectures on Rhetoric and Belles Lettres*, delivered fifty or so years later (1759–60), the grounds for appreciation, and the critical vocabulary used, are still recognizably Addisonian: 'Milton's great and distinguishing excellence is, his sublimity',[120] Blair claims. But by this stage a realignment has taken place in the relation between classical and vernacular literature (and, indeed as we have seen, between notions of imitation and originality) which allows for the dislodgement of a larger number of classical forebears than Addison had conceived possible. Where he had excepted Homer from the list of poets who were 'triumphed over' by Milton's sublimity, Blair claims that Milton 'perhaps excels Homer; as there is no doubt of his leaving Virgil and every other Poet, far behind him'.

Blair turns for his examples of sublimity to passages in *Paradise Lost* which were first singled out by Addison and have since become synonymous with the Miltonic grand style. 'The First and Second Books of *Paradise Lost* are continued instances of the sublime', he claims: (p. 474)

The prospect of Hell and the fallen Host, the appearance and behaviour of Satan, the consultation of the infernal Chiefs, and Satan's flight through Chaos to the borders of this world, discover the most lofty ideas that ever entered into the conception of any Poet.

There is indeed an implied preference, in what both Addison and Blair say, for books which concern Satan: sublimity is frequently associated with the soaring of Satan through the heavens, or his plummeting through space. Sometimes this

---

[119] J. Addison, *Spectator*, 279 (19 Jan. 1712), in *The Spectator*, ed. with introd. and notes, D. F. Bond (5 vols., Oxford, 1965), ii. 587.
[120] *Lectures on Rhetoric and Belles Lettres* (2 vols., London, 1783), lecture 44, ii. 473–4.

involves a daring equation of Satan's perspective with Milton's own—as in Gray's 'The Progress of Poesy', where Milton is likened to Satan spying on 'the secrets of the abyss'.[121] At other times, it is connected more straight-forwardly with an appreciation of the expansiveness of Milton's spatial meta-phors, or with his dramatic counterpointing of dark and light.

From the first, there is a tendency in Milton appreciations to internalize the cosmology of *Paradise Lost*—that is, to follow Satan's own practice of reading heaven and hell as subjective states. When Addison writes of the imagination as distending itself with great ideas, he is locating sublimity in the mind—or, more specifically, in the elasticity of mental space. Johnson, similarly, claims that 'Milton's delight was to sport in the wide regions of possibility', and he goes on to expand the metaphorical connection between space and imaginative potential: 'He sent his faculties out upon discovery, into worlds where only imagination can travel'.[122] Such comments point forward to the identification made by Coleridge between sublimity and reflexivity: 'the sublimest parts of Paradise Lost are the revelations of Milton's own mind, producing itself and evolving its own greatness'.[123] They are closely paralleled in some of the observations made by Burke, whose important treatise, *A Philosophical Enquiry into the Origin of our Ideas of the Sublime and Beautiful*, grounded much of its analysis of sublimity of language in passages taken from *Paradise Lost*.

I shall be returning in Chapter 6 to Burke's famous critique of the 'signifi-cant and expressive uncertainty' which characterizes Milton's description of Death, in *Paradise Lost* Book II; and I shall be offering an extended analysis of the ways in which eighteenth-century commentary on the sublime (particularly with reference to this passage) paves the way for an aesthetic of indeterminacy, through its foregrounding of subjectivity (Milton's and the reader's). I do, however, want to take note of the passage here, since its importance is not to be underestimated, as part of the process whereby key passages of Miltonic lan-guage are received as touchstones of sublimity, thereby ensuring an increas-ingly close associative bond between the Miltonic imagination and the idea of the sublime.

Burke quotes in full the passsage which begins 'The other shape | If shape it might be called which shape had none | Distinguishable, in member, joint, or limb ...', and goes on to observe that 'in this description all is dark, un-certain, confused, terrible, and sublime to the last degree'.[124] He thus makes an important connection between sublimity and obscurity—between the power and grandeur of ideas and the insufficiency of language to express them. It is this connection which makes possible the internalization of sublimity as a function of the subjective mind, since it draws attention to the fact that, as Kant later puts it, 'ideas of sublimity cannot be contained in any sensuous

[121] l. 97.   [122] *Johnson Life*, 178.
[123] 'Lecture on Milton and the Paradise Lost', 4 Mar. 1819, in *Romantics on Milton*, 245.
[124] *Burke Enquiry*, 59.

form'.[125] But, conversely, it is this connection, also, which allows ideas of power and grandeur to be sustained as potentially tyrannical forces, since the human subject is thereby reminded of its littleness in the face of something tremendously bigger than itself. The language of *Paradise Lost*, by vividly enacting the inexpressibility of terrible and awe-inspiring ideas, is drawn, by Burke's analysis, into a power system which underwrites 'the structure and psychology of transcendence'.[126]

In his 'The Fragment of an Intended Commentary on Paradise Lost', Cowper discusses the subjective dimension of limitlessness. Commenting on the lines in Book II where Milton describes the fall of Mulciber, he quotes 'and to this hour | Down had been falling'. This expression, he claims, 'is like a fathoming-line put into our hands by the poet for the purpose of sounding an abyss without a bottom'.[127] Cowper sees Milton as exploiting the reader's sense of limitation, in order to enhance their capacity to conceive the limitless—a procedure which I shall later suggest is crucial to the pleasure-in-displeasure of the Kantian sublime. Thus, despite the impossibility of imagining Mulciber's fall as something that could conceivably take as long as Milton suggests, the reader is none the less given access to a subjective dimension, in which space and time both become endless. This is made possible, as Cowper implies, because the 'fathoming-line' offered by Milton himself belongs to an eternal perspective, beyond the text itself. His commentary continues: 'Nor is this the only passage in which Milton sublimely and with great effect, by the help of a mere supposition, assists our apprehension of the subject. In the 6th book we find one similar to this, where describing the battle of the angels ... he says—"All heav'n | Resounded, and had earth been then, all earth | Had to her centre shook."' Once again, it is the sudden shift of temporal perspective, together with its diminution of human capacity and its shrinkage of human significance, which for Cowper constitutes the Miltonic sublime.

Sublimity, then, is particularly associated with Satanic passages in *Paradise Lost*, and with the opening up of subjective or mental space, through the use of a language of obscurity. But, in the readings offered by both Burke and Cowper, this obscurity works finally to diminish the power of the human subject, in the face of supersensible ideas; it is, in other words, ideologically appropriated by Milton, as a means of mystification—bringing home to the reader a magnified sense of the power of God. For this reason, the boundary between sublimity and divinity is a narrow one, where discussions of Miltonic language are concerned; and the subordination of sublimity to devotional purpose is more or less standard in accounts of Milton belonging to the later part of the eighteenth century. Indeed, after the publication in 1787 of Bishop Lowth's *Lectures on the Sacred*

---

[125] *The Critique of Judgement*, trans. with analytical indexes, J. C. Meredith (Oxford, 1952; repr. 1978), 92.

[126] I refer to the title of T. Weiskel's influential *The Romantic Sublime: Studies in the Structure and Psychology of Transcendence* (Baltimore, 1976).

[127] Cowper's *Milton*, ii. 457.

Poetry of the Hebrews, it becomes almost impossible to separate Miltonic sublimity from the generic attributes of 'prophecy' as Lowth defined them.

Lowth's *Lectures* consistently maintain the view that Hebrew poetry proves the
inferiority of all other nations in attempting to treat the greatness of God;[128] and
Milton features only in passing comparisons (often footnotes) with the Old
Testament passages which Lowth is commenting on. What matters here, then, is
not Milton's named presence in discussions of the sublime so much as Lowth's
appropriation of sublimity as a subspecies of sacred poetry. Lowth affirms that
'the original office and destination of Poetry' is religion (p. 36), and that sacred
poetry is far superior to either nature or art. 'Nothing in nature', he claims, 'can
be so conducive to the sublime, as those conceptions which are suggested by the
contemplation of the greatest of all beings' (p. 169). He acknowledges, as Burke
does, the close connection between obscurity of language and sublimity of
conception; but he is more explicit in giving it the divinely authoritative dimension which lies in the background of Burke's aesthetic. 'Some degree of obscurity', he claims, 'is the necessary attendant upon prophecy' (p. 200); and parts of
the future must inevitably be repressed or withheld from the reader.

When it comes to defining the effectiveness of sublime language, as a vehicle
for conveying ideas of divinity, Lowth finds in the Holy Scriptures two different
species of the sublime. The first uses 'the grandest imagery that universal nature
can suggest, and yet this imagery, however great, proves totally inadequate to the
purpose' (p. 353). The reader thus comes up against ideas of limitlessness which
he cannot handle, and responds along Burkean lines: 'The mind seems to exert
its utmost faculties in vain to grasp an object, whose unparalleled magnitude
mocks its feeble endeavours.' The second kind of sublimity depends on a
comparison between the qualities of divinity and either natural objects or
human attributes. These latter, precisely by being inadequate to the conceptions
they are meant to embody, allow for an enlightening comparison with the
greatness of God:

From ideas, which in themselves appear coarse, unsuitable, and totally unworthy of so
great an object, the mind naturally recedes, and passes suddenly to the contemplation of
the object itself, and of its inherent magnitude and importance.   (p. 364)

Lowth's analysis of sublimity thus adopts two routes for underwriting divine
authority. It sees both kinds of language, whether grand or humble, as inadequate to the purpose of describing God; and it sees sublimity as consisting in the
acknowledgement of our human inadequacy, in the face of supersensible ideas.
Here, as in Burke and Cowper, humiliation of the subject is built into the
structure of the sublime.

Lowth's analysis of prophecy adapted itself readily to *Paradise Lost*, if only
because of the applicability of its general claims to poetry with an overtly religious tenor. Its evident influence on the reception of Milton could be seen to play

[128] *Lowth Lectures*, i. 347–9.

an important part in maintaining a connection between concepts of divinity and the sublime, for some time after this latter might otherwise have become an autonomous aesthetic. Even without Lowth, however, it is probable that the religious ideas embodied in *Paradise Lost* would have been importantly present, in the minds of Milton's pre-Romantic and Romantic readers, whenever they turned to him as a model of sublimity; and this is the case even when their allusions appear to work on a purely secular or aesthetic level. Hazlitt's comment that in *Paradise Lost* 'the power of [Milton's] mind is stamped on every line'[129] suggests a coalescence between authorial identity and creative product, which bears out the Keatsian sense of what it is that distinguishes Milton's imagination from Shakespeare's.[130] The oppressive aura of authority which surrounded this 'power of mind', and which, in the eyes of his eighteenth- and nineteenth-century readers, gave Milton the status of God, can be seen to derive from a merging between his sublime poetic stature, his Puritanical reputation, and his sacred subject. Cowper offers a clear analysis of this in his commentary on *Paradise Lost*:

The sublimest of all subjects was reserved for Milton, and bringing to the contemplation of that subject not only a genius equal to the best of [the ancients], but a heart also deeply impregnated with the divine truths ... it is no wonder, that he has produced a composition on the whole, superior to any, that we have received from former ages.[131]

It is clear how far Cowper has progressed beyond the neo-classicism of Pope, Addison, and Johnson: Milton is not being claimed as the equal of Homer and Virgil, but as their superior; and it is precisely his Christianity which puts him in a class of his own: 'Milton's divine subject afforded him opportunities of surpassing in sublime description all the poets his predecessors, and his talents were such as enabled him to use those opportunities to the best advantage' (p. 438).

In Cowper's view, *Paradise Lost* holds no interest for the atheist or agnostic reader, since its audience, fit though few, is determined by membership of the Christian elect. Indeed, the sense Cowper has of Milton as a mind 'impregnated with divine truths' makes the study of *Paradise Lost* a Puritan task—a test of the religious devotion of its reader:

he, who addresses himself to the perusal of this work with a mind entirely unaccustomed to serious and spiritual contemplation, unacquainted with the word of God, or prejudiced against it, is ill-qualified to appreciate the value of a poem built upon it, or to taste its beauties. (p. 427)

Aesthetic enjoyment and religious awe are seen as twin aspects of the Miltonic sublime, and to separate tenor and vehicle is, in Cowper's view, to do irreparable damage to the 'very soul' of *Paradise Lost*:

---

[129] 'On Shakespeare and Milton', in *Romantics on Milton*, 381.   [130] See n. 151 below.
[131] Cowper's *Milton*, ii. 427.

Milton is the poet of Christians: an Infidel may have an ear for the harmony of his numbers, may be aware of the dignity of his expression, and in some degree of the sublimity of his conceptions, but the unaffected and masculine piety, which was his true inspirer, and is the very soul of his poem, he will either not perceive, or it will offend him. (pp. 427–8)

This view was shared by Hayley, whose *Life of Milton* is significant in the genesis of Blake's prophecy, and who plays a prominent part in confirming Milton's reputation for spiritual perfection. Hayley goes further than Cowper, however, in suggesting a coalescence between aesthetic and religious categories. He sees a possibility for the inducement of devotional piety through the enhancement of a sense of beauty. Again, actual converts will be few, since 'A devotional taste is as requisite for the full enjoyment of Milton as a taste for poetry';[132] but there is, of course, room for improvement, even amongst the fit and few: 'To a reader who thoroughly relishes the two poems on Paradise', Hayley claims, 'his heart appears to be purified, in proportion to the pleasure he derives from the poet, and his mind to become angelic.'[133] Interestingly, Hayley makes an implicit connection here between the experience of poetic sublimity and the process of spiritual sublimation. Milton becomes a vehicle for the human capacity to move up what Coleridge will later call 'the ascent of being', into an angelic state.[134] The poet's dual nature is thus replicated within the imagination of the reader, who realizes his or her divine potential in the act of reading. Something of this idea is present, also, in Coleridge's observation of the stylistic ingredients in *Paradise Lost* which encourage vigilance. 'A reader of Milton', he claims, 'must be always on his Duty. He is surrounded with sense.'[135] He goes on to suggest a distinction between 'that vicious obscurity which proceeds from a muddled head', and the obscurity which is 'complaisant to the reader'. Here he presumably means that the vigilance which Milton encourages is both educative and pleasurable: as Lowth, Cowper, and Hayley would all agree, it improves the reader's capacity for devotion.

I have already discussed the democratization in the literary canon, for which *Paradise Lost* may be partly responsible, in its challenging of the supremacy of Homer and Virgil. Far more significant, however, is the levelling effect which Milton's religious authority has on the Holy Scriptures themselves. Comparisons between *Paradise Lost* and the Scriptures abound in eighteenth-century commentaries on Milton. Thomas Newton, for instance, writes that 'throughout the whole the author appears to have been a most critical reader and a most passionate admirer of Holy Scripture'.[136] And he goes on to offer a playful

---

[132] 'Conjectures on the Origin of Paradise Lost', 278.   [133] Ibid.

[134] 'Our Almighty Parent hath therefore given to us Imagination ... that still revivifies the dying motive within us, and fixing our eye on the glittering summits that rise one above the other in Alpine endlessness still urges us up the ascent of Being' (*Coleridge Lectures*, 235).

[135] *The Notebooks of Samuel Taylor Coleridge*, ed. K. Coburn (4 vols., New York, 1957–61), i. 280; in *Romantics on Milton*, 159.

[136] *Paradise Lost*, ed. Newton, ii. 446–7.

reworking of the battle between the Ancients and the Moderns, in which classical literature is altogether overlooked: 'Whoever has any true taste and genius, we are confident, will esteem this poem the best of modern productions, and the scriptures the best of the ancient ones'.[137] This is a view not so very distant from Bishop Lowth's. Alongside it one might put Hayley's comment that Milton's poetry 'flowed from the scripture, as if his unparalleled poetical powers had been expressly given him by Heaven for the purpose of imparting to religion such lustre as the most splendid of human minds could bestow'.[138] Here we have a suggestion, slightly more daring than Newton's, not only that Milton is the vessel of God's word, and therefore in a line directly descended from the Scriptures, but that in some respects his function is to improve on the material he inherits: he *imparts to* religion a 'lustre' which comes from the splendidness of his human mind. Cowper similarly acknowledges the indebtedness of *Paradise Lost* to the Bible, 'as well for the beauty of the stile and sentiments, as for the matter of his poem';[139] and he too stresses the expansion of Milton's imagination beyond the bare ingredients of the biblical text: Scripture, he observes, supplies only 'a lake of Fire and Brimstone', 'yet what a world of woe has [Milton] constructed by the force of an imagination ... the most creative, that ever poet owned' (p. 430).

By the end of the eighteenth century there has emerged a view of Milton as arguably more sublime than the Scriptures. This elevation of status is, of course, helped along by two claims Milton himself makes, that he has received instruction from the Holy Spirit and that *Paradise Lost* has been dictated to him by the heavenly muse: together, these establish that his epic is a transcription of the divine word.[140] But such a view is dependent, also, on the increasingly high premium that is placed on imagination and sublimity, in responses to devotional writing; and on the realignment of secular and classical literature previously discussed. Thus, when Hayley presents his climactic description of Milton in the *Essay on Epic Poetry*,[141] he gives him a role that is importantly double. Not only does the author of *Paradise Lost* bring to its apogee the classical epic; he also seizes a sacred theme which no one else has dared to touch, and in so doing eclipses both religious and secular competition, at a single blow. In a description that is shot through with echoes from Collins's 'Ode on the Poetical Character' (to be discussed at length in Chapter 7), Hayley stresses the distance of Milton from his kind: 'Apart, and on a sacred hill retir'd ... the mighty Milton sits'. He invokes the extraordinary nature of his genius ('beyond all mortal inspiration fir'd'), and the daringness of his aspiration: 'To grasp with daring hand a Seraph's lyre'. He affirms the angelic status which Milton achieves; and he points to the process of improvement the poet initiates in his readers, through

---

[137] Ibid. 447.   [138] *Hayley Life*, 219.   [139] *Milton*, ii. 461.
[140] See *PL* i. 6–26; vii. 28–31; ix. 20–4.
[141] Hayley, *Essay on Epic Poetry*, epistle 3, ll. 411–32 (pp. 64–5).

his 'soul-subduing themes'. Milton becomes a model of the aspiring imagination, which achieves divine status in the process of celebrating divinity.

This conflation of Milton with God proves fruitful to the emergence of
Romanticism because it provides a monolithic version of authority against
which the Romantics can fight, and a set of moral and religious absolutes against
which they can choose to define themselves. But this 'revisionary' aspect of
Romanticism, powerfully and influentially conveyed by Harold Bloom's theory
of influence, should not be emphasized at the expense of evident continuities in
tradition. Alongside the questioning of Puritan values which we see at its most
urgent, for instance, in Blake's *The Marriage of Heaven and Hell*, there is in
Romanticism a strong perpetuation of two eighteenth-century traditions
identified in the course of my analysis of sublimity. The first of these can be
characterized as deferential and awe-stricken: a dwarfed and humiliated response to the obscurity of Milton's prophetic style. The second can be seen as
potentially liberating, in that it sees the possibility for moving up the ascent of
being, towards godhead itself, by taking Milton as a role model of poetic aspiration. A close connection between these two ideas establishes Milton as an
exemplar, at one and the same time, of the rivalrous and the unrivalled imagination; and, as I shall show in my later analysis of allusive practices, this double
role creates some problems and ambiguities for critical interpretation.

DEHUMANIZATION

Not surprisingly, the sublimity and loftiness of Milton's conceptions were seen
as removing him from human concerns. 'Apart, and on a sacred hill
retir'd | Beyond all mortal inspiration fir'd',[142] he became a model of the
abstracted imagination which works at a distance from its kind. Responses to
this removedness, or abstraction, are an important means, for Milton's
followers, of defining their own imaginative identity; and indeed, much of the
interest of eighteenth-century commentary derives from the debate it conducts,
at the level of Miltonic invocation, on the issue of commitment or non-
commitment to human concerns. When Johnson, for instance, writes of Milton
that 'He sent his faculties out upon discovery, into worlds where only imagination can travel' (*Life*, p. 178), his approval is more complex than at first appears.
One must recall the suspicion with which he regarded imagination—in *Rasselas*,
particularly, where it has explicit connections with madness, obsession, and
alienation.[143] In his emphasis on Milton's boundlessness, and in his backhan-
ded compliments—'Milton sometimes descends to the elegant, but his element

---

[142] Ibid. 64.
[143] See esp. ch. 44 of *Rasselas*, headed 'The dangerous prevalence of Imagination', where
Johnson writes: 'All power of fancy over reason is a degree of insanity'; *The Yale Edition of the Works
of Samuel Johnson* (16 vols., New Haven, Conn., 1958–80), xvi: *Rasselas and Other Tales*, ed. G. J.
Kolb (1980), 150.

is the great'; 'reality was a scene too narrow for his mind' (*Life*, pp. 177, 178)—one must see a clear rebuke for Milton's neglect of the real world. Johnson asserts, categorically, that in *Paradise Lost* 'the want of human interest is always felt' (p. 183); and according to his own terms, there is something culpable, even hubristic, in such oversight.

Pope took a rather more balanced view. He is reported by his friend Joseph Spence to have conceded that Milton's style was not natural but 'exotic';[144] and yet, unlike Johnson, he stressed the adaptability of Miltonic language to human subject-matter:

As his subject lies a good deal out of our world, [the exotic style] has a particular propriety in those parts of the poem; and when he is on earth, whenever he is describing our parents in Paradise, you see he uses a more easy and natural way of writing.

This was not, however, a characteristic perspective on Milton. By and large, eighteenth-century commentary seemed determined to account for the distinctiveness and oddity of Milton's language rather than to explain it away. Philip Neve is closer to the norm when he uses oddity to claim originality—'Milton's language is so peculiarly his own, that the style of no former, or contemporary writer bears any resemblance to it'[145]—a tactic which is adopted also by Hugh Blair when he observes that Milton has 'chalked out for himself a new, and very extraordinary road, in Poetry':

As soon as we open his *Paradise Lost*, we find ourselves introduced all at once into an invisible world, and surrounded with celestial and infernal beings. Angels and Devils are not the machinery, but principal actors, in the poem; and what, in any other composition would be the marvellous, is here only the natural course of events.[146]

The defamiliarizing effect of sublimity is registered in Blair's sense that *Paradise Lost* is uncategorizable. A subject 'so remote from the affairs of this world' is, in his view, alien to the epic genre; he therefore turns to the notion of imagination, or genius, as a way of explaining the anomalous qualities of Milton's style: 'By whatever name it is to be called, it is, undoubtedly, one of the highest efforts of poetical genius'.

According to Knight's influential essay on taste, however, Milton 'viewed nature through the medium of books, and wrote from the head rather than the heart':[147] this explained his preference for the strained inversions of sublime poetic diction, instead of the plain word-order of natural language.

---

[144] Joseph Spence, *Observations, Anecdotes, and Characters, of Books and Men*, arr. with notes, E. Malone (London, 1820); in J. T. Shawcross (ed.), *Milton 1732–1801: The Critical Heritage* (London, 1969), 132.

[145] *Cursory Remarks on some of the Ancient English Poets, particularly Milton* (London, 1789), 121.

[146] *Lectures on Rhetoric and Belles Lettres*, ii. 471.

[147] R. P. Knight, *An Analytical Inquiry into the Principles of Taste* (London, 1805), 126.

Wordsworth, in a mood of impetuosity that is almost Blakean, wrote in the margin of his own copy of Knight's essay, alongside the comment just quoted,

Milton wrote chiefly from the Imagination which you may place where you like in head heart liver or veins. *Him* the Almighty Power hurled headlong etc. See one of the most wonderful sentences ever formed by the mind of man.[148]

He thus places himself on Blair's side of the debate over rhetoric. Even to the author of *Lyrical Ballads* and its 1800 'Preface', there is justification for the baroque inversions of Miltonic language, in the 'imaginative and impassioned' nature of his sublime subject. Knight's opposition between head and heart is immaterial, in Wordsworth's view, since Milton's 'imagination' belongs to a category that is removed from either. For Keats, on the other hand, there is something oppressively artificial in the Miltonic style: 'The Paradise Lost though so fine in itself is a corruption of our Language—it should be kept as it is unique—a curiosity. a beautiful and grand Curiosity.' When he abandons 'Hyperion', it is because his own language has become cluttered with inversions: 'Miltonic verse cannot be written but in an artful or rather Artist's humour,' he writes, in tones that remind one of Johnson or Knight.[149]

As the stress on sublimity grew, Milton became less and less associated with human emotions, a process which was reinforced by what one might call the 'Satanizing' of *Paradise Lost*. Adam and Eve thus diminished in importance, as Satan took on increasingly heroic dimensions, himself becoming the tragic human centre of Milton's poem:

> —His form had not yet lost
> All her original brightness, nor appear'd
> Less than archangel ruined, and the excess
> Of glory obscured:
>
> (*PL* i. 591–4)

Wordsworth once said that he could read this description of Satan 'Till he felt a certain faintness come over his mind from the sense of beauty and grandeur': Hazlitt, reporting the comment, saw 'no extravagance in it, but the utmost truth of feeling', and himself observed of the same lines that 'the mixture of beauty, of grandeur, and pathos, from the sense of irreparable loss, of never-ending, unavailing regret, is perfect'.[150] A clear separation emerges, then, between the capacity of Milton's imagination to sympathize with Satan, on grounds of sublimity, and the incapacity of his imagination to present the human predicament from other than a divinely abstracted perspective. Even now, a view persists that

---

[148] Annotations (Mar.–Apr. 1802) to Knight's *Principles of Taste*; in *Romantics on Milton*, 378.

[149] To G. and G. Keats, 24 Sept. 1819 (*Keats Letters*, 325); to J. H. Reynolds, 21 Sept. 1819 (ibid. 292).

[150] Reminiscence of Hazlitt (before 19 Apr. 1808) in *Romantics on Milton*, 119; and 'On Shakespeare and Milton', ibid. 378.

the first two books of *Paradise Lost* are the best, and that its intensity decreases when the focus shifts from Satan to Adam and Eve.

The dehumanized caricature of Milton emerges most clearly by contrast with Shakespeare, who is frequently invoked as his opposite, particularly by Romantic readers. The two come to stand as complementary figures, who demonstrate contrasting tendencies in the creative mind, or symbolize radically different kinds of poetic genius. Shakespeare is associated with pathos and tenderness, Milton with the sublime; Shakespeare can enter fully into human frailties whereas Milton stands at a distance from them; Shakespeare is all relativism and openness whereas Milton is hidebound by religious absolutes, from which he is unable to break free. Keats, for instance, ascribes to Shakespeare the capacity to remain 'in uncertainties, Mysteries, doubts, without any irritable reaching after fact & reason',[151] whilst he sees in Milton a denial and closure which he finds stifling: 'I have but lately stood on my guard against Milton, Life to him would be death to me'.[152] The greatness of Milton's capacity as a philosopher is never, for Keats, in question, but his lack of 'negative capability' means that he can never 'think into the human heart' as deeply as did Shakespeare or Wordsworth.

Variations on this contrast abound in Romantic criticism. One of Coleridge's most pithily suggestive observations makes an alignment between the two different kinds of imagination, and the immanent/transcendent models of divinity: 'Shakspeare is the Spinozistic Deity, an omnipresent creativeness. Milton is Prescience; he stands *ab extra*, and drives a fiery coach and four, making the horses feel the iron curb which holds them.'[153] Wordsworth makes a similar contrast, but on the more familiar basis of division between human and divine subject-matter. Thus, in the Preface to *Poems* (1815): 'the grand storehouses of enthusiastic and meditative Imagination, of poetical, as contradistinguished from human and dramatic Imagination, are the prophetic and lyrical parts of the holy Scriptures, and the works of Milton. The 'human and dramatic Imagination', on the other hand, is to be found in Shakespeare.[154]

Interestingly, the claim that Wordsworth makes here depends on divesting Milton's poetry of its classicism, which he sees as merely its surface interest. He is wary of paganism (Coleridge's 'godkins and goddesslings');[155] in particular,

---

[151] To G. and T. Keats, 27 Dec. 1817; *Keats Letters*, 43.

[152] To G. and G. Keats, 24 Sept. 1819; ibid. 325.

[153] *Table Talk*, i. 125 (9 May 1830) in *Romantics on Milton*, 270. Cf. Coleridge's comment that, whereas Shakespeare 'darts himself forth, and passes into all the forms of human character and passion', Milton 'attracts all forms and things to himself, into the unity of his own IDEAL' (*Biographia*, ii. 27–8).

[154] See *Wordsworth*, 634, 635.

[155] Coleridge distinguishes between the religious poetry of the Greeks, which addresses Genii and Dryads (Godkins and Goddesslings) and that of the Hebrews, 'For whom each Thing has a Life of it's own, & yet they are all one life'; see *Coleridge Letters*, ii. 865–6. For a discussion of this letter in relation to Coleridge's later definition of the Fancy, see ch. 4 of my *Coleridge, Wordsworth and the Language of Allusion* (Oxford, 1986).

he repudiates the imagination's bondage to definite form. Where Greek poetry is in this respect idolatrous, the Holy Scriptures and Milton are 'sublime'. That is, in the terms adopted by Bishop Lowth, the latter either consider God 'simply and abstractedly, with no illustration or amplification' or they compare God with human or natural attributes, in such a way as to cause the understanding to refer continually 'from the shadow to the reality'.[156] Either way, there is no confusion of God with the natural forms He animates or transcends; and the imagination is allowed maximum freedom, in its oscillation between the physical and the spiritual. By placing Milton in the tradition of religious sublimity which Lowth has defined, Wordsworth does more than make an alignment of content and method between the Scriptures and *Paradise Lost*: he suggests, further, that Milton is a model for the poetic imagination, whose divinity consists in its transcendence of the vehicles it uses. Milton thus becomes, as in Coleridge's phrase, the deity who 'stands *ab extra*', and he offers a fitting model for the 'Wordsworthian, or egotistical sublime'.[157]

Metaphors of revelation and incarnation were used frequently by Milton's Romantic readers, as a means of characterizing the paradoxical nature of his genius, which appeared to work on a divine level, whilst clearly being of human origin. A comment of De Quincey's, for instance—'In Milton only, first and last, is the power of the sublime revealed'[158]—implies a Christ-like dimension to Milton himself, through the metaphor of revelation. Wordsworth's sonnet 'Milton! Thou shouldst be living at this hour' similarly turns on the conjunction of conflicting ideas of permanence and mutability, infinitude and limitation. But even when it is not coupled with Christian association, metaphor can give Milton a status that is quasi-divine, as in the almost hysterical language of apotheosis adopted by De Quincey:

Milton is not an author amongst authors, not a poet amongst poets, but a power among powers, and the *Paradise Lost* is not a book amongst books, not a poem amongst poems, but a central force amongst forces.[159]

Milton is here removed from a purely textual realm, and seen in terms of elemental power, much as he is in Wordsworth's sonnet of 1802: 'Thou hadst a voice whose sound was like the sea; | Pure as the naked heavens, majestic, free . . .'. In such contexts it is by virtue of his sublimity, which abstracts him from the human sphere and absorbs him into nature, that Milton achieves a kind of honorary divinity.

So customary was it to think of Milton in these terms that the dramatic origins, as well as qualities, of *Paradise Lost* tended to be overlooked. In those

---

[156] *Lowth Lectures*, i. 353, 360.

[157] Coleridge's comment is in *Table Talk*, i. 125 (cf. also his observation that 'the egotism of such a man [as Milton] is a revelation of spirit'; *Romantics on Milton*, 277). Keats writes that 'The Wordsworthian or egotistical sublime is a thing per se and stands alone'; to R. Woodhouse, 27 Oct. 1818 (*Keats Letters*, 157).

[158] J. E. Jordan (ed.), *De Quincey as Critic* (London, 1973), 44.   [159] Ibid. 253–4.

rare instances when Milton's human sympathy is observed by his critics, it is cause for surprise, and a language is needed to describe its emotive power which puts it in a category of its own: 'Milton is godlike in the sublime pathetic', Keats observes in one of his annotations: 'In Demons, fallen Angels, and Monsters the delicacies of passion living in and from their immortality, is of the most softening and dissolving nature.'[160] The distinction between two kinds of imaginative terrain is itself 'dissolved' by the anomalous category of the 'sublime pathetic', which mediates between Shakespearian tenderness and Miltonic aloofness. Keats can be seen in this comment to be realizing a duality in Milton, which is more thoroughly expanded in the processes of allusion and imitation I shall be exploring later in this book. He experiences a similar shock of tenderness in seeing the visible memento of human frailty, a lock of Milton's hair. This experience he turns into a spot of time, allowing ideas of eternity and transience to converge, in an uncomfortable idiom one might label the 'bathetic sublime': 'For many years my offering must be hushed, | When I do speak, I'll think upon this hour'. Transformed by Keats's idolatry, the lock of hair becomes an icon—a fragment of Milton that survives as testimony to his humanity and his divinity, at one and the same time.

An analogous duality in Milton is suggested by Charles Lamb, who is somewhat more ironic about his own bardolatry. Lamb recalls with mock horror the occasion when he first looked at the manuscript of 'Lycidas', only to discover that Milton's genius was as fallible as other mortals:

There is something to me repugnant, at any time, in written hand. The text never seems determinate. Print settles it. I had thought of the Lycidas as a full-grown beauty—as springing up with all the parts absolute—till, in evil hour, I was shown the original copy of it ... How it staggered me to see the fine things in their ore! interlined! corrected! as if their words were mortal, alterable, displaceable at pleasure! as if they might have been otherwise, and just as good! as if inspirations were made up of parts, and those fluctuating, successive, indifferent![161]

The passage functions on its most obvious level as a parodic undermining of romantic clichés—inspiration, spontaneity, organicism, fragmentariness—and as a nostalgic return to the classical values of harmony and completeness. But working against this is Lamb's playfulness at his own expense: we see this in the building up, to absurdity, of his naïve expectations; the Miltonic allusion ('in evil hour') which turns anticlimax into a version of the Fall; and the incredulous exclamation of facts which are self-explanatory: 'as if their words were mortal ... as if inspirations were made up of parts'. The voice which refuses Romantic values is ironized just as effectively as are the Romantic values themselves: what remains stable is the perceived dichotomy between expectation and actuality, between imagination and the written word, between the sublime conceptions of

[160] Annotations to *Paradise Lost* (*c.*1818); the comment appears alongside *PL* ii. 546–561 (*Romantics on Milton*, 557).

[161] *London Magazine*, Oct. 1820; in *Romantics on Milton*, 298.

Milton and the contingencies of language. The discovery that Milton was fallible and mortal stands, in Lamb's account, as further testimony to the grandeur, authority, and unattainability of Milton's imaginative world; and the Burkean apprehension of linguistic insufficiency is thereby built into his definition of the Miltonic sublime.

It has become clear from my study of the reception of *Paradise Lost* that Milton stands in his readers' minds both for the capacity to express the inexpressible and for the inexpressible itself: he is, in other words, at once the vehicle of sublimity and himself a sublime phenomenon. It has also become clear that the strength of the Milton myth is dependent on the intersection of ideas of divinity and humanity which we see in Lamb's and Keats's anecdotes, and which bears an important figural relationship to Romantic ideas about the creative imagination. Despite this duality, however, it is noteworthy that the tendency of all the mythologizing processes this chapter has examined is to subordinate humanity to divinity, and that the author function is of paramount importance in maintaining a stable model of authority on which this myth of Milton rests. Paradoxically, then, it is through the extraordinary power which 'Milton the man' exerts over his literary reception that he comes to be read as a synecdoche of God. The full irony of this paradox will emerge in Blake's *Milton*: a poem which systematically undoes the reception processes I have here analysed, deconstructing Milton as divine authority, and rewriting both God and Milton as man. The reader who turns to my last chapter will find that I have there analysed *Milton* in the context of his eighteenth-century reception, and have offered Blake as its strongest critic: this symmetry of argument would indeed make it possible to proceed forthwith to my conclusions. However, the revisionary strategies which Blake evolves will seem less like a sudden and dramatic reversal of reception tactics if they are read in the light of subtle allusive practices which are common to all of the followers of Milton featuring in this book. It is with these allusive practices that my intervening chapters are concerned.

2

Allusion

'What is the price of experience?' Enion asks, in Night the Second of Blake's *Vala*, 'Do men buy it for a song, | Or wisdom for a dance in the street?' No, comes her careful, deliberative answer:

> it is bought with the price
> Of all that a man hath, his house, his wife, his children:
> Wisdom is sold in the desolate market where none come to buy,
> And in the withered field where the farmer ploughs for bread in vain.[1]

Spelt out thus baldly, in the language of economic exchange, Enion's post-lapsarian vision must strike the reader as one of the bleakest of its kind: more chillingly familiar, for instance, because more laconically presented, than Michael's forecast of the 'ghastly spasm, racking torture, qualms | Of heart-sick agony' which are the consequence of Adam and Eve's fall (*PL* xi. 481–2); more objectively conceived than the personal hell of Wordsworth's London, with its 'trivial objects, melted and reduced | To one identity by differences | That have no law, no meaning, and no end';[2] and more inclusive than the nightmare world of Coleridge's Ancient Mariner, 'Alone on a wide wide sea'.[3] Yet, for all its extremity, it is not despairing. Enion's bitterness is tempered by something more affirmative than resignation: a valuation of 'wisdom' (here significantly synonymous with experience) whose roots are deeply embedded in Christian humanism. As Jerome McGann puts it,

The lines, with their implicit allusion to the New Testament admonishment to sell all that one hath in order to follow Jesus, drive the reader toward an expansion of his understanding. ... The poetic genius is the faculty which experience, and all imaginative growth entails. ... This Experience, which Enion laments, becomes for her a failed invitation to apocalypse.[4]

There is, then, behind Enion's initial question, an assumption common to most Romantic writing: experience, however costly, is worth paying for; no price is considered too high. To prove that this assumption is crucial, in defining what one means by 'Romanticism', is far too broad and nebulous a task to be em-

---

[1] *Vala, or the Four Zoas*, ii. 607–11. [2] *Prelude*, vii. 703–5.
[3] 'The Ancient Mariner', l. 233.
[4] 'The Aim of Blake's Prophecies', in S. Curran and J. Wittreich (eds.) *Blake's Sublime Allegory: Essays on 'The Four Zoas', 'Milton' and 'Jerusalem'* (Madison, Wis., 1973), 18.

barked on here. What might in a more limited way be demonstrated, however, is the amplification by Romantic writers of a phenomenon which has its most obvious origins in *Paradise Lost*, and which is perhaps best exemplified in Michael's parting words to Adam and Eve: 'Then wilt thou not be loath | To lose this Paradise, but shalt possess | A Paradise within thee, happier far' (*PL* xii. 585–7). In a straightforwardly theological reading of these words, they refer to the coming of Christ and humankind's redemption through Him; but they can also suggest the expanding of inner resources (especially imagination and love) which more than compensate humanity for the loss of Eden. In what follows, I shall be using the notion of a 'fortunate fall' in this wider-than-theological sense, to identify and describe the paradigm of gain through loss which Enion unwittingly affirms, and which becomes a persistent feature of Romantic writing. My aim is to demonstrate an important continuity between Milton and the Romantics: a continuity that has been largely ignored, under-standably by Miltonists (who are concerned with the intended meaning of *Paradise Lost* rather than with its reception), but more perplexingly and damag-ingly by Romanticists, whose studies of influence and allusion have so far suffered from an investment in proving discontinuity, or even rupture and rebellion.

At one extreme, Romantic allusion does indeed take the form of deliberate 'misreading': Blake's too famous pronouncement, in *The Marriage of Heaven and Hell*, that Milton was 'of the devil's party without knowing it'[5] offers a startling inversion—or, as Harold Bloom would put it, a *transumption*[6]—of Milton's original terms. But shading outwards from this are numerous more subtle manifestations of the Romantics' preference for fallen human values (imagin-ation, suffering, love) as opposed to the stasis of innocence preserved. In regis-tering the various degrees of 'revision' involved in these allusions, the reader becomes increasingly aware of the degrees of 'continuity' that are also implied. This awareness has the interesting effect of qualifying the stability, or deter-mined meaning, both of *Paradise Lost* itself and of the texts which are dependent on it. Just how far, one begins to wonder, did Milton himself share the Romantics' valuation of experience? To what extent are Romantic readings of *Paradise Lost* anticipated in, and justified by, the language of the poem? Are they '*mis*readings' at all?

A thorough investigation of these questions would have to include an account of Milton's carefully untraditional treatment of the fortunate fall, and the detailed study of a wide range of Romantic allusions, neither of which can be accomplished within a single chapter. I have chosen to concentrate here on the

---

[5] 'The reason Milton wrote in fetters when he wrote of angels and God, and at liberty when of devils and Hell, is because he was a true poet, and of the Devil's party without knowing it' (*MHH*, pl. 5, ll. 52–5).

[6] The term, which is Harold Bloom's, means 'outdoing a precursor, by absorbing and transcen-ding his terms'; there are numerous examples of Milton's own 'transumption' of Homer and Virgil: see esp. *PL* ix. 27–47.

surprising implications of allusive patterns within *Paradise Lost*, and on their significance for later writers. I want to suggest that, unless one sees this continuity, one tends either to dismiss Romantic interpretation as perverse or to overstress (and overvalue) the 'transumptive' qualities which are present at its Satanic extreme. The image of a Milton dramatically divided against himself— in fetters when writing of angels and heaven, at liberty when of devils and hell[7]—has tended to obscure the more subtle and pervasive ways in which his ambiguous allusions, cross-references and self-echoes allow a 'Romantic' reading to emerge.

TEXTUAL CHOICE

The subtext of *Paradise Lost* offers a valuation of the fallen world which is integral to its meaning. All readers, at some level or other, respond to the insistent pressure of this subtext: it is the price of experience that they should do so. But there are different ways of dealing with the response once it has been acknowledged. Broadly speaking, Milton criticism faces a choice between two kinds of interpretation. (These one might see as having their origins in the metaphorical split between Milton as human being and Milton as God, which emerged as a feature of his eighteenth-century reception.[8]) Is the text controlled, as Stanley Fish would argue, by an omniscient narrator, who betrays his reader into fallen assumptions as part of a humiliating programme of education and reform?[9] Or alternatively (as Bloom, following Blake, would see it) are fallen implications celebrated, by poet and reader alike, as the defeat of 'Our Great Forbidder' Reason (the superego) by Desire (the id)?[10] Choosing between these opposite readings is especially fraught when the critical discussion centres either on Milton's own allusions or on Miltonic allusions in others. For it is in the process of alluding that choice presents itself as such, both to the poet and to the reader. Christopher Ricks saw this clearly, if not first. Writing of the moment when Satan is compared with Jacob, in *Paradise Lost* Book III (ll. 510–15), he commented: 'The length and power of the allusion forces us to choose between damaging irrelevance, or likeness turning grimly into disparity'.[11] A further option, which he failed to mention, is to see disparity turning suggestively into likeness. In Fish's terms, this last might be regarded as an educative temptation, whether succumbed to or resisted. In Bloom's, it is at once the poet's 'strong misreading' of the Bible (Jacob Satanized) and the reader's creative 'misprision' of Milton himself.

[7] As in Blake's proposition, quoted in n. 5 above.
[8] See my discussion of the conflict between politics and religion in Ch. 1.
[9] *Surprised by Sin: The Reader in 'Paradise Lost'* (Berkeley, Calif., 1967).
[10] Bloom's reading of Milton, which has its origins in *MHH*, forms the basis of his entire theory of poetic influence; for the clearest statement, see *The Anxiety of Influence: A Theory of Poetry* (Oxford, 1973).
[11] *Milton's Grand Style* (Oxford, 1963; repr. 1983), 128.

On both sides of this debate, the limitations one sees in critical method stem from a distortion of the ways in which allusive language works. Stanley Fish's interpretation of *Paradise Lost*, on the one hand, and Harold Bloom's, on the other, opt for singleness rather than doubleness of meaning. The subtext, according to the one, must always be subordinate to didactic truth; and didactic truth, according to the other, is inevitably less compelling than the subtext. Both arrive at these positions by reading allusion as though it were always revision. Bloom's theory of 'transumption' thus aids and abets a crudely intentionalist line. It is clear, however, that all allusion—whether Miltonic or not—requires the reader to perceive the co-presence of similarity and difference in conjunctions made by images and concepts, characters and situations, or phrases and words. It implies choice, and it depends on choice not being made. Take, for example, the conclusion to Wordsworth's description of the Simplon Pass in Book VI of *The Prelude*:

> Tumult and Peace, the darkness and the light,
> Were all like workings of one mind, the features
> Of the same face, blossoms upon one tree,
> Characters of the great apocalypse,
> The types and symbols of eternity,
> Of first, and last, and midst, and without end.[12]

As the Norton editors point out, the last line is drawn almost verbatim from Milton's description of God in *Paradise Lost* Book V: 'Him first, Him last, Him midst, and without end' (l. 165).[13] But the all-important word 'Him' has dropped, leaving it open to the reader to interpret the one mind as Wordsworth's own. God is present, in so far as Miltonic echo inevitably conjures him up. But He is absent, in the sense that Wordsworth's revision of the line has dispensed with Him as Him. The conjunction of likeness and difference gives us ambiguity, which is the allusion's meaning.

An ideal reading of *Paradise Lost* would consistently hold opposites in tension. Narrative, however, works through alternation, and language involves the reader in choice. The best visual parallel for this is to be found in *Gestalt*: Wittgenstein's 'duck-rabbit'[14] is the most famous example (see Fig. 1). Seeing the duck first, Wittgenstein demonstrates, is likely. Seeing the rabbit second is what he calls 'the dawn of an aspect'. Seeing one and not the other is 'aspect blindness'. But only in theory is it possible to see both at the same time: one has to see each in a kind of oscillation in order to know that both are there. *Paradise Lost* opens the same gap between theory and practice. Unless the reader suffers

[12] ll. 567–72.

[13] *Prelude*, 218 n. 6. The reader's interpretation of this Miltonic allusion is determined by wider considerations. The idea of continuity supports the Norton editors' pantheistic account of Wordsworth—in this context underlined by millenarian suggestion. The idea of revision, on the other hand, helps to imply a Wordsworth whose semi-atheism led him to assert the mind's similarity to (rather than coalescence with) the godhead.

[14] *Philosophical Investigations*, trans. G. E. M. Anscombe (Oxford, 1958; repr. 1963), 194.

I shall call the following figure, derived from Jastrow, the duck-rabbit. It can be seen as a rabbit's head or as a duck's.

And I must distinguish between the continuous 'seeing' of an aspect and the 'dawning' of an aspect.

The picture might have been shewn me, and I never have seen anything but a rabbit in it.

FIG 1. Wittgenstein's 'duck-rabbit', from L. Wittgenstein, *Philosophical Investigations*, trans. G. E. M. Anscombe (Oxford, 1958; repr. 1963).

The idea of a duality such as air and water can be expressed in a picture by starting from a plane-filling design of birds and fish; the birds are 'water' for the fish, and the fish are 'air' for the birds. Heaven and Hell can be symbolised by an interplay of angels and devils. There are many other possible pairs of dynamic subjects—at least in theory, for in most cases their realisation meets with insuperable difficulties. MCE

FIG 2. M. C. Escher, 'Sky and Water 1' (1938). © 1938 M. C. Escher/Cordon Art, Baarn, Holland. Rubric quoted from M. C. Escher, *Twenty-nine Masterprints*, published by Harry N. Abrams, 1981, New York.

from what Wittgenstein calls 'aspect blindness', or decides (like Bloom and Fish) to subdue one interpretation to the other, he or she is likely to see opposite possibilities, and to see them alternately. Milton's rhetoric, considered in terms of the overall structure of *Paradise Lost*, encourages such oscillation. Meanwhile, the local effects achieved by allusion frequently guide the reader toward an interpretative choice. Here again, a visual parallel might be helpful. Escher's drawing of bird shapes turning into fish shapes (Fig. 2) presents the 'dawn of an aspect' in more gradual terms than the duck-rabbit or rabbit-duck. Whereas Wittgenstein's example involves a moment of awareness, in which the new aspect is suddenly revealed, Escher lets the observer in by stages, as it were, to the final image. This process of merging, or assimilation, is a feature of Milton's allusive language which I shall be examining in detail: Eve becoming Narcissus (*PL* iv. 460–91) or Satan becoming Jacob (iii. 501–15) offer the most obvious illustrations.

It is the central contention of this chapter that *Paradise Lost* contains an abnormal degree of indeterminate poetic modes—modes, that is, in which likeness and difference coexist, create readerly indecision, allow for implications which conflict with a didactic reading. Allusion to other writers is one of these; anticipation and self-echo are others. Cross-references, linking heavenly activities with those in hell, may be intended as ironic parallels, but what the reader frequently responds to is the human feelings which opposites share. Parody, when complicated by these human feelings, becomes an imaginative conflation which undoes moral extremes. Similes, too, suggest a merging of opposites and a dissolving of boundaries which repeatedly unsettle the moral design. In analysing the workings of these poetic modes, I shall be arguing that it is their cumulative pressure which allows a 'Romantic' reading of *Paradise Lost* to emerge—and that it emerged, what is more, long before the Romantics started reading.

It is not my purpose, nor indeed would it be possible, to establish whether Milton was finally 'in control' of the effects produced by his textual ambiguities, nor whether they could be said to amount to an authorial strategy or intention. But I do hope to be justified in making the apparently anachronistic claim that they provoke in the reader what Keats called 'negative capability'—the capacity, that is, to remain in 'uncertainties, Mysteries, doubts, without any irritable reaching after fact & reason'.[15] Keats evolved this important model of creativity, not with reference to Milton, whose commitment to absolutes he found as oppressive as Coleridge's, but in relation to Shakespeare, whose imagination he saw, by contrast, as flexibly human, adaptable, and open-ended. In borrowing his term, and thus 'Shakespearianizing' *Paradise Lost*, I hope to bring out an aspect of the Romantics' reading of this poem which would certainly be overlooked, if one accepted at face value the contrast between sublimity and human-

[15] In its context, it is Shakespeare and not Milton whom Keats identifies as being 'posessed [*sic*] so enormously' of this quality; see *Keats Letters*, 43.

ity ('enthusiastic and meditative Imagination ... poetical, as contradistinguished from human and dramatic Imagination') that they frequently present,
in their polarization of Milton and Shakespeare.[16] The evidence I have discovered, and will be presenting in the remainder of this book, would indeed
suggest a significant inconsistency in Romantic responses to Milton: while in
their role as critics the Romantics may have felt it necessary to caricature him as
authoritarian and absolutist, in their role as practising writers they admired,
imitated, and closely reproduced the indeterminacies of his style and meaning.

In the analysis that follows, I hope to show that the incremental effect of
Miltonic ambiguity is such as to place the reader of *Paradise Lost* in a position
which Keats's definition of 'negative capability' adequately describes. Faced
with a sequence of textual choices—faced, indeed, with a plot which turns on a
single moment of irrevocable choice—Milton's reader is, I believe, encouraged
by his allusive habits to take up an intermediate position, in which no final
'decision' is reached. It is not simply that moral categories are repeatedly
blurred or confused by pleasurable complexity, but that the suspension of choice
emerges in itself as a subtle kind of 'truth'. This process involves a considerable
elevation in the value of that aesthetic category of indeterminacy which, as I
shall argue in Chapter 6, is closely connected with Romantic ideas of the
sublime. The validation of this aesthetic is all the more surprising for the moral
and religious context it challenged, but from which it none the less emerged.

CLASSICAL AND SHAKESPEARIAN ALLUSION

It is a measure of Bloom's powerful influence on literary criticism that even the
straightforward Miltonists—those coming to *Paradise Lost* from a non-
Romantic angle—should have to take his theory of poetic influence into
account.[17] And as I suggested in my Introduction, it is perhaps proof of their
anxiety that the vast majority of them choose to oppose his views. One important
aspect of this anti-Bloom trend in Milton studies is that it is accompanied by the
submission to an extreme intentionalist approach. Whether or not this is derived
from Fish, its effect on critical method is baleful. Milton broods, God-like, over
his own text, forbidding and foreknowing. Didactic significance is paramount;
multiple meanings are denied. Allusions, far from being models of ambiguity,
are seen instead as check-points, whereby the erring reader adjusts his or her
perspective to fit with Milton's own.

A sequence of books on intertextuality has shown a hardening of this line.
Barbara Lewalski's *'Paradise Lost' and the Rhetoric of Literary Forms* is the most

[16] The quotation comes from Wordsworth's 'Preface' to *Poems* (1815), in *Wordsworth*, 634; but
the distinction between Miltonic and Shakespearian kinds of genius is standard in Romantic
criticism (see Ch. 1).

[17] See esp. B. Lewalski, *'Paradise Lost' and The Rhetoric of Literary Forms* (Princeton, NJ, 1985);
and P. Stevens, *Imagination and the Presence of Shakespeare in 'Paradise Lost'* (Madison, Wis., 1985). I
reviewed these and other books on Milton in *The Times Literary Supplement* (8 Aug. 1986).

impressive, confronting Milton's text as a complex generic hybrid and seeking
to understand allusion as more than semantic play. Imitative strategies in *Paradise Lost*, she argues, are 'essentially heuristic'. The reader is not so much
'entangled' as instructed, through awareness of multiple genres and genre
transformations, to see Milton's purpose in a clearer light. This purpose is
emphatically and conclusively defined as Christian: it guides the reader through
what otherwise would be an intertextual maze, providing multiple perspectives
upon the various personages and incidents, and engaging them in the process of
comparison and evaluation.[18] Whereas the reader is in an educated position
(having at his or her fingertips a full panoply of classical texts), Milton's characters are ignorant and ineducable: not only are they shown to be humanly implicated in actions they cannot fully comprehend, but they are belittled by a
range of allusions whose end is essentially ironic.

Lewalski's powerful and learned reading of *Paradise Lost* must stand or fall
on its treatment of Satan. Here, generic references are in open conflict with the
character they describe, and therefore potentially subversive of moral design. In
Lewalski's view, Satan is measured according to the heroic standards embodied
in classical epic, romance and tragedy, against all of which he is found wanting.
The poet's intention, she argues, is neither to debase those genres nor to exalt
Satan as hero; it is, rather, to make evil humanly comprehensible, and at the
same time to convey how far Satan has perverted what in him was good.[19] This
approach yields suggestive parallels—with Achilles, with Prometheus, and with
Odysseus; but when they are in danger of upsetting the moral scheme, Lewalski
interprets them as parody. The reader is expected to respond to them, not as
though they elevated Satan, nor even as though they introduced a pleasing
incongruity in his character, but rather in terms of their ironic devaluation of
his pretensions to heroic status. Conveniently and reductively, disturbing likeness is seen as the ironic confirmation of reassuring difference, by which it is
finally subdued.

Similar issues are raised by Milton's relationship with Ovid—seen by
Richard DuRocher as 'the heroic, at times perilous struggle between poetic
fiction and Christian truth';[20] and with Shakespeare, whose imagination
(according to Paul Stevens) was merely 'creative', whereas Milton's own was the
instrument of God.[21] In both these studies, intra-poetic relationship is conceived to be not just revisionary but stalwartly dismissive of pagan and imaginative temptation: it engages the reader in acts of refusal, wherever the overarching
values of Christianity appear to be unsettled by alternative points of view.
Moving a little further afield, R. A. Shoaf takes didacticism to its limit, arguing
for the necessity of perpetual vigilance on the part of the reader. We must be on
guard, he claims, against the seductive duplicity of Milton's puns, if we are to

---

[18] Lewalski, *Rhetoric of Literary Forms*, 17–28.   [19] Ibid. 55–78.
[20] *Milton and Ovid* (Ithaca, NY, 1985), 218.
[21] See *Imagination and the Presence of Shakespeare*, esp. ch. 2.

resist the temptation to see likeness where difference should be, and so to replicate the fall through mental confusion. Milton's puns are there to test our allegiance to his Christian values. 'More than any other text I know', Shoaf concludes, '*Paradise Lost* is intended. ... To deconstruct would necessarily be to transgress'.[22]

What all these readings suggest is a Milton who subjugates fictive play to didactic tenor, manipulating intertextual reference so as to underline the powerful and abiding coherence of Puritan ideology. The origins of such an argument can be traced back to *Areopagitica*, where Milton himself offers a model of reading-as-temptation, or reading-as-trial. Good and evil, in his view, grow up together in 'the field of this World ... almost inseparably'. The knowledge of good is 'involved and interwoven with the knowledge of evil', and is in 'many cunning resemblances hardly to be discerned'. The capacity to distinguish between them can only come through knowing both; and it is the advantage of books that they allow the reader access to ever-widening experience:

It was from out the rinde of one apple tasted, that the knowledge of good and evill as two twins cleaving together leapt forth into the World. And perhaps this is the doom which *Adam* fell into of knowing good and evill, that is to say of knowing good by evill. As therefore the state of man now is; what wisdome can there be to choose, what continence to forbeare without the knowledge of evill? He that can apprehend and consider vice with all her baits and seeming pleasures, and yet abstain, and yet distinguish, and yet prefer that which is truly better, he is the true warfaring Christian.[23]

This stress on the responsibility of the reader, with regard to processes of moral discrimination, is famously extended by Locke in his *An Essay Concerning Human Understanding*, where its role is central in confirming the paramount status of reason. Locke's argument rests on a distinction between 'Wit', whose function is to perceive likeness where it is not intended, and 'Judgement', which distinguishes differences in things apparently alike:

Judgement lies ... in separating carefully, one from another, Ideas wherein can be found the least difference, thereby to avoid being misled by Similitude, and by affinity to take one thing for another. This is a way of proceeding quite contrary to Metaphor and Allusion, wherein, for the most part, lies that entertainment and pleasantry of Wit, which strikes so lively on the Fancy, and therefore so acceptable to all People; because its Beauty appears at first sight, and there is required no labour of thought, to examine what Truth or Reason there is in it.[24]

Locke goes so far as to allow metaphorical language a certain independence from moral categories: 'it is a kind of an affront, to go about to examine it, by the severe Rules of Truth, and good Reason: whereby it appears, that it consists in some-

---

[22] *Milton, Poet of Duality: A Study of Semiosis in the Poetry and the Prose* (New Haven, Conn., 1985), 57.

[23] Milton, *Areopagitica* (London, 1644), in *Milton Prose*, ii, ed. E. Sirluck (New Haven, Conn., 1959), 514–15.

[24] *An Essay Concerning Human Understanding*, ed. with introd. P. H. Nidditch (Oxford, 1975), 136.

thing, that is not perfectly conformable to them';[25] but he does this grudgingly. The sense he conveys is that metaphors and allusions are potentially subversive of morality, since by their very nature they are the vehicles of deceit.

Writers such as Fish, Lewalski, DuRocher, and Shoaf write in a Lockean tradition, as though there had been nothing in the intervening centuries to cause a reassessment of the merits of wit and judgement. They conceive of the reader as someone who must be thoroughly armed against the temptations of fallen language, and so against their own potential for sin, by learning to distinguish like from unlike: the duplicity of metaphor must, in other words, be subdued to the higher demands of judgement. But what of the ambiguous workings of allusion itself, and what of the author's part in allowing them? Shoaf claims that 'to deconstruct would necessarily be to transgress'; but we do not need the language of deconstruction to see that, for Milton, the process of alluding and of understanding allusions must logically involve rather than resist the seductive temptation which is inherent in metaphor. If learning to distinguish like from unlike is a matter of experience, then it depends (as *Areopagitica* makes clear) on reading as a kind of aesthetically distanced falling: the power to discriminate derives from the initial awareness of similarity, which itself invites the suspension of 'judgement'. Even within the Miltonic framework, then, allusion *is* transgression.[26]

If one is interpreting classical reference in *Paradise Lost*, it is evasive (even repressive) to convert ambiguity into irony. When Milton suggests a likeness between Satan and Odysseus, he steps outside—*literally* transgresses—the Christian framework, altering the poem's scale and engaging a different order of sympathy in the reader. To suggest, as DuRocher puts it, that Satan is 'the hero of an epic tradition that the poem ultimately disavows'[27] is to ignore the homage to that tradition which the poem repeatedly pays—not only as a means of self-definition but as a way of including values that in themselves are attractive, whether or not they are seen finally as subordinate to higher truth. Those words 'ultimately' and 'finally' are indeed misleading. When a likeness is suggested, or a pagan context is invoked, it creates in the reader a response which cannot later be retracted. Milton may choose to put a marker outside the passage involved, as he does, for instance, with the dismissive comment, 'thus they relate, | Erring' which follows Mulciber's fall:

---

[25] Ibid. 157.

[26] There is a potential conflict between Milton's moral seriousness and the (pagan) modes and genres with which he experiments; but intentionalists claim that such conflict is resolved: see e.g. C. Brown, *John Milton's Aristocratic Entertainments* (Cambridge, 1985). Brown argues that, for Milton, 'the way to moral definition was through the delights of fictive play' (p. 61); and that the pastoral mode was paradoxically a means by which aristocrats could 'prescribe to themselves ... the kind of godliness which could be exemplary to a nation' (p. 57). Although more subtle than many such, his thesis underplays the extent of Milton's own 'transgression'.

[27] *Milton and Ovid*, 119.

> From morn
> To noon he fell, from noon to dewy eve,
> A summer's day; and with the setting sun
> Dropped from the zenith like a falling star,
> On Lemnos the Aegean isle: thus they relate,
> Erring.

(PL i. 742–6)

But, if Waldock's intuitions are correct, the so-called 'damage' has already been done.[28] Imaginatively, both writer and reader have given in to the Ovidian spell; it cannot be unsaid. The presence of the marker has, in fact, a tendency to emphasize, antagonize, and so heighten the emotion previously felt, just as, within a simile, one's interest in stated likeness may be intensified by contrast that is implied.

What one sees here in a limited context is true of allusive patternings in the poem as a whole. Classical reference, rather than ironically confirming the Christian message, repeatedly complicates it. The reader responds to this complication with pleasure, sometimes in ways that are subversive, because it implies a subtler than moral perspective. Shakespearian echoes work in a similar fashion: Satan as Macbeth, for instance, draws the reader into a human dilemma, commands sympathy at a tragic level. Milton's mind, as John Carey puts it, 'turns to Shakespeare at moments of compassion'.[29] 'Thrice he essayed, and thrice in spite if scorn, | Tears such as angels weep, burst forth', the poet writes of Satan in Book I. A hint of Isabella, pleading with Angelo for Claudio's life, adds to the moment its dignity and pathos:

> But man, proud man,
> Dressed in a little brief authority,
> Most ignorant of what he's most assured,
> His glassy essence, like an angry ape,
> Plays such fantastic tricks before high heaven
> *As makes the angels weep.*[30]

Tragic soliloquy, even when specific echoes cannot be detected, gives Milton access to this Shakespearian world:

> That space the evil one abstracted stood
> From his own evil, and for the time remained
> Stupidly good, of enmity disarmed,
> Of guile, of hate, of envy, of revenge.

(PL ix. 463–6)

[28] Waldock argues, with specific reference to the speeches of Satan and Belial, that they contain 'guarding phrases' and retrospective corrections, whose intent is to neutralize the reader's response to diabolic attractiveness. This 'systematic degradation' of the Satanic impulse is not, he claims, as effective as Milton might wish it to be; see ch. 4 of A. J. A. Waldock, *'Paradise Lost' and its Critics* (Cambridge, 1959).

[29] I am quoting from one of a course of lectures on Milton given by Prof. Carey at Oxford University.

[30] *Measure for Measure*, II. ii. 117–21.

After this discovery of the latent compassion in Satan—pleasurable, precisely because it makes him subtly human—the reader is guided, indeed *required*, to check his or her sympathy against a flatter, more stereotyped perspective: 'Fierce hate he recollects, and all his thoughts | Of mischief, gratulating, thus excites' (*PL* ix. 471–2). But, having once introduced the complexity of a Satan who still has the potential for good, one can hardly accept the crudity of straightforward evil. Shakespearian tragedy cannot be 'belittled', as DuRocher seems to think, by Christian epic: this is not a case of one-upmanship, anxious or otherwise, but rather of what Charles Lamb, in a different context, referred to as 'a following of the spirit, in free homage and generous subjection'.[31] Nor is it a case of the didactic Milton somehow 'winning out' over the tragic, since an underlying sense of tragedy continues to qualify and enrich the moral perspective. To argue, therefore, that the reader is involved in 'choosing' between two opposing viewpoints, and that Milton guides us towards the one that is 'correct', is to opt for a crude model of intentionality, in which the voice of the epic narrator is given the final say.

If, rather, it is in the oscillation between two different perspectives that meaning resides, we can fairly replace the didactic models of intertextuality offered by Fish and others with an alternative that is open-ended. Adapting Lewalski's analysis to these ends, it becomes possible to read *Paradise Lost* as an intertextual and inter-generic collage, in which several species of response are simultaneously called for, and several kinds of allegiance compete for attention. Such a reading depends on hearing the epic voice of the narrator as one of many voices, raising its own expectations, and taking its place in a temporal sequence where no final authority is or can be established. The reader does indeed respond, in such a reading, to Satan as 'Faustian hero, degenerating into villain-hero driven by ambition', to Satan as Romance hero, entering the garden of Eden , to Satan as Achilles, Prometheus, and Odysseus, and to Satan as Macbeth.[32] All of these Satans are present, and none of them are reduced by any final act of transvaluation, on Milton's part, in relation to the traditions from which they are drawn.

Measured against the standards of *An Essay Concerning Human Understanding*, this dialogic reading of *Paradise Lost* is self-evidently anachronistic. It would be difficult to find anything in eighteenth-century Milton criticism to which it overtly corresponds; although a plausible argument has recently been offered, by Leslie E. Moore, for seeing 'sublimity' as a term which registered the eighteenth century's inability to categorize Milton, or to cope with the generic hybrid it was faced with, in *Paradise Lost*. The interest of critics at this time in generic laws and rules made them, in Moore's view, 'especially aware of the processes by

---

[31] Lamb is reviewing Wordsworth's *The Excursion* for the *Quarterly Review* (1814): 'Those who hate the Paradise Lost will not love this poem. The steps of the great master are discernible in it, not in direct imitation or injurious parody, but in the following of the spirit, in free homage and generous subjection'; *Lamb as Critic*, ed. R. Park (London, 1980), 200.

[32] Lewalski, *Rhetoric of Literary Forms*, 63–71.

which genres were transformed'.[33] He goes on to argue that what the genre explained was often less interesting than what it did not, and that critics were often most interested in the infringement of implicit rules; but that, 'whereas in the twentieth century we take pleasure in the *concordia discors* of competing generic conventions', eighteenth-century readers 'expressed a reserved admiration tempered by anxiety, as disparity between expectation and result led them again and again to confront the question of generic stability'.[34] The 'sublime', in this context, becomes the only adequate term to describe a form which incorporates multiple genres but (by remaining uncategorizable under any of their headings) subsumes them all.

In Romantic literature, with its strong inclination towards the sublime, it became possible to read Milton's allusiveness pluralistically, and to respond to the challenge of generic mixtures and indeterminacies, precisely for the imaginative freedom they allow. But, to make this response possible, it was necessary that the rationalist suspicion towards metaphor's seductive duplicity should be partially suspended. If the ground for a dialogic reading of Milton is prepared anywhere, then, it is in the gradual evolution of an affirmative attitude towards the imagination, which replaces Locke's 'Wit', as the mental faculty which allows likenesses to triumph over differences, and opposites to be dissolved. This process of evolution is already discernible in Bishop Lowth's lectures on Hebrew poetry:

As accuracy of Judgement is demonstrated by discovering in things, which have in general a very strong resemblance, some partial disagreement, so the genius or fancy is entitled to the highest commendation, when in those objects, which upon the whole have the least agreement, some striking similarity is found out.[35]

Such 'commendation' prepares the way for a Romantic concept of the imagination, which is epitomized by this phrase of Wordsworth's: 'a dark | Invisible workmanship, that reconciles | Discordant elements, and makes them move | In one society',[36] or by these sentences from Shelley's 'A Defence of Poetry': 'Reason respects the differences, and imagination the similitudes of things. Reason is to Imagination as the instrument to the agent, as the body to the spirit, as the shadow to the substance.'[37] In such comments it is possible to see a permissiveness towards the metaphorical ideal of assimilation which would have been impossible for Locke, and which is denied by didactic readers of Milton in our own century, but which is none the less discernible in the allusive practices of *Paradise Lost*.

ANTICIPATION AND ECHO

Self-echo, like allusion, invites choice on the part of the reader, and can be interpreted in intentionalist or non-intentionalist terms. If one wishes, for instance, to posit a 'purpose' for Milton's verbal anticipations, then it makes sense to

[33] *Beautiful Sublime: The Making of 'Paradise Lost', 1701–1734* (Stanford, Calif., 1990), 13.
[34] Ibid.   [35] *Lowth Lectures*, i. 264–5.   [36] *Prelude*, i. 352–5.   [37] *Shelley*, 480.

argue that he 'intends' to preserve or sharpen distinctions between fallen and unfallen perspectives. But the effect of this device on the reader is a different matter. Very frequently it causes distinctions to dissolve. Foreshadowing Eve's fall, in Book II, Milton writes of Sin,

> Thus saying, from her side the fatal key,
> Sad instrument of all our woe she took;
>
> (ll. 871–2)

And foreshadowing it again, in Book IX, of Eve:

> Thus saying, from her husband's hand her hand
> Soft she withdrew,
>
> (ll. 385–6)

Her lapse, when it finally comes, sounds familiar—its gestures and rhythms are already known:

> So saying, her rash hand in evil hour
> Forth reaching to the fruit, she plucked, she ate:
>
> (ix. 780–1)

But even here, despite the finality of the language, we have not reached conclusion. A further echo, fifty or so lines on, seems for a moment to re-enact the climax of Eve's choice—'So saying, from the tree her step she turned' (ix. 834)—ironically suggesting a denial of temptation, even as it verbally repeats her fall. Milton's 'imagination' cannot rest content with portraying the single momentous crisis in Eve's tasting of the apple, but eliminates temporal distinctions in a much more ambiguous treatment of loss. The effect is not only, as one might expect, to heighten dramatic irony, but to offer several versions of the Fall which become conflated in the process of reading. As each echo is heard, one is aware of the singularity of the moment within a larger pattern of repetition. And the moments, although distinct, tend to fuse.

Another example is Eve's blush, in Book VIII, which raises questions about the nature and extent of her sexual innocence before the Fall. Adam, having given his account of the creation of Eve, describes their first lovemaking:

> 　　　　　　　　　　　　to the nuptial bower
> I led her, blushing like the morn; all heaven,
> And happy constellations on that hour
> Shed their selectest influence; the earth
> Gave sign of gratulation, and each hill;
> Joyous the birds; fresh gales and gentle air
> Whispered it to the woods, and from their wings
> Flung rose, flung odours from the spicy shrub,
>
> (viii. 510–17)

The context, and Milton's moral pointers, make it clear that both lovers are 'pure of sinful thought'; but the eroticism of the language is not easily freed from its fallen associations. This problem has been approached, again and again, by critics wishing to separate the poem's godly intention from its post-lapsarian subtext. C. S. Lewis, for instance, would have us believe that Milton saw a clear dividing line between fallen and unfallen sexuality, and that he meant this passage to be contrasted in the reader's mind with the one in Book IX, where sex is corrupted by lascivious desire.[38] Any temptation, he implies, that there might be to regard sex as fallen in the first instance is corrected by our subsequent experience of it in a context that is technically post-lapsarian. Stanley Fish, though coming to the same conclusions, argues the other way round. Far from preserving a distinction between fallen and unfallen sex, he suggests, Milton traps the reader into projecting sinfulness onto the text, so as to make him aware of his fallen state. This is part of an overall design, in his view, whereby the reader is humiliated into learning.[39]

The stress placed on intention by such interpretations is repressive, and ignores the indeterminacy of Milton's poetic effects—achieved, in the passage in question, by verbal anticipation. When Milton, punning on Eve's name, has Adam say 'To the nuptial bower | I led her, blushing like the morn', he is indeed describing unfallen, unshameful pleasure. But when the pun recurs in Book XI, it is with portents of the Expulsion all around: 'Nature first gave signs, impress-ed | On bird, beast, air, air suddenly eclipsed | After short blush of morn' (ll. 182–4). In the first instance, Eve blushes like the innocent morn; in the second, by implication, morn blushes like the fallen Eve. This contrast is heightened by a further connection in Milton's mind between the joy nature feels at the consummation of marriage in Book VIII: 'the earth | *Gave sign of* gratulation' (ll. 513–14) and her birth-pangs at the moment of the Fall in Book IX: 'Earth felt the wound, and nature from her seat | Sighing through all her works gave signs of woe, | That all was lost' (ll. 782–4)—a link which is then picked up, and confirmed, in the lines from Book XI already quoted: 'nature first *gave signs*, impressed | On bird, beast, air' (ll. 182–3). Anticipation and echo bring out connections between these three passages which are designed, one might concede, to highlight the contrast between fallen and unfallen sexuality. But is this how they actually work? As one reads the passage in Book VIII, one is aware both of unshamefulness and of the fallen possibility of shame. Eve's blush in the first case seems already half-fallen, while morn's blush in the second ironically recalls an innocence that is lost. The two moments mirror each other, and in so doing seem to merge.

The effect of verbal anticipation, then, is to support the subversive impli-

---

[38] *A Preface to 'Paradise Lost'* (Oxford, 1942; repr. 1979), 70; but Lewis admits that Milton 'has made the unfallen already so voluptuous and kept the fallen still so poetical that the contrast is not so sharp as it ought to have been' (ibid.).

[39] *Surprised by Sin*, 129–30.

cations of Milton's erotic language by offering proleptically fallen sexuality in the blush. From a temporal standpoint, this means that the blush can be seen as transitional; but it is also ambiguous from a moral point of view. The whole problem is made more complex, not less, by Raphael's blushing, also in Book VIII. One should perhaps give his 'smile that glowed | Celestial rosy red, love's proper hue' (viii. 618–19) an angelic reading; but the pleasure of the moment depends on our apprehension (inappropriate of course) that Raphael is vulnerable and weak. The involuntariness of the blush is reassuringly human: angels too can be embarrassed—and, what is more, a third of them fell.

The patterning of Milton's language, in both the cases I have discussed, should be seen as part of his general tendency, often noticed by critics, to show fallen human impulses emerging before the Fall. Two famous examples are Eve's ringlets, wanton before they should be, and the garden itself, which surprisingly is 'tending to wild' (ix. 912). Another, discussed by Christopher Ricks,[40] is the river of Book IV which, anticipating 'Kubla Khan',[41] runs 'with mazy error under pendent shades' (l. 239). The evil meaning of error, as Ricks sees it, is 'consciously and ominously excluded'. The word reminds us of the Fall, but only because it takes us back to 'a time when there were no infected words because there were no infected actions'. This is an ingenious view, but Ricks fails to demonstrate how it is possible, in either the writing or the reading process, to exclude fallen meanings. His use of the words 'consciously' and 'ominously' implies a sophisticated double awareness which is itself 'fallen'.

A more important passage, which has been consistently misunderstood, is Adam's speech in Book IX as he faces the choice between living with Eve and obeying God:

> How can I live without thee, how forgo
> Thy sweet converse and love so dearly joined,
> To live again in these wild woods forlorn?
>
> (ll. 908–10)

Tillyard, in 'The Crisis of Paradise Lost', muses over the sympathy we feel for Adam, and, he claims, ought not to. 'In actual reading', he writes,

we are not profoundly shocked, and the reason is that Adam's innocence at this point is only nominal. ... he has really crossed the frontier, and no abstention from eating the fruit can put him back the other side.[42]

This is tempting, but only half true. As Adam speaks, one responds on two different levels to the significance of his choice. He is to fall, and be cast out from Eden, for the love he feels *in his unfallen state*; but the very intensity of his love seems to declare him already fallen. The momentousness of his decision is

---

[40] *Milton's Grand Style*, 110.
[41] 'Five miles meandering with a mazy motion' ('Kubla Khan', l. 25).
[42] 'The Crisis of *Paradise Lost*', in *Studies in Milton* (London, 1951; repr. 1973), 28–9.

paradoxically heightened, not diminished, by its tacitly having been made before. As with the echoes that surround Eve's fall, one should be aware that a singular moment can be intensified by the larger pattern to which it belongs, at the very point where the merging takes place.

Davis Harding is more sophisticated about the meaning of Milton's anticipations. 'To accomplish by artifice what could not be accomplished in fact', he writes,

Milton sought to implant in the minds of his readers a secret, furtive, tentative uneasiness about Adam and Eve—not so much doubts as the shadows of doubts—while simultaneously maintaining the illusion of their entire sinlessness.[43]

He is only one step away, here, from the didacticism of Stanley Fish, who claims that these 'doubts' and 'shadows of doubts' are planted by Milton in the reader's mind to show that, 'just as the fallen consciousness infects language, so does it make the unfallen consciousness the mirror of itself'.[44] *Paradise Lost*, Fish insists, is 'a primer designed to teach the reader how to interpret it', especially 'at the point where the characters perform that action which made its writing and reading necessary'.[45] Milton's own consciousness, by implication, is either spotlessly innocent or fallen in real life but somehow immune to temptation when in the act of writing. Either way, the poet (as distinct from the narrator) is omniscient, which conveniently allies him with God.

De Quincey offers an answer to Tillyard, Harding, and Fish which moves in quite the opposite, affective, direction. 'Amongst the oversights in the *Paradise Lost*', he writes, in a footnote to 'Suspiria de Profundis',

some of which have not yet been perceived, it is certainly *one*—that, by placing in such overpowering light of pathos the sublime sacrifice of Adam to his love for his frail companion, he has too much lowered the guilt of his disobedience to God.

The possibility of overdetermining the passage's meaning is neatly avoided, here, by dodging the question of intentionality and focusing instead on reader response:

All that Milton can say afterwards does not, and cannot, obscure the beauty of that action; reviewing it calmly, we condemn; but taking the impassioned station of Adam at the moment of temptation, we approve in our hearts.[46]

This places a clearer than usual emphasis on the fact that Adam falls (albeit selfishly) for love. It also dispenses with the idea that sympathy can be retracted. Stanley Fish, though stopped short in his didactic reading by the intensity of Milton's engagement with Adam, persists none the less in seeing the reader as

[43] *The Club of Hercules: Studies in the Classical Background of 'Paradise Lost'* (Urbana, Ill., 1962), 68–9.
[44] *Surprised by Sin*, 103.   [45] Ibid. 162.
[46] *Confessions of an English Opium Eater and Other Writings*, ed. with introd. G. Lindop (Oxford, 1985), 101.

trapped, the poet as omniscient, the text itself as a deliberate and clever snare. De Quincey's comment is corrective. Intensities of this kind, he argues, are not subdued by overall design: the poet's commitment, once given, cannot be withdrawn. Mulciber's fall, as we have seen, offers a simple and small-scale anticipation of this pattern. Adam's speech, by chronologically superimposing fallen and unfallen perspectives, confirms it on a subtler level, and at the dramatic climax of the poem.

The effect of anticipations and echoes in *Paradise Lost* is significantly to reveal Milton's fallen perspective. Not in Fish's crude sense, for this would turn the poet into a sinner, but in the more subversive and imaginative sense implied by De Quincey's comment, or by an extension of Blake's famous misreading. In them, Milton's 'imagination' turns and returns to the Fall because he is compelled by its human implications. They are not (as Harding sees them) 'shadows of doubts' deliberately manœuvred, but moments of affirmation dangerously allowed.

LIKENESS AND DIFFERENCE

Writing on the subject of simile and cross-reference in *Milton's Grand Style*, Christopher Ricks is particularly concerned with the conflict of likeness and difference in the poet's imagination. His central example, which I have already touched on briefly, is the passage in Book III where Satan, looking up at the palace gate from the limbo of fools, is compared to Jacob, when he too saw Heaven's gate:

> The stairs were such as whereon Jacob saw
> Angels ascending and descending, bands
> Of guardians bright, when he from Esau fled
> To Padan-Aram in the field of Luz,
> Dreaming by night under the open sky,
> And waking cried, *this* is the gate of heaven.
>
> (ll. 510–15)

Ricks has this to say:

Satan is the arch-enemy of God, Jacob was the chosen hand of God. If a contrast of this kind is not present, then we ought to deprecate the passage (however beautiful), since it would seem to suggest either that Satan was good, or that Jacob was bad.[47]

'The length and power of the allusion', he concludes, in a sentence already quoted, 'forces us to choose between damaging irrelevance or likeness turning grimly into disparity.' This claim is elegant, and its implicit subjugation of 'wit' to judgement would no doubt have been approved by Locke; but it is incomplete, as an account of the range of possible choices involved. Aside from the fact that

---

[47] *Milton's Grand Style*, 128.

Jacob, too, is morally ambiguous—not above deception himself[48]—there is a much subtler interplay between the two figures than Ricks allows. Disparity, undeniably present, is there throughout, the point being that the reader watches it turning into likeness. Milton is intrigued, as we have seen, by the fallen potential of an angel's blush; he is also compelled by the thought of Satan and Jacob becoming one. 'Qualities', as Wordsworth puts it, 'pass insensibly into their contraries, and things revolve upon each other'.[49] The didactic Milton might agree with Ricks, but within the simile itself there is a moment of imaginative fusion when the longings of God's arch-enemy and chosen hand come to be shared.

A comparable passage, which again encloses allusion within simile, occurs in Book IV. Eve, giving her account of life before Adam, is tacitly compared with Narcissus:

> As I bent down to look, just opposite,
> A shape within the watery gleam appeared
> Bending to look on me, I started back,
> It started back, but pleased I soon returned,
> Pleased it returned as soon with answering looks
> Of sympathy and love;

(ll. 460–5)

Fish, in what sounds like an echo of Ricks, claims that the reader is obliged to make a choice:

One can either conclude with Miss Bell that 'we have glimpsed a dainty vanity in "our general mother" which the serpent will put to use' or contrive, with Peter and Harding, to disengage her from the pejorative connotations of the myth.[50]

But once again this is a simplification. The reader is aware, as with Satan and Jacob, of an underlying incongruity in the comparison, even as he or she becomes conscious of its more dangerous implications. Milton may indeed be using allusion to draw attention to moral choice, but his own imagination seems to hover between two extremes. To opt for one alternative or the other is to deny a conjunction of opposites in the poetry's meaning which is essential to its intellectual complexity.

To put the case more generally: there are two different ideals to which a Miltonic simile can aspire, rather than two different kinds of Miltonic simile. On the one hand is the ideal of incongruity—described by De Quincey, in a passage which Ricks suggestively quotes, as 'the principle of subtle and lurking antagonism' between images: 'Each image, from reciprocal contradiction,

---

[48] See Gen. 27–8.
[49] 'Essay upon Epitaphs' (essay ii); *The Prose Works of William Wordsworth*, ed. W. J. B. Owen and J. W. Smyser (3 vols., Oxford, 1974), ii. 53.
[50] *Surprised by Sin*, 217.

brightens and vivifies the other. The two images act, and react, by strong re-
pulsion and antagonism.'[51] On the other hand is the ideal of assimilation, or
merging, which Wordsworth—in his famous simile in 'Resolution and Independence'—claims is fulfilled as 'the Stone is endowed with something of the
power of life to approximate it to the Sea-beast, and the Sea-beast stripped of
some of its vital qualities to assimilate it to the stone'. The final effect, he goes on
to suggest, is created at 'the point where the two objects unite and coalesce in just
comparison'.[52] One could argue that Wordsworth's description works for Jacob
and Satan, De Quincey's for Narcissus and Eve, but it is more complicated than
that. The two processes remain ideals because in practice they are able to coexist,
and therefore to modify each other. When they do so, a perplexity in the reader's
response (the equivalent of what Burke calls 'judicious obscurity' in a poet's
style)[53] ensures that no final decision is made. The 'danger' of these similes lies,
not in one's apprehension that Eve is vain, or Satan good, but in one's response
to the attractiveness of the human values which emerge.

Moving back into echoes, after similes, one observes how closely related they
are. A telling moment, mishandled by Rajan as straight burlesque,[54] comes in
Book X. Sin, addressing her son and lover, Death, celebrates the divinity which
the fall appears to give her: 'Methinks I feel new strength within me rise, |
Wings growing, and dominion given me large | Beyond this deep' (ll. 243–5).
Her words, as Alastair Fowler points out,[55] contain an echo from Book IX,
where Adam and Eve, intoxicated by their fall, 'fancy that they feel | Divinity
within them breeding wings' (l. 1010). The main point, undoubtedly, is to
underline the illusory and sinful nature of fallen man's sense of elation. But
there are subtler implications. As her address to Death continues, Sin takes on a
moving resemblance to the fallen Adam: 'Thou my shade | Inseparable must
with me along: | For death from sin no power can separate' (x. 249–51)—her
language, in its tenderness, recalling his to Eve: 'Our state cannot be severed, we
are one, | One flesh; to lose thee were to lose myself' (ix. 958–9). Milton may
intend one merely to apprehend Sin as a diabolic version of Adam (a variation
on his usual practice of linking her with Eve),[56] but to see parody alone is to opt
for a limited reading. For a moment, Sin and Adam, like Jacob and Satan, are at
one: united not only in their aspiration but in the love which is both a cause of
their fall and the abundant recompense it brings.

[51] 'On Milton' (1839, 1857), in *De Quincey as Critic*, ed. J. E. Jordan (London, 1973), 257.

[52] 'Preface' to *Poems* (1815); *Wordsworth*, 633.

[53] The phrase is used by Burke to describe the uncertainty which he regards as an essential
ingredient of the sublime. It is applied to Milton's description of Death in *PL* ii, in which, Burke
comments, 'all is dark, uncertain, confused, terrible, and sublime to the last degree' (*Burke Enquiry*,
59). For further discussion of the connection between Burkean sublimity and interpretative indeterminacy, see Ch. 6.

[54] B. Rajan, *'Paradise Lost' and the Seventeenth-Century Reader* (London, 1947), 45.

[55] See *PL*, p. 520.

[56] Cf. the connection between *PL* i. 1–3 and ii. 872; and between ii. 871–2 and ix. 385–6.

Parody in Milton frequently complicates itself in this way. The address of Sin to Death in Book X is mirrored, in Book II, by a moment of equal ambivalence. On this occasion, it is to her father, Satan, that Sin is speaking:

> Thou art my father, thou my author, thou
> My being gavest me; whom should I obey
> But thee, whom follow? thou wilt bring me soon
> To that new world of light and bliss, among
> The gods who live at ease, where I shall reign
> At thy right hand voluptuous, as beseems
> Thy daughter and thy darling, without end.

(ii. 864–70)

Coming so soon after the horrific account of her rape, this gentleness of tone, modulating into formal utterance, takes one by surprise. Rajan and others are right to point out that the speech is a parody of the Nicene creed, and that Sin—in a moment of blasphemous transumption—usurps Christ's place beside God (Satan).[57] But the revelation of human need in her questioning works on a different level. Sin's words, 'whom should I obey | But thee, whom follow?', are a distant anticipation of Adam's: 'How can I live without thee, how forgo | Thy sweet converse?' (ix. 908–9), themselves echoed later, more reproachfully, by Eve: 'forlorn of thee, | Whither shall I betake me, where subsist?' (x. 921–2). Human relationship creates a bond between opposites which is stronger than the opposition itself. The reader feels surprise, pleasure—even perhaps relief—in noticing that Milton has broken down the stability on which parody normally depends.

It is a process one can also watch in the recurrence of key words, single and paired. Satan's description of hell in Book I, for instance, as 'yon dreary plain, forlorn and wild' (l. 180), is echoed by Adam's phrase in Book IX, 'to live again in these wild woods forlorn' (l. 910). More interesting still is the connection between Sin, 'with terrors and with clamours compassed round' (ii. 862), and Milton himself, 'in darkness and with dangers compassed round' (vii. 27). Echoes such as these belong to the intricate network of parallels, connecting the activities of heaven, earth, and hell, with which *Paradise Lost* is held together. When pointed out by Rajan, details such as the parody of Creation in the building of the causeway, and the paired councils in hell and heaven, are easily understood in terms of a stable, binary system of oppositions.[58] The frequency with which they occur, he would argue, habituates the reader to the Miltonic habit of seeing contrast within analogy. But the system is undermined by the presence of words that resonate much more freely, giving the impression of easy movement from one state into another and creating subtle, unexpected conflations.

'Wandering' is a good example. Stanley Fish, who follows the word, through

---

[57] *Seventeenth-Century Reader*, 47–8, 50.   [58] Ibid. 44–52.

its many permutations, across the entire text of *Paradise Lost*, establishes for its first occurrence in Book I a neutral meaning which is later displaced. Except, he argues, when used to describe aspects of Paradise before the Fall, 'wandering' has for Milton very clear negative implications. This is increasingly so after Book VII. An access of Christianity, however, in Fish's view, guides the poet as he brings the epic to an end, with the result that fallen words are redeemed: 'Under Providence', he says,

through the medium of faith, the word is able to include all its meanings, even those which are literally contradictory, and is thus returned, after many permutations, to its original purity and innocence.[59]

This is a kind of profit-and-loss criticism, in which it is assumed that each of Milton's references to wandering relates to all the others, and that—when the adding of goodness and subtracting of badness has taken place—a final reckoning can be made. In practice, of course, language does not work like that. Only some of the wanderings echo each other, and when they do so, a more subtle relationship is being implied. Belial's anguish in Book II—'for who would lose, | Though full of pain, this intellectual being, | Those thoughts that wander through eternity' (ll. 146–8) is barely qualified by the moralizing un-resonance of a later line: 'And found no end, in wandering mazes lost' (ll. 561), though Milton the Great Forbidder might intend it to be cancelled out. Other wanderings, however, seem to resonate among themselves, and it is to this group that Belial's use of the word belongs.

When Adam and Eve depart from paradise—'They hand in hand with wandering steps and slow | Through Eden *took their solitary way*' (xii. 648–9)—an echo from Book II connects them with Beelzebub, asking the fallen angels 'Who shall tempt with wandering feet | The dark unbottomed infinite abyss | And through the palpable obscure find out | *His uncouth way*? (ii. 404–7). Fish, drawing attention to a similar echo, would have us believe that 'the contrast is all'.[60] But this cannot be so. There is, in Milton's allusive language, a balance of adjustment and retention which allows for similarity to emerge despite difference and for affinity to be underlined. Delight and liberty, accompanied in each case by loneliness and fear, draw Satan and the fallen humans together. They go out to confront danger; they also go out to create new worlds.

ROMANTIC INTERPRETATION

Romantic readings of *Paradise Lost* respond both to the alternating possibilities in its overall structure and to the conflationary tendencies of its local rhetorical effects. They seize on the mighty opposites it contains, but they are also excited by the extent to which Milton himself seems prepared to transgress moral

---

[59] *Surprised by Sin*, 141.   [60] Ibid.

boundaries. Belial's speech in Book II is a reminder of how subtly, in meta-phoric as well as allusive language, this lapse can take place:

> For who would lose,
> Though full of pain, this intellectual being,
> Those thoughts that wander through eternity,
> To perish rather, swallowed up and lost
> In the wide womb of uncreated night,
> Devoid of sense and motion?

(ll. 146–51)

Imagery works strangely here, juxtaposing infinite distance with fallen associ-ation and human immediacy, as Belial, who has not himself experienced birth, imagines re-entering a womb that widens and darkens into a night that has yet to be created. As one reads, it is the womb—human and out of place—that draws attention to itself. In place of the warmth and fertility one might expect, it evokes non-relationship, non-being. As on other occasions, Milton has made a connection between falling and being born.[61] In his acceptance of pain, Belial refuses to go backwards—values the world of restlessness, suffering, aspiration, over the stasis that may be called either innocence or death. In the poet's imagination, there is a threshold between two worlds. There is also a choice to be made. Satan, looking into 'the secrets of the hoary deep' later in Book II, stands on a more palpable brink, but one that is equally symbolic, for it is only in leaving hell behind that his potential can be fulfilled. Adam, in Book IX, is also poised—the threshold is not seen here, but imagined—as he chooses between duty and human love.

It is to moments of choice such as these that the Romantics frequently return, especially in their narrative poetry; and in so doing they adopt Milton's allusive language as their own. Charles Lamb once referred to Wordsworth as 'the best knower of Milton':[62] it is perhaps no surprise, then, that the opening of *The Prelude*, itself a threshold experience of sorts, should provide an in-stance of carefully imitative Miltonic conflation. Wordsworth's playful re-working of Adam and Eve's departure from paradise, is, of course, well known: 'The world was all before them, where to choose | Their place of rest, and Providence their guide' (*PL* xii. 646–7). But it goes hand in hand with an unnoticed echo from Sin's address to Death: 'Nor can I miss the way, so strongly drawn | By this new felt attraction and instinct' (*PL* x. 262–3). The effect Wordsworth creates is one of exultation, which exactly matches that of both Sin and Eve, as they revel in the new found 'divinity' which is an after-effect of falling:

---

[61] See *PL* ix. 780–84, ix. 997–1001.

[62] The phrase appears in Lamb's hand on the fly-leaf of the first edition of *Paradise Regained*, given by him to Wordsworth in 1820, and now in the Wordsworth Library, Grasmere.

> *The earth is all before me*—with a heart
> Joyous, nor scared at its own liberty,
> I look about, and should the guide I choose
> Be nothing better than a wandering cloud
> *I cannot miss my way.*[63]

Released from the hell of an imprisoned state of mind, Wordsworth writes of the inner creative power which excites him: 'I breathe again— | Trances of thought and mountings of the mind | Come fast upon me' (*Prelude* i. 19–21). Sin's elation, as she watches the building of the causeway from earth to hell, might easily follow on: 'Methinks I feel new strength within me rise, | Wings growing, and dominion given me large | Beyond this deep' (*PL* x. 243–5). By thus conflating Miltonic opposites, in a carefully Miltonic manner, Wordsworth not only pays tribute to his literary model; he also succeeds in suggesting a parallel between the Fall and the birth of imagination: in Chapter 7, I shall return to the wider Romantic implications of this comparison.

Romantic allusions are frequently of this careful Wordsworthian kind. But even when they are boldly and thematically conceived, instead of closely and verbally echoic, they are far from suggesting a revisionary '*mis*reading' of *Paradise Lost*. Instead, they imply a subtle amplification of Miltonic indeterminacy, which places the reader in a position of suspended choice. He or she becomes aware of the coexistence of moral opposites, perceives the implication that a choice might be made, and comes to the conclusion that not making it is a subtler kind of truth. *The Marriage of Heaven and Hell*, for instance, may appear to make a choice, by inverting Milton's terms and privileging the subtext of his poem. But it does so, misleadingly, in order to arrive at the superior position of ambivalence—the truly Miltonic conjunction of opposites—which its title promises.[64] As Jerome McGann reminds us, Blake's poetic strategies are 'precisely designed to foster ambivalent perspectives—to tease us out of thought'. Providing a route to 'fourfold vision', they encourage the perception of similarities and differences in perpetual (infinite) oscillation.[65] The method adopted by Mary Shelley, in *Frankenstein*, is similar, though more straightforward. 'Remember that I am thy creature', the monster warns his creator at one point: 'I ought to be thy Adam; but I am rather thy fallen angel, whom thou drivest from joy for no misdeed.'[66] The monster sees Adam and Satan as alternatives. The reader, encouraged by sustained allusive patterns, sees them as both opposite and complementary. Frankenstein, too, is a conflation—like Adam in his curiosity and ambition, like God in his capacity to create.

---

[63] *Prelude*, i. 15–19.

[64] Blake would have found a straightforward reversal of *Paradise Lost* unsubtle. *MHH* depends for its subversiveness on disconcerting (Swiftian) techniques; see e.g. the 'Proverbs of Hell', which first exhilarate then shock the reader through sheer contrariness: 'Sooner murder an infant in its cradle than nurse unacted desires' (pl. 10, l. 67). Some aspects of Blake's technique will be examined in Ch. 4.

[65] 'Blake's Sublime Allegories', 13, 16.   [66] *Frankenstein* (London, 1976), 82.

The open-endedness of Romantic allusions can thus be seen as closely re-sembling, if not deriving from, a 'negative capability' which is inherent in *Paradise Lost* itself: Geoffrey Hartman has renamed this a 'spirit of accommoda-tion', which allows 'two different, even contrary ideas to coexist'.[67] It can be discerned, not only in the allusive strategies I have closely analysed, but in some of the broader conceptual ambiguities which Milton allows. Possibilities for intellectual relativism are, indeed, invited by the slightest Miltonic devices of hesitancy and indeterminacy:

> though what if earth
> Be but the shadow of heav'n, and things therein
> Each to other like, more than on earth is thought?

> (*PL* v. 574–6)

As Virginia Mollenkott reminds us, 'the possibility of earth as heaven's exact shadow is one that Milton cannot positively assert because of his respect for the absolute authority of Scripture, which is silent on the topic; but he cannot exclude it either'.[68] Here as elsewhere, the author of *Paradise Lost* is using what Mollenkott calls the technique of 'multiple choice', to include transgressional ideas within a more neutral framework. In so doing, Milton prepares the ground for Coleridge, who must be similarly hesitant about making philosophical enquiries which could tamper with the unknowable absolute. When, in 'The Aeolian Harp', he poses his daring panentheistic question, 'And what if all of animated nature | Be but organic Harps diversely fram'd?',[69] he is using a rhetorical device closely modelled on Milton's own. Both writers allow them-selves the pleasure of a speculative activity which is, strictly speaking, out of bounds; and in Coleridge's case there is the added playfulness which derives from allusion.

Steven Knapp, in his illuminating analysis of personification and the sub-lime, has observed of *Paradise Lost* that it is 'filled with moments of imaginative leisure that indulge ... in fictional possibilities of apostasy', and that the modern reader 'turns to such moments—the epic similes, the pagan allusions, Belial's speech in Book II, Eve's account of her first awakening, the invocation to Book VII—for images of poetic self-consciousness'.[70] Knapp argues, as I have done, for a refusal of the closure embodied in the voice of the epic narrator, and for an indulgence towards fictive play:

While the narrator takes as much pleasure in cancelling such alternatives as he does in presenting them—'thus they relate, | Erring'; 'But all was false and hollow'; 'For thou art Heavenly, she an empty dream'—the momentary oscillation between fiction and truth gives an illusion of genuine mediation.[71]

---

[67] 'Adam on the Grass with Balsamum', *English Literary History*, 36 (1969), 178.
[68] 'Milton's Technique of Multiple Choice', *Milton Studies*, 6 (1974), 103.
[69] ll. 44–5.
[70] *Personification and the Sublime: Milton to Coleridge* (Cambridge, Mass., 1985), 48.
[71] Ibid.

In this 'momentary oscillation between fiction and truth' one might see a model for the Romantic imagination, which, although attempting to secure for itself a purely aesthetic status, repeatedly subjects itself to the pressures of truthfulness and morality. Keats's moments of 'imaginative leisure' are just as threatened as Milton's are: witness his observation that 'the fancy cannot cheat so well | As she is famed to do, deceiving elf'.[72] Yet the oscillations he repeatedly allows— between dreaming and waking, illusion and reality, escapism and engagement—can be seen, like Milton's, to be creating 'an illusion of genuine mediation' between worlds that are disjoined. The mediating principle is, in both cases, 'poetic self-consciousness', or subjectivity, which earns its right to be amoral by remaining purely speculative:

What shocks the virtuous philosop[h]er, delights the camelion Poet. It does no harm from its relish of the dark side of things any more than from its taste for the bright one; because they both end in speculation.[73]

The 'spirit of accommodation' which the Romantics inherit from Milton emerges all the more strikingly as a result of the transgressional implications with which it is supplied, not only by its moral and religious context, but also by the eighteenth century's suspicion of metaphor. I shall be suggesting in Chapter 6 that there is an important connection between allusion and indeterminacy, in the emphasis they both place on the subjectivity of the reader. It will therefore be appropriate to end, here, by tracing the growth of subjectivity back to Milton himself, via the Romantics' preoccupation with transgression. 'In all modern poetry in Christendom', writes Coleridge, in a lecture of 1819,

There is an underconsciousness of a sinful nature, a fleeting away of external things, the mind or subject greater than the object, the reflective character predominant. In the Paradise Lost the sublimest parts are the revelations of Milton's own mind, producing itself and evolving its own greatness.[74]

The ambiguity of his language is worth noting: 'an underconsciousness of a sinful nature' means both 'an underlying awareness of sin' and 'a sinful (i.e. fallen) unconscious'; and it is noticeable, too, that Coleridge's emphasis is not on Satanic energy but on human potential: what he sees in the loss of paradise is the evolution of imaginative worlds. Milton, anticipating Coleridge, is the first Romantic reader of *Paradise Lost*. The Fall, visited and revisited by his echoic imagination, as it will be interpreted and reinterpreted by later writers, offers a moment of absolute loss which is also one of human gain. Cross-references, echoes, and allusions draw attention, repeatedly and insistently, to this doubleness, revealing a valuation of the fallen world which conflicts with the poem's moral design. It is in the subtext of *Paradise Lost* that we find its Romantic meaning. If, as the intentionalists would argue, Milton *designs* this subtext, so

---

[72] 'Ode to a Nightingale', ll. 73–4.
[73] To R. Woodhouse, 27 Oct. 1818; *Keats Letters*, 157.
[74] 'Lecture on Milton and Paradise Lost', 4 Mar. 1819, in *Romantics on Milton*, 245.

that we may 'see and know and yet abstain',[75] the reader, like Adam and Eve, is fortunately free to fall.

[75] DuRocher, *Milton and Ovid*, 217. For the Miltonic passage on which DuRocher bases his proposition, see *Areopagitica:* 'He that can apprehend and consider vice with her baits and seeming pleasures, and yet distinguish, and yet prefer that which is truly better, he is the true warfaring Christian' (cited above, n. 23).

3

Politics

It has been customary to simplify what the Romantics saw as the political meaning of *Paradise Lost*: first, by overemphasizing the heroic values identified in Satan (most famously by Blake); secondly, by equating these too specifically with the republicanism championed in Milton's political pamphlets (then later espoused by the young Wordsworth and Coleridge); and thirdly, by applying a blanket conception of Romanticism to a range of different writers, whose political complexions were not only distinct but were themselves coloured by changing circumstances. Christopher Hill refers, in *Milton and the English Revolution*, to 'the view of Blake, Shelley, Belinsky—all romantic radicals, we note—that Satan is the hero of *Paradise Lost*, or that he is the first Whig'.[1] The main effect of this and similar simplifications has been to suggest that, by virtue of its association with republican values, the Romantics regarded Satanic energy as of necessity positive, and so to overlook some of the hesitancies and ambiguities which register a Romantic mistrust of political extremism. This mistrust emerges, for instance, in Shelley's repudiation of 'the taints of ambition, envy, revenge, and a desire for personal aggrandisement, which in the Hero of *Paradise Lost* interfere with the interest';[2] or in Coleridge's comment:

The character of Satan is pride and sensual indulgence, finding in self the sole motive of action. It is the character so often *seen in little* on the political stage. It exhibits all the restlessness, temerity, and cunning which have marked the mighty hunters of mankind from Nimrod to Napoleon.[3]

It must be evident—not just from Shelley's and Coleridge's comments, but also from the characterization of such figures as Falkland in *Caleb Williams*, Rivers in *The Borderers*, and Robespierre in *The Prelude*—that Satanic allusion can function as a register, not only of moral approval for a particular political stance, but also of moral ambiguity or even revulsion, in a particular set of circumstances. It must, furthermore, be apparent that Romantic writers turn

---

[1] *Milton and the English Revolution* (London, 1977), 367.

[2] 'Preface' to *Prometheus Unbound*; *Shelley*, 133. The revisionary implications behind Shelley's characterization of Prometheus are discussed in Ch. 4.

[3] 'Lecture on Milton and the Paradise Lost', 4 Mar. 1819; in *Romantics on Milton*, 244. Cf. Coleridge's comment on Satan in *The Statesman's Manual* (1816): 'in its utmost abstraction and consequent state of reprobation the will becomes Satanic pride and rebellious self-idolatry. ... Alas, too often has it been embodied in real life. Too often has it given a dark and savage grandeur to the historic page' (*Romantics on Milton*, 228).

back to Milton with added interest, at moments when they are perplexed by the relation between politics and morality, or intrigued by the nature of individual motivation, or fascinated (as in the Coleridge comment quoted above) by the distinctive characteristics of the tyrant. Instead of isolating Satanic energy from its larger Miltonic context, then, as though it could somehow float free of ethical questions, one should be restoring to each Satanic reference an ambivalence which originates in the complex argument of *Paradise Lost*.

In reading *Paradise Lost* as a political poem, Romantic writers found in it nothing so coherent or unified as republican allegory, though some commentators have wished this to be the case. What they found, instead, was a troubled and divided treatment of the relation between earthly politics and religious truth, which gave a by no means systematic explanation for the origin of evil. The range and complexity of responses available to the reader of *Paradise Lost* emerges most clearly from an examination of the political appropriations of Satan and God, which have been a constant feature of Milton criticism since the eighteenth century, and which appear to be invited by connections between Milton's prose writings and the language of his later epic. When discussing the affinities that exist between Satan's 'republicanism' and Milton's own, critics have, for instance, drawn attention to resemblances between *The Readie and Easie Way to Establish a Free Commonwealth* (1660) and Satan's political ideas. Milton's plea against the return to monarchy has, in particular, been stressed as a source for Satan's repudiation of heavenly tyranny:

It may well be wonderd that any nation, styling themselves free, can suffer any man to pretend right over them as thir lord; whenas by acknowledging that right, they conclude themselves his servants and his vassals, and so renounce thir own freedom.[4]

The parallels with Satan's position are clear enough;[5] but they have been handled in such a way as to reveal sharp distinctions of ideology between the critics who discuss them.

On one side of the debate, William Empson in *Milton's God* and Christopher Hill in *Milton and the English Revolution* have sustained a tradition which begins with Godwin and Blake. Associating God with monarchical rule, and Satan with republican ideals, Hill in particular reads *Paradise Lost* as a political allegory in which the allusions are 'veiled' but 'not indecipherable'.[6] Milton, he claims, 'does not *identify* with Satan and the rebel angels, who embody and criticize the defects of the military leaders of the Revolution'; instead, he uses them to explore the reasons for the failure of the Good Old Cause. 'Satan *is* heroic: as heroic as Milton still thinks the English Revolution had been', but he also embodies 'selfish Reason', and as such can be closely aligned with Crom-

---

[4] *Milton Prose*, vii, ed. R. W. Ayers and A. H. Woolrych (New Haven, Conn., 1980), 362–3.
[5] Satan's refusal to submit to the tyranny of heaven is best epitomized in his rallying call to the fallen angels (see esp. *PL* i. 98, 111–12, 322–3), the language of which is similar to Milton's own.
[6] *Milton and the English Revolution*, 365.

well.[7] If Hill stresses the moral distance which Milton puts between himself and the leaders of the Revolution, he is also interested by the bond of anger and disappointment which Milton shares with Satan:

the magnificent Satan of the early books of the epic does convey some of the defiance which Milton himself must have felt tempted to hurl in the face of onmipotence as the republic crashed about his ears. The rebellious energy ebbs in the later books, after the restoration of Charles II has brought Milton to recognize the full magnitude of the rethinking that is required.[8]

Milton persists, in such a reading, as a loyal republican—despite the sense of betrayal which the collapse of the Commonwealth must have caused him, and in the face of personal threats to his safety posed by the return of the monarchy. If the Revolution had utterly failed, 'It had failed because the men were not great enough for the Cause';[9] but Hill is emphatic that 'we must, however, not take Milton's condemnation of Satan as condemnation of rebellion'.[10]

On the other side of the debate, Satan is given a timeless and abstracted status, as the ultimate tyrant of Milton's poem. In Merritt Hughes's influential reading, he is 'the destroyer opposed to cosmic order', who has affinities with 'a Renaissance tyrant', with modern Turkish sultans, with Cromwell, with Charles I, and with Macbeth.[11] Hughes is concerned to steer clear of the 'attribution of any topical political intention to Milton's epic plan', which in his view would involve 'irreconcilable hypotheses';[12] but it is important that his identification of Satan as tyrant can be seen to work compatibly alongside anti-republican readings. In other words, Satan can be identified in absolute moral terms as evil, at the same time as voicing Milton's earlier political ideals—the point being that he registers the extent of Milton's withdrawal from republicanism in the face of its betrayal. For a clear statement of this position, we can do worse than to recall the Tory challenge, made in the *London Chronicle* 1763:

How could Milton better refute the good old cause he was such a partisan of and such an advocate for than by making the rebellion in the poem resemble it, and giving the same characteristics to the apostate angels as were applicable to his rebel brethren?[13]

Such a reading depends on seeing in a purely ironic light the affinities which exist between Milton's republican language and Satan's own. The subtlest and most convincing case for this view is made by Blair Worden, who argues that Milton is at pains not only to 'implant his republicanism in *Paradise Lost*' but

[7] Ibid. 367; Hill goes on to claim that Satan is like Cromwell in 'pleading "public reason just, | Honour and empire" to justify an aggressive foreign policy' (p. 368). This alignment of Cromwell | Satan with perverted reason is illuminating, esp. in view of Wordsworth's later portrayal of the Satanic Rivers as one who uses Godwinian reason to disguise his own irrational compulsions.

[8] Ibid. 368.   [9] Ibid. 367.   [10] Ibid. 368.

[11] *Ten Perspectives on Milton* (New Haven, Conn., 1964), 171.

[12] Ibid. 173.

[13] 12–13 Nov. 1763; quoted by J. DiSalvo, *War of Titans: Blake's Critique of Milton and the Politics of Religion* (Pittsburgh, Pa., 1983), 29.

also to 'expose the falsity of Satan's application of it'.[14] Worden sees the point-
edness of this exposure in terms of topical moral exemplum: there is for him a
clear alignment between Satan as the type and Cromwell as 'the most eminent
and destructive example' of 'the Puritan hypocrite', who disguises his personal
craving for power with self-righteousness.[15] He also sees, in *Paradise Lost*'s
ironic use of self-quotation, evidence for the personal education Milton had
been through in witnessing the humiliating collapse of the Commonwealth. A
cyclical pattern of events had proved only how pathetically mistaken is any
human attempt to interfere with providence: Cromwell had become a substitute
sovereign, and monarchy had been restored. If what had once been identified in
political terms as good could turn so readily into evil, through the fallibility of
politicians and the unworthiness of the British people, then perhaps it did
follow that only the absolute religious categories would stand the test of time:

> in 1657–63 it was the turn of the Puritans themselves to confront the lesson in which
> Milton had instructed the royalists: the lesson of the measureless difference of proportion
> between temporal politics and eternal verities. In those years ... Milton does not merely
> return to his right hand, from prose to poetry: he withdraws from politics into faith.[16]

Evidence for the moral relativism of *Paradise Lost* lies not just in the poem's
adaptability to both these arguments, which would seem to locate ideology solely
in the reader's interpretation. It is present also in the fact that Milton gives
counter-signals in the text itself, as though to draw attention to the interchan-
geability of moral values when measured with a political yardstick, and of
political values when measured against a stable moral grid. Thus, as my
summary of the debate has suggested, the character of God Himself is not
exempt from politics. He can be appropriated by readers wishing to see a pro-
republican argument, as a monstrous exemplar of monarchical tyranny: this
view is well rehearsed by Empson, Hill, and DiSalvo (the latter drawing attention to heaven as 'an elaborate feudal court', a 'full-fledged theocracy'[17]).
Alternatively, He can be understood as offering divine justification for monarchical rule. Furthermore, some of the topical political references work both
ways: the divine right of kings is famously embodied (some would say sanctioned) in God's choice of His son as the appropriate vessel for His providential
plan;[18] but it is also echoed by Satan himself in the claim that he holds 'imperial
titles which assert | [His] being ordained to govern, not to serve'.[19] As Joan
Bennett persuasively argues in *Reviving Liberty*, Satan is the mouthpiece for the
royalist belief that 'whoever currently holds power over a people, whether just or
unjust according to any heretofore accepted national or natural law, can rightly

---

[14] 'Milton's Republicanism and the Tyranny of Heaven', in G. Bock, Q. Skinner, and M. Viroli
(eds.), *Machiavelli and Republicanism* (Cambridge, 1990), 240.
[15] Ibid. 241–2.   [16] Ibid. 244.   [17] *War of Titans*, 249.
[18] For God's election of Christ the Son, as the inheritor of His 'effectual might', see *PL* iii.
168–70 and v. 604–15.
[19] See Satan's corrupt version of republicanism, *PL* v. 795–802.

by virtue of his strength control his subjects' behaviour'.[20] Or, as the Whig contributor to the *London Chronicle* in 1763 had put it, 'the Tory plan, where man assumes a right of dominion over man, was nearer related to Satan's aim of setting himself in glory over his peers'.[21] Textual evidence for such readings is easily found: Milton's description of Satan as seated 'High on a throne of royal state' would appear to be exposing the monarchical and imperialist designs in Satan himself, at the expense of a straightforwardly republican identification.[22]

The central contradiction of *Paradise Lost* can be simplified thus: on the one hand, Milton sees good and evil as moral absolutes, existing outside a political structure, and determined by the Christian perspective which validates or belittles all human endeavour; on the other hand, he appears to be suggesting that good and evil are themselves politically determined: the labels contingently applied to a given cause by opposing factions in their bid for power. In this second reading, the straightforward equations of heaven with royalism and hell with republicanism, which have been encouraged at both ends of the political spectrum by allegorical appropriations of the text, can be seen to break down under the influence of Milton's mirroring and echoing devices. The reader is drawn into a political identification which its balancing opposite serves to cancel out.

Theoretically, it should be possible to see the second of these views as reconcilable with the first. If Milton did indeed write *Paradise Lost* with the full consciousness of how far the republican cause had miscarried, not simply because of the fallibility of politicians but because in itself it stood for man's misguided attempt to anticipate God's will, he might well have been retreating from politics altogether, into the trustable absolutes of religious conviction— what Worden refers to as the 'eternal verities'. It would then be plausible to suppose that he was inviting the reader to make false political identifications on a local level, in order that these should be checked against the larger religious perspective offered in the poem as a whole. The function of the text's two-way indeterminacies would thus be to imply the dangerous moral relativism which stems from ideology and, further, to suggest that notions of good and evil are finally resistant to political appropriation. One factor which makes this resolution problematic, however, is the nature of Milton's dramatization. If the 'eternal verities' are outside politics, then it is surely confusing to the reader that their representatives (God and Satan as types of Good and Evil) should be contaminated by allusion to topical political concerns. And, even if those topical references are neutralized, is there not something uncomfortably paradoxical in having protagonists who at once embody moral absolutes and signal moral relativism? In this respect, as in others,

[20] *Reviving Liberty: Radical Christian Humanism in Milton's Great Poems* (Cambridge, Mass., 1989), 46.
[21] See n. 13 above.   [22] *PL* ii. 1.

Milton's dramatic technique has precisely the opposite effect from that identified by Johnson:[23] it makes his epic characters overly human, overly involved in the ideologies they are intended to rise above.

But there is another reason for finding the two views incompatible: whilst the first implausibly supposes that Milton made a rupture with his political past, the second more credibly suggests a distanced accommodation of ambivalence and change. Writers who revise their earlier positions usually do so with considerable difficulty, and much self-justification, since the act of revision is itself bound up with a larger sense of themselves as continuous beings. It seems no more likely, therefore, that Milton resigned his political ideals in 1660 and retired to a separate world of eternal verities than that Wordsworth substituted imagination for revolutionary zeal in circa 1797.[24] Both were forced by disillusioning circumstances to take a long cool look at the miscarriage of their earlier beliefs; and both rechannelled their hopes in the light of what they had learnt. But the vestiges of each poet's political origins remain visible, even within their later objectives. As Jackie DiSalvo sees it, there is evidence in *Paradise Lost* for a Milton who is 'the engaged polemicist still hoping to prepare his countrymen for the next round of battle'. DiSalvo outlines the possibility that when 'defeated political tendencies' are seen to 'retreat into culture', this is 'not as a mode of surrender, but of survival, as a means of preserving their goals for revival at a more opportune moment'.[25] Religious quietism was not, then, a *replacement* for Milton's republicanism (any more than were retirement and imagination for Wordsworth's). His earlier position was absorbed and subsumed in the later one, making it, not less political than it had ever been, only differently so.

It is my contention that Satan provides a meeting-point, but not a reconciliation, of the two counter-arguments I have been outlining. On the one hand, his assumption of sovereignty is a parody of earthly claims to divinity, whether these are identified as overtly monarchical (Charles I, Charles II, the divine right of kings) or surrogately so (Cromwell). In this respect, Milton does indeed evince a levelling scorn for politics, finding opposing factions to be equally culpable in their usurpation of divine status and their abuse of power. On the other hand, however, Satan speaks very specifically in the language of republicanism earlier adopted by Milton himself. This is a register, not only or necessarily of how far

[23] Johnson complains that in *Paradise Lost* 'The want of human interest is always felt'; and observes that 'The reader finds no transaction in which he can be engaged, beholds no condition in which he can by any effort of imagination place himself; he has, therefore, little natural curiosity or sympathy' (*Johnson Life*, 183, 181).

[24] That there might be difficulties (for Milton, at least) in the process of self-revision is clearly acknowledged by Worden, who argues that 'the pain and complication of that process are characteristically kept hidden from us' ('Milton's Republicanism', 244). For a comparison between the responses of Milton and Wordsworth to the failure of revolution, see J. Wordsworth, *William Wordsworth: The Borders of Vision* (Oxford, 1982), 107–9; and for the transformation of Wordsworth from 'poet of social protest' to 'prophet of apocalypse', see N. Roe, *Wordsworth and Coleridge: The Radical Years* (Oxford, 1988), 144.

[25] DiSalvo, *War of Titans*, 29.

Milton has come to repudiate those views, but of the extent to which ideals may persist, despite the corrupt character of those who are their spokesmen, and alongside the contingent evils which have caused them to miscarry. Satan need not and should not be assimilated into a single consistent reading of Milton's political standpoint; he must instead be allowed the troubling ambiguity which for three centuries has so excited, and divided, readers of *Paradise Lost*.

MOTIVATION

It would seem simplistic, then, in the face of the text's multiple indeterminacies, to argue either that Milton made Satan heroic by aligning him with republican ideals or that he wished to 'frame' republicanism by making Satan its mouth-piece. It is more likely that, in choosing the Fall as his subject, he wished to trace the process whereby good turned gradually from potential to actual evil— wished, in other words, to come to terms with the fallibility of human beings, which his own political experience had taught. Read in this way, the study of motivation in *Paradise Lost* suggests a forward-looking possibility: if what is good may be the origin of what is evil, then what is evil may none the less still have access to what is good. The moral ambiguity of Satan allows Milton to go on believing that, however far the Commonwealth had failed, there was still the chance of a political outcome which might genuinely implement the divine plan.

What the radical poets of the 1790s found in the character of Satan was a treatment of the origin of evil which reflected their own moral and political concerns. They too sought an explanation for the disappointing outcome of the French Revolution—an explanation that might leave intact the ideals out of which it had grown, and in which so much had been invested. Satan provided the focus for what turned out to be a sequence of psychological studies in motivation—Falkland, Rivers, Frankenstein, Beatrice Cenci, Cain, Manfred, to name only the most obvious. Each of these studies raises the question asked by Milton in *Paradise Lost*: if the miscarriage of revolutionary ideals lies in the transition from good to bad motivation, who is finally to be held responsible— the individuals who wield earthly power, the circumstances which act upon their characters, or the divinity which shapes their ends?

One might expect Milton's answer to be very different from that of his Romantic followers, and in its theological formulation this is indeed how it sounds: the potential for evil, as explained in *De Doctrina Christiana*, is planted within man by God, and even its realization is foreknown; but culpability rests squarely with the individual consciousness that makes choices and takes actions. Thus, although the Fall can be used to rationalize the emergence of evil as part of the larger good toward which (in accordance with God's plans) man is tending, it cannot excuse the initial choice of evil, for which man is himself wholly responsible. In practice, however (that is, when writing *Paradise Lost*), it is precisely because he places so strong an emphasis on the *felix culpa* that Milton

qualifies the absoluteness of the evil man chooses. And, furthermore, it is
because of his Shakespearian interest in motivation that he provides circum-
stantial details which explain, and to some extent diminish, human culpability.
To my question—who is finally to be held responsible for political error?—
Paradise Lost gives all three of the available answers: the Commonwealth failed,
not because its ideals were in themselves evil, but because they were implemen-
ted wrongly. The responsibility for this lay with the individuals who chose to
abuse power, but there were mitigating circumstances; and, what is more, their
wrongdoing was neither final nor absolute, since in God's plan evil will eventually bring forth good.

Milton's qualifying of moral absolutes must have seemed particularly appropriate to the generation of young writers who had recently encountered the ideas
of Godwin. There is, in the radical thought of the late eighteenth century and
onwards, a strong emphasis on the social conditioning of individuals: human
motivation, it was argued, should be seen in terms of the collocation of social
influences by which it is shaped and determined, and not in terms of an innate
propensity for evil. Thus, according to *Political Justice*, a murderer is made such
by the pressures upon him: punishment for his crime is wholly inappropriate.[26]
As Coleridge puts it, in a formulation which owes much to the necessitarian
thinking of David Hartley, but might equally well be Godwinian: 'Vice originates not in the man, but in the surrounding circumstances.'[27]

Hazlitt, expanding this idea two decades later, concentrates on the disjunction between society's distanced, objective judgement of a given crime, and a
criminal's informed, subjective account of it: 'no man answered in his own
mind . . . to the abstract idea of a *murderer*', he asserts:

He may have killed a man in self-defence, or in 'the trade of war', or to save himself from
starving, or in revenge for an injury, but always 'so as with a difference', or from mixed or
questionable motives. The individual, in reckoning with himself, always takes into
account the considerations of time, place, and circumstance, and never makes out a case
of unmitigated, unprovoked villainy, of 'pure defecated evil' against himself.[28]

[26] 'A man of certain intellectual habits is fitted to be an assassin; a dagger of a certain form is fitted
to be his instrument. . . . The assassin cannot help the murder he commits, any more than can the
dagger. . . . Nothing can be more absurd than to look to [punishment] as a source of improvement'
(pp. 632–3, 671).

[27] In Coleridge's view, this belief characterizes the 'thinking and disinterested patriots' who have
'encouraged the sympathetic passions until they have become irresistible habits' (*Coleridge Lectures*,
12). Patton and Mann draw attention to Coleridge's debt to Hartley (ibid. n. 4), but not to the
Godwinian parallel. However, notwithstanding Coleridge's animosity towards Godwin's atheism,
his proposal for the ideal method of dealing with crime has a distinctly Godwinian flavour: instead
of punishing the offender, he argues, the disinterested patriot 'by endeavouring to alter the circumstances removes, or by strengthening the intellect disarms, the temptation' (ibid.). For a careful
discussion of Coleridge's politics during 1795, see Roe, *Radical Years*, 210–17.

[28] Hazlitt, 'On the Knowledge of Character', in *Selected Writings*, ed. with introd. R. Blythe
(Harmondsworth, Middx., 1970), 113. Hazlitt's use of quotation marks around the phrase 'pure
defecated evil' tacitly acknowledges his debt to Burke's *Letter to a Noble Lord*; for the passage in
question, see p. 110.

The sympathetic familiarity which human beings naturally have with themselves is capable, Hazlitt argues, of extending to others by acts of identification, love, and imagination. Thus, where the moral character of family or friends is concerned, we 'know too much to come to any hasty or partial conclusion. ... We suspend our judgments altogether, because in effect one thing unconsciously balances another.'[29] Hazlitt clearly approves of the suspension of judgement: 'Perhaps this obstinate, pertinacious indecision would be the truest philosophy in other cases', he argues, 'where we dispose of the question of character easily, because we have only the smallest part of the evidence to decide upon.' By implication, the inadequacy of the penal system is its crude reduction to clarity of issues which are complexly indeterminate.

From a slightly different perspective—that of the 'genteel reformer'[30]—Byron, too, argues against the reductivism of 'cant', which he sees as a 'vile substitute' for morality. It is his own 'respect for morals', he argues, that makes him capable of sympathizing with men whom 'this good natured world' chooses to dismiss as wicked:

We are all the creatures of circumstance ... the greater part of our errors are caused, if not excused, by events and situations over which we have had little control; the world see the faults, but they see not what led to them: therefore I am always lenient to crimes that have *brought their own punishment*, while I am little disposed to pity those who think they atone for their own sins by exposing those of others, and add cant *and hypocrisy to the catalogue of their vices.*[31]

Byron's tales of guilty adventurers are all, as Jerome McGann puts it, 'exercises in which sympathy is evoked for the hero by forcing the reader to consider all the circumstances of the case'.[32] Whereas the hero-villains of Gothic fiction are sentimental, because their authors submit to a sense of prevenient order—reining in their questionings and setting their reader's consciousness at rest—Byron's plays are 'actively intellectual works', perceiving problems that cannot be solved, and sceptically refusing closure.[33] In this respect, McGann argues, they are deeply Miltonic; for 'Milton's mind is not only not made up, it positively avoids "argument" on a system of "proof" for a set of fixed ideas'.[34]

Milton's study of the origin of evil provided the ideal starting-point for writers who were deeply preoccupied with moral philosophy, and who wished to explore its political implications. The Fall narrative could be adapted to this end by the use of two different modes of Miltonic allusion: straightforwardly, and by metaphorical extension, it could suggest the way in which individual lapses explained themselves in terms of the social pressures acting on development. Writers using this mode—we might consider the fall of Falkland, or Rivers, as examples—are doing little more than translating Milton's account of the Fall

[29] Ibid. 112.
[30] The phrase is J. McGann's; see *'Don Juan' in Context* (Chicago, 1976), 27.
[31] *Lady Blessington's Conversations of Lord Byron*, ed. E. J. Lovell, Jr (Princeton, NJ, 1969), 172–3.
[32] *'Don Juan' in Context*, 27.   [33] Ibid. 30.   [34] Ibid. 30–1.

into the arena of earthly politics, as a way of underlining their determinist views. Implicit in their method is the depressing possibility that the fallen condition itself determines a repetition of the Fall: we might see this as a politicization of the idea of original sin, used to explain the cyclical patterns of tyranny and revolution observable through history.

More radically, through the revision or undermining of Milton's terms, it was possible to expose God Himself as the origin of evil. Writers using this second approach—and Blake is the outstanding example—are enabled by their critique of Milton's system to uncover the roots of societal oppression, and at the same time to suggest a different explanation for the cycles of history: moral categories, according to this view, should be read as the contingent products of warring ideologies, and not as entities in themselves. God is the origin of evil, since He is the creator of a repressive order which invites rebellion. The fall from grace is necessary, as an expression of the autonomy of the individual. Rebellion can be identified as good from a radical, bad from a conservative, angle. The emergence of evil as a separate category from good is therefore an expression of the status quo's will to power. By giving evil its bad name, the status quo attempts to isolate and contain what it is threatened by, and in so doing perpetuates the hierarchy which invites rebellion.

To some extent, these two modes of allusion cross over or coincide within individual Romantic texts or writers, and in so doing replicate the ambiguity which I have suggested is central to *Paradise Lost*. But I shall look at them separately in the two chapters that follow, because I want to suggest that the second is, at least partly, a chronological development of the first, as well as being a more thoroughgoing treatment of the problems. In other words, Satanic motivation was the starting-point for the writers of the 1790s, as they attempted to justify the ends of the revolution whilst witnessing its miscarriage through evidently unscrupulous means; and a more general analysis of the problem of evil followed, as attention was shifted from these specific anxieties to the larger issues. Despite tracing this development, however, what I want to stress throughout the discussion that follows is the *consistent* tendency of Romantic interpretation towards a mapping of the specific and the political onto the generic and the moral. What interests the Romantics in Satan, even as early as the 1790s, is the material he provides for their intellectual enquiry into problems of moral philosophy; and in a sense, this means that the strictly political origins of their interest begin to be elided, from the start. I do not wish to go as far as to claim an incipient conservatism in this elision, but I am interested in showing that the process of interiorization which characterizes High Romantic argument is a relatively early phenomenon.

ENERGY

'Society is indeed a contract', Burke proclaims, in his *Reflections on the Revolution in France* (1790): 'It is a partnership in all science; a partnership in all art; a partnership in every virtue, and in all perfection.' Supporting his view of social cohesiveness with the medieval metaphor of the Great Chain of Being, he sounds remarkably like Raphael lecturing Adam on the virtue of knowing his place in the divine scheme of things:

Each contract of each particular state is but a clause in the great primaeval contract of eternal society, linking the lower with the higher natures, connecting the visible and invisible world, according to a fixed compact sanctioned by the inviolable oath which holds all physical and all moral natures, each in their appointed place.[35]

'This law', he admonishes the reader, 'is not subject to the will of those, who by an obligation above them, and infinitely superior, are bound to submit their will to that law.' And he turns to the French Revolution (as Raphael does to the war in Heaven) to demonstrate the appalling consequences of making this 'submission to necessity' into an object of choice:

the law is broken, nature is disobeyed, and the rebellious are outlawed, cast forth, and exiled, from this world of reason, and order, and peace, and virtue, and fruitful penitence, into the antagonist world of madness, discord, vice, confusion, and unavailing sorrow.[36]

Burke's lofty register, his ominous tone, his diction, the vocabulary of fall and expulsion which he exploits, are all in themselves Miltonic; but over and above these general resemblances there is a distinct verbal allusion to *Paradise Lost*. It is an allusion which draws on the implicitly monarchical authority of Milton's God (at the moment when he appoints his son as viceregent), to warn against revolution:

> him who disobeys
> Me disobeys, breaks union, and that day
> Cast out from God and blessed vision, falls
> Into utter darkness, deep engulfed, his place
> Ordained without redemption, without end.
>
> (*PL* v. 611–15)

Such is the conservative appropriation of Milton's narrative. But, as Blake points out, the history of *Paradise Lost* 'has been adopted by both parties'[37]—and nowhere more evidently than in its application to history. Alongside Burke's

---

[35] *Reflections on the Revolution in France*, ed. with introd. C. C. O'Brien (Harmondsworth, Middx., 1968; repr. 1986), 194–5.

[36] Ibid. Burke's diction and vocabulary suggest a distinct analogy between the revolution and the fall of the angels. For a possible Coleridgean parallel, see my discussion of 'The Ancient Mariner' in Ch. 4.

[37] *MHH*, pl. 5, l. 41. The ambiguity of *Paradise Lost* distinguishes it from Milton's prose, which, as Coleridge points out, conveys a more explicit political message: 'Admirable to the very height of praise as Milton's prose works are, yet they are of a party, in country, in religion, in politics and even in MORALS ... a party, indeed, to which in all respects I cleave, with head, heart, and body; but yet, it is a *party*. But the poetry belongs to the whole world!' Annotation (28 Mar. 1808) to Birch's edn. of Milton's prose; in *Romantics on Milton*, 181.

organicist defence of the monarchy and the aristocracy, one should place the
rationalist argument of Godwin's *Political Justice* (1793): 'Why did Satan rebel
against his maker?' asks Godwin; 'It was, as he himself informs us, because he
saw no sufficient reason for that extreme inequality of rank and power which
the creator assumed.'[38] The Creator can, of course, only be thought to
'assume' rank and power by an atheist, and it is as such that Godwin is writing.
The presence of that word 'reason' should remind us of the philosophy which
underpins all his comments on and allusions to *Paradise Lost*: religion, as he
saw it, was politically unacceptable because intellectually enthralling; only by
evolving the freedom of the individual mind could society proceed, non-
violently, towards justice and equality. Satan's account of events is to be
trusted, in Godwin's view—the words 'as he himself informs us' confirming
this—because his grounds for complaint have a rational basis. According to
this account, God wrongly 'assumes' rank and power when he promotes
Christ, having earlier treated the arch-fiend as his right-hand angel.[39] Satan's
legitimate sense of grievance is the direct cause of his revolt, but it is also the
root cause of his ability to sympathize with Eve—whose subjugation to Adam is
similarly arbitrary—and so incite her to rebel. Read atheistically, Genesis too
had presented the Fall as a political narrative, because in it the acquisition of
knowledge is a bid for power. But Milton creates a significant bond between
Satan and Eve, which makes inequality a central thematic concern.

For Godwin, it is this sympathetic treatment of the motives for rebellion that
provides the central interest of *Paradise Lost*. Satan is emblematic of innate
human virtues, thwarted by adverse circumstances: 'a sense of reason and
justice was stronger in his mind than a sense of brute force ... he had much of
the feelings of an Epictetus or a Cato, and little of those of a slave.' In his
struggle against tyranny, he becomes a heroic figure who 'bore his torments
with fortitude, *because* he disdained to be subdued by despotic power', and who
'sought revenge, *because* he could not think with tameness of the unexpostulating authority that assumed to dispose of him'.[40] Godwin is not simply
appropriating Satan as a spokesman for republican views, or making a facile
equation between the hero of *Paradise Lost* and its author. He is using Milton's
symbolic narrative on two different levels as supporting evidence for the argument of *Political Justice*: by examining the circumstances which motivate an
individual to commit a particular 'crime', he seeks to highlight the illogic of a
legal system which looks only at effects, not at causes. And by bringing

---

[38] *Political Justice*, 309. Since Blake engraved *MHH* in 1793, and moved in the same radical
London circles as Godwin, there is a possibility that they exchanged ideas about Satan, as well as
much else; see R. Sharrock, 'Godwin on Milton's Satan', *Notes and Queries*, n.s. 9 (Dec. 1962),
463–5.

[39] For the angelic version of Christ's promotion, which accords him and his Father monarchical
status (and which underpins Burke's support of the monarchy), see Raphael's account of events
leading up to the war in heaven (*PL* v. 600–17).

[40] *Political Justice*, 309.

Milton's God down to earth, he exposes religion itself as the model for other forms of political tyranny.

But there is a personal aspect to Godwin's interest in the moral ambivalence of Satan, and this is symptomatic of the particular era out of which *Political Justice* grows. Godwin felt, in common with many radicals during the 1790s, a keen sense of regret and responsibility for the miscarriage of revolutionary ideals: this might have centred, as it did for Wordsworth and Coleridge, on the leaders of the Revolution who initially had right on their side, but who allowed evil to become their good. Instead, it takes the more generalized form of an interest in great bad men—tyrants whose potential for benevolence was misdirected:

We shall find that even Caesar and Alexander had their virtues. There is great reason to believe that, however mistaken was their system of conduct, they imagined it reconcilable, and even conducive, to the general interest. If they had desired the general good more earnestly, they would have understood better how to promote it.[41]

Godwin believes that 'wherever ... a strong sense of justice exists, it is common and reasonable to say that in the mind exists considerable virtue', and he believes this all the more strongly because it is his intention to prove that 'the individual, from an unfortunate concurrence of circumstances, may, with all his great qualities, be the instrument of a very small portion of benefit'.[42] But he has before him, in the tyrannical figures mentioned, a warning of what might happen as a result of placing too much faith in the innate goodness of the individual.

Godwin's belief in Satan's potential 'to proceed from a sense of justice to some degree of benevolence' is qualified, therefore, by the acknowledgement that 'his energies centred too much on personal regards'.[43] He attempts, like Blake, to establish that energy is innately good—'great talents are great energies, and great energies cannot but flow from a powerful sense of reason and justice'[44]—but he is unable to deny that the misuse of energy produces evil effects. The band of robbers in *Caleb Williams*, for instance, show signs of 'benevolence and kindness', and are 'strongly susceptible of emotions of generosity'; but they have become 'habituated' through adverse circumstances to the use of violence.[45] In their favour, Godwin claims that they 'frequently displayed an energy, which from every partial observer would have extorted veneration':

Energy is perhaps of all qualities the most valuable; and a just political system would possess the means of extracting from it thus circumstanced its beneficial qualities, instead of consigning it as now to indiscriminate destruction. We act like the chymist who

---

[41] Ibid.   [42] Ibid. 308–9.   [43] Ibid. 309.   [44] Ibid.
[45] *Caleb Williams*, 218.

should reject the finest ore, and employ none but what was sufficiently debased to fit it immediately to the vilest uses.[46]

And yet he is quite categorical in his condemnation, not just of the violent means adopted by these outlaws, but also of the ends they have in view: 'The energy of these men', he concludes, 'was in the highest degree misapplied, unassisted by liberal and enlightened views, and directed only to the most narrow and contemptible purposes.'

In theory, then, education and enlightenment are the key to a 'just political system', since they 'extract' from energy its 'beneficial qualities', making it available for the general good. But *Caleb Williams* is not *Political Justice*: it deals with 'Things as they are', not as they ought to be, and it offers no easy blueprint for reform. Indeed, the fallen world Godwin chooses to depict is one in which moral categories have become wholly confused. The Satanic anti-hero, Falkland, makes good his evil: at one time the model of benevolence, he turns murderer and tyrant through too extreme a pursuit of personal honour. The hero, on the other hand, makes evil his good— refusing until the last moment to betray the murderer who is his master, and perpetuating in the process his own enthralment: 'I will never become an informer. I will never injure my patron; and therefore he will not be my enemy. With all his misfortunes and all his errors, I feel that my soul yearns for his welfare.'[47] This loyalty may be misguided, but it remains until the final pages of the book the one steadfast value in a world turned upside down. In true Godwinian fashion, Caleb laments of Falkland, 'If he have been criminal, that is owing to circumstances; the same qualities under other circumstances would have been, or rather were sublimely beneficent.'[48] To know (at first or second hand) this tragic gap between potential and actual 'energy' is to re-enact the Satanic condition: its logical conclusion, as Godwin shows, an extreme relativism grounded in the observation that moral categories are only subjectively perceived. 'Does a firm persuasion that a thing is so make it so?' asks Blake in *The Marriage of Heaven and Hell*.[49] To which Caleb gives, unconditionally, the answer that is the price of his personal experience:

'He [Falkland] might yet be a most excellent man, if he did but think so. It is the thinking ourselves vicious, then, that principally contributes to make us vicious!'[50]

---

[46] Ibid. 218–19.   [47] Ibid. 137.

[48] Ibid. For the survival of Caleb's loyalty, grounded in Godwin's own belief that adverse circumstances foster crime, see the 'Postscript' to *Caleb Williams*, which contains the following lament for Falkland's wasted potential: 'A nobler spirit lived not among the sons of men. Thy intellectual powers were truly sublime, and thy bosom burned with a godlike ambition. But of what use are talents and sentiments in the corrupt wilderness of human society? It is a rank and rotten soil from which every finer shrub draws poison as it grows' (p. 325).

[49] Pl. 12, l. 27.   [50] *Caleb Williams*, 137.

REVOLUTION

Caleb's regret for ideals that have miscarried, his faithfulness to personal qualities that exist only in memory, his frightened but questioning addiction to
charisma and leadership, are (as I shall argue in my next chapter) evidence of the
hold which Godwin believes that anachronistic and pernicious social systems
continue to exert over the mind, long after their basis has been outwardly
eroded. The irony is that, even in the circumstances of the overthrow of tyranny
through revolution, these mind-forged manacles can survive transference to
another, equally unworthy, object. Godwin's novel does nothing so explicit as to
identify Falkland with Robespierre; but it does offer in Caleb a fictionalized
representation of the troubled responses made by many English radicals to the
worst atrocities in France. In some respects, the characteristics of Caleb Williams are shared by Wordsworth, as features of his own 'sympathy with
power'—a sympathy which, as Nicholas Roe has demonstrated, persisted in his
attraction to Robespierre long after the acknowledgement of his evil deeds.[51] I
shall draw on Roe's argument in what follows, but my own emphasis will be on
the emotional and moral ambivalence which persistently emerges in Satanic
parallels and allusions.

Wordsworth was by no means the only British radical to feel attracted by
Robespierre. In John Thelwall's lecture 'On the Prospective Principle of Virtue', qualities which have their literary analogues in Milton's Satan are celebrated as Robespierre's natural attributes: 'He had a soul capacious,' Thelwall
claims, 'an imagination various, a judgement commanding, penetrating, severe.
Fertile of resources, he foresaw, created, and turned to his advantage all the
events that could possibly tend to the accomplishment of his designs.'[52]
Lamenting the terrible outcome of these resources, he treats Robespierre's
downfall as though it had its own ineluctable momentum: 'Who knows when
you once begin a system of massacre, where you can stop?' And, sounding just
like Caleb, he goes on to offer the only justification which a faithful Friend of
Liberty can give: 'I do not believe that *Robespierre* meditated, in the first instance,
those scenes of carnage into which he at last was plunged.'[53]

The Fall of Robespierre, written by Coleridge and Southey while they were
undergraduates, is probably the immediate source of some of the details in
Thelwall's portrait. As its title suggests, the play presents Robespierre in Miltonic terms; but the authors hedge their bets more than Thelwall does when it
comes to deciding if their hero is innately evil or tragically flawed: 'a man', the
'Dedication' calls him, 'whose great bad actions cast a disastrous lustre over his
name'.[54] This 'disastrous lustre' is reminiscent of the light which shines from

[51] Roe, *Radical Years*, ch. 6.
[52] J. Thelwall, 'On the Prospective Principle of Virtue', *The Tribune* (3 vols., London 1795–6) i.
259; cited by Roe, *Radical Years*, 207.
[53] *Tribune*, i. 259; cited in ibid. 204.
[54] 'Dedication' to *The Fall of Robespierre, CPW*, ii. 495.

Milton's ruined archangel, but with an important difference: in the syntax of the sentence the 'lustre' is a superficial covering for evil, not the remnant of former goodness; whereas in *Paradise Lost* Satan's 'original brightness' is only partially obscured by his fallen state:

> [He] above the rest
> In shape and gesture proudly eminent
> Stood like a tower; his form had not yet lost
> All her original brightness, nor appeared
> Less than archangel ruined, and the excess
> Of glory obscured

(i. 589–94)

If the revision is a conscious one, its point might be that Robespierre was a 'great bad man' who achieved greatness because of, not despite, his 'great bad actions'. And yet the play's opening speech describes him more favourably, restoring innate Satanic grandeur through a closer recollection of Miltonic language: 'rising awful 'mid impending ruins; | In splendour gloomy, as the midnight meteor, | That fearless thwarts the elemental war'.[55] Clearly, whatever limits Coleridge wished to impose on it, he too felt 'a kind of sympathy with power'.

The controlling and directing of power is Coleridge's central concern in the 'Moral and Political Lecture' he delivered in Bristol in 1795, soon afterwards revising it for publication as the 'Introductory Address' in 'Conciones ad Populum'. Here he sets out to define not only what went wrong with the French Revolution but also what he sees as potentially abortive in English radicalism. Broadly speaking, his argument is a Christian one: God is the only trustable absolute; all violence is pernicious (whatever its objectives), and all political activism is dangerous without the systematic adherence to 'fixed principles' deriving from religious faith.[56] Godwinian ideas are therefore disapproved of, for all their apparent similarity with Coleridge's own, because of the atheism on which they are grounded; and any system that smacks of deism is similarly held at arm's length.[57] In some of its finer details, however, the lecture appears hesitant and undoctrinaire. Coleridge's pronouncements on Robespierre's character, for instance—his mixture of 'glowing ardour' and 'cool ferocity'—evince a fascination with charisma worthy of Caleb Williams; and his response to the political objectives of this great bad man is by no means

---

[55] *The Fall of Robespierre*, I. i. 5–7.

[56] 'It will therefore be our endeavour, not so much to excite the torpid, as to regulate the feelings of the ardent: and above all, to evince the necessity of *bottoming* on fixed Principles' (*Coleridge Lectures*, 5).

[57] Coleridge's attack on Godwin grounds itself in his hostility to the latter's atheism; but in 'Conciones ad Populum' (ibid. 47) he is also vocal in advocating the 'domestic affections' which he sees as nurturing benevolence, and which Godwin mistrusts. This aspect of Coleridge's political theory is fully explored in K. Everest, *Coleridge's Secret Ministry: The Context of the Conversation Poems, 1795–1798* (Brighton, 1979), esp. chs. 2–3. For Coleridge's response to deism, see introd. to *Coleridge Lectures*, p. lvi.

unequivocal; indeed, it closely resembles Godwin's own comments on Caesar, Alexander, and Falkland:

What [Robespierre's] end was, is not known: that it was a wicked one, has by no means been proved. I rather think, that the distant prospect, to which he was travelling, appeared to him grand and beautiful; but that he fixed his eye on it with such intense eagerness as to neglect the foulness of the road.[58]

When it comes to defining the point at which Robespierre's idealism miscarried, Coleridge is interestingly ambivalent in assigning a cause. He begins by asserting that it is 'power' in the abstract which corrupts: 'If however his first intentions were pure, his subsequent enormities yield us a melancholy proof, that it is not the character of the possessor which directs the power, but the power which shapes and depraves the character of the possessor.' In the next breath, however, he moves in the opposite direction, conceding that in Robespierre the 'influence' of power was '*assisted by the properties of his disposition*' (my italics). The next two sentences follow the same oscillatory pattern: Coleridge first lumps together as blinkered all species of political idealism, implying that Godwinian ideals, too, might be self-defeating, if too enthusiastically pursued: 'the ardour of undisciplined benevolence seduces us into malignity: and whenever our hearts are warm, and our objects great and excellent, intolerance is the sin that does most easily beset us.' He then goes on to establish the faults in Robespierre's character which made inevitable the miscarriage of high ideals:

This enthusiasm in Robespierre was blended with gloom, and suspiciousness, and inordinate vanity. His dark imagination was still brooding over supposed plots against freedom—to prevent tyranny, he became a Tyrant—and having realized the evils which he suspected, a wild and dreadful tyrant.—Those loud-tongued adulators, the mob, overpowered the lone-whispered denunciations of conscience—he despotized in all the pomp of Patriotism, and masqueraded on the bloody stage of Revolution, a Caligula with the cap of Liberty on his head.[59]

The combination of Miltonic association and self-identification in this portrait should alert us to the cautionary status Robespierre is being accorded. It is significant that, in posing the troubled question of who is to be held responsible for the abuse of power, Coleridge should invoke the presence of Milton's Satan, whose enthusiasm is similarly blended with gloom, and whose most glaring faults are suspiciousness and inordinate vanity. It is equally important that, when describing Robespierre's political objectives, Coleridge uses vocabulary which from a very early stage in his career is associated with the expansiveness of the creative imagination. The 'distant prospect, to which [Robespierre] was travelling', and which appeared to him so 'grand and beautiful' that he neglected the 'foulness of the road', is not so very different in this respect from the inner compulsion which fixes our eye on the 'glittering Summits that rise one

58 Ibid. 35.   59 Ibid.

above the other in Alpine endlessness', and which, as Coleridge argues in his 'Lecture on the Slave-Trade', urges us 'up the ascent of Being' by diverting us from the 'ruggedness of the road' with 'the beauty and grandeur of the ever-widening Prospect'.[60]

Coleridge, already troubled by the ambivalence of that 'restless faculty', imagination, sees it as a meeting-point for the moral extremes represented on the one hand by the 'wild and bloody tyrant', Robespierre, and on the other by 'that small but glorious band of disinterested patriots' who alone are capable of leading his country towards liberty.[61] Like Godwin on the subject of 'energy', he is pulled first in one direction, then in the other, in the philosophical claims he is making: imagination must be innately good, he implies, because planted in us by 'our Almighty parent' (not an argument Godwin would have approved); but innate goodness appears incompatible with some of the effects of visionary idealism: 'Such and so noble', he writes in his slave trade lecture, 'are the ends for which this restless faculty was given us—but horrible has been its misapplication.'[62]

There is, however, for Coleridge if not for Godwin, some educational benefit to be derived from witnessing phenomena such as the Terror, for 'man can only acquire the right use of God's gifts by experiencing the effects of having perverted them'.[63] The figure of Robespierre, brooding darkly in a Satanic world of tyranny and violence, is offered as a cautionary reminder of the excesses to which such perversion can lead. Only by learning from his terrible mistakes will English radicalism be ready to recognize as its true leaders those 'disinterested patriots' who 'never hurry and never pause', but who use their imaginations in the humble submission to God's will. For them, revolution is a gradual process, not a distant visionary goal:

theirs is not that twilight of political knowledge which gives us just enough light to place one foot before the other; as they advance the scene still opens upon them, and they press right onward with a vast and various landscape of existence around them.[64]

The secret, then, as Coleridge sees it, to the controlling and directing of power is patience—the patience which Milton, too, had advocated as he turned from *Paradise Lost* to *Samson Agonistes*.[65] Imagination need not be rejected as solipsistic, so long as it is kept in place, made socially responsible, through submission to God. The innate goodness which is shared by Satan, by Robespierre, and by the small band of patriots to which Coleridge himself belongs, can thus be given the chance to triumph over corrupting circumstances. Such at least is

---

[60] 'Lecture on the Slave Trade', ibid. 235.   [61] 'A Moral and Political Lecture', ibid. 12.
[62] Ibid. 235–6.   [63] Ibid. 236.   [64] 'A Moral and Political Lecture', ibid. 12.
[65] Christopher Hill demonstrates that mid-17th-c. readers were accustomed to political applications of the Samson myth, and especially to Samson being taken as a figure for the army or the revolutionary cause (*Milton and the English Revolution*, 430). The play is not pessimistic, in his view; rather, it leaves to providence the question of whether or not the chosen nation is now capable of fulfilling its promise (ibid. 439).

Coleridge's optimism in the early phase of his career: a more complicated picture is to emerge later, when his belief in original sin, and his diminishing faith in Priestleyan necessitarianism, lead to a more mistrustful analysis of imagination.

VIOLENCE

For Wordsworth, meanwhile, there are no steadfast religious absolutes against which to measure earthly politics, or to correct the wayward potential of his sympathy with power. He writes, for this reason, in a spirit that is openly tolerant of moral ambivalence, whether in reacting to events as they unfold or in accounting for the contradictions of response which retrospectively emerge. Satanic allusion, in this context, functions as a register of the unsettled nature of the debate which Milton had begun and Wordsworth continues—a debate which explores the problematic relation between morality and politics, or, more specifically, means and ends.

'Alas,' Wordsworth laments, in his 'Letter to the Bishop of Llandaff' of 1793, 'the obstinacy & perversion of men is such that [Liberty] is too often obliged to borrow the very arms of despotism to overthrow him, and in order to reign in peace, must establish herself by violence.' And he continues, in a tone of cool expedience, to assert that 'Political virtues are developed at the expence of moral ones'; that there is indeed an 'apparent contradiction between the principles of liberty and the march of revolutions'; and, even more bleakly, that 'if, at this moment [in any European nation], the original authority of the people should be restored, all that could be expected from such restoration would in the beginning be but a change of tyranny'.[66] These observations are not made, however, as concessions to anti-radicalism. They are there to show the toughness, the practicality, and the patience (though not in a Christian sense) of Wordsworth's revolutionary ideals. His message comes across, loudly and clearly: there is no reason 'to reprobate a convulsion from which is to spring a fairer order of things'. Given that in the longer (Godwinian) perspective, education will succeed in rectifying 'the erroneous notions which a habit of oppression ... may have created', violence must be tolerated in the shorter term as the justifiable means to a glorious end.[67] The note of pragmatism which sounds here may seem out of keeping with the Wordsworth who, three years later, in *The Borderers*, exposes the use of violence as pernicious, and offers a searching critique of the cyclical patterns observable in recent history. But it serves as a useful reminder that we should not, like Marilyn Butler, see Wordsworth as reactionary from the first—a perspective which

---

[66] 'A Letter to the Bishop of Llandaff', in *The Prose Works of William Wordsworth*, ed. W. J. B. Owen and J. W. Smyser (3 vols., Oxford, 1974), i. 33–4, 38.

[67] Ibid. 34.

overlooks the revolutionary zeal of this early phase.[68] Rather, we should take into account the extent to which political idealism was at first capable of triumphing over moral scruples, not blindly and hastily, but in the context of a thoughtful and rigorous intellectual discussion.

The Borderers represents a transitional stage in Wordsworth's thinking, as well as a conscious revision of his earlier position. Marilyn Butler is right to see in the play 'a stylised account of the French revolution', and there is some truth in her claim that it 'explores the part played in the revolutionary crime by intellectuals; it depicts the wickedness, prematurity or arrogance of political action and those who seek cerebrally to initiate or justify it'.[69] But her reading is too categorical: in overlooking Wordsworth's own status as intellectual radical, she neglects his evident identification with Rivers, the play's Satanic hero; and in caricaturing Rivers as one of 'those sinister, subversive intellectuals who haunt the propaganda and fiction of conservative Europe',[70] she moves Wordsworth further to the right than he deserves. Most damaging of all, however, is Butler's assumption that an earlier ideological position can be relinquished without doubts or regrets: here she falls into a trap which is reminiscent of conservative appropriations of Milton. Wordsworth has no more succeeded in outrightly rejecting Godwinian rationalism, by the time he writes *The Borderers*, than Milton has straightforwardly repudiated his early republican views when he writes *Paradise Lost*. Rivers and Satan are both spokesmen for their creators' revolutionary ideals; and the language they speak continues to be compelling and persuasive, even in a context which frames them as immoral. In each case, the poetic process of self-dramatization involves nostalgic attraction as much as oppositional revision, internal debate as much as critique.

The insufficiency of Butler's reading can be easily demonstrated by putting alongside Wordsworth's portrait of Rivers an almost exactly contemporaneous caricature by Edmund Burke of the radical intellectual who throws off his fear of God. According to Burke's 'Letter to a Noble Lord' (1796), 'a more dreadful calamity cannot arise out of Hell to scourge mankind':

Nothing can be conceived more hard than the heart of a thoroughbred metaphysician. It comes nearer to the cold malignity of a wicked spirit than to the frailty and passion of a man. It is like that of the principle of Evil himself, incorporeal, pure, and unmixed, dephlegmated, defecated evil.[71]

---

[68] Butler stresses Wordsworth's truth to 'the humanist spirit of classicism' and has him, in the 'Preface' to *Lyrical Ballads*, 'putting rational thought, moral intention and social utility above the subjective, emotional side of the mind, and above the claims of self-expression'; see *Romantics, Rebels and Reactionaries: English Literature and its Background, 1760–1830* (Oxford, 1981), 59–60.

[69] Ibid. 64, 65.   [70] Ibid. 64.

[71] Edmund Burke, *A Letter to a Noble Lord on the Attacks made upon him and his Pension, in the House of Lords, by the Duke of Bedford and the Earl of Lauderdale, Early in the Present Sessions of Parliament* (London, 1796); in M. Butler (ed.), *Burke, Paine, Godwin and the Revolution Controversy* (Cambridge, 1984), 57.

In some of its finer details, this hysterical portrait corresponds with Coleridge's analysis of Robespierre: Burke's revolutionaries, for instance, 'never see any way to their projected good, but by the road of some evil ... Their humanity is at their horizon, and like the horizon, it always flies before them'[72]—a description which one might put alongside Coleridge's; 'The distant prospect, to which [Robespierre] was travelling, appeared to him grand and beautiful; but he fixed his eye on it with such intense eagerness as to neglect the foulness of the road.'[73] But there is no room in Burke's analysis, as there is in Coleridge's, for a compassionate understanding of the circumstances and motives which cause the transformation of innate good into pragmatic evil. Capable of refusing 'the compunctuous visitings of nature', and of 'eradicating humanity from his breast', Burke's characterization of wickedness bears more resemblance to Iago or Edmund than to Satan or Macbeth.[74]

Wordsworth's message in *The Borderers* is, in some superficial respects, comparable to Burke's. He offers a critical analysis of qualities which in 'A Letter to the Bishop of Llandaff' he had himself evinced—namely, the tolerance of violent means in favour of glorious ends, and the capacity to remain fired by a distant visionary goal, however sordid the immediate outcome. These are the very qualities Burke dismisses as pernicious in his description of the 'bravoes and banditti' who 'are ready to declare that they do not think two thousand years too long a period for the good they pursue'.[75] Furthermore, in his handling of Rivers, Wordsworth sets out to expose the appalling consequences of putting Reason before humanity—a demonstration not just of the inadequacies of Godwinian thinking, but if we take a Burkean perspective, of the Revolution as a whole. Wordsworth's explanation for the emergence of pragmatic evil is, however, quite different in kind from Burke's, laying emphasis as it does not on the 'cold malignity of a wicked spirit' but on the 'frailty and passion of a man': not on the motiveless malignity of an Iago, but on the complexity of the fallen Satan.

The imaginative appeal of Rivers derives from his experience of guilt and suffering. Indeed, in dramatizing criminal compulsion, Wordsworth borrows those aspects of Milton's Satan which make him intensely sympathetic, because humanly fallible: the dissatisfaction with arbitrary authority which is the root cause of his being tricked into murder; the feelings consequent on this action, first of confusion and guilt, then of abiding grievance—this latter driving him to repeat his own fall through another; the imagination which gives access to a moral world he can no longer claim as his own; and the remorse which must of necessity be disguised as hardness of heart. He further expands our sympathy by giving Satanic depth and grandeur to Rivers's consciousness: 'Three sleepless nights I passed in sounding on, | Through words and things, a dim and perilous way',[76] and by suggesting his Wordsworthian receptivity to the language of nature:

[72] Ibid. 58.   [73] *Coleridge Lectures*, 35.   [74] *Letter to a Noble Lord*, 57.
[75] Ibid. 58.
[76] *The Borderers*, ed. R. Osborn (Ithaca, NY, 1982), IV. ii. 102–3.

> In these my lonely wanderings, I perceived
> What mighty objects do impress their forms
> To build up this our intellectual being ...

The echo of Belial, here—'for who would lose, | Though full of pain, this intellectual being,' (*PL* ii. 146–7)—does not suggest straightforward diabolism, any more than it does in its original Miltonic context; nor does it signal Wordsworth's repudiation of the 'sinister intellectual' whom, in Butler's reading, Rivers represents. Instead, it vividly enacts Wordsworth's continuing attraction to the Godwinian argument—his reluctance to lose 'the intellectual being' which his faith in rationality has built up.

Wordsworth appears at least partly approving, too, of Rivers's impatience with mental constraints: 'And, whereso'er I turned me, I beheld | A slavery compared to which the dungeon | And clanking chains are perfect liberty' (IV. ii. 104–6); of his political optimism: 'I saw that every possible shape of action | Might lead to good' (IV. ii. 108–9); and of the beneficent potential of his fallen energy: 'And yet I had within me evermore | A salient spring of energy; I mounted | From action up to action with a mind | That never rested' (IV. ii. 118–22). Even the famous Godwinian speech, in which Rivers congratulates Mortimer for murdering Herbert, is given a power and sense of conviction that openly conflict with the moral repugnance we might otherwise feel:

> You have obeyed the only law that wisdom
> Can ever recognize: the immediate law
> Flashed from the light of circumstances
> Upon an independent intellect.

(III. v. 30–3)

By the time Wordsworth adapts these lines for *The Prelude*, he has moved a long way beyond believing in the 'independent intellect', though he still retains his fundamental reverence for 'the freedom of the individual mind': in their later context, therefore, the lines function ironically, as a reflection on the extent to which Wordsworth had been misled by the Godwinian thinking he now disowns.[77] In 1796, however, the identification with Rivers is less thoroughly distanced, and the mistrust of Godwin less systematically worked through.

Nicholas Roe has shown how Robespierre and Godwin come together in the poet's retrospective account of his radical years[78]—an imaginative conflation which is appropriate, given their parallel emphasis on reason, their intoxicating extremism, and their symbolic status as fallen idols. To this one might add an observation on their positioning in the Miltonic design of *The Prelude*, at the point in Wordsworth's life which is represented as his personal 'fall'. Both are

---

[77] For the significance of these lines in their new context, and for the lightness of Wordsworth's mockery, which is 'quite as much against his former self as at Godwin', see J. Wordsworth, *Borders of Vision*, 266.

[78] *Radical Years*, 221.

envisaged as successful Satanic tempters—Robespierre explicitly, in an allusion which makes him 'Chief regent' of the 'foul tribe of Moloch', and Godwin by implication, in that his elevation of the human intellect is seen as both presumptuous and specious:

> Tempting region that
> For zeal to enter and refresh herself,
> Where passions had the privilege to work,
> And never hear the sound of their own names.[79]

It would be misleading, however, to suggest that Satanic allusion has by this stage become a means of signalling wholesale moral repudiation: although more 'damning'[80] than they had been earlier, such references preserve a sympathy with Satanic aspiration which makes them emotionally (as well as historically) true to the complexity of Wordsworth's original response. Thus, even from a decade's disillusioned distance, he is still capable of acknowledging the attractiveness of a philosophy 'That promised to abstract the hopes of man | Out of his feelings, to be fixed thenceforth | For ever in a purer element' (x. 806–9), and of rescuing from the debris of his revolutionary ideals 'Something to glory in, as just and fit, | And in the order of sublimest laws' (x. 412–13).

MISTRUSTFUL HOPE

No writer on the subject of revolution sounds a note so sustainedly hysterical as Burke's. And yet there is, in the writing of both Coleridge and Wordsworth, a revulsion from bloodshed and anarchy which is comparably strong, and which makes similar use of an apocalyptic frame of reference:

> The horse is taught his manage, and the wind
> Of heaven wheels round and treads in his own steps,
> Year follows year, the tide returns again,
> Day follows day, all things have second birth;
> The earthquake is not satisfied at once[81]

It would be wrong to conclude that the Burkean strand in Wordsworth's and Coleridge's thinking makes them into reactionaries, as Butler's levelling comparisons seem to suggest. It is important, however, to acknowledge that, when

[79] *Prelude* ix. 810–13. The word 'tempting' has a distinctly Miltonic resonance. Wordsworth may well have in mind the self-deception of the fallen angels, whose parliamentary style of debating in *PL* ii conceals the true motivation behind their proposals and decisions. For a discussion of hell's 'totalitarianism', and the abuses of democratic assembly in Satan's demagogic addresses to the devils, see Hughes, *Ten Perspectives on Milton*, 187.

[80] Roe argues that when Wordsworth 'confounds Robespierre with Satan', this is an 'effort to damn Robespierre' (*Radical Years*, 221). Such a reading underestimates the moral and political ambivalence which makes Satan so potent a symbol to and for the Romantic imagination.

[81] *Prelude* x. 70–4. The lines refer to Wordsworth's return to Paris in 1792, a month after the September Massacres. The editors of the Norton Critical Edition note the 'apocalyptic' flavour of the passage.

they make their radical claims for the individual, they do so in contexts which carefully admonish against extremity; and that, in evolving their moral and political theory, they attempt to preserve the social connectiveness of self.

As I have shown, Coleridge is more consistently outspoken in his repudiation of violence than Wordsworth: he envisages the process of perfectibility as a 'bloodless fight',[82] and he explicitly condemns 'the bloody stage of revolution'.[83] Wordsworth's critique, on the other hand, is ambivalent. *The Borderers* is weighted in a revolutionary direction by the Satanic energy of Rivers; but the evident powerlessness and pathos of Herbert (who, as Marilyn Butler has pointed out, can be read as a dramatic representation of Louis XVI)[84] acts as a counterbalance to the reader's sympathy with a Satanic perspective. One is unlikely to respond to the plan for Herbert's murder with other than revulsion, given that Wordsworth accords him so marginalized a position in the power structure. This revulsion has the effect of steering one toward a conservative estimate of Rivers, and towards a morally distanced disapproval of the abuse of power.

In Shelley's *The Cenci*, moral ambivalence works the other way round. As outlined in theory, his repudiation of violence is far clearer, and more categorical, than any statement on the subject made by Wordsworth: his purpose is to show that 'revenge, retaliation, atonement, are pernicious mistakes', and that 'if Beatrice had thought in this manner she would have been wiser and better'.[85] In practice, however, his treatment of Beatrice's tragic dilemma complicates the moral issues. Beatrice is more compelling than Rivers, for all the latter's Satanic attractiveness, because more evidently a tragic victim, who is 'violently thwarted from her nature by the necessity of circumstance and opinion'.[86] Indeed, the grounds she has for murdering her father are considerable. Not only does his exploitation of power and status establish him, unlike Herbert, as a political tyrant (which for the Milton of *The Tenure of Kings and Magistrates* would in itself be sufficient justification for his removal);[87] but he is also exposed as a monstrous travesty of fatherhood who, by raping his daughter, provokes in her a similarly violent response.

Beatrice Cenci is as much a descendant of Milton's Satan as are Byron's reprobate heroes; and, in true Byronic tradition, she stands as testimony to the

[82] See 'Reflections on Having Left a Place of Retirement': 'I therefore go, and join head heart and hand, | Active and firm, to fight the bloodless fight | Of Science, Freedom, and the Truth in Christ' (ll. 60–2; *Coleridge Poems*, 80–1).

[83] *Coleridge Lectures*, 35.

[84] The 'old, blind, helpless Herbert, a father-figure who might stand generally for the *ancien regime* or more specifically for Louis XVI himself' (*Romantics, Rebels and Reactionaries*, 65).

[85] 'Preface' to *The Cenci* (*Shelley*, 240).

[86] Ibid. 238. Shelley's emphasis on the shaping influence of circumstances is clearly Godwinian.

[87] Milton argues that a tyrant responsible for 'innumerable wrongs and oppressions of the people, murders, massacres, rapes, adulteries, desolation, and subversion of Cities and whole Provinces' may be *lawfully* dealt with by the people 'as a common pest, and destroyer of mankinde'; see *The Tenure of Kings and Magistrates* (13 Feb. 1649), *Milton Prose*, iii, ed. M. Y. Hughes (New Haven, Conn., 1962), 212.

fact that 'the greater part of our errors' are indeed 'caused, if not excused, by situations over which we have had little control'.[88] The moral questions which Shelley leaves us asking are, furthermore, intellectually speculative in the same ways as Byron believed *Paradise Lost* to be. They cannot be answered by dogma, and they 'prove nothing'.[89] In *Cain*, Byron very nearly succeeds in justifying murder, simply by virtue of the intense sympathy which he awakens on behalf of his hero. The appeal of Cain lies, as does that of Milton's Satan, in a love of liberty which is recognized to be at once courageous and self-destructive: it is this 'fatal paradox', as Jerome McGann argues,[90] that works itself out in terms of Cain's murder of Abel—an act which Byron overtly condemns, even while he delineates its circumstances with compelling psychological insight and sympathy. But if Byron succeeds in 'exciting compassion' for Cain, as Milton did for Satan, in giving him 'human passions', and making him out an 'injured personage',[91] then Shelley's *The Cenci* goes further along this pro-Satanic line. The intensity of sympathy with which his drama examines the outrage of Beatrice, her sense of defilement, and her last desperate resort to murder, is a far cry from the cool and distant tones of the 'Preface', where he mentions 'the restless and anatomising casuistry with which men seek the justification of Beatrice, yet feel that she has done what needs justification'.[92] The play leaves little room, by contrast with *The Borderers*, for a balancing sympathy with the tyrant-victim, who has none of Herbert's pathos; so that, against Shelley's conscious design, Beatrice ends by being a persuasive and convincing advocate for the use of violence in countering the abuse of power.

More even than Rivers, Beatrice and Cain are evidence that one must register the genuine conflict which Milton's Satan dramatizes if one is to appreciate the way in which Romantic writers use his complexity (or 'meaningful obscurity')[93] to explore their own moral ambivalence, in relation to the problems of tyranny, of revolution, and of violence in a revolutionary cause. I have shown that there is an important connection between imagination and corruptible power, which emerges in the ambivalence of Satanic allusions as they apply to unfolding

[88] Byron's remarks to Lady Blessington are quoted in full on p. 99 above.

[89] According to Byron, Milton's 'great epics that nobody reads prove nothing.' Milton 'excites passion for Satan, and endeavors to make him out an injured personage—he gives him human passions too, makes him pity Adam and Eve, and justify himself much as Prometheus does'. But Byron remains 'very curious to know what [Milton's] real belief was'; see *Medwin's Conversations of Lord Byron*, ed. E. J. Lovell, Jr (Princeton, NJ, 1966), 77–8.

[90] *'Don Juan' in Context*, 33.   [91] See n. 89 above.

[92] *Shelley*, 240. S. Curran has drawn attention to the correspondence of phrasing between the 'Preface' to *The Cenci* and the 'Preface' to *Prometheus Unbound*: the former mentions the 'restless and anatomising casuistry' of Beatrice's defenders, while the latter refers to the 'pernicious casuistry' of those who argue in favour of Satan. See 'The Siege of Hateful Contraries: Shelley, Mary Shelley, Byron and *Paradise Lost*', in J. A. Wittreich, Jr (ed.), *Milton and the Line of Vision* (Madison, Wis., 1975), 222, 225.

[93] See R. Osborn, 'Meaningful Obscurity: The Antecedents and Character of Rivers', in J. Wordsworth (ed.), *Bicentenary Wordsworth Studies in Memory of John Alban Finch* (Ithaca, NY, 1970), 393–425. The phrase 'meaningful obscurity' is presumably intended to recall Burke's 'judicious obscurity', and thereby to accrue associations with the sublime.

political events; and I have, in particular, stressed that Coleridge's and
Wordsworth's 'sympathy with power' should be seen both historically (as an
accurate reflection of their complicated attraction to Robespierre and to Godwin) and in broader terms, as an explanation for the problematic status which
imagination is accorded throughout their œuvres. We should not underestimate the further ramifications of this connection, either as the first-generation Romantics move into a less overtly political phase, or in the context of
second-generation Romanticism, which looks back on the French Revolution
from a vantage point that sees history as cyclical, and tyranny as repetition
compulsion.

Disillusionment with the revolution is usually portrayed as resulting in a
compensatory hopefulness about imagination—the 'Paradise within' being
envisaged as 'happier far' than the republican ideal. But this reading is inadequate on two counts: firstly, it ignores the awkwardness of the transition, suggesting that a process of internalization can take place without a sense of loss.
(One could do worse than go to *The Prelude* itself for a corrective to this
assumption: 'I lost | All feeling of conviction', Wordsworth writes of his trau-
matic period of betrayal, 'and, in fine, | Sick, wearied out with contrarieties, |
Yielded up moral questions in despair.'[94]) Secondly, such a reading overlooks
the fact that an investment in imagination is from the first almost as problematic
as political faith. Power, in whichever direction it is channelled, is *potentially*
dangerous; the process of internalization removes only the most obvious of
threats, thus replacing violence with solipsism. The disappointed revolutionaries who persistently crop up in Wordsworth's poetry—the recluse in 'Lines
Left upon a Seat in a Yew-Tree', whose 'visionary views' feed on fancy and
self-pity till his eye streams with tears;[95] the solitary in *The Excursion*, who
broods over his past; even the Arab Quixote, 'crazed | By love and feeling and
internal thought | Protracted among endless solitude'[96]—all these act as ironic
reminders of the difficulty involved in transferring political optimism from a
public to a private arena; they admonish against the selfishness, the exclusivity,
of imagination.

Paul Hamilton has argued that, for Wordsworth, the apocalyptic drive of
imagination is symbolically associated with revolution; and that the poet's response to this drive, as to the Terror itself, is one of exultation checked by fear.[97]
This is certainly borne out by the cautious restraint imposed on imaginative
activity when it is seen to be getting out of hand. In 'Nutting', for example, an act

[94] *Prelude* x. 897–900.
[95] l. 41. For debate on the extent of anti-Godwinism implied in this poem, see M. Jacobus,
Tradition and Experiment in Wordsworth's 'Lyrical Ballads', 1798 (Oxford, 1976), 31–2; L. Newlyn,
Coleridge, Wordsworth, and the Language of Allusion (Oxford, 1986), 21; Roe, *Radical Years*, 231.
[96] *Prelude* v. 144–6.
[97] *Wordsworth* (Brighton, 1986), 41–6. In keeping with Blake's observation, that we see in
Wordsworth 'the Natural man rising up against the Spiritual man', Hamilton claims that the poet
invests *nature* (rather than mind), with 'the authority of the visionary imagination to exceed inherited
cultural restraints in the articulation of the self' (ibid. 46).

of plunder performed in childhood is transformed by Wordsworth's adult gaze into a Satanic invasion of paradise—a rape of passive and innocent nature. A symbolic connection is thus implied between violent exploitation and the access of imaginative power.[98] Less extreme, but equally significant, is the presence of heavily accented political resonances in the 'Climbing of Snowdon' episode, in *The Prelude* Book XIII. Nature is 'usurped upon, as far as sight could reach', by the mist which symbolizes the imagination's transforming activity. The real sea seems to 'dwindle, and gives up its majesty' to a metaphorical power which proves greater than itself, and the mind 'exerts domination' on the outward face of things.[99] The imperialist associations of Wordsworth's language carry a particularly heavy charge of irony, in view of the democratic alignment which had at an earlier stage been possible for the imagination. One thinks of the parallel irony in *Paradise Lost* itself, as Satan takes on regal pretensions, through an attempt at usurpation.

Wordsworth is not alone in seeing a tyrannical potential in the mind's creative powers. Coleridge shows a similar ambivalence in 'Kubla Khan', drawing attention to Kubla's act of appropriation, in constructing a pleasure house for his own uses ('twice five miles of fertile ground' are girdled with walls and towers),[100] and pointing to its repetition, within the imagination of the poet, who seeks to replicate this paradisal construction in language. As in *Paradise Lost*, two-way indeterminacy allows a mirroring process to take place, which elides specific political alignments even as it sets them up: Kubla's imperialism associates him with the tyranny of heaven, while the poet's ambition has Satanic overtones; but the latter becomes a reflex of the former, within the act of imitation itself. Ironically, then, the poetic act requires an assertiveness of self, which implicates it in the power structure it attempts to unsettle.

It would be possible to discuss numerous passages in Romantic literature in the light of a cyclical pattern (tyranny–rebellion–tyranny) which has its literary origins in Milton's portrayal of Satan.[101] But I hope it will be sufficient, here, to conclude that the mistrustful hope the Romantics accord to the imagination echoes or replicates their ambivalent response to the Satanic power of revolution. In *Paradise Lost*, Milton had established Satan as a paradigm for self-critique, at the point of transition in his own career when the revolutionary impulse had become most problematic. The Romantics, in re-using this paradigm, exploit Satanic allusion to register the problems, not only of revolution itself,

---

[98] G. Hartman underplays the erotic violence—'all is handled lightly', he claims, 'with only an overtone of sexuality and lust'—preferring to see the action in the poem as 'almost purely psychological'; see *Wordsworth's Poetry: 1787–1814* (Cambridge, Mass., 1964; repr. 1987), 74. Hamilton reads the poem as a critique of 'capitalist notions of relationship', and observes that it 'reveals a violence inherent in the common language of sexual engagement' (*Wordsworth*, 70).

[99] *Prelude* xiv. 50–1, 77–8.　　　[100] 'Kubla Khan', ll. 6–7.

[101] Curran writes that Shelley was 'indebted to Milton for his own comprehension of a reductive, self-consumed, and self-consuming evil'; 'Siege of Hateful Contraries', 214. This comprehension (which extends to Byron also) is especially noticeable in those writers who witness the rise of Napoleon, and are therefore prone to seeing the cyclical repetitions of history.

but of the process of internalization which attempts to contain and reformulate revolutionary energy. 'Think and endure,' Lucifer urges Cain, 'and form an inner world | In your own bosom, where the outward fails.'[102] These are stirring words, but it proved no easier for the Romantics to follow this advice than it had done for Milton.

[102] Byron, *Cain*, II. ii. 463–4.

4

Religion

It is central to the structure and meaning of *Paradise Lost* that there exists a disjunction between the linear conception of time which is accorded to the human characters involved and the eternal perspective from which God sees, all at once, the repetitions and cycles of history. Verbal echo may invite the reader to make links between different parts of the unfolding narrative, blurring temporal distinctions and causing successive versions of the Fall to converge; but these connections are made at the expense of the limited perspectives of characters caught up in events as they unfold. At each new reading of the narrative, it becomes possible to make more connections, and to make them with greater authority: the reader becomes increasingly god-like, because more in touch with the Providential plan which Milton's epic narrator discloses. And the greater the reader's authority becomes, the more difficult it is to resist the quasi-divine authority embodied in the epic voice, which points to dramatic ironies, fore-warns characters of the consequences of their actions, and, most importantly of all, anticipates the ultimate redemption of fallen man through the coming of Christ. Acceptance of Milton's epic voice is, indeed, constitutive of submission to the authority of Christian truth, and (as I showed in Chapter 2) it is only by refusing or resisting the absoluteness of this voice that the reader can have access to the plurality of alternative voices which the poem contains.

When Adam is granted the privilege of seeing into futurity, in Books XI and XII, he becomes the reader of a text that is already written by God: a text that embodies the higher truth in which he is required to believe. Read from his limited human perspective, this text presents a bleak view of mankind's history as an unending cycle of tyrannies, each replacing the other; but read through the eyes of Michael, it offers a justification of God's providential plan. 'Know withal,│Since thy original lapse, true liberty│Is lost', Michael explains to Adam (*PL* xii. 82–4); and, having placed the blame on man's shoulders, he goes on to suggest a parallel between mental and political oppression:

> Reason in man obscured, or not obeyed,
> Immediately inordinate desires
> And upstart passions catch the government
> From reason, and to servitude reduce
> Man till then free. Therefore since he permits
> Within himself unworthy powers to reign
> Over free reason, God in judgement just

> Subjects him from without to violent lords;
> Who oft as undeservedly enthral
> His outward freedom: tyranny must be,
> Though to the tyrant thereby no excuse.
>
> (*PL* xii. 86–96)

It is crucial that these words are spoken from the eternal perspective, by one who can see that the cycles of tyranny will be broken when Christ's resurrection undoes the effects of the Fall. This redemptive certainty makes acceptable the nonchalant illogic of those final words: 'tyranny must be, | Though to the tyrant thereby no excuse'. Without it, Adam might begin to question the justice of God's judgement in sentencing man to an external oppression which replicates the tyranny inside his mind.

But questioning this justice is precisely what the Romantic reader of *Paradise Lost* is prone to do; and it is here, in Adam's vision of the successive tyrannies of the Old Testament, that one might posit a source for some of Romanticism's angriest repudiations of Milton, as well as for some of its most troubled and ambiguous treatments of the Fall. In Blake's ballad, 'The Mental Traveller', mankind is shown to be without redemptive possibility, eternally trapped in compulsive repetitions, each revolutionary overthrow of tyranny establishing a new and equally oppressive status quo. Cycles are observed macrocosmically, in the historical evolution of successive religions; and microcosmically, in the exploitation of man by woman, and woman by man. Blake's allusive handling of myth allows for a fusion of narrative levels, so that political, religious, psychological, and sexual possibilities coincide—their common thread being the mutual need which binds together the oppressor and the oppressed:

> Her fingers number every nerve
> Just as a miser counts his gold;
> She lives upon his shrieks and cries—
> And she grows young as he grows old,
>
> Till he becomes a bleeding youth
> And she becomes a virgin bright;
> Then he rends up his manacles
> And binds her down for his delight.[1]

The poem provides a fitting comment on the texts with which this chapter will be concerned, most of which share some kind of cyclical perspective, even at times going so far as to present tyranny and servitude as twin halves of a single, inevitable drive. It also poses their central question—namely, who or what can be held responsible for 'evil', once the cycles have begun?

For the Romantics, interest in the corrupting influence of circumstances on human motivation frequently evolves into a larger and more abstract concern with the problem of evil. But the question of accountability—the individual's

[1] ll. 17–24.

accountability to himself, to society, to nature, and to God—remains of paramount importance to all those who have an interest in proving or ensuring the responsibility of imagination. One might claim of each of the texts I will examine that they bear a more or less 'revisionary' relation to Michael's theory of oppression, depending on the degree of redemptive hopefulness they are capable of envisaging, and the degree of responsibility they wish to accord to mankind. For in their interpretation of history as an unending cycle of rebellions, each reversing the one before it, and in their psychologizing of political events (especially in respect of the inevitability of tyranny), the Romantics borrow a vision which is either clearly justifiable in terms of its providential patterning or clearly unjust in terms of the human perspective from which it is viewed. The interpretative choices invited by *Paradise Lost* are, here, more than usually dramatic, since more than usual is at stake.

At one extreme, I shall be examining the ways in which Milton's portrayal of God is amplified by Romantic writers so as to expose the systematized oppression for which they hold religion responsible. Earthly tyranny is shown to be constructed along heavenly lines, following the example of a divine role model who proves to be inappropriately human. As the unknowable absolute, He ought not to be capable of anger, or to feel the desire for revenge, or to make jokes at the expense of his trusted servants, or to rail at man for showing the fallibility expected of him by his omniscient creator: 'Ingrate, he had of me | All he could have: I made him just and right, | Sufficient to have stood, though free to fall' (*PL* iii. 97–9). As Empson demonstrates, it is these human characteristics which make it difficult to accept either the unknowability of Milton's God or His absolute justice: they bring Him down to earth, and in so doing upset the stable morality on which Milton's theodicy ought to rest.[2] Whether or not these foibles should be seen as part of a conscious authorial strategy is a matter for debate. I am concerned here with the fact that, in his function as poet and dramatist, Milton is *inevitably* involved in giving human attributes to God, and that these can be and are seized on as tyrannical, by readers disposed to question religion.

At a less pugnacious extreme, and examining the subtler implications of narrative mode and authorial perspective, I shall demonstrate that questioning the justice of God, as propounded in Michael's theory, implicates the Romantic reader in a number of deconstructive activities, where the epic narrator of *Paradise Lost* is concerned. For challenging divine authority, and unsettling the notion of a providential plan, are activities which also call into question the status of the author as a version of God, and therefore of his reader as the submissive recipient of higher truth. In the narratives I shall be examining, the finality and absoluteness of *Paradise Lost* are undermined by strategies which resist the authority of its epic narrator, and so disclose the plurality of perspectives which he restrains. Here, as elsewhere, it becomes possible to read Romantic texts as both revisionary and imitative, for this perspectivism is

[2] *Milton's God* (Cambridge, 1961), esp. ch. 3.

anticipated in those features of *Paradise Lost* which clearly challenge the epic voice. Indeed, one of the most remarkable and influential features of Miltonic method is its expansion of biblical narrative, not along the single line one might expect (especially from a poet who claimed to be transcribing the word of God) but along several different lines in turn, each of them offering a fresh perspective on the Fall. This transformation of monolithic biblical authority into kaleidoscopic narrative bears a close resemblance to the demystifying tactics of Thomas Paine in *The Age of Reason*, and it has, for the Romantics, an obvious appeal: it makes the subjectivity of experience apparent and, by removing the officialdom of 'truth', demotes authority.[3] It is therefore unsurprising to find that multiple perspectives proliferate in Romantic texts, especially where the problem of indeterminacy is being consciously explored.

I have been obliged to be more selective, on the all-embracing topic of religion, than I would wish; but I hope that this chapter will explore a representative variety of texts, and demonstrate the range of methods for questioning religion which were made possible to Romantic writers through their engagement with *Paradise Lost*. Coleridge's treatment of the origin of evil takes Miltonic theodicy as its starting-point, and 'The Ancient Mariner' provides a norm against which to measure the more problematic studies of responsibility which arise when religion is being overtly questioned—by Godwin and Mary Shelley, for instance, in their troubled psychological novels, or by Blake and Shelley in their radically revisionary myths. *Caleb Williams* and *Frankenstein* demonstrate the perplexities which emerge through psychologizing Milton's God; while *The Marriage of Heaven and Hell* and *Urizen* use a range of experimental devices to undermine biblical and Miltonic authority, thereby exposing the basis of religious oppression, and enabling the Fall to be rewritten along lines that are more favourable to human potential. I shall conclude with a discussion of Shelley's *Prometheus Unbound*, which attempts to cast off the 'mind-forged manacles' of religion, defining human redemption in terms of the cancellation of binary oppositions, and thereby removing the repetition compulsion of history, as prophesied by Michael.

CRIME AND PUNISHMENT

It would be difficult to find a writer more exercised by the problem of evil than Coleridge, who once wrote that 'A *Fall* of some sort or other—the creation, as it were, of the Non-Absolute—is the fundamental *Postulate* of the Moral History of Man'.[4] Hard task though it is to separate one area of his thought or writing

---

[3] Paine's systematic de-authorization of the Bible, in Pt. i of *The Age of Reason* (1794), begins: 'These books, beginning with Genesis and ending with Revelation (which, by the bye, is a book of riddles that requires a revelation to explain it) are, we are told, the Word of God. It is, therefore, proper for us to know who told us so, that we may know what credit to give to the report. The answer is that nobody can tell, except that we tell one another so' (*Thomas Paine Reader*, 409).

[4] *Table Talk*, i. 106 (25 Apr. 1830).

from another, one can observe in the letters and notebooks around 1797–8 an unusually intense and focused preoccupation with the sources and causes of evil. 'I believe most steadfastly in original sin,' he writes on one occasion: 'that from our mothers' wombs our understandings are darkened'.[5] The idea had not until this stage struck him so forcibly. He now faced the problem of reconciling his faith in the perfectibility of mankind (a faith founded on the contingent nature of evil, and the power of circumstances to alleviate vice) with the acknowledgement of a sinfulness endemic in the human condition.[6] The three 'supernatural' poems which belong to this period—'The Ancient Mariner', 'Kubla Khan', and 'Christabel'—show him examining sin and guilt from a variety of angles, each of them involving a different kind of Miltonic allusion, and different assumptions about the Fall. In later chapters, I shall be looking at his careful study of psychological motivation in 'Christabel', and at his treatment of guilty imaginative power in 'Kubla Khan'. My concern here is with 'The Ancient Mariner', which I see as as a troubled and divided exploration of responsibility, in which Coleridge attempts the difficult task of sustaining necessitarian optimism alongside his 'steadfast belief' in the innate corruptibility of man. I would suggest that his recent analysis of the French Revolution gives a 'conservative' bias to his presentation of expanding individualism; but that there is, running counter to the overt moral of the poem, an unease about divine authority which might be seen to have radical implications, especially in the light of other Romantic texts.

There is a political dimension to 'The Ancient Mariner' that one might regard as Burkean, though only in the loosest possible sense. Nothing in the narrative lends support to the detailed ramifications of Burke's system—his upholding of aristocracy and monarchy as the earthly embodiment of man's fixed compact with God. But there is none the less a meeting-point for the two writers (Burke from his orthodox perspective and Coleridge from within the dissenting tradition of Unitarianism) in their subjugation of earthly politics to religious truth. Both place their ultimate faith in 'the inviolable oath which holds all physical and moral natures, each in their appointed place'.[7] Thus, in his symbolic reworking of the Fall narrative, Coleridge posits a thoughtless act of violence, disrupting the pre-ordained harmony of things, as the origin of evil. By shooting the albatross, the rebellious mariner breaks 'that great primeval contract of eternal society' which Burke sees as 'linking the lower with the higher natures, connecting the visible and the invisible world'. Having broken this law, and 'disobeyed nature', he is 'outlawed, cast forth and exiled' from a

---

[5] Letter to Revd G. Coleridge, 10 Mar. 1798 (*Coleridge Letters*, i. 396).

[6] In a note to the first of Coleridge's 'Lectures on Revealed Religion', Patton and Mann write that his views during 1794–6 on evil and vice are 'not notable for their consistency', but that 'The common underlying assumption is that evil is not absolute, but contingent and induced'. They observe that 'by 1798 C had moved toward the traditional Christian view of evil as personal, innate, absolute, and prior to all conditions and circumstances'; see *Coleridge Lectures*, 107.

[7] Burke, *Reflections on the Revolution in France*, ed. with introd. C. C. O'Brien (Harmondsworth, Middx., 1968; repr. 1986), 195.

world of 'reason, and order, and peace, and virtue' into 'the antagonist world of madness, discord, vice, confusion, and unavailing sorrow'.[8]

Coleridge is not interested here (as Wordsworth had been in *The Borderers*, and as he himself would be, when he came to write 'Christabel' Part I) in examining the motivation which causes the fall to take place. The shooting of the albatross is therefore unexplained: we have no build-up before it, no suggestion of overweening curiosity, no study of the restlessness of the unfallen state. The bareness of the narrative suggests an almost fatalistic attitude towards the moment of transgression, as though it were somehow involuntary. Yet we are invited by the poem's larger symbolic pattern to interpret it as a failure of responsibility on the mariner's part. Read in terms of Coleridge's specific pre-occupations during this period, it embodies an upsetting of the harmonious interconnectedness of all things. Whether this is seen in Priestleyan terms, as a crime against the 'One Life',[9] or in Miltonic terms, as a disruption of organic hierarchy, or in Burkean terms, as a rebellion against the social order, it betokens an assertion of selfhood which fails to acknowledge God. The potential for evil is thus defined as the carelessness of good—a definition which neatly side-steps the more radical charge made by Mary Shelley in *Frankenstein*, or Blake in *Urizen*, namely that God must be the origin of evil, if everything is assumed to originate in God.

The sufferings undergone by the mariner himself, although extreme, can be explained on this moral level by the loss of cohesion which arises out of a disconnection from the One Life. Reasserting harmony is a matter of ceasing to ignore good, of perceiving the God whose absence makes the universe seem anarchic. Water-snakes may initially seem ugly, but their beauty is realized in the moment of the mariner's blessing—an act of selfless and involuntary love, through which he comes to perceive his own inclusion in the divine scheme of things.[10] But although this reading is relatively coherent, so long as one is concentrating exclusively on the mariner himself, it begins to be less so as we turn to the other members of his crew. Does Coleridge see the death of two hundred innocent people as strictly necessary for the enlightenment of one individual? Or is he hinting at the arbitrary injustice of God's ways? It was not until 1799 that he clarified his reservations about Priestleyan necessitarianism; but, as Patton and Mann point out, there is enough in his 1796 lectures to suggest that 'he could not long have remained content with dry and abstract

---

[8] Ibid. 48. This passage is quoted in Ch. 3, to illustrate Burke's monarchical appropriation of the Fall narrative.

[9] For an account of the Priestleyan content of Coleridge's early poetry, see H. W. Piper, *The Active Universe: Pantheism and the Concept of Imagination in the English Romantic Poets* (London, 1962), 29–59.

[10] I. Wylie's *Young Coleridge and the Philosophers of Nature* (Oxford, 1989) throws light on the transformative power of this moment, reading it in the context of scientific discoveries which connected sea-luminescence with fundamental processes of life and death: 'The light of the moon ... transforms the uncreated parasites of a decaying ocean into protoplastic larval forms, imbued with vitality to grow and develop' (p. 161).

complacencies of Priestley on the themes of evil and suffering'.[11] The formulation of discontent with which, in April 1799, he greeted the death of his son Berkeley is therefore very much to the point in the context of 'The Ancient Mariner': 'That God works by *general* laws are to me words without meaning or worse than meaningless,' he writes emphatically: 'What and who are these horrible shadows necessity and general law, to which God himself must offer *sacrifices*—hecatombs of Sacrifices? I feel a deep conviction that these shadows exist not . . . I confess that the more I think, the more I am discontented with the doctrine of Priestley.'[12]

Coleridge frames his discontent in terms of the inadequacy of one theological explanation, but beneath this intellectual restlessness there is surely a much deeper questioning of God's ways. The idea of an unjust God—one for whom 'hecatombs of sacrifices' are necessary—is explored not only in 'The Ancient Mariner' but in the prose fragment from which it had evolved, 'The Wanderings of Cain'.[13] Here Coleridge envisages the appalling possibility that earthly injustice might be a pale reflection of divine injustice, and that faith in the afterlife would prove useless, if the innocent continued to suffer, while the guilty got off scot-free. In a reversal of roles which brings this nightmare possibility vividly alive, Coleridge confronts the living Cain with the tormented spirit of his dead brother:

Cain said, 'Didst thou not find favour in the sight of the Lord thy God?' The Shape answered, 'The Lord is God of the living only, the dead have another God.'[14]

William Denis Horn has seen 'in Blake especially, and in the darker side of the other Romantic writers . . . a strain of Gnostic defiance that grew in part from the Romantic reaction to Milton'.[15] Certainly, the thought voiced by Coleridge's 'Shape' that there might be two Gods—or, in other words, that 'the Creation of the non-absolute' might extend to the divine principle, as well as to fallen man—is one that haunts him in his most troubled moments, unsettling his Neoplatonist faith in a good creation, and taking him uncomfortably close to the gnostic belief that 'the created world and hence his Creator were evil'.[16]

In 'The Ancient Mariner', too, the deity has power to inflict suffering and

[11] *Coleridge Lectures*, p. lxvi.
[12] *Coleridge Letters*, i. 482. Coleridge felt qualms about Priestley's necessitarianism as early as Mar. 1796, when Sara's pregnancy pains caused 'uneasy doubts respecting Immortality'. In a letter to Edwards, he complains that 'the pangs which the Woman suffers, seem inexplicable in the system of optimism—Other pains are only friendly admonitions that we are not acting as Nature requires—but here are pains most horrible in consequence of having obeyed Nature' (ibid. 192).
[13] For Coleridge's account in 1828 of the genesis of 'The Wanderings of Cain', see *CPW*, i. 285–7.
[14] Ibid. 291.
[15] 'Blake's Revisionism: Gnostic Interpretation and Critical Methodology', in D. Miller, M. Bracher, and D. Ault (eds.), *Critical Paths: Blake and the Argument of Method* (Durham, NC, 1987), 84.
[16] Ibid. 83.

death on the innocent many, whilst preserving only one for continuing life.
Though framed in terms of the mariner's internalized guilt, the poem betrays an
unspoken questioning of God's inscrutable ways, which is underpinned by
gnostic possibilities:

> An orphan's curse would drag to hell
> A spirit from on high;
> But oh! more horrible than that
> Is the curse in a dead man's eye!
> Seven days, seven nights, I saw that curse,
> And yet I could not die.

> (ll. 257–66)

In this sense, the poem bears out the truth of Anne Mellor's observation that
'Coleridge desperately wanted to believe in the absolute validity of an ordered
Christian universe but *could not*, could not because his own intelligence perceived the existence of underlying chaos'.[17] Schizophrenically, the text offers
two alternative Gods for our choosing: the just God whose actions are explicable
according to a system of optimism, and the capricious, arbitrary God, whose
ways cannot be justified, no matter how hard one tries.

   In attempting to answer its own questions about suffering, the poem relies on
Miltonic patternings which work on a symbolic level. If the mariner represents
Adam, and the killing of the albatross re-enacts the tasting of the apple, then the
death of the crew need not be read literally: it can be seen as the symbolic
consequence of the Fall, which 'Brought death into the world, and all our woe'
(*PL* i. 3). Suffering is explained by the symbolic dimension of Coleridge's
narrative, which offers a redemptive principle in the mariner's reawakening to
love. Miltonic theodicy can thus be used to assuage the perplexities raised by a
more literal reading of the text, and to present the mariner's experience as a sort
of fortunate fall. This amplified Miltonic reading makes the killing of the
albatross and the blessing of the water-snakes into paired and opposite climaxes
in the narrative, representing the twin halves of human subjectivity: the first
demonstrates the destructive potential of the self when it expands beyond its
proper bounds; the second suggests the capacity to 'lose and find all self in
GOD'.[18] The mariner's sufferings, 'alone on a wide wide sea', are symbolic of
the burden of consciousness which fallen man inherits; and his potential lies, as
it does for the fallen Adam, in the capacity for love/imagination which constitutes the 'Paradise within'. Although the blessing of the water-snakes reveals
this redemptive potential, allowing the mariner to be re-included in the One
Life, it does not lift him permanently out of his fallen state. While the goodly
company goes to church to pray, he wanders like night from land to land,
compelled by what he has seen and known. The loss of innocence is absolute,
this pattern reminds us, and fallen man is forever displaced.

---

[17] *English Romantic Irony* (Cambridge, Mass., 1980), 137.   [18] *Biographia*, i. 283.

In so far as he is able to do so, then, Coleridge quells his suspicions of divine injustice, in 'The Ancient Mariner', by using a circular argument very similar to Michael's in *Paradise Lost* Book X: the torment undergone by the mariner and his crew is 'explicable' (even while it seems disproportionate) both in terms of his individual cycle of crime–punishment–redemption and as part of the larger pattern of fall–oppression–salvation which is God's plan for mankind. The mariner's compulsion to repeat his story, and so implicate an innocent bystander in his fall from grace, is allied to his initial compulsion to repeat the Fall itself: both are given a sense of underlying purpose by Miltonic theodicy, and by Coleridge's valuation of experience as the route to salvation. This purposiveness somewhat mitigates the mariner's original sin, making it a necessary stage in his education towards responsibility.

Years after publishing the poem, Coleridge came to feel that 'The Ancient Mariner' had too obvious a moral: he would have preferred the story-line to be held together by a magic that was inconsequential and therefore un-allegorizable.[19] The envying account he offers to Mrs Barbauld of an *Arabian Nights* story (in which a chain of events is set in motion by a chance happening) brings to consciousness the alternative (gnostic) possiblities which hover in the background of 'The Ancient Mariner''s theodicy, subverting its control. This gives us a poem much closer to the *Arabian Nights* than Coleridge was aware: a poem in which the mariner's journey is governed by forces just as unpredictable—the polar spirits who move his boat along, the deathly crew who dice for his life—all of them working, it seems, on behalf of a deity who resembles the Old Testament God in his capricious vengefulness. It is, indeed, in the improbability of the poem's supernatural machinery that we find the more radical implications of Coleridge's thinking: his difficulty in reconciling disproportionate suffering with beneficence; his questioning of divine justice; his suspicion that man's irresponsibility might be a reflex of God's. In a corner of his imagination, there was certainly room for the mischievous and arbitrary deity who later crops up as Blake's Nobodaddy, and whom Empson sees as presiding over *Paradise Lost*.[20]

If 'The Ancient Mariner' is more open-ended than its 'moral' (or Coleridge's later comment) would suggest, this is partly because it raises different and competing narrative expectations. Reading the poem as a study in the psychology of guilt, we might find it easy to rationalize its supernatural happenings as projections of the mariner's paranoid consciousness: an interpretation which

[19] 'It ought to have had no more moral than the story of the merchant sitting down to eat dates by the side of a well and throwing the shells aside, and the Genii starting up and saying he *must* kill the merchant, *because* a date shell had put out the eye of the Genii's son'; *Table Talk*, i. 272–3 (31 Mar. 1832).

[20] 'Any angel instructed in theology will realize that God has intended throughout all eternity to spite Satan, so that when he presents his plan as new he is telling a lie, which he has also intended to tell throughout all eternity (*Milton's God*, 145–6). In Empson's view, it is the characterization of Milton's God which accounts for something Kafkaesque in *Paradise Lost*: 'Perhaps I find him like Kafka merely because both seem to have had a kind of foreknowledge of the Totalitarian State' p. 146).

grows plausibly out of Coleridge's source material,[21] and which has the further advantage of sitting comfortably alongside other psychological studies of this period—'The Three Graves', for instance, or (an even more intriguing comparison) Wordsworth's study of a crazed old sea-captain, 'The Thorn'.[22] Reading the poem as a myth of the Fall, however, we naturally make causal connections between crime and punishment, which then raise doubts about the probability of the narrative and the reasonableness of God's ways. This oscillation between literal, figurative, and allegorical possibilities creates in the reader an unease which is the poem's defence against reductive interpretation. Moreover, the framing device (introduced by means of the wedding guest) has a distancing function, as though Coleridge's intention is 'to destroy what one might call the realist illusion', setting the narrative 'within a framed and fictional space'.[23]

Romantic irony is, indeed, much more crucially integrated into the poem's theological questionings and ambiguities than has been allowed.[24] Coleridge provokes in his reader an awareness of the suspension of disbelief which is necessary, if one is to listen to the mariner's story like 'a three year's child'. The presence of this disbelief works to unsettle our comfortable faith in divine order, and to support the gnostic subtextual possibilities which the poem raises. The factual gloss on events which Coleridge adds later has the additional effect of admonishing against tidy-minded reading habits which leave no room for imaginative activity.[25] Thus, on a formal as well as a thematic level, Coleridge's questions remain largely unanswered, even by the Miltonic theodicy on which he relies. A psychologized and internalized version of the Fall coexists with a moral allegory which itself has political implications. The origin of sinfulness is left unexplained.

[21] In Shelvocke's *A Voyage Round the World by Way of the Great South Sea* (London, 1726), the captain who shoots the 'disconsolate black albatross' is prone to 'melancholy fits', and assumes that the albatross is an 'ill omen'. Shelvocke stresses his 'superstition', and the loneliness and dejection experienced by the crew (p. 73). This account provided Coleridge with the psychological details necessary for him to make his poem into a study of madness or paranoia.

[22] 'The Thorn' is, as Wordsworth's 'Note' tells us, a study in superstition. It observes the suffering of Martha Ray through the gossipy narrative of a retired sea captain, provoking the reader's sympathy with her predicament while at the same time ironizing the narrator's perspective. Its use of romantic irony is like that of 'The Ancient Mariner', in requiring the simultaneous suspension and activation of disbelief.

[23] I quote T. Rajan, somewhat out of context, since she is here discussing Keats, but with relevance to a mode of irony which Coleridge also adopts; see *Dark Interpreter: The Discourse of Romanticism* (Ithaca, NY, 1980), 107.

[24] Mellor's otherwise excellent study plays down the degree of Coleridge's rhetorical control, in order to emphasize the metaphysical *angst* which his poems register: 'Coleridge could respond to the ontology of romantic irony, to a vision of the universe as alternating between chaotic abundance and limited, man-made systems, only with anxiety' (*English Romantic Irony*, 164). Her reading therefore neglects the ways in which irony might be construed as an ideal vehicle for Coleridge's exploration of *angst*.

[25] For the successive devices of glossing, framing, and distancing which Coleridge introduces into the poem during revision, see K. M. Wheeler, *The Creative Mind in Coleridge's Poetry* (London, 1981), 42 f.

INJUSTICE AND OPPRESSION

Godwin's handling of the Fall in *Caleb Williams* raises similar problems of generic classification.[26] But whereas it is relatively simple to accept the competing implications of a largely symbolic poem, it is difficult to assimilate one symbolic strand into a narrative which otherwise functions literally. How do we interpret the religious components of a novel whose political meaning is clearly foregrounded? We can take as straightforward social commentary Godwin's exposure of the tyranny of landlords, the injustice of the legal system, and the appalling conditions which prevail in prisons, since all these add up to an explicit indictment—graphically and powerfully illustrated—of 'things as they are' (the novel's subject-matter, according to the title page of 1794). But at what level, conscious or unconscious, symbolic or otherwise, does the analogy between Falkland and God, Caleb and Adam/Satan, operate? Are we to take it that religion is the model for social tyranny, as Godwin spells it out in *Political Justice*? Or does the portrayal of the novel's central relationship function more ambiguously? The complications of Godwin's personal history make interpretation doubly complex:[27] the atheist might be expected to triumph over the ex-Calvinist minister, in which case Caleb's worship of Falkland might be taken as a critique of religion which functions on the conscious and rationalist level alone. But it is also plausible that the novel unconsciously enacts his own feelings for the God he has rejected—in which case the Falkland–Caleb relationship explores the magnetism of servitude in a way that is very far from being consciously controlled:

Do you know what it is you have done? To gratify a foolishly inquisitive humour you have sold yourself. You shall continue in my service, but can never share in my affection. I will benefit you in respect of fortune, but I shall always hate you. If ever an unguarded word escape your lips, if ever you excite my jealousy or suspicion, expect to pay for it by your death or worse. It is a dear bargain you have made. But it is too late to look back. I charge and adjure you by everything that is sacred and that is tremendous, preserve your faith![28]

Further complexities arise out of the novel's structure, which gives the Fall motif a different function, according to the perspective from which events are viewed. In Part I, we are asked to regard with sympathy Falkland's degeneration

---

[26] These difficulties are explored by B. J. Tysdahl in *William Godwin as Novelist* (London, 1981). For Tysdahl, *Caleb Williams* is 'an example of Empson's most radical kind of ambiguity' (p. 32), in that it offers both 'a picture of the kind of society which Godwin attacks in his political philosophy' (p. 34) and a Fall narrative, constructed along biblical lines (pp. 52–6). Godwin, according to Tysdahl's reading, 'was obviously not fully conscious of the extent to which he was writing a desperate and tortuous version of Calvinism between the covers of *Caleb Williams*' (p. 56).

[27] Godwin's Calvinist background, his Sandemanian beliefs, his career as a minister, and his final abandonment of religion, are briefly summarized in ibid. 11–13.

[28] *Caleb Williams*, 136.

from exemplar of chivalry to murderer. As in *The Borderers*, this sympathy is
stimulated by a study of psychological motivation, which makes entirely plausible—even perhaps inevitable—his Satanic fall. The repeated provocations he
receives from Tyrrel are sufficient to explain his having eventual recourse to
violence; he thereby demonstrates the argument supplied by *Political Justice*,
that crime is the product of circumstances acting on the individual and not of
that individual's innate propensity for evil. In Part II, however, our sympathies
are engaged in two directions at once: we are being asked to understand Caleb's
curiosity as well as Falkland's status as damaged archangel. Although the
narrative perspective is Caleb's own, our sympathy for Falkland lingers on,
producing an oscillatory effect reminiscent of the middle books of *Paradise Lost*.
As the novel progresses further, it could be said of Falkland that he undergoes a
'systematic degradation' similar to Satan's.[29]

Caleb's fall from grace is made plausible, as are those of Adam and Eve, by
virtue of the obstacles placed in the way of his growth towards experience: 'To
do what is forbidden always has its charms, because we have an indistinct
apprehension of something arbitrary and tyrannical in the prohibition' (p. 107).
The unknown contents of Falkland's 'fatal trunk', like the forbidden fruit of the
tree of knowledge, incite and provoke Caleb into knowing more. Curiosity
therefore becomes associated, as in the overtly sexual narrative of Lewis's *The
Monk*,[30] with irrepressible desire:

The mind is urged by a perpetual stimulus; it seems as if it were continually approaching
the end of its race; and, as the insatiable desire of satisfaction is its principle of conduct,
so it promises itself in that satisfaction an unknown gratification, which seems as if it
were capable of fully compensating any injuries that may be suffered in the career.
(p. 122)

The 'Great Forbidder', who at once represses and tempts desire, is, of course,
Falkland himself, who by Part II of the novel has acquired a dual status, playing
both God and Satan to Caleb's Adam. His moral ambivalence is an important
ingredient of his emotional power. It is because we can still recall the sympathetic perspective of Part I that we, like Caleb, are held by his reputation and
charisma—and are reluctant, even, to have the truth of his crime brought to our
attention. Godwin plays just as cleverly with the reader's own compulsion to
idolize as he does with Caleb's, and he thus exposes as misguided, not just
religion, but those analogous systems of loyalty which are used by conservatives
such as Burke to underwrite oppression.

In *Political Justice*, Godwin had thought vigilance and rationality sufficient
precautions against the tyranny a master could exert over his servant, or a father
over his son:

---

[29] See A. J. A. Waldock, *'Paradise Lost' and its Critics* (Cambridge, 1947), ch. 4.
[30] For the excitement of prohibition, see esp. *The Monk*, ed. H. Anderson (Oxford, 1973), 84.

Comply, where the necessity of the case demands it; but criticise while you comply. Obey the unjust mandates of your governors; for this prudence and a consideration of the common safety may require; but treat them with no false lenity, regard them with no indulgence. Obey; this may be right; but beware of reverence.[31]

In *Caleb Wiliams*, however, he is more pessimistic: rational and critical obedience get Caleb nowhere; neither do rebellion, flight, or the eventual betrayal of his tormentor. More terrifying than the subjection Falkland can exact from his servant, by virtue of a legal system rigged in his favour, is the reverence which insidiously survives in Caleb's emotional attachment to his master, despite all the suffering he undergoes. 'I came hither to curse, but I remain to bless,' Caleb declares, after telling the 'plain and unadulterated tale' which condemns Falkland to death:

I came to accuse, but am compelled to applaud. I proclaim to all the world that Mr. Falkland is a man worthy of affection and kindness, and that I am myself the basest and most odious of mankind! Never will I forgive myself the iniquity of this day. The memory will always haunt me, and embitter every hour of my existence. In thus acting I have been a murderer, a cool, deliberate, unfeeling murderer.   (p. 323)

The praise and forgiveness which, in return for this outpouring, Falkland lavishes on his servant provide the novel's most subtle irony: 'You have conquered,' he declares (p. 324), but by this very act of forgiveness he binds Caleb to him in the perpetual servitude of remorse. 'His figure is ever in imagination before me,' Caleb laments; 'Waking or sleeping I still behold him. He seems mildly to expostulate with me for my unfeeling behaviour' (p. 325).

The ending Godwin originally planned for the novel has its own powerful logic: Caleb's exposure of his master's crime proves unavailing in the face of a legal system corrupted through and through. He is imprisoned yet again, and the final pages of the book, written as a diary, record his slow degeneration into madness: 'well then,—it is wisest to be quiet, it seems—Some people are ambitious—other people talk of sensibility—but it is all folly!' (p. 334). The ending as it was revised and published is, however, more radical in its implications. Replacing the literal chains of imprisonment with the 'mind-forged manacles' of guilt, Godwin leaves us with a savage indictment of Christianity—in his view the most pernicious, because the most disguised, of all systems of oppression.[32] Every detail in the magnificent final scene, down to the mildness of Falkland's expostulation, is used by Godwin to press home his political point: If Christianity's central tenet is forgiveness, then forgiveness must be exposed as hypo-

·

---

[31] p. 242.

[32] Godwin writes that 'the system of religious conformity is a system of blind submission', and 'the tendency of a code of religious conformity is to make men hypocrites' (*Political Justice*, 569, 570).

crisy and sham—a weapon manipulated by those in authority to maintain their monopoly on power.

If Milton's theory of oppression reverberates through the pages of *Caleb Williams*, then, it is ironically. Godwin's underlying assumption, here as in *Political Justice*, is an equation of liberty with reason, which the archangel Michael would surely approve;[33] but he is a long way from seeing tyranny as evidence of God's 'judgement just' on man for sinning against reason. Whilst ironically keeping intact Michael's parallel between external and internal oppression, he manages to point the finger in quite the opposite direction. There can be no escape, Godwin argues, from the cycles of tyranny which repeat themselves through history, so long as religion (or any other form of superstition) maintains its tyrannical hold over the human mind. No form of tyranny is excusable, and the ultimate model of tyranny is God himself. It seems, however, that, from his sternly radical perspective, Godwin accuses the servile Caleb, as much as the overweening Falkland, for the compulsive patterns of rejection/love, flight/pursuit, betrayal/guilt which they keep repeating—like embattled lovers, or parent and child—over and over again. He appears to see as an inevitable compulsion this mutual need which binds together the tyrant and the oppressed—a compulsion which appears stronger, and more lasting, than rationality. Indeed, the closing pages of *Caleb Williams*, with their portrayal of Caleb's illogical, guilty, masochistic, and above all enduring faith towards his master, supply a darkly supportive comment on Michael's fatalistic words, 'tyranny must be, | Though to the tyrant thereby no excuse' (*PL* xii. 95–6).

The political and social atrocities which Godwin exposes in *Caleb Williams* take place sometimes as the background to, and sometimes in the foreground of, the central relationship between Falkland and Caleb. It is not always easy to keep track of the hybrid genre which Godwin has produced, in thus conflating psychological narrative with social realism; but the Miltonic roles adopted by the novel's protagonists help to sustain both the momentum of the story and the larger symbolic point being made. Significantly presented in terms both of the servant's obligation to his master and of man's bondage to God, the Caleb–Falkland relationship stands for those twin systems of oppression, religion and social hierarchy, which together provide the foundation of British society. So long as oppression is internalized, Godwin implies, it will maintain its hold both on individual consciousness and on the collective mentality. Where *Political Justice* offers a programme for the reform and ultimate perfectibility of the human mind, however, *Caleb Williams* pessimistically reflects a closed system, in which tyranny is self-perpetuating, and miscarriages of 'justice' preserve the status quo.

Moral relativism is adumbrated in the cyclical structure of the novel (Falkland thus changes places with Tyrrel, 'benevolence' being renamed tyranny); in the ambiguities and conflations produced by Miltonic allusion

---

[33] See Michael's discussion of the role played by reason in preventing servitude (*PL* xii. 82–96).

(Falkland is both Satan and God, Caleb both Adam and Satan); and, finally, in the multiple perspectives through which the narrative is allowed to emerge. There is, indeed, no pretence of an authoritative narrative, nor of an impartial narrator, after Collins's version of events comes to an end. Caleb's subjective account (into which Falkland's confession is embedded) is the only proof we have that Falkland is a murderer—a fact we are reminded of when Caleb surmises about 'the contents of the fatal trunk from which all [his] misfortunes originated':

I once thought it contained some murderous instrument or relique connected with the fate of the unhappy Tyrrel. I am now persuaded that the secret it encloses is a faithful narrative of that and its concomitant transactions, written by Mr. Falkland, and preserved in case of the worst, that, if by any unforeseen event his guilt should come to be fully disclosed, it might contribute to redeem the wreck of his reputation.   (p. 315)

In what, though, does a 'faithful narrative' actually consist? Caleb is still naïve enough to suppose that Falkland's story would back up his own—at least in its confession of the central events surrounding the murder. But Godwin's own position is surely more sceptical. The sequence of trials which thread their way through the novel are a disturbing reminder of the adaptability of truth to the teller: Falkland's narrative could be faithful in his own terms, whilst still purveying only the 'official' truth.

RESPONSIBILITY

The question of narrative faithfulness had been posed implicitly, by Milton himself, in the successive versions of events which *Paradise Lost* contains; and Coleridge makes use of a related device in 'The Ancient Mariner', where the story is at two removes from its reader—told by the mariner to the spellbound wedding guest, who then relays it to us. The effect is such as to draw the reader into a close identification with the dramatized listener, but at the same time to cast doubt on the factual validity of the mariner's tale. Its imaginative power is therefore in no way bound up with notions of truthfulness: it is a 'faithful' narrative without being verifiable.

It is in the Gothic novel, however, that the full potential of this Miltonic method is realized, in an explosion of juxtaposed perspectives, fictional editors, unreliable narrators, and tales within tales.[34] The relativism which these formal devices underline is neither wholly applauded nor outrightly condemned by those who use them. Like many other products of Romanticism, the Gothic

---

[34] Such a method is employed by, among others, J. Hogg in *The Private Memoirs and Confessions of a Justified Sinner* and C. Maturin in *Melmoth the Wanderer*—this latter being an extreme example of dialogism. As A. Hayter points out, in her introduction to the Penguin edition (Harmondsworth, Middx., 1977), Maturin's mode of narration was, from the first, 'condemned as Chinese-box perversity—story within story within story, a perpetual shift and distancing of narrator from reader which chills the latter's interest and belief' (p. 25).

novel thus reveals a fundamental ambivalence towards the subjectivity it releases, aligning itself with a 'conservative' need to quell individualism, but also with a 'radical' impulse to release energy or desire. *Frankenstein* takes its place in the genre both as a typical product of the Gothic and as a self-conscious commentary on Romanticism. It shares with both 'The Ancient Mariner' and *Caleb Williams* its hybrid form, being interpretable as political commentary, psychological narrative, and moral fable. It adds the further ingredient of conscious and sustained Miltonic allusion, manipulated in such a way as to suggest a revisionary reading of *Paradise Lost* alongside a questioning of religion.

The central ambivalence of *Frankenstein* is reflected in its structure, which amplifies the possibilities of Godwin's double narrative focus, to offer two overlapping interpretations of the Fall. The first narrative (Frankenstein's) can be accommodated within a conservative Christian framework. Along with those other moral fables it resembles, Genesis and *Faust*, it concerns the danger of overweening curiosity, presenting Frankenstein as a human overreacher who wrongfully appropriates divine power. The fallibility of man is thus seen to derive from a culpable need to break that 'inviolable oath' which, in Burke's view, 'holds all physical and moral natures, each in their appointed place';[35] and the moral, clearly underlined by Frankenstein in his admonition of Walton, has a flavour of reactionary insularity:

Learn from me, if not by my precepts, at least by my example, how dangerous is the acquirement of knowledge, and how much happier that man is who believes his native town to be the world, than he who aspires to become greater than his nature will allow.[36]

Mary Shelley adds a humanist complexity to this moral, however, through her sympathetic treatment of psychological motivation: in this, she closely follows those aspects of Miltonic characterization which had been imitated by Wordsworth and Godwin. Curiosity is shown to begin as an innate potential—'earnest research to learn the hidden laws of nature, gladness akin to rapture, as they were unfolded to me, are *among the earliest sensations I can remember*' (p. 27; my italics)—which becomes overdeveloped through education, and which ends as an uncontrollable drive:

when I would account to myself for the birth of that passion, which afterwards ruled my destiny, I find it arise, like a mountain river, from ignoble and almost forgotten sources; but, swelling as it proceeded, it became the torrent which, in its course, has swept away all my hopes and joys.   (p. 29)

In this respect, Mary Shelley's treatment of Frankenstein's motivation clearly resembles Godwin's psychological study of Caleb, making a suggestive association between mental aspiration and erotic desire—'The world was to me a secret which I desired to divine' (p. 27); 'a fervent longing to penetrate the

[35] See nn. 7–8 above.   [36] *Frankenstein* (London, 1976), 41.

secrets of nature' (p. 29)—both of them intensified by the excitement of pro-hibition.[37]

The monster's narrative, on the other hand, has far more radical impli-cations. The focus of sympathy has shifted, as it does in *Caleb Williams*, along with the Miltonic roles each character plays in the second half of the novel. Frankenstein is now a confused, partly unsympathetic, and wholly tyrannical God, where before he was a curious Adam (though with occasional Satanic overtones). The monster, meanwhile, is at once an Adam to be admired and a Satan to be pitied: from his creator's point of view, the Satanic aspect is upper-most. Mary Shelley is concerned with the fall of the monster, from innate good to violent and destructive evil. Following the argument of *Political Justice*, she sees evil as the product of circumstances acting on the individual—a view which she carefully expands, on two interrelated levels. Psychologically, through the monster's own eyes, we see how his innate capacity for love is thwarted at every stage by his creator, who made him ugly, then rejected him and denied his needs: 'Accursed Creator! Why did you form a monster so hideous that even *you* turned from me in disgust?' (p. 109).[38] On a social and political level, again through the innocent observations of the monster ('I heard of the division of property, of immense wealth and squalid poverty; of rank, descent and noble blood'), we are encouraged to see a parallel form of exclusion and repudiation, operating in society at large:

I learned that the possessions most esteemed by your fellow-creatures are high and unsullied descent united with riches. A man might be respected with only one of these advantages; but without either, he was considered ... as a vagabond and a slave, doomed to waste his powers for the chosen few! (p. 100)

Mary Shelley's point is not to write a symbolic narrative whilst incidentally producing a critique of societal values; it is, rather, to demonstrate the clear connections that exist between two systems of oppression. The oscillation between literal and symbolic modes is as disconcerting as it is in *Caleb Williams*, but more powerfully manipulated to ironic effect: we are repeatedly drawn into comparisons which we might be in danger of finding favourable to ourselves,

---

[37] See the erotic language used by Godwin to describe the climactic discovery that Falkland is a murderer: 'In the very tempest and hurricane of the passions, I seemed to enjoy the most soul-ravishing calm' (*Caleb Williams*, 130).

[38] For Bloom, Victor Frankenstein's tragedy is that a failure of responsibility leads him to abhor his creature: the hideousness of the monster is 'no part of [Victor's] intention', and can be read as a product of the moral idiocy which Bloom assigns to discoverers in general; see H. Bloom, *The Ringers in the Tower: Studies in Romantic Tradition* (Chicago, 1971), 124. By contrast, S. Gilbert and S. Gubar approach Frankenstein's predicament from a psycho-sexual angle, reading the creation scene in terms of Mary Shelley's fears and fantasies about motherhood: 'Like Eve's fall into guilty knowledge and painful maternity, Victor's entry into what Blake would call the realm of "gener-ation" is marked by a recognition of the necessary interdependence of ... sex and death'; see *The Madwoman in the Attic: The Woman Writer and the Nineteenth-Century Literary Imagination* (New Haven, Conn., 1979), 232.

only to have our complacency undermined. 'Listen to my tale,' begs the monster, appealing to his master for leniency, after the assassination of William and the unjust execution of Justine:

when you have heard that, abandon or commiserate me, as you shall judge that I deserve. But hear me. The guilty are allowed, by human laws, bloody as they are, to speak in their own defence before they are condemned. Listen to me, Frankenstein. You accuse me of murder; and yet you would, with a satisfied conscience, destroy your own creature. Oh, praise the eternal justice of man!   (p. 83)

The moral to be derived from these repeated comparisons is a clear one. Just as we are encouraged to see responsibility for the monster's crimes as residing with his creator, who made the conditions out of which evil could spring, so we must see our own responsibility for the social and political systems of oppression which are man's creation, and which in their turn produce monsters: 'I was benevolent and good; misery made me a fiend. Make me happy, and I shall again be virtuous' (p. 82).

But how does religion figure in this replication of injustice? Does Mary Shelley use the Fall narrative to reinforce conservative Christian values, as the first part of the novel leads us to expect, or does she intend a Godwinian exposure of the tyrannical hold religion has on human consciousness? The answer to this question must hinge on whether we choose to read Frankenstein's oppression of his monster as an accurate critique of the central values of Christianity or as a departure (itself monstrous) from them. The effect of Miltonic allusion is to repeat and accentuate this choice of interpretations. *Paradise Lost* is the monster's Bible: he reads it 'as a true History' (p. 108); and it teaches him the values by which he measures both himself and his creator. Comparison between himself and Adam reveals a painful disparity in their lots, which at first seems to reflect favourably on Milton's God:

Adam had come forth from the hands of God a perfect creature, happy and prosperous, guarded by the especial care of his Creator; he was allowed to converse with, and acquire knowledge from, beings of a superior nature: but I was wretched, helpless, and alone. (p. 109)

And yet we are cleverly reminded, in the same breath, of the inequity which prevails in *Paradise Lost*, for God's benevolence does not extend to the outcast Satan, with whom the monster feels his true affinities to lie: 'Many times I considered Satan as the fitter emblem of my condition; for often, like him, when I viewed the bliss of my protectors, the bitter gall of envy rose within me.' This contrast between Satan and Adam is frequently referred to, as a reminder of Frankenstein's neglected obligations: 'Remember, that I am thy creature: I ought to be thy Adam; but I am rather the fallen angel, whom thou drivest from joy for no misdeed' (p. 82). But such reminders, wherever they occur, have a twofold effect: they reflect badly on Frankenstein, who is shown to be an irresponsible creator by comparison with God; but they also reflect badly on

God, who by implication maltreats Satan. Even when Satan's misery is seen as preferable to the monster's—'he had his companions, fellow-devils to admire and encourage him, but I am solitary and abhorred'—the effect is rather more complex than one might expect.

Mary Shelley's method depends on the use of parallel and interlocking lines of satire. One is directed towards society, whilst apparently being directed towards Frankenstein himself: the fallibility and corruptness of the legal system are thus shown to be a pale reflex of the capricious judgement passed on the monster by his creator; but as I have shown, this scarcely lets the legal system off the hook. The other is directed at religion (more specifically, at Milton's God), by way of unfavourable contrast with the behaviour of a man who usurps and abuses God-like powers. Again, the implication must be that religion itself has a lot to answer for, if God's behaviour in *Paradise Lost* is even remotely comparable to Frankenstein's.[39] The link that Mary Shelley thus suggests, between political and religious oppression, is rather more subtle than we find in *Caleb Williams*. Instead of presenting Frankenstein's tyranny over his monster as a religious paradigm for atrocities perpetrated in the name of religion, she unsettles the stability of the God/man comparison, to produce a more disconcerting sequence of unflattering reflections. If one seeks to allegorize the novel's formal qualities as well as its themes, then one might see in this two-way mirroring process a satirical comment on the evasion of responsibility which characterizes both God and man, each of them blaming the other for the origin of evil.

To the question, is Frankenstein a parody of God, or of the man who thinks he is God? one has, I think, to answer that he is both: the novel is written from two overlapping perspectives, and it would be reductive to claim that either dominates. The warning against curiosity which is offered by Frankenstein as the 'moral' of his tale is therefore interpretable on two quite different levels. It can be read sympathetically, as the pronouncement of a man who has transgressed, and who (like the Ancient Mariner) preaches from his post-lapsarian perspective to the chosen few, who themselves become sadder and wiser from hearing his tale. But it could also be delivered as from the mouth of a suspect deity, thus providing an ironic comment on the scapegoat mentality which pervades Genesis and *Paradise Lost*. God safeguards his power by punishing man for the upstart sin of curiosity—this despite the fact that man's curiosity must by definition be innately good, because it originates in God. A morality which rests on so unreasonable a basis has to be flawed: one side of Mary Shelley's argument might well suggest that we should regard as suspect any such

---

[39] C. Baldick notes that to some of the early readers of *Frankenstein* it seemed that the novel was 'calling into question the most sacred of stories, equating the Supreme Being with a blundering chemistry student'. In Baldick's reading, Milton lays himself open to this impious and heretical treatment, since 'by submitting God's providence to rational debate' he had 'inadvertently exposed the foundations of his religion to subversion'; see *In Frankenstein's Shadow: Myth, Monstrosity, and Nineteenth-Century Writing* (Oxford, 1987), 40–1.

warning—particularly since, as Caleb Williams had observed, the 'indistinct apprehension of something arbitrary and tyrannical' in the prohibition heightens the charm of doing what is forbidden.[40]

Of all the features which *Frankenstein* and *Caleb Williams* have in common, the most interesting is their double focus, which in each case allows their tyrannical anti-hero to function simultaneously as man and God. The prehistory given to both Falkland and Frankenstein makes them just as human, just as fallible, as the powerless figures they later torment; and it is our awareness of their past transgressions which magnifies the injustice and hypocrisy of their behaviour. The God of *Paradise Lost* plays a crucial part in suggesting this double focus, for, as I suggested at the beginning of this chapter, he too gives signs of humanness which uncomfortably qualify his divinity. The point about Godwin's and Mary Shelley's reactions to *Paradise Lost* is thus not primarily that they 'misread' or 'revise' Milton because they wish to compete with him, but that they use the radical indeterminacy of his text as a way of themselves exploring the interface between politics and religion.[41]

In doing so, they enlarge on the possibilities of Miltonic ambiguity, in two major respects. Firstly, whereas the instability of *Paradise Lost* works in only one direction—God seeming inappropriately human—in *Caleb Williams* and *Frankenstein*, it works in both. The tyrants in these novels are at once gods exhibiting human fallibility and humans claiming god-like status. Secondly, in considerably magnifying the humanness of their 'God'-figures, they are more successful than Milton at understanding tyranny from the inside. Falkland and Frankenstein are not just gods with feet of clay, they are gods tormented by the full consciousness of their guilt—Satanic gods, whose motivation is fully and sympathetically realized—for whom we can feel more pity than we accord to Satan. Neither Godwin nor Mary Shelley sets out to 'justify the ways of God to man', but they both use a carefully Miltonic method of portraiture, which paradoxically allows us to understand the injustice and oppression for which religion is responsible from God's point of view, as well as man's.

Both the similarities and the differences between Godwin's vision and that of Mary Shelley are sharply realized in the apocalyptic closing scenes of *Frankenstein*, where the interlocking narratives of monster and creator finally converge, each becoming the mirror image of the other's loneliness and despair. 'All my speculations and hopes are as nothing', Frankenstein confides to Walton, in their final exchange, 'and like the archangel who aspired to omnipotence, I am chained in eternal hell' (p. 179). To which the monster's words sound like a reproachful echo when he contemplates the violent demise of his creator at his

---

[40] *Caleb Williams*, 107.

[41] Gilbert's and Gubar's revisionary reading is none the less ingenious, seeking to place Eve at the centre of a text from which she is at first sight excluded: '*Frankenstein* is ultimately a mock *Paradise Lost* in which both Victor and his monster, together with a number of secondary characters, play all the neo-biblical parts over and over again—all except, it seems at first, the part of Eve' (*Madwoman in the Attic*, 230).

own hands and torments himself with unavailing regret and remorse: 'When I run over the frightful catalogue of my sins', he laments 'I cannot believe that I am the same creature whose thoughts were once filled with sublime and transcendent visions of the beauty and the majesty of goodness. But it is even so; the fallen angel becomes a malignant devil' (p. 187). Further to underline the narrative's cyclical repetitions, Walton is himself driven by curiosity and loneliness, and undergoes a fall: 'Thus are my hopes blasted by cowardice and indecision; I come back ignorant and disappointed. It requires more philosophy than I possess to bear this injustice with patience' (p. 182). Injustice, however, seems in Mary Shelley's vision to be as much the product of unavoidable human compulsion as it is of systematized oppression: indeed, she would share Michael's view that the two are one and the same. But she has taken over the darker implications of his psychological theory, without being able to find an acceptable substitute for the Christian redemptive principle which offsets its gloom. She sees no way out of history's endlessly self-perpetuating cycles of oppression, except through the self-consuming violence of 'sacrificial' death; and this makes hers an even darker, because more acquiescent, vision than Godwin's.

AUTHORITY

The sense in which Blake would agree with Michael's view of tyranny is much closer to Godwin's oppositional irony than to Mary Shelley's pessimism. Blake takes further than Godwin does, for instance, the refusal of oppression; and this means subjecting all modes of authority, especially religious authority, to critique. His radical treatment of the problem of evil can be seen as a creation myth turned upside down. For him, as for Mary Shelley, there is a 'monster' produced by man's creative spirit which is an ugly replica of humanity, but which, far from being marginalized as a pitiable figure, rebellious from oppression, is welcomed and institutionalized by society. This 'monster' is religion itself, whose development Blake presents as the gradual degeneration of good into evil, through successive stages of 'abstraction':

> The ancient poets animated all sensible objects with gods or geniuses ...
> Till a system was formed, which some took advantage of and enslaved the vulgar by attempting to realize or abstract the mental deities from their objects. Thus began priest-hood—choosing forms of worship from poetic tales.
> And at length they pronounced that the gods had ordered such things.
> Thus men forgot that all deities reside in the human breast.[42]

If God is tyrannical, Blake shows us, then the responsibility is none the less man's, since God is made in man's image and, though benign in His origins, has become corrupted and malformed by political abuse. This is an adaptation,

---

[42] *MHH*, pl. 11, ll. 8–16.

then, of the Godwinian 'corruption by circumstances' argument, applied in an unexpected direction.

Morality, the by-product of religion, is in Blake's view a contingently produced ideology, disguised as an eternal set of absolutes: it works by encoding within individual consciousness a system of enslavement, which remains unobserved because it has been successfully internalized. Political oppression and psychological repression must therefore have the same roots; and the only radical means of unlocking these 'mind-forged manacles' is to turn language on its head, since language, by concealing the political basis of morality, works on behalf of the oppressor. What is usually termed 'evil', Blake therefore calls 'energy' or 'desire', and what is customarily seen as 'good', he labels 'reason': 'Good is the passive that obeys reason: Evil is the active springing from energy. Good is Heaven; Evil is Hell' (pl. 3, ll. 11–13). He thus returns to their original state the 'contraries' which are 'necessary to human existence', defamiliarizing language so as to defeat the traditional moral expectations which language encodes:

> Those who restrain desire do so because theirs is weak enough to be restrained; and the restrainer or reason usurps its place and governs the unwilling.
> And being restrained it by degrees becomes passive, till it is only the shadow of desire.
>
> (pl. 5, ll. 30–4)

Milton is useful to Blake as the model purveyor of Christian values, and therefore the prime representative of restraint—'The history of this is written in *Paradise Lost*, and the governor (or reason) is called Messiah' (pl. 5, ll. 35–6)—but Milton's unconscious was actually, in Blake's view, on the side of Satan, liberty, and 'eternal delight', so he ought to have known better than to betray them.[43]

In the microcosm of Milton's imagination, divided as it is between conscious restraint and unconscious desire, Blake produces a replica of the oppression he sees as operating in society at large. Milton's divided imagination also provides Blake with an instance of contraries that might be properly used in the service of 'progression', but are prevented from so doing by the narrative method of *Paradise Lost*. By undoing the restraints imposed on energy, Blake's aim is to restore to its original integrity Milton's divided imagination. In proposing the 'marriage' of heaven and hell, he does not, however, envisage a *reconcilement* of contraries, for 'opposition is true friendship', but rather a reinstating of Satan's genuine oppositional power. Imaginative integrity could thus be defined as the balancing in perpetual creative tension of what Blake terms the 'prolific' and the 'devourer', for 'the prolific would cease to be prolific unless the devourer as a sea

---

[43] Wittreich repudiates the 'vulgar' reading of this passage (i.e. one that aligns Blake with Satan), claiming that it is the energy of Satan that Blake admires, not Satan himself. The devil, like the angel, merely turns the world upside down, whereas Blake wants to find a truth transcending the 'partiality of party affiliation'; see *Angel of Apocalypse: Blake's Idea of Milton* (Madison, Wis., 1975), 214.

received the excess of his delights' (pl. 16, ll. 114–15). In other words, the dominance of either contrary is to be seen as oppression; whilst 'Religion is an attempt to reconcile the two' (l. 121).

The rewriting of *Paradise Lost*, so as to reverse the effects of restraint, is partly metaphor: Blake's larger project is to restore man's integrity, by undoing the effects of the Fall. One of his primary targets is 'the notion that man has a body distinct from his soul' (pl. 14, ll. 75–6): this arbitrary division he sees as religion's way of ensuring the weakening of desire. By 'an improvement of sensual enjoyment' (ll. 73–4) man will be enabled to reassert the balance he has lost, for 'If the doors of perception were cleansed everything would appear to man as it is—infinite' (ll. 80–1), whereas man 'has closed himself up, till he sees all things through narrow chinks of his cavern' (ll. 82–3). To make the improvement of sensual enjoyment possible, however, morality must be reconceived, since guilt operates as an internalized form of oppression. Guilt is personified as the covering cherub of *Paradise Lost*, who prevents fallen man from re-entering Eden, and who repeats God's original act of prohibition against sin. If the notions of sin and guilt were abolished, Satan could be reintegrated, and the Fall could be reimagined as the fulfilment of energy and eternal delight:

the cherub with his flaming sword is hereby commanded to leave his guard at the Tree of Life; and when he does, the whole creation will be consumed, and appear infinite and holy, whereas it now appears finite and corrupt.　(ll. 67–72)

Blake's optimism is such—at least in 1790—that he believes it possible to rewrite the Fall along these lines, and so eradicate the notion of original sin. He uses a variety of shock tactics to expose the arbitrariness of moral terminology, and to destabilize the official authority of biblical truth. So, religious dictates and sanctions are parodied in his 'Proverbs of Hell', which juxtapose and conflate 'good' and 'evil':

> Exuberance is beauty.
> Sooner murder an infant in its cradle than nurse unacted desires.
>
> (pl. 10, ll. 64, 67)

The Bible, like *Paradise Lost*, is shown to be merely partial in its recording of a history which can be adopted by both parties: Blake adjusts the balance by confidently citing Christ as the spokesman of Blakean ideals—'I tell you no virtue can exist without breaking these ten commandments. Jesus was all virtue, and acted from impulse, not from rules' (pl. 23, ll. 281–2)—and by claiming that the 'diabolic' subtext of the Old Testament is just as valid as its conventional meaning:

Note. This angel, who is now become a devil, is my particular friend. We often read the Bible together in its infernal or diabolical sense, which the world shall have if they behave well.

I have also the Bible of Hell—which the world shall have whether they will or no.
(pl. 24, ll. 288–92)

Blake's jocular conversations with angels and devils suggest a familiarity with
the divine which is at once parodic of humans claiming prophetic status
(including Milton, Swedenborg and himself) and subversive of the supernatural machinery used to enforce moral codes.[44]

The truculent, confrontational tactics of *The Marriage of Heaven and Hell*
depend on Blake's faith that language can undo its own tyrannical hold on
morality, simply by turning accepted truths upside down. The foundations for
such a faith are, however, shaky so long as language itself remains unredeemed,
and it will continue to be so while biblical authority maintains its univocal claim
on linguistic origins. It follows that Blake's most urgent task is to challenge the
logocentric assumptions of Genesis, and to reclaim language for the 'eternal
delight' of mankind. He therefore leaves behind the *Marriage*'s bizarre and
somewhat piecemeal strategies of defamiliarization, and moves on in *Urizen* to
the wholesale rewriting of the Bible's account of Creation. He begins, not by
positing God as the Logos—'in the beginning was the Word, and the Word was
with God'—but by positing the origin of God as an act of silent, self-conscious
separation:

> Lo, a shadow of horror is risen
> In Eternity. Unknown, unprolific,
> Self-closed, all-repelling.

> (pl. 3, ll. 1–3)

Language comes later, along with those pernicious systems of religion,
morality, and repressed sexuality by means of which this 'shadow of horror',
Urizen, consolidates his power. The origin of evil is thus shown to be the first
act of division through which the creative principle asserts itself, whilst the
Creation itself is reconceived as a myth of the Fall.

Indeed, the closest parallel for Urizen's separation from the Eternals is
Satan's expulsion from heaven in *Paradise Lost*. Blake underlines the comparison by giving two separate accounts of this single event: one from the 'Eternal'
perspective, which sees Urizenic activity as pride—'unknown and horrible, | A
self-contemplating shadow'—and which corresponds in some of its details to
Raphael's narrative of the war in heaven; and one from Urizen's own perspective, which makes him the centre and origin of unfolding events. This latter
parodies Satan's retrospective account of the Fall, suggesting that the claims
Urizen makes to omnipotence may be as empty and ungrounded as Satan's own
claim to be 'self-begot':[45]

---

[44] See Milton's claim in the proem to *PL* vii that he receives nightly visitations from Urania, the
heavenly muse; also the use made by God of Raphael, to warn Adam and Eve against temptation. For
a parallel in Pope's *The Rape of the Lock*, see Ch. 5.

[45] 'We know no time when we were not as now; | Know none before us, self-bigot, self-raised'
(*PL* v. 859–60).

First, I fought with the fire, consumed
Inwards, into a deep world within—
A void immense, wild, dark and deep,
Where nothing was, nature's wide womb.
And self-balanced stretched o'er the void
I alone, even I, the winds merciless
Bound.

(pl. 4, ll. 58–64)

Blake's aim is to reintegrate Satan, however, not to repudiate him, so these Satanic references work in more than one direction: their function is to draw God and Satan closer together, creating an imaginative conflation of the 'good' and 'evil' principles which have become separated in official accounts of the Creation. Blake is not, therefore, in the crude sense, making God responsible for evil: he is exposing the evils for which the Genesis account of God is itself responsible. In this respect *Urizen* is more coherently analytic than either *Caleb Williams* or *Frankenstein*, both of which it closely resembles in its anti-authoritarian implications. There is an inventiveness in Blake's account of the Creation as Fall which manages, more successfully than they do, to fuse and make sense of different narrative expectations: Urizen, like Falkland and Frankenstein, has competing claims to divinity and humanity, since the moment that he separates himself off from the Eternals is the moment at which 'God' comes into being, through his 'fall' into consciousness. Blake's Creation myth works two ways at once: as an account of how God made man and an account of how man made God—a possibility which neither Godwin nor Mary Shelley is able to pursue. As a result, responsibility for evil devolves on the misrepresentation of God which Genesis purveys, and which Blake sees as having ossified through repetition.

Within this myth, the advantage of Satanic allusion is twofold: it allows Blake to challenge biblical authority in the most outrageous way, by pointing to the features that God and Satan have in common, and it establishes a method for demonstrating the pernicious effects of religion. The way is prepared for this in Blake's parody of Mosaic law, constructed by Urizen to repudiate sin, but having the adverse effect of nurturing it through repression:

Here alone I, in books formed of metals,
Have written the secrets of wisdom,
The secrets of dark contemplation
By fightings and conflicts dire
With terrible monsters sin-bred,
Which the bosoms of all inhabit—
Seven deadly sins of the soul.

(pl. 4, ll. 68–74)

At this stage in the Fall, however, no humans exist to take the blame for sin; and religion as such—by which is meant 'The ecclesiastical control of men's beliefs and lives'[46]—has not formally emerged. Blake reserves his most subtle observations for the penultimate stage of the Fall, when the net of religion is woven out of Urizen's inadequacy and loneliness:

> A cold shadow followed behind him,
> Like a spider's web, moist, cold, and dim,
> Drawing out from his sorrowing soul,
> The dungeon-like heaven dividing ...
>
> Till a web dark and cold throughout all
> The tormented element stretched
> From the sorrows of Urizen's soul ...
> None could break the web—no wings of fire,
>
> So twisted the cords, and so knotted
> The meshes, twisted like to the human brain.
> And all called it *The Net of Religion*.

(pl. 25, ll. 456–9, 462–4, 466–9)

From a linear perspective, religion precedes the human race in Blake's account of the Fall; but its successive stages happen all at once within Urizen's consciousness. Blake's likening of religion to the human brain is a metaphor of the adaptability of the human brain to religion: he further extends the paradox by showing how 'the shrunken eyes' of human beings, clouded over by the Fall, 'Discerned not the woven hypocrisy'. Humanity conspires with Urizen to eclipse eternal vision altogether.

   Blake's study of responsibility is even-handed. He demonstrates the mutual adaptability of religion and blinkered servitude, and he implies that modes of oppression which originate in Urizen are not to be seen as consciously and malevolently constructed by him: they are, rather, at once the involuntary products of his fall into division and psychic projections from his tormented, Satanic unconscious. Blake's conflation of God with Satan allows him to humanize, personify, and psychologize those aspects of religion he finds most repugnant and, by this method of anti-abstraction,[47] to diminish their tyrannical hold on consciousness. In this respect, as in others, his myth allows him to go one stage further than either Godwin or Mary Shelley.

REDEMPTIVE POSSIBILITIES

In *Prometheus Unbound*, Shelley formulates a more optimistic answer than do any of the writers I have so far examined to the questions raised by Michael's theory of oppression in *Paradise Lost*. He sees religion as the supreme example of

---

[46] W. H. Stevenson draws attention to Blake's distinction between the 'inspiration of religion', and the 'ecclesiastical control of men's beliefs and lives' (*Blake Poems*, 267): it is to the latter that Blake objects.

[47] Pl. 11 of *MHH* traces (and seeks, thus, to reverse) the process of abstraction which has succeeded in making forms of worship out of poetic tales.

systems of enslavement for which mankind is alone responsible; and he looks to a transformation in the human mind for a possible solution to both earthly and heavenly tyranny. The only 'revolution' which can undo the cycles of history is, he claims, one that is energized by love, rather than by opposition. Like Blake in *The Marriage of Heaven and Hell*, he seeks to cut through what he sees as Milton's binary moral scheme (itself a system of enslavement, with cyclical repercussions); and, like Blake, he redraws our moral categories by a process of defamiliarization. But in identifying a redemptive principle which subsumes the polarities of good/evil, Christ/Satan, energy/reason, he arrives at a vision of human perfectibility which is closer to Blake's mature prophecies than it is to the other texts with which I have been concerned. The most obvious parallel for *Prometheus Unbound* is indeed *Milton*, and I shall be making several comparisons between the two in the discussion that follows. Detailed analysis of *Milton* is, however, reserved until my last chapter, for reasons there explained.

In opting for a classical hero, rather than one drawn from either of the two Miltonic extremes, Shelley does not refuse the evaluative choice with which *Paradise Lost* faces every reader (a choice, that is, between outright rejection of and tacit support for the 'tyranny of heaven');[48] rather, he negotiates a careful critical position, which allows him to repudiate the moral failings both of Milton's God and of his Satan, so as to define as redemptive a human potential which lies beyond them both, and thus to cast off the restraints of religion altogether. His 'Preface' is indeed designed in such a way as to expose heaven's tyrannical features, as if incidentally, during a discussion of the comparative merits of Prometheus and Satan. Prometheus is, Shelley claims, 'a more poetical character' than Satan because 'in addition to courage and majesty and firm and patient opposition to omnipotent force, he is susceptible of being described as exempt from the taints of ambition, envy, revenge, and a desire for personal aggrandisement, which in the Hero of *Paradise Lost* interfere with the interest'.[49] He goes on to argue that Milton's portrayal of Satan is such as to engender in the reader's mind a 'pernicious casuistry' which leads us to 'weigh his faults with his wrongs and to excuse the former only because the latter exceed all measure'.[50] Having casually introduced (as though it is to be taken for granted) this reference to Satan's immeasurable wrongs at the hands of God, Shelley proceeds both to accuse Milton and to unsettle his acquiescent readers, by implying that such 'pernicious casuistry' is less damaging than the tolerance towards oppression which is engendered by 'those who read that magnificent fiction with a religious feeling'. His rhetorical deftness is such as to alert the reader to the dangers of too passive a reception of Satan's heroic qualities, while

---

[48] As I suggested in Ch. 3, this choice is determined by the ideological perspective of the reader.

[49] *Shelley*, 133. For a discussion of Prometheus's resemblance to Satan, see T. Webb, *Shelley: A Voice not Understood* (Manchester, 1977), 144.

[50] Ibid. For a discussion of the connections between this sentence and one in the 'Preface' to *The Cenci*, see Ch. 3, n. 92.

at the same time establishing reasonable grounds for rejecting both Milton's portayal of God and religion itself.

In its dialogue with *Paradise Lost*, Shelley's drama, like his Preface, is not the less revisionary (or allusive) for its choice of a classical model. It does not enter so frequently as Blake's *Milton* does into open correction of or opposition to Milton's method, but it does play constantly on the audience's awareness of ways in which Miltonic patterns are being modified, avoided, or put on one side. This obliqueness is carefully judged, and it provides an appropriate vehicle for the undoing of binary opposition which is Shelley's project. It allows him to retain those generic or universal ingredients of Satan's predicament which are useful to his exposure of religion as tyranny, whilst moving beyond the servitude which is implied by a wholesale espousing of Satan's particular (and, in Shelley's terms, forlorn) cause. Prometheus's opening address to Jupiter thus avoids calling to mind any specific soliloquy in *Paradise Lost*, but offers instead a summation of legitimate reasons why the reader can and ought to sympathize with Satan, for the wrongs he suffers at God's hands:

> regard this Earth
> Made multitudinous with thy slaves, whom thou
> Requitest for knee-worship, prayer and praise,
> And toil, and hecatombs of broken hearts,
> With fear and self contempt and barren hope;
>
> (I. i. 4–8)

Even as it does so, however, Shelley's language calls attention to the inadequacy of reproach and protest as revolutionary tools. Prometheus is barren in hope, and 'eyeless in hate' (l. 9), impotently frozen into a rebellious attitude which merely underscores his own oppression; and in this sense his resemblance to Satan provides a model of servitude which will be discarded as the play unfolds.

Indeed, within only fifty or so lines of the opening, Prometheus begins the process which will allow him to reject a Satanic solution (one that creates its own hell out of implacable revenge) and move toward the redemptive compassion which Shelley is offering as the only valid alternative: 'I speak in grief, | Not exultation,' he claims, 'for I hate no more, | As then, ere misery made me wise' (I. i. 56–8). In seeking to 'recall' the curse he had breathed on Jupiter, Prometheus reveals both the sense in which he is still locked into the memory of his rebellious action and the sense in which he is now ready, by revoking his anger, to move forward. This ambiguity is central to the meaning and the dramatic unfolding of the first act, since it allows a promise for the future to be envisaged, even while a reprise of Prometheus's past actions takes place. Furthermore, it juxtaposes two alternative roles for Prometheus to choose between: the implication is that if he were to persist as a version of Satan he would remain trapped in repetition compulsion, whereas by purging himself of Satanic anger he will succeed in undoing the cycles of history. True revolution must take nothing in its own past as the precedent for change; on this point, as on others, Shelley would agree with Paine.[51]

In the ensuing confrontation with Jupiter's Phantasm, Prometheus 'recalls' (in both senses) the curse which has bound him to his rock, having Jupiter play it back to him in much the same way as an echo or mirror might be used to confirm a self-image of power. Shelley is interested, here, by the sense in which oppressor and oppressed represent twin halves of a single compulsion: the curse acts as a metaphor of the double bind in which both Jupiter and Prometheus are caught,[52] its pronouns working interchangeably for the original voice of the curser and the echoic voice of the cursed:

> Fiend, I defy thee! with a calm, fixed mind,
>   All that thou canst inflict I bid thee do;
> Foul Tyrant both of Gods and Humankind,
>   One only being shalt thou not subdue.

> (I. i. 262–5)

One might see the symbolic significance of this scene as analogous to the interlocking needs of master and servant, creator and creation, as they are dramatized in *Caleb Williams* and *Frankenstein*. Indeed, Shelley makes a Miltonic conflation which is distinctly reminiscent of those novels when, at lines 381–3, Prometheus laments of Jupiter, 'I gave all | He has, and in return he chains me here | Years, ages, night and day'. In this pivotal acknowledgement of his own responsibility for Jupiter's tyranny, we can hear not just the tones of Milton's self-righteous Jehovah, upbraiding man for his rebellion: 'Ingrate, he had of me | All he could have' (*PL* iii. 97–8) but the regretful tones of Satan, reproaching himself for his ingratitude to God: 'He deserved no such return | From me, whom he created what I was | In that bright eminence' (iv. 42–4). Shelley amalgamates Miltonic opposites to expose the entrapment of tyranny, which like religion remains blind to the redundancy of its moral polarities, even when they evidently cancel each other out. His devices of echoing, mirroring, and conflation allow for a deconstruction of these polarities, throwing into ironic relief the double significance of Prometheus's statement that 'Evil minds | Change good to their own nature' (ll. 380–1). Turned back upon itself, this statement contains the redemptive potential that Prometheus seeks, and that his revoking of the curse will bring about.

Shelley's implicit repudiation of Milton is at once confirmed and widened in scope by his rejection of Christ as a model for the redemptive process he is seeking to define. Christ's image is summoned by the Chorus, at lines 545–72, as

[51] In *The Rights of Man*, Paine conducts a reasoned argument against the speciousness of precedents, concluding: 'The fact is, that portions of antiquity, by proving everything, establish nothing. It is authority against authority all the way' (*Thomas Paine Reader*, 215).

[52] For 'the ambiguities of identity between Prometheus and Jupiter', see G. McNiece, *Shelley and the Revolutionary Idea* (Cambridge, Mass., 1969), 223; and for an even closer identification between the two figures, see Webb, *A Voice not Understood*, 147–8.

a warning to Prometheus of the evils which are committed in the name of religion. Christianity is held responsible for the cycles of tyranny–rebellion–tyranny which are observable through modern history, of which the most recent example is the French Revolution (see I. i. 568–72). Still more tellingly, it is exposed as a system of enslavement which works unobtrusively, through 'hypocrisy and custom', to conceal from mankind its own potential for change: 'They dare not devise good for man's estate | And yet they know not that they do not dare' (I. i. 623–4). In a staggering echo of Christ's dying words on the cross, Shelley accuses Christianity of disempowering man, by removing from him a sense of accountability for his actions:

> Many are strong and rich,—and would be just,—
> But live among their suffering fellow men
> As if none felt: they know not what they do.
>
> (I. i. 629–31)

Indeed, the sacrifice and atonement of Christ are figured by Shelley as mankind's abnegation of responsibility for the continuance of evil: only through a reversal of the ignorance to which Christ has condemned them can mankind awaken to their own potential for reform. Prometheus therefore recognizes in Christianity a 'curse' (l. 604), which, like his own, must be undone.

The remaining action of the play can be seen as an attempt to revise Milton's inadequate conception of the redemptive process, along lines that are considerably more favourable to human potential. It envisages the possibility of what M. H. Abrams has called 'a sudden right-angled break-through from misery to felicity',[53] thereby avoiding Michael's long-drawn-out historical process, with its tolerance of suffering, and its cycles of tyranny and rebellion; and it emphasizes the fundamental importance of an integration between masculine and feminine elements, in the achievement of genuine liberation. In these and other respects, it resembles Blake's *Milton*, which brings forward the Second Coming of Christ, and the redeeming of Albion, by having Milton descend from Heaven to be reconciled with the humanity (and particularly the femininity) he has neglected.[54]

The first act of Shelley's drama had ended with the emergence into consciousness of Prometheus's need for Asia, the female complement from whom he has been divided by his curse, and with whom he must be reunited to make redemption possible. The second act focuses on her descent into the underworld, to encounter Demogorgon and initiate his dethronement of Jupiter. In placing the female principle at the centre of the redemptive process, and in envisaging this as a descent rather than an ascent, Shelley revises Milton

---

[53] M. H. Abrams, *Natural Supernaturalism: Tradition and Revolution in Romantic Literature* (New York, 1971), 300.
[54] See Ch. 8.

along markedly Blakean lines; but he gives greater autonomy to Asia than Blake does to Ololon; and in some ways his treatment of the feminine can be seen as more concretely corrective than Blake's, in that it makes allusive parallels and contrasts between Asia and Eve which appear to be stressing the deficiencies of Milton's conception of women (not just his neglect of femininity).

In the opening scene of Act II, for instance, Shelley empties out the fallen associations of Eve for which Milton is infamous—associations which I shall be analysing at length in my next chapter—by approaching two crucial passages in *Paradise Lost* from a perspective different to Milton's own. Panthea's recounting of her dream to Asia suggestively recalls Eve's recounting of hers to Adam; but whereas Eve's dream confirms a Satanic tendency in the female unconscious, in its foreshadowing of the Fall, Panthea's puts Asia in touch with her own dream, through which redemptive possibilities are disclosed.[55] Similarly, in the scene that ensues, Shelley offers a reversal of the passage in *Paradise Lost* where Eve gazes at her own image in the lake, and is likened to Narcissus.[56] When Asia looks into Panthea's eyes, she sees more than her 'own fairest shadow imaged there':

PANTHEA: Why lookest thou as if a spirit past?
ASIA: There is a change: beyond their inmost depth
           I see a shade—a shape—'tis He.

(II. i. 118–20)

The suggestions of vanity in Eve are here stripped away, and Asia is shown to be capable of that powerful attraction to what is beyond the self, which Shelley describes in his essay 'On Love'.[57] The 'mirroring' scene between her and Panthea offers a marked contrast to Prometheus's narcissistic confrontation with the phantasm of Jupiter in Act I, and shows that, far from being solipsistic, Asia can realize the redemptive impulse that Prometheus only dimly conceives.

It is indeed Asia's function, in *Prometheus Unbound*, to bring important truths to consciousness; and in the questions and answers between her and Demogorgon, she stands symbolically for the intelligence of mankind, asking for 'the rationale of all human history and experience'.[58] Shelley plays deftly, here, with Miltonic expectations: for in the parallel question-and-answer sequences of *Paradise Lost*, Adam and Eve are made the passive recipients of God's univocal truth, as relayed to them by his archangels, Raphael and Michael; whereas Asia is shown playing an active role in constructing the truth as it is humanly known.

[55] Cf. *PL* v. 28–94.
[56] *PL* iv. 449–91. This passage is much imitated in 18th-c. poetry, presumably because of its playful underwriting of sexist assumptions about female vanity: see e.g. Pope's *The Rape of the Lock*, i. 125–6 (discussed in Ch. 5); and Gray's 'Ode on the Death of a Favourite Cat', ll. 6–18, 25–6. Both Shelley and Mary Shelley use it, however, to revisionary ends: the latter, in *Frankenstein*, to draw attention to the emerging subjectivity of the monster (p. 95), and the former to suggest a power of love in Asia which is not equalled by Prometheus himself.
[57] *Shelley*, 473.
[58] Abrams, *Natural Supernaturalism*, 304.

M. H. Abrams explains the relevance of the scene to Shelley's scepticism, suggesting that 'Demogorgon, who simply acts as he must without knowing why, responds to Asia's queries with riddling utterances that merely stimulate her to answer her own questions, by specifying as knowledge what she had already possessed as obscure presentiment'.[59] But we may also see in the scene a pro-feminist parody of *Paradise Lost* that is worthy of Mary Wollstonecraft, especially in its insistence on female intelligence. It is also significant, as Abrams points out, that Asia, and not Demogorgon, should tell the prehistory of the drama in which she is involved: here we may see another marked reversal of Miltonic practice, for the narrative of God's Creation, followed by the fall of the angels, is delivered from the Eternal perspective of Raphael, and bears no trace of woman.

The content of Asia's exchange with Demogorgon, although enigmatic, is crucial in expanding some of the insights which Shelley has prepared in Act I. Asia frames the question of accountability for tyranny as though it were part of a larger question, about the origin of good and evil (II. iv. 12–28); but at the point where Demogorgon resists pointing the finger at God, and instead gives the enigmatic answer 'He reigns', Asia is confronted with man's responsibility for his own actions. Her question, 'Who is the master? Is he too a slave?' (II. iv. 109) allows an open-ended reply, in which the mirroring of Jupiter and Prometheus can be ominously suggested: 'All spirits are enslaved who serve things evil; | Thou knowest if Jupiter be such or no' (ll. 110–11). Indeed, all Asia's questions are framed to yield the answers she intuits, confirming that bondage is created by and within the mind; that master and slave are mirrors for each other; and that only 'Eternal love' outlasts the evils of mortality. These answers have already been metaphorically suggested, by the confrontation of Prometheus and Jupiter's phantasm, in Act I; but Asia brings them to full consciousness, and in so doing undoes the 'curse' of ignorance which disempowers mankind.

Redemption is made possible, in *Prometheus Unbound* as in *Milton*, by a cancelling of the binary system of moral polarities which has been authorized by the Bible and perpetuated in *Paradise Lost*. Blake brings this about through the 'mutual self-annihilation' of Milton's law-giving God and his vilified Satan, as I shall show in Chapter 8; while Shelley uses Demogorgon as a personification of Neccessity (and so as neutral 'third term', neither oppressor nor oppressed) to exile Jupiter and so end for ever the cyclical patterns of history. 'The tyranny of Heaven none may retain | Or reassume, or hold succeeding thee', Demogorgon proclaims, in Act iii (i. 57–8). This statement, apparently unaccompanied by violence, is sufficient to bring Jupiter to an end which recalls the fall of Satan in *Paradise Lost*, but is pathetically emptied of Satanic glory: 'The elements obey me not ... I sink ... | Dizzily down—ever, forever, down—' (III. i. 80–1). The way is now clear for the reuniting of Prometheus and Asia, and the re-creation of an Edenic innocence which consists in their companionship and love, but

[59] Ibid.

which includes also the knowledge of mortality. Here Shelley resembles Blake yet again; for although he conceives of the redemptive process as one in which all things put off their evil nature (Scene iv), the 'paradise' he envisages is none the less an earthly one, as is the garden at Felpham in which the apocalyptic closing scenes of *Milton* take place. Indeed, it is central to the vision of both poets that 'paradise' is an internalized condition, in which the fullness of humanity can be realized only at the point where limitation is acknowledged. Thus, although 'chance and death and mutability' are for Shelley 'clogs' on man's aspiring mind, which 'else might oversoar | The loftiest star of unascended Heaven' (III. iv. 202–3), yet still

> The loathsome mask has fallen, the man remains
> Sceptreless, free, uncircumscribed—but man:
> Equal, unclassed, tribeless and nationless,
> Exempt from awe, worship, degree,—the King
> Over himself; just, gentle, wise—but man:
>
> (III. iv. 193–7)

Just as the Spirit of the Hour greets the arrival of a 'paradise within' in this language of qualified triumph, so Demogorgon warns us, in his closing speech in Act IV, that evil may reawaken; that the serpent, Destruction, threatens Eternity; but that none the less there are human 'spells' (Gentleness, Virtue, Wisdom, and Endurance) which may be uttered, 'to reassume | An empire o'er the disentangled Doom' (IV. 568–9). The presence of these muted reminders of human limitation and human responsibility is such as to dampen the operatic euphoria of Act IV, and to replace the liberated certainties of an achieved present with 'timeless admonitions'[60] suggestive of latent or continuing possibilities in the human mind. Shelley's claims for the redemptive process are none the less more absolute, as well as more humanist, than those made by Michael in *Paradise Lost*: more absolute, in the sense that *Prometheus Unbound* envisages as genuinely achievable mankind's contemplation of 'the melancholy ruins | Of cancelled cycles' (IV. 288–9); and more humanist, because it conceives of this liberation from history as an empowering of men and women which can dispense with the Christian props of sacrifice and atonement, and which needs no help from God.[61]

---

[60] See D. Reiman's note, *Shelley*, 210.

[61] Webb writes, 'Man must learn not to pay homage to divinities which are merely nebulous but to recognise within himself those truly divine potentialities which deserve his devotion and worship' (*A Voice not Understood*, 151).

5

Sex

INEQUALITY

When Godwin refers to 'the extreme inequality of rank and power' assumed by the Creator in *Paradise Lost*,[1] his purpose is to explain the motivation which lies behind Satan's rebellion. But he might just as easily be pleading the cause of Eve. Grievances which Satan has against God—His establishing of a fixed hierarchy in Heaven, His promotion of Christ—are similar in kind to Eve's, for God repeats His practice of arbitrary subjection (on earth as it is in heaven), by constructing a human hierarchy, in which woman is placed below man. However, whereas Satan's sense of resentment is made credibly sympathetic, in terms of the republican values which Milton had earlier espoused, the issue of authorial sympathy in Eve's case is more problematic. Historical and biographical evidence would seem to suggest not only that Milton presupposed the inequality of man and woman but that he was in some repects misogynist; and the textual evidence in *Paradise Lost* itself might appear in several places to bear this out:

> For contemplation he and valor formed
> For softness she and sweet attractive grace,
> He for God only, she for God in him;

> (iv. 297–9)

As early as 1792, in *A Vindication of the Rights of Woman*, Mary Wollstonecraft uses Milton's portrayal of Eve to demonstrate all that is pernicious and debilitating in male preconceptions of the 'feminine'. Commenting brusquely on the passage quoted above, she writes:

I cannot comprehend his meaning, unless, in the true Mahometan strain, he meant to deprive us of souls, and insinuate that we are beings only designed by sweet attractive grace, and docile blind obedience, to gratify the senses of man when he can no longer soar on the wing of contemplation.[2]

The focus of Wollstonecraft's critique is Milton's stress on beauty and submissiveness as requisites for womanhood. More specifically—and with particular pertinence to her discussion of Rousseau and education—she complains that Milton denies to Eve the reasoning powers that would put her on a par with

---

[1] *Political Justice*, 309.   [2] *Wollstonecraft Works*, v. 88.

Adam, and so reduces her to the status of a child. 'Children, I grant, should be innocent; but when the epithet is applied to men, or women, it is but a civil term for weakness.'[3] The infantilization of women by men becomes one of her main targets of attack; but she is habitually shrewd in pointing to the ways in which women collude with men by adopting childlike airs, and so underwrite their own oppression.[4]

Milton inserts himself, thus, into feminist debate. In a work that proves massively influential, Wollstonecraft succeeds in establishing certain key passages in *Paradise Lost* (iv. 634–8; viii. 381–92) as touchstones of misogyny, coupling Milton with Rousseau as the patriarchal enemies of female emancipation.[5] Yet to take Wollstonecraft's reading as the norm in feminist responses to *Paradise Lost* would be to oversimplify the complex history of that poem's reception; for, as Joseph Wittreich has recently argued, there is a powerful counter-tradition, amongst eighteenth-century women readers in particular, which establishes Milton's epic as 'a forging ground for their own ideal of educated and responsible womanhood', and which responds to the contradictions and inconsistencies in Milton's presentation of Eve as puzzles that are 'deftly planted so as to erode the orthodoxies the poem ought to espouse'.[6] Far from being a monster of misogyny, then, Milton is conceived by his early female readership as an 'ally' in the enterprise of 'rising up against the patriarchal tradition of scripture'.[7]

Wittreich's concern is specifically with the place of women in Milton's reception, and I am fully persuaded by his argument that 'in Milton studies women have a history and have had an influence of their own'.[8] My concern, however, in this chapter, will be to establish that those aspects of *Paradise Lost* which mark themselves out as 'contradictory' and 'inconsistent' on the question of gender are as readily appropriable by a sympathetic male readership as they are by women readers. I shall hope to demonstrate, therefore, that there is a *male* line of pro-feminist writing which descends directly from Milton through Pope, and which leads on into the major Romantic poets—Blake, Coleridge, Keats, and even Byron. I shall argue that this tradition is established, not as the result of a conscious political alignment (or revisionary choice) on the part of individual authors so much as through the closely imitative habits of allusion with which this book is predominantly concerned. In other words, I shall be claiming a readiness on the part of Milton's poetic language to 'erode orthodoxies', which is sufficiently strong to establish a pro-feminist sympathy in *Paradise Lost* itself. This can be used to counter the

---

³ Ibid. 89.   ⁴ See esp. *Vindication*, ch. 4.

⁵ In outlining a programme for female education and emancipation, Wollstonecraft makes Rousseau's *Émile* her prime target of attack. The 'captivating' but 'grossly unnatural' character of Sophia is further evidence that Rousseau believes women 'so weak that they must be entirely subjected to the superior faculties of men' (ibid. 93–4).

⁶ J. A. Wittreich, Jr, *Feminist Milton* (Ithaca, NY, 1987), 4, 14.   ⁷ Ibid. 7.
⁸ Ibid., p. ix.

objections raised by Wollstonecraft and others to the evident sexism of Milton's epic narrator.

In Chapter 2, I examined the ways in which the moral equilibrium of *Paradise Lost* could be said to be disturbed, perhaps even subverted, by moments of textual choice; and I claimed for these moments a response on the reader's part which was 'negatively capable'—one, that is, which left indeterminacy intact, rather than opting for either of the two available forms of closure: authoritarian on the one hand and revolutionary on the other. I suggested that the Romantics preserved and prolonged the subversive implications of *Paradise Lost* by imitating Milton's ambiguous poetic modes: his practice, for instance, of drawing together moral opposites, such as Jacob and Satan, or Sin and Eve; and his use of cross-references to dissolve the boundary between fallen and unfallen states. I implied that these conflationary techniques were compatible with Romantic theorizing about the imagination; and I concluded that a reading of *Paradise Lost* which stresses the fortunate fall is not so much a *misreading* as a careful amplification of the ambiguities which Milton himself presents. Continuing this argument here, I want to look in detail at one of the pairs of polar opposites that Milton chooses to conflate—namely, Satan and Eve—concentrating first on the implications of this conflation for *Paradise Lost* itself, then pursuing them further in a number of post-Miltonic poems which centre on the fall of woman.

It is, I shall argue, precisely in the merging of Satan and Eve that the feminist possibilities of *Paradise Lost* reside. Eve is given the same legitimate cause for grievance as Satan, and the same ambitious potential. She can be understood and played on by Satan, because she has within her the yearning for equality that makes him a sympathetic figure. In this respect, Milton considerably expands on the bare ingredients of the biblical account, and might well be seen (as Wittreich puts it) 'rising up against the patriarchy of scripture'. Genesis offers the Fall as a political narrative by exposing the acquisition of knowledge as a bid for power, and it takes for granted the subjection of woman to man. Indeed, the effect of the story, if not its purpose, seems to be to frame Eve as the guilty party, thereby offering a rationalization of her inferior status. But Milton has accentuated the theme of inequality, by creating an important bond between Satan and Eve. The narrative sequence of *Paradise Lost* causes the reader to focus on her subjugation with an interest that is heightened by Satan's fall: inevitably, then, our response to her frustrations and aspirations reflects back on the arch-rebel, for whom our sympathies have already been roused.

As is frequently the case with Milton's indeterminacies, the reader is faced with a choice between what I have earlier called the supertext and the subtext. If we see Milton as to some extent ironizing his early republicanism by using Satan as his mouthpiece, this casts a dubious light on any other kind of egalitarianism the text might imply. If, on the other hand, we see him as maintaining sympathy with the republican cause, we will be ready to see the feminist implications of *Paradise Lost*. In the same way, the reader who makes a connection between

Milton and his authoritarian God is likely to see in *Paradise Lost* a continuation of the Genesis 'framing' of Eve: all the signs of her fallenness before the Fall will then add up to a judgement on Milton's part against woman—an exposure of the incipient sinfulness which causes her to transgress. Her wanton ringlets, for instance, will register authorial disapproval of seductiveness; her similarity to Narcissus will imply vanity; her dream of flying through the heavens with Satan will suggest not just an eagerness to succumb to temptation but an imagination which is already presumptuous and damned. The reader who chooses instead to give the subtext a more generous reading will be drawn into sympathy with Eve's subjection: these signs of fallenness may then be read as the register of her dissatisfaction with the unfallen state, and her striving for liberation. The 'Narcissus' passage will show her imaginative playfulness; it will also prove that she has a self-sufficient life before Adam. The dream of her flight with Satan will show her understandable aspiration, her desire to see as a God sees—her refusal, in other words, to remain content with the place assigned to her by her 'Great Forbidder'.[9]

Milton's republicanism may indeed draw him into unconscious sympathy with Eve's bid for power; but there are equally good reasons for his *choosing* to make her fall more detailed and compelling than Adam's. A reading of the poem which accentuates Eve's imaginative potential is to some extent compatible with the broader and more openly conceived humanism which emerges from Milton's untraditional treatment of the Fall. As I argued in Chapter 2, falling is not just loss but gain; it involves the realization of the self as subject or, in Romantic terms, the emergence of consciousness and imagination. If Eve is more responsible than Adam for their transgression, this is not necessarily to be held against her, as though Milton were the misogynist that cliché would have him be; it can be seen also in terms of the good which will ultimately emerge from the Fall, and which in humanist terms is valued more highly than a 'fugitive and cloister'd virtue'.[10] As Wollstonecraft herself argues, 'innocence' is 'a civil term for weakness': all the possibilities for Eve's strength and emancipation lie, paradoxically, in the resemblance with Satan which makes her fallible, and which therefore allows her to grow toward experience and self-knowledge.

Eve's likeness to Satan was not, however, something that Wollstonecraft perceived. In a footnote commenting on the 'pleasing picture of paradisiacal happiness' which Milton portrays in the conjugal affection of Adam and Eve, she confesses: 'instead of envying the lovely pair, I have, with conscious dignity, or

---

[9] N. Frye traces the mother-centred myths on which *Paradise Lost* draws, concluding that, whereas the father-myth is 'inherently conservative', the mother-centred myth is more naturally revolutionary, and that this shows how near Milton is to 'the mythology of Romanticism'; see 'The Revelation to Eve', in B. Rajan (ed.), *'Paradise Lost': A Tercentenary Tribute* (Toronto, 1969), 46.

[10] For Milton's personification of untested virtue as a woman who 'never sallies out and sees her adversary, but slinks out of the race' see *Areopagitica, Milton Prose*, ii, ed. E. Sirluck (New Haven, Conn., 1959), 515.

Satanic pride, turned to hell for sublimer objects'.[11] This proud and dignified choice significantly indicates Wollstonecraft's radical sympathies, and also the extent of her investment in laying claim to a traditionally 'masculine' terrain.[12] Ironically, however, it sets up a stronger division than there need be between the 'sublime' world of Satan and the 'beautiful' world of Eve, with the consequence that, in Wollstonecraft's reading, the latter is culpably demeaned. *Paradise Lost* itself is not nearly so categorical in the divisions it proposes; indeed, in Milton's ambiguous and flexible language there is constant room for comparison/conflation between different and gendered worlds.

I would be wary of going so far as to argue that *Paradise Lost* is a feminist text, but I am, like Catherine Belsey, interested that it can be laid claim to on both sides of the debate.[13] In recent years, the practice of ideological appropriation has, practically speaking, given to this issue of literary criticism the flavour of a pamphlet war; and it is well to take heed of Diane McColley's warning, that 'whenever we appropriate the poem for our own textual politics, we exploit Eve as text object'.[14] On one side of the debate, critics such as Marcia Landy have seen in Eve an 'excessive curiosity', a 'vulnerability to flattery', and a 'capacity to forget her role as future wife and mother', which evidence Milton's conservative disapprobation of women who refuse to take seriously their function in a system of kinship.[15] On the other side, Barbara Lewalski defends Milton from feminist hostility by claiming that he 'did not make of women either sex objects or mother-figures'.[16] Against all those who complain of Eve's inequality, Lewalski insists that she is given the same education as Adam, an equal share in the work and responsibility of running Eden, and the joint honour and dignity of

[11] *Wollstonecraft Works*, v. 94.

[12] Burke's categories of the sublime and the beautiful are given heavily accented gender alignments, supportive of (and on occasion underwritten by) Milton's division between masculine and feminine characteristics. The following passage especially riled Wollstonecraft: 'so far is perfection, considered as such, from being the cause of beauty; that this quality, where it is highest in the female sex, almost always carries with it an idea of weakness and imperfection. Women are very sensible of this; for which reason, they learn to lisp, to totter in their walk, to counterfeit weakness, and even sickness. In all this they are guided by nature' (*Burke Enquiry*, 110). Wollstonecraft replies in *Vindication of the Rights of Men* (see *Wollstonecraft Works*, v. 45).

[13] See *John Milton: Language, Gender, Power* (Oxford, 1988), 58–60. Belsey contrasts the 'fictional denunciation of Milton's sexism' which emerges from novels such as Robert Graves's *Wife to Mr Milton* and Charlotte Brontë's *Shirley* with feminist appropriations of *Paradise Lost* in recent criticism. Her own reading, like mine, is one in which 'The text can be seen at certain points to exceed the utterances of its own narrative voice'. Cf. R. Corum, 'In White Ink: *Paradise Lost* and Milton's Ideas of Women', in J. Walker (ed.), *Milton and the Idea of Woman* (Urbana, Ill., 1988), 120–47. Corum detects a 'residue' in *Paradise Lost* which makes Milton's epic 'a fallen poem, and of interest to fallen readers'; he aims to recover an invisible Milton 'who hides unrepentantly in the text of Milton's ideological perfection' (ibid. 121).

[14] 'Eve and the Arts of Eden', in Walker (ed.), *Milton and the Idea of Woman*, 101.

[15] 'Kinship and the Role of Women in *Paradise Lost*', *Milton Studies*, 4 (1972), 3–18. Landy concludes that 'Milton is not a misogynist, but he conveys a very clear sense of how the family structure becomes the basis for models of authority, social order, and sanctioned behaviour' (ibid. 17).

[16] 'Milton on Women—Yet Once More', *Milton Studies*, 6 (1974), 3–20.

becoming one of the progenitors of the human race. If anything, she is more important than Adam, Lewalski argues, because she is made 'a type of the Messiah's redemptive love', exonerating man by taking the burden of guilt upon herself.[17]

Such arguments have the air of special pleading, and are less useful than an attempt, such as Susanne Woods's, to discriminate between Milton's inherited cultural assumptions and his personal and political beliefs:

Milton's profound respect for human liberty has the ultimate effect of subverting his patriarchal assumptions. He is too thoughtful to accept cultural assumptions without question, yet he has no frame of reference for responding to biblical authority in this matter. The curious result is that the dignity and intelligence he gives his female characters strains against the inferior social position in which they find themselves.[18]

This analysis seems to me to be sound; and although I would myself wish to place a stronger stress than Woods does on the (possibly involuntary) textual ambiguities which support Milton's unorthodoxy, I shall take her argument as a starting-point for my own, and return to the feminist issues at the end of this chapter. My concern in the mean time will be to demonstrate the continuity of Milton's ambiguous poetic modes, and the perpetuation of interpretative choices for the reader, in a number of post-Miltonic poems—all of them using the 'fall' of woman to explore their writers' concern with female sexuality/ morality, and each in their different way making an important alignment between imagination and the female psyche. Focusing on *The Rape of the Lock*, *Thel*, and 'Christabel', 'The Eve of St Agnes', and Cantos II–IV of *Don Juan*, I will show that complications in these texts break down the notion of a straightforward progression from innocence to experience, thereby replicating the moral and political questions which Milton himself had raised in *Paradise Lost*. Verbal allusions—most of them intricate, complex, and sustained—will show that, for his followers as for Milton himself, the qualifying of opposites creates indeterminacy, which in its turn allows for a sympathetic reading of the Fall.

REPRESSION

> Say what strange motive, Goddess! cou'd compel
> A well-bred *Lord* t'assault a gentle *Belle*?
> Oh say what stranger Cause, yet unexplor'd,
> Cou'd make a gentle *Belle* reject a *Lord*?[19]

[17] Ibid. 9. Lewalski's position is persuasively answered by J. Halley, who argues that female heterosexuality is not natural but socially constructed; and that in *Paradise Lost* 'A prior masculine understanding or meaning both incorporates and transcends the mere imagery of the female figure'; see 'Female Autonomy in Milton's Sexual Politics', in Walker (ed.), *Milton and the Idea of Woman*, 249.

[18] 'How Free Are Milton's Women?', in ibid. 19. 'Far from being a misogynist,' Woods claims, 'Milton was ahead of his time in granting to women a dignity and responsibility rarely conceded in the seventeenth century' (ibid. 15).

[19] *The Rape of the Lock*, i. 7–10.

The serious issues Pope raises in *The Rape of the Lock* are sometimes neglected, and with them the context in which his references to *Paradise Lost* might accrue a significance beyond lexical play. Critics, while being prepared to grant Belinda a measure of dignity, have tended to do so only in limited terms. Emphasizing the power of Pope's imagination in expanding and transforming the world of the 'feminine', they have preserved a suspicion that in itself this world is trivial. Such approaches neglect the powerful study of sexuality and emotional repression which the poem sustains, and in which Milton's treatment of the fall of woman has a subtle and influential part to play.[20]

The answer Pope gives to the opening questions of *The Rape of the Lock* is both moral and psychological. Marriage, between those who are mutually attracted, is the central positive of the poem: it is pride that motivates Belinda's rejection of the man she loves, and the Baron's practical joke on her is a punishment for the sin she shares with Satan and Eve. Pope's attitude to the rape itself is best represented by Clarissa, who advocates a sense of proportion, 'good humour', in the face of loss.[21] The impressiveness of the poem, though, lies not in the urgency of this simple moral, but in the depth given to Belinda herself. Pride, as in *Paradise Lost*, has subtle origins: Pope is interested in sexual politics, in the structures of power and codes of repression which dictate Belinda's behaviour. He takes his reader behind the 'outward Part' of her social world, to uncover the 'craving void left aking in [her] breast'.[22] The presence of Milton plays a crucial part in this process, for it draws attention to one sense at least in which the loss of Belinda's lock might be seen as a fortunate fall.

The curtain rises on a Miltonic tableau. Belinda, asleep and dreaming, is the yet unfallen Eve, whose dream anticipates her temptation and introduces her to post-lapsarian feelings. Ariel, whispering in her ear, is the toad-shaped Satan, who squats beside her and sows the seeds of her fall. Like Satan, he is both inside and outside her 'morning dream'. In the role of 'guardian spirit', he prolongs her balmy rest, conjures the dream into existence, and determines what it contains; in that of fantasy lover, he is part of the dreamwork itself. Glittering and seductive—again like Satan, whose 'dewy locks distilled | Ambrosia' (*PL* v. 56–7)—he tempts Belinda with words that 'ev'n in Slumber caus'd her Cheek to

[20] D. Fairer, by reading the sylphs as allegorical of Fancy, overlooks the fact that Ariel is the guardian of Honour, and so neglects the complexity of Belinda's inner world. Commenting on the scene of Belinda at her dressing table, he observes that its disorder 'may outrage our moral preconceptions and strain decorum to breaking point' but that the disorder is 'fundamentally an imaginative profusion'. Equating Belinda with imagination, Fairer judges both as 'brilliant, unstable, alluring, and independent of morality'; see *Pope's Imagination* (Manchester, 1984), 67, 70. He is thus sensitive to the gendering of imagination which typifies the 18th c., but not to Pope's observation of societal conditioning.

[21] Clarissa does not appear in the 2-canto version of the poem (1712) and, according to a note of Pope's in the 5-canto version (1714), she is 'A new character introduced ... to open more clearly the MORAL of the Poem' (*Pope Poems*, 237).

[22] See Pope's 'Epistle to Miss Blount with the Works of Voiture', l. 55, and 'Eloisa to Abelard', l. 94. Both poems expose the constraints in which woman, the 'suffering sex', remains, offering a psychological reading of female sexuality.

glow' (i. 24). For Milton, blushing and dreaming alike raise important questions, because they register transitional stages and indeterminate states of mind.
Pope too, as Belinda's dream-blush suggests, is interested by the moment of
recognition which turns unconscious transgression into guilt. If blushing were
merely involuntary, who would be surprised by its happening in sleep? When
Pope writes '*ev'n* in slumber' the surprise is there, by implication, because
feelings of shame or guilt are normally the prerogative of the conscious mind.

Minor though it may seem, this detail takes one to a central ambiguity in the
poem. Ariel is not straightforwardly Satan, and the dream he induces is
'tempting' only in a special sense. His role is that of a repressor, rather than a
fulfiller, of sexual desires. 'What guards the purity of melting maids?', he asks,
and the answer is both supernatural ('Tis but their *Sylph*, the wise Celestials
know') and moral, or psychological: '*Honour* is the Word with Men below' (i. 71,
76–7). Ariel stands for internal scruples, which are the expression of external
prohibitions, which in their turn reflect the scruples themselves. Appropriately,
given Ariel's status as guardian, the Satanic references with which his speech
begins are superseded by angelic ones. In parodying the sex life of Milton's
angels—'For spirits, freed from mortal laws, with ease, | Assume what Sexes
and what Shapes they please' (i. 69–70)—and in foretelling Belinda's fate, he is
meant to remind us of Raphael. In addition, there is his witholding of vital
information, 'But Heav'n reveals not what, or how, or where' (i. 111), which is a
witty comment on Raphael's own practice of half-revealing, half concealing,
God's plans. His final words—'Beware of all, but most beware of Man!'
(i. 114)—at once reproduce Raphael's warning and nicely upset for a minute the
crudely authoritarian assumption that Satan and Eve are to blame for the Fall.

Aside from the playfulness of a parodic intention, what can be inferred from
this conflating of Satan and Raphael? One answer comes in *Paradise Lost* itself.
The Argument to Book V tells us that 'to render man inexcusable [God] sends
Raphael to admonish him of his obedience, of his free estate, of his enemy near
at hand; who he is, and why his enemy, and whatever else may avail Adam to
know'. The partial education which follows is an incitement to curiosity, so that
the effect, if not the function, of Raphael's warning is ironically parallel to that
of Eve's Satanic dream. (Whether or not this irony is intended, it incidentally
supports an Empsonian reading of God.)[23] Pope, seeing the implications, has
taken them a stage further, by conflating dream and warning. He plays beauti-
fully on Ariel's ambivalence—'Hear and believe! thy own importance know, |
Nor bound thy narrow Views to Things below' (i. 35–6)—suggesting that
Ariel Satanically excites ambition, whilst also ascetically encouraging the sublimation of desire. (The two impulses are one and the same, in so far as they
crave angelic status as transcendence.) In Canto II, the mode of Ariel's address
to the sylphs is again Miltonically double-edged: 'Ye *Sylphs* and *Sylphids*, to

---

[23] For the 'grisly jokes' played by God on His Angels and on man, see ch. 3 of *Milton's God*
(Cambridge, 1961; repr. 1980).

your Chief give Ear, | *Fays, Fairies, Genii, Elves*, and *Daemons* hear!' (ll. 73–4). For it parodies both the biblical words of God Himself—'Thrones, dominations, princedoms, virtues, powers' (*PL* v. 601)—and their demonic echo in Satan's address to the angels (*PL* v. 772). The recurrence of these patterns of conflation suggests how alert Pope is to Milton's own allusive language. The effect, as in *Paradise Lost* itself, is a dissolving of moral extremes, and their internalization as psychological impulses within Belinda herself. Ariel controls Belinda as both forbidder and tempter: he is, in effect, a fusion of what Blake saw as the opposing principles of reason and desire.

'Those who restrain desire', Blake claims, in *The Marriage of Heaven and Hell*, 'do so because theirs is weak enough to be restrained.' And being so, he went on, 'it by degrees becomes passive, till it is only the shadow of desire. The history of this is written in *Paradise Lost*.'[24] Belinda's restraint takes the form of flirtation: 'Favours to none, to all she Smiles extends, | Oft she rejects, but never once offends' (ii. 11–12). When 'awful Beauty puts on all its Arms' (i. 139), it is at once predatory and passive: the 'purer blush' produced by rouge attracts the male eye with cosmetic freshness, but disguises true sexuality. The petticoat, 'stiff with Hoops, and arm'd with ribs of Whale' (ii. 120) invites male admiration, only to repel it. The locks which hang (more artfully than Eve's wanton ringlets) 'in equal Curls' are nourished 'to the Destruction of Mankind' (ii. 19), at once tempting and prohibiting. Belinda's narcissism recalls Eve in *Paradise Lost* Book IV, worshipping her own image before she knows of Adam:

> A shape within the watery gleam appeared
> Bending to look on me, I started back,
> It started back, but pleased I soon returned ...
>
> (ll. 461–3)

Pope lovingly reproduces Milton's rhythms: 'A heav'nly Image in the Glass appears, | To that she bends, to that her Eyes she rears' (i. 125–6), and he uses the Miltonic suggestion of vanity to expose Belinda's 'sacred Rites of Pride' (i. 128). But from a psychological angle, what interests him most is the 'pining' that 'vain desire' entails (*PL* v. 466). Belinda conceals her genuine feeling for the Baron behind the airs of a coquette, till it becomes, as Blake would put it, only the shadow of feeling.

It is a measure of Pope's 'romantic' faith—a faith, that is, in powerful human emotion—that desire in *The Rape of the Lock* is *not* weak enough to be restrained.[25] As the poem's climax approaches, Ariel, who is guarding

---

[24] *MHH*, pl. 5, ll. 30–4.
[25] The strength of Pope's romanticism is best conveyed in Eloisa's celebration of unrestrained love: 'O happy state! when souls each other draw, | When love is liberty, and nature, law: | All then is full, possessing and possest, | No craving Void left aching in the breast' ('Eloisa to Abelard', ll. 91–5).

Belinda's locks from the Baron, 'watche[s] the ideas rising in her mind'. One
idea gets past his censorship, and inhibitions are at an end:

> Sudden he view'd, in spite of all her Art,
> An Earthly Lover lurking at her Heart,
> Amaz'd, confus'd, he found his Pow'r expir'd,
> Resign'd to Fate, and with a Sigh retir'd.

>   (iii. 143–6)

Pope had cleverly raised the possibility, in Canto II, of reading the Fall as a
triumph of Satanic guile;[26] but a much more troubling interpretation emerges
here. If, as Belinda's 'seducer', the Baron resembles Satan, he is also presented by Pope as God's agent in punishing her for her pride: in which case,
the rape does indeed depend (to resort to the classic response of sexist judges)
on the complainant's 'asking for it'. This potentially unsympathetic reading
should not be ignored simply on the grounds that one wishes Pope to be
single-mindedly sensitive to the feminist issues involved. His commitment is
to undoing codes of repression, and to establishing an equality of desire which
is disallowed by the social mores of his time. This takes him, as it later does
Blake, into areas which inevitably make the modern reader squeamish;[27] but it
also allows him to explore a double focus in the issues involved.

According to the poem's overarching system of values, then, the Baron reads
Belinda correctly, and in taking the lock asserts the primacy of human feeling.
As if to underline the moral message, Clarissa hands him the scissors: one
could have no clearer indication that the 'rape' itself is to be viewed as a
fortunate fall. Pope's subtlety, however, depends on an expanding of sympathy
for Belinda that is in tension both with the poem's moral and with one's own
sense of proportion. The language moves deftly from Miltonic parody at
l. 150—'Fate urg'd the sheers, and cut the *Sylph* in twain, | (But airy substance
soon unites again)'—to the tragic finality of loss: 'The meeting Points the
sacred Hair dissever | From the fair Head, for ever and for ever!' (iii. 153–4).
The triviality of the literal event throws into relief its intensity on figurative
and allusive levels. Tillotson's note rightly acknowledges the sense in which,
at this point especially, Pope is writing 'about life and death';[28] but one should
not forget the sexual dimension, which deepens and darkens as Belinda's
'Screams of Horror rend th'affrighted Skies' (iii. 156). In *Paradise Lost*, there
is twice a connection in Milton's mind between falling and giving birth: first

---

[26] ll. 29–32.

[27] See esp. *Visions of the Daughters of Albion*, pl. 7, where Oothoon celebrates free love by
imagining herself using 'silken nets' and 'traps of adamant' to catch girls for Theotormon, watching
'their wanton play | In lovely copulation, bliss on bliss' (ll. 198–201). The passage causes equal
discomfiture in male and female readers. See B. Webster, 'Blake, Women and Sexuality', in D.
Miller, M. Bracher, and D. Ault (eds.), *Critical Paths: Blake and the Argument of Method* (Durham,
NC, 1987), 223–4; and D. Fuller, *Blake's Heroic Argument* (New York, 1988), 47.

[28] *The Twickenham Edition of the Poems of Alexander Pope*, gen. ed. J. Butt (11 vols., London,
1961–9); ii, *'The Rape of the Lock' and Other Poems*, ed. G. Tillotson (London, 1940; repr. 1966), 179.

when Eve tastes the apple, and again at the moment of Adam's fall. In each case, it is Nature who registers human pain:

> Earth trembled from her entrails, as again
> In pangs, and nature gave a second groan,
> Sky loured and muttering thunder, some sad drops
> Wept at completing of the mortal sin
> Original;

(ix. 1000–4)

In much the same way, in Pope, the skies enact Belinda's suffering—'affrighted', as she is, but also 'rent' by her screams of terror, as though in sympathy for her violation. All the brutality happens metaphorically and by inference, just as in Canto V it takes place on the level of allusion: '*Restore the Lock!* she cries; and all around | *Restore the Lock!* the vaulted Roofs rebound' (v. 103–4). Pope's imagination has returned here to the rape of Sin by Death in *Paradise Lost* Book II: 'I fled, and cried out Death; | Hell trembled at the hideous name, and sighed | From all her caves, and back resounded Death' (ll. 787–9). Taken in conjunction with *The Rape*'s more jocular tones, Belinda's reaction seems absurd. But Pope's allusive language allows him to laugh at her for her vanity, while sympathizing in the language of implication.

Pope's parody of the classical underworld in Canto IV complements his imitation of Eve's dream in Canto I. He uses both to explore the unconscious, and to make observations about repression. The Cave of Spleen contains figures that are at once allegorical and true to life (Spleen, Affectation); but in addition there are more fantastical figures who enact the return of the repressed: 'Men prove with Child, as powerful Fancy works, | And Maids turn'd Bottels, call aloud for Corks' (iv. 53–4). Pope's sympathy is even-handed, presenting male and female frustration as two sides of a single coin. Condemned, by women's refusals, to control their sexuality, men fantasize about being with child themselves. Women, meanwhile, are forced by the societal code of honour to play hard to get; but their sexual desires (as the innuendo suggests) function crudely and healthily in the liberated world of the unconscious. This scene allows Pope, more explicitly than anywhere else in the poem, to answer his opening questions: the gentle belle rejects the lord because she is trained in the art of repression; the well-bred lord assaults the gentle belle because his procreative urge must be fulfilled.

Pope returns from the unconscious as he brings Canto IV to an end. Belinda's lament shows the helplessness and repining of an immediately post-lapsarian state:

> For ever curs'd be this detested Day,
> Which snatched my best, my favourite Curl away!
> Happy! Ah ten times happy, had I been,
> If *Hampton-Court* these eyes had never seen!

(iv. 147–50)

The echo of Adam's lament to Eve in *Paradise Lost* Book IX—'O might I here | In solitude live savage, in some glade | Obscured' (ll. 1084–6)—is both comical and touching, for something of the depth of Miltonic regret is carried over in the language: 'Oh had I rather unadmir'd remain'd | In some lone Isle, or distant *Northern* Land' (iv. 153–4). But despite his evident sympathy, Pope probably intends us to see Belinda's refusal of experience as mistaken and regressive. This is implied in the allusion itself, which recalls Adam indulging the sin of despair by contemplating suicide; and it is later made explicit, by Clarissa, when she advocates a responsible acceptance of mortality and loss:

> But since, alas! frail Beauty must decay,
> Curl'd or uncurl'd, since Locks will turn to grey,
> Since painted, or not painted, all shall fade,
> And she who scorns a Man, must die a Maid;
> What then remains, but well our Pow'r to use,
> And keep good Humour still whate'er we lose?

> (v. 25–30)

There can be no doubt that this is the proper attitude to fallenness, both in Pope's terms and in those of *Paradise Lost* itself. Adam reaches this level of acceptance only after Michael has shown him what the fallen world contains; Eve achieves it with him as they leave paradise hand in hand. Clarissa is in literary terms a Michael figure, in that she offers Belinda the education Adam underwent, but her wisdom comes also from experience, and the voice she uses is Pope's own.

My reading of *The Rape* has concentrated on the poem's inner world of psychology, morals, and sexuality, rather than its outer world of society, behaviour, and manners. The limitations of reading exclusively in this way are evident if one turns to the closing lines of Belinda's speech in Canto IV: 'Oh, hadst thou, Cruel! been content to seize | Hairs less in sight, or any Hairs but these!' (iv. 175–6). The innuendo reminds one that loss of virginity, which I have been treating as an event, 'happens' only on the level of implication and allusion. The lines are shocking, partly because they are a spoken acknowledgement of sexual need, partly because they pin-point the hypocrisy on which Belinda's sexual morality depends. She has been trained by a society concerned with public appearances, not private morals: it is reputation, rather than chastity, that matters to her most. In arguing for a Miltonic reading, I do not wish to overlook the satire on manners and morals which Pope is evidently offering. I do, however, wish to acknowledge different (and perhaps competing) levels in the poem. Milton's presence provides a genuine 'subtext' for *The Rape of the Lock*, in that it opens up the world of Belinda's unconscious: this allows for a sympathetic portrayal of her individual predicament, alongside a more general satire on the fragile values ('honour', 'virtue') of which she is both the representative and the unwitting victim.

STASIS AND PROGRESSION

Blake's *Thel* and Coleridge's 'Christabel' were written within a single decade, and at the far end of the century which saw the publication of the extended *Rape of the Lock*.[29] Their use of female consciousness and sexuality to explore the mind's potential for liberation has behind it a weight of authority, for during the intervening years there is a marked tendency in English poetry to equate imaginative activity with the feminine.[30] This tradition, for which Pope is partly responsible, can be traced back to *Paradise Lost*. As Diane McColley observes, 'Eve embodies and performs the process that Milton elsewhere attributes to Poetry itself'; she is 'the special carrier of fancy, which is both subsequent and precedent to understanding', and she 'figures forth Milton's own art'.[31] As one might expect of Enlightenment thinking, there is a suspicion, even mistrust, of the world of imagination, which is powerfully conveyed in eighteenth-century male poets' use of the female gender to signal wayward or uncontrollable creative activity.[32] Romanticism turns this mistrust to revisionary ends, exploiting more recent connections between the feminine and Revolution to place female consciousness at the centre of a programme for humankind's emancipation: a

[29] *Thel* was written in 1789–90, and 'Christabel' pt. i in 1797–8 (pt. ii was composed in 1800).

[30] S. Gilbert and S. Gubar stress the negative and mostly biological associations of creativity with the feminine; see *The Madwoman in the Attic: The Woman Writer and the Nineteenth-Century Literary Imagination* (New Haven, Conn., 1979), 30–4. Their study goes back to Spenser's Error and Duessa (and to Milton's Sin) as precursors of Swift's monstrous and disgusting females; Pope's Dulness, on the other hand, is seen as de-creative—symbolizing 'the failure of culture, the failure of art'. A counter-tradition is, however, discernible: in e.g. Pope's praise for the 'quick poetic eyes' of the Muse in *The Rape of the Lock* (v. 24); in Collins's portrayal of Fancy (see my discussion of 'Ode on the Poetical Character' in Ch. 7); and in Akenside's description of the creative mind (*The Pleasures of Imagination*, iii. 380–1). For a discussion of the association between women and imagination during the 18th c., see Fairer, *Pope's Imagination*, 82–112.

[31] 'Eve and the Arts of Eden', 103. Cf. J. M. Webber, 'The Politics of Poetry: Feminism and *Paradise Lost*', *Milton Studies*, 14 (1980), 3–24. Webber argues that 'subjectivity is seen in *Paradise Lost* as a female characteristic, and external knowing as a male one. Eve's first act is to contemplate herself, and Adam's to contemplate the heavens' (p. 19).

[32] According to Fairer, Pope's ambivalence toward imagination is registered in a characteristically Enlightenment mistrust of fiction. A century later, Wordsworth's distinction between imagination and fancy shows itself to be equally the product of Enlightenment thinking. Imagination (un-gendered, but clearly masculine) is 'conscious of an indestructible dominion'; while fancy (explicitly female) is 'unstable and transitory'. The latter has 'winning' characteristics: she is 'capricious ... surprising, playful, amusing, tender, and ludicrous'; and she 'prides herself upon the curious subtilty and the successful elaboration with which she can detect ... lurking affinities'; see 'Preface' to *Poems* (1815), in *Wordsworth*, 636. A parallel for Wordsworth's distinction might be made, in Locke's implicitly gendered discrimination between judgement and wit; see *An Essay Concerning Human Understanding*, ed. with introd. P. H. Nidditch (Oxford, 1975), 156.

programme which begins with the 'mind-forg'd manacles' of authoritarian and patriarchal morality.[33]

Despite the evident literary developments and political transformations which have taken place since the publication of *The Rape of the Lock*, there is a striking continuity in the way Pope and his Romantic successors make use of Eve. Both Blake and Coleridge explore sexuality in terms of the complex relation between innocence and experience, and both suggest a tension between attitudes to falling. *Thel* does so in the framework of myth, rather than in the social context offered by Pope. It does not, therefore, negotiate problems such as reputation; though it implies much about the inner world of the female psyche in which inhibition plays an important part, and examines the complex ways in which sexuality is constructed by conventions and expectations.[34] 'Christabel', on the other hand, makes playful use of the Gothic mode, to mediate between the 'private' world of the psyche (Part I) and the 'public' world of family relations (Part II). Blake's and Coleridge's female protagonists offer contrasting perspectives on innocence: Thel is like Belinda, in that she refuses the humanity that Experience would give her; while Christabel moves out of stasis, into a higher, though more painful, consciousness. Yet both poets (albeit with a slightly different perspective from Pope's) suggest qualified preference for the 'fallen' over the 'unfallen' state.

In *Thel*, the emergence of a 'fortunate fall' pattern is achieved by setting up Miltonic expectations only to disappoint them. Leaving behind the daughters of Mne Seraphim, and seeking 'in paleness the secret air', Thel seems at first to be a version of Eve, wandering away from Adam to find a workspace of her own—an assertion of independence which Milton sees as as foreshadowing the Fall.[35] Like Eve, she is also curious. The insistent questionings which take up Plates I and IV do not openly acknowledge dissatisfaction with Edenic life, but they betray a curiosity that is inappropriate to the existence she might otherwise be leading: 'Is this a worm? I see thee lay helpless and naked weeping, | And none to answer, none to cherish thee with mother's smiles' (pl. iv, ll. 79–80).

---

[33] R. Paulson argues that two opposite categories of femaleness are connected with Revolution by Burke and subsequently deconstructed by Wollstonecraft. Marie Antoinette offers 'an image of passive beauty' that Burke can approve, whereas he recoils from the 'horrible, ugly, violent, agressive women ... of the Parisian mob who march to the royal palace and bring back the king and queen—women who in effect *are* the Revolution'; see *Representations of Revolution (1789–1820)* (New Haven, Conn., 1983), 81–2. Shelley exploits this woman-as-revolution paradigm in *The Cenci*, and also places female consciousness at the centre of the revolutionary process in *Prometheus Unbound*.

[34] The Matron Clay indoctrinates Thel with stereotypical ideas of passive, fulfilling motherhood, but as B. Webster argues, these are undermined by the threat of death posed by the lily and the clod; the poem thus points to 'the implicit degradation and forced submission of the woman' ('Blake, Women and Sexuality', 223).

[35] As I showed in Ch. 2, the words 'Thus saying, from her husband's hand her hand | Soft she withdrew' (*PL* ix. 385–6) are clearly anticipatory of the moment of the Fall itself: 'So saying, her rash hand in evil hour | Forth reaching to the fruit, she plucked, she ate' (*PL* ix. 780–1). Depending on the degree of fortunateness which readers assign to falling, Milton's dramatic irony can be read either in terms of an authorial disapproval of female independence or as the reverse.

Adam and Eve, when they question Raphael, want to know how the universe works, and his answers are educational, as well as an encouragement to devotion. Thel's enquiries are more probing: they suggest, even before she has experienced them, an awareness of pain, suffering, and the injustice of God's ways. The function of the clod of clay is to condition Thel towards an acceptance of the inequality of women, specifically in their maternal role. 'My bosom of itself is cold and of itself is dark', says the Matron Clay, on behalf of her weeping child, the worm, 'But he that loves the lowly pours his oil on my head' (pl. iv–v, ll. 86–7). The message is one that Raphael would have approved: the ways of God, it suggests, cannot be comprehended; finite beings can only wonder at the mystery of Grace: 'But how this is, sweet maid, I know not and I cannot know, | I ponder, and I cannot ponder; yet I live and love' (pl. v, ll. 91–2).

As in Milton, this question-and-answer sequence is designed to lead the interlocutor to a better understanding. But (again as in Milton) the invitation to accept God's ways seems like a disguised temptation to know more. Pope, similarly perceiving the irony of Raphael's likeness to Satan, had used it to create an ambivalent Ariel, who was both forbidder and tempter. Blake's use of conflation has rather different implications. The clod of clay is given affinities with Milton's instructing angels, and at the same time with Satan himself, because experience in its own right is what is being valued. At stake here is both the meekness of acceptance and the maturity and ripeness it implies. When Thel says:

> That God would love a worm I knew, and punish the evil foot
> That wilful bruised its helpless form. But that he cherished it
> With milk and oil I never knew, and therefore did I weep

> (pl. v, ll. 95–7)

the Matron Clay judges her to be ready for experience. (Michael does the same, when he has finished instructing Adam in the suffering which the fallen world contains.) 'Wilt thou, O Queen, enter my house', Clay continues, '' tis given thee to enter | And to return. Fear nothing; enter with thy virgin feet' (pl. v, ll. 102–3). Plate V ends, in this way, with a sort of temptation. What Thel is being offered (like Adam in Book XII) is the chance to realize her humanity by entering the fallen world.

Plate VI is a masterpiece of Miltonic conflation. 'The eternal gate's terrific porter lifted the northern bar' (l. 104), it begins, invoking Sin, porter of hell gates, as she opens them for Satan in Book II of *Paradise Lost*: 'Thel entered in', it continues, extending the parallel, 'and saw the secrets of the land unknown' (l. 105). For a moment, Thel's identity merges with that of Satan, poised on hell's brink and looking into 'The secrets of the hoary deep, a dark | Illimitable ocean without bound' (*PL* ii. 891–2). At this point, double allusion begins to complicate the pattern:

> She saw the couches of the dead, and where the fibrous roots
> Of every heart on earth infixes deep its restless twists—
> A land of sorrows and of tears where never smile was seen.

(ll. 106–8)

Milton fuses Sin with Eve;[36] Blake merges Satan with Adam. Confirming patterns of allusion which began to appear in Plate V, the language takes one back to *Paradise Lost* Book XI, and to Michael's bleak prophecy of sickness and death:

> Immediately a place
> Before his eyes appeared, sad, noisome, dark,
> A lazar-house it seemed, wherein were laid
> Numbers of all diseased ...
> Dire was the tossing, deep the groans, despair
> Tended the sick busiest from couch to couch;

(ll. 477–80, 489–90)

This vision is offered to Adam as a forewarning of what the fallen world contains; and he, despite the future's grimness, leaves paradise with a sense of the world before him. Blake conflates him with Satan because what both figures share is a threshold experience in which forward movement demands courage. Both of them accept the challenge; for Thel, on the other hand, fears of sex and mortality intervene.

   Wandering first in a land of clouds (as Satan had through chaos—'wander' is a fallen word) she sees evidence of death, as opposed to the transience which puzzled her in the vale of Har. Chancing next on her grave, she is horrified by the voice of sorrow which comes back to her as an echo , but which speaks from an older and darker perspective than her own:

> Why cannot the ear be closed to its own destruction,
> Or the glistening eye to the poison of a smile?
> Why are the eyelids stored with arrows already drawn,
> Where a thousand men in fighting ambush lie?

(pl. vi, ll. 114–16)

These questions form a sequence, enacting the progress of a relationship and climaxing in a sexual fall: 'Why a tender curb upon the youthful burning boy? | Why a little curtain of flesh upon the bed of our desire?' (pl. vi, ll. 122–3). Thel's revulsion from death accompanies fear of sexuality; but beyond this there is dissatisfaction with sex itself. The tender curb and curtain of flesh create impediments to fulfilment. They are fallen humanity's disguise of its own desires.

   The last lines of the poem reverse Miltonic expectations, as Thel draws back in horror from experience, into the security of innocence prolonged: 'The Virgin started from her seat, and with a shriek | Fled back unhindered till she

[36] See Ch. 2.

came into the vales of Har' (ll. 124–5). She might be compared, at this moment, to three Miltonic figures, each of whom achieve a dimension through experience which is unavailable to her. Most obviously, she is an antithetical version of Eve: an Eve who becomes scared at the last minute, and will not bite the apple. But she also resembles a fearful Satan, turning down the challenge of Chaos; and an Adam who is afraid of mortality, choosing instead to retreat into the safety of a Paradisal world. This tripling of resemblance suggests an underlying concern in Blake with the idea of growth through experience: a concern that cuts through conventional moral boundaries, and transcends the categories (paradise/earth; heaven/hell) used to symbolize them. Read in isolation, the text might be taken straightforwardly as a critique of, or warning against, the limitations of innocence. But the dark and negative associations of the experienced state are proleptically implied in the final plate; and when the poem is read in conjunction with its sequel, *Visions of the Daughters of Albion*, it becomes apparent that Blake is deeply divided on the central issue. Thel's counterpart in the later poem, Oothoon, goes further than she does, daring to 'pluck the flower' of experience, rather than remain embalmed in her virgin state. But she falls prey to an exploitative system of male values, and to codes of sexual morality which thwart her potential for liberation.[37] The later text casts a shadow over the early one, in much the same way as the *Songs of Innocence* are problematized by their experienced counterparts.[38] One is left, in *Thel*, with a sinister underlying awareness of inadequacies in the Matron Clay's understanding of the world of generation, and with a sense that her reassurances are not to be trusted.

Christabel is quite the opposite of Thel: indeed, the Blakean figure she more closely resembles is Oothoon, in that she embraces the world of experience as an inevitable stage of growth. Her fall, though it depends on a Satanic catalyst, is voluntary in the same sense as Eve's; and, within the context of Part I, it promises also to be 'fortunate', however odd that statement might later appear. Coleridge's critics, distracted by the poem's incompleteness, have failed to see that Miltonic patternings make sense (even if not unity) of its separate halves. In the form of a Gothic tale, Part I perfectly complements 'The Ancient Mariner': that is, it offers a female version of events leading up to the fall, with complexities of psychology and motivation included. Part II goes on to deal with the consequences of having fallen—what it actually feels like to be living in 'a world of sin', with no evident means of undoing the mind-forged manacles of experience, and thereby winning through to redemption.

Coleridge follows *Paradise Lost* in making his heroine an ambiguous figure. Like Eve, she is oppressed by prolonged innocence—'The spring comes slowly up this way' (l. 22)—and like Eve, she wanders off alone—conscious, as the

---

[37] The outrage of Oothoon's rape by Bromion is compounded by Theotormon's jealous possessiveness towards her, which reduces her to an object. Despite attempts at liberation, Oothoon remains entrapped by male fantasies until the final plate (see n. 27).

[38] The shadowing of innocence by experience, a distinctly Miltonic phenomenon, is discussed in Ch. 6 as a function of subjectivity.

words 'a furlong from her father's gate' remind us, of the beginnings of transgression. The sexual aspect of her adventure is touched in lightly, with the reference to 'her lover that's far away' (l. 30). And though it is no more than a momentary flicker of cross-reference, one notices that the dreams she had 'all yesternight' (l. 27) resemble Eve's.[39] Jonas Spatz has drawn attention to the lines Coleridge erased from the poem before publication—'Dreams that made her moan and leap | As on her bed she lay in sleep'—which suggest, as he puts it, that 'they have upset, confused, and perhaps erotically stimulated her'.[40] They are not projected (so far as we know) by a Satanic figure, as in Milton and Pope; but in some sense they initiate the fall. Their effect on waking life, too, has Miltonic overtones. When Coleridge writes 'She stole along, she nothing spoke, | The sighs she heaved were soft and low' (ll. 31–2), he is suggesting a state of anxiety that is carried over from dream. One recalls the 'tresses discomposed', 'glowing cheek', and 'startled eye' with which Eve awakes, after having gone through all the motions of her fall in an unconscious state (*PL* v. 10, 26).

The use of Miltonic hints and undertones encourages in the reader a questioning frame of mind. If Christabel's innocence is already qualified, then hers is not a world of moral polarities, black against white, but of more indeterminate shades of grey. With this in mind, one approaches the poem's temptation scene expecting something more subtle than pure seduction. The stage is set, allusively, for a repeat of Satan's dalliance with Eve: 'Hush, beating heart of Christabel! | Jesu, Maria, shield her well!' (ll. 53–4) And when Geraldine is discovered behind her tree, she fulfils Satanic expectations: the tactile eroticism of her bare neck and arms is quickened by the visual detail of her blue-veined, unsandalled feet; and the 'gems entangled in her hair' (l. 65), glamorous enough in themselves, might also be a sign of nobility or former riches. (They glitter wildly: Coleridge uses the word 'glitter', as in 'The Nightingale' and 'The Ancient Mariner', to signal access to experience that is exciting and compelling.) Geraldine is as sexy as Satan himself—and as overtly so; but her gender causes an unsettling of the expectations which are normally brought to bear on a seductive scenario.[41]

To suggest that Geraldine is at once Satan and Christabel's fallen other is not for a minute to detract from the plausibility of lesbian or vampiric interpretations.[42] It is, rather, to opt for a symbolic rather than a literal approach. Looked at from a broad perspective, the design of Part I can be seen as reflecting Coleridge's lifelong preoccupation with polarities. For here we have a symbolic

---

[39] See *PL* v. 28–135.

[40] 'The Mystery of Eros: Sexual Initiation in Coleridge's "Christabel"', *PMLA* 90/1 (Jan. 1975), 112.

[41] A mischievous rumour circulated in Coleridge's lifetime, that Geraldine was a man in disguise.

[42] R. Basler discusses 'the traditionally sexual mystery of vampires, lamias, mermaids, fairies, elves, and witch-women in general' in *Sex, Symbolism, and Psychology in Literature* (New Brunswick, NJ, 1948); for his analysis of 'Christabel', see esp. 33–40.

enactment of that reconciliation of opposites on which all his thinking depends. 'EVERY POWER IN NATURE AND IN SPIRIT', he writes in *The Friend*, '*must evolve an opposite, as the sole means and condition of its manifestation:* AND ALL OPPOSITION IS A TENDENCY TO REUNION.'[43] Or, as Boehme puts it, in a passage which influenced not only Coleridge but clearly also Blake: 'A thing that has only one will has no divisibility. If it finds not a contrary will, which gives occasion to its exercising motion, it stands still.'[44] Meanwhile, on an allegorical level which is consistent with these larger implications, the poem is an account of falling as growth. Christabel is trapped in a Thel-like stasis, Geraldine is the experienced older self she must become: 'Stretch forth thy hand (thus ended she) | And help a wretched maid to flee' (ll. 102–3).

Preceded by a pause, the momentous line 'Then Christabel stretched forth her hand' (l. 104) takes one to the climax of Eve's fall—the actual moment of plucking the fruit. But, true to Miltonic practice, Coleridge makes this only one in a sequence of lapses before her final transgression at the end of Part I. The next occurs at the castle gate:

> They crossed the moat, and Christabel
> Took the key that fitted well;
> A little door she opened straight,
> All in the middle of the gate;
> The gate that was ironed within and without
> Where an army in battle array had marched out.

> (ll. 123–6)

Coleridge's imagination, returning to *Paradise Lost* Book II, re-creates the most famous and most echoed of threshold experiences: 'the gates wide open stood, | That with extended wings a bannered host | Under spread ensigns marching might pass through' (*PL* ii. 884–6). Following Milton's own conflationary patterns, he has made Christabel into a fusion of Sin and Eve: Sin, who opens hell gates, to let Satan into chaos: 'Thus saying, from her side the fatal key, | Sad instrument of all our woe she took' (*PL* ii. 281), and Eve, whose fall Sin verbally foreshadows: 'So saying, her rash hand in evil hour | Forth reaching to the fruit, she plucked, she ate' (*PL* ix. 780–1). Geraldine, by implication, is the Satan who leaves hell, voyages through chaos, enters paradise, and destroys the happiness it once held. Or rather, she is the Satan who is *about* to do all that: part of the power of this moment depends on the potentiality it contains.

The doubleness of the allusion is important: in suggesting a Duessa aspect to Christabel herself, and in preparing the reader for further ambiguities. As the

---

[43] *The Friend; Collected Coleridge*, iv, ed. B. Rooke (2 vols., Princeton, NJ, 1969), i. 94 n.

[44] Quoted by T. McFarland, *Romanticism and the Forms of Ruin: Wordsworth, Coleridge, and Modalities of Fragmentation* (Princeton, NJ, 1981), 324.

narrative continues, innocence and experience draw ever more closely together. Christabel becomes active and seductive—offering Geraldine hospitality, carrying her (like a husband his newly wed wife) over the threshold, leading her upstairs to her bedroom, giving her cordial wine, and leaning up in bed to watch her undress. Geraldine, meanwhile, is passive in relation to Christabel; but in her effect on her surroundings she is vital and energetic:

> The brands were flat, the brands were dying,
> Amid their own white ashes lying;
> But when the lady passed, there came
> A tongue of light, a fit of flame

(ll. 156–9)

In the seduction scene itself, Coleridge dramatizes the poignancy of Satanic fallenness. When Geraldine 'in wretched plight [sinks] down upon the floor below', she feels the indignity of Satan's transformation in *Paradise Lost* Book X:

> His visage drawn he felt to sharp and spare,
> His arms clung to his ribs, his legs entwining
> Each other, till supplanted down he fell
> A monstrous serpent on his belly prone,

(ll. 511–14)

This Ovidian metamorphosis repeats itself, once just before the seduction, when Geraldine bows, rolls her eyes round slowly, and draws in her breath, and again in Part II, when she and Christabel turn into snaky forms, mirroring each other. Waldock has seen the serpent scenes in Milton as part of his 'systematic degradation' of Satan: what Blake defined as the weakening of desire.[45] Coleridge may well be repeating the pattern, in the sense that Geraldine's alluring qualities are diminished by this revelation of the reptile behind her disguise; but compassion makes this more than straight humiliation. As the scene continues, her real resemblance is to an earlier, more tragic Satan than the hissing serpent of Book X. She reveals herself as fallen but remorseful: compelled, like Satan or Rivers, to repeat her own fall through another, but compelled against her better instincts:

> Deep from within she seems half-way
> To lift some weight with sick assay,
> And eyes the maid and seeks delay;
> Then suddenly, as one defied,
> Collects herself in scorn and pride,
> And lay down by the Maiden's side!—

(ll. 257–62)

---

[45] See A. J. A. Waldock, *'Paradise Lost' and its Critics* (Cambridge, 1947), ch. 4; *MHH*, pl. 5.

Satan's moment of abstraction from evil, 'stupidly good' in the face of Eve's purity, could not be more movingly re-created.[46] Coleridge has taken over Milton's practice of qualifying innocence, humanizing evil, and thus abolishing moral extremes.

The Conclusion to Part I is a commentary on the narrative so far, drawing attention to Miltonic practices of this kind. Different stages of the female fall are telescoped into a single night, and images of innocence and experience are juxtaposed, so as to suggest mirroring and conflation. We begin with two images of Christabel—one recalling her in the wood before she has met Geraldine, the other describing her asleep in Geraldine's arms. An act of recollection thus presents the unfallen state from a fallen point of view. Christabel, 'kneeling in the moonlight, | To make her gentle vows' (ll. 284–5), offers an image of innocence which is qualified, first by the agitation of her heaving breast, then by the reference to her being 'resigned to bliss or bale' (l. 288)—passively accepting, that is, rather than (like the lady in *Comus*) resisting; and finally by the careful observation, 'And both blue eyes more bright than clear | Each about to have a tear' (ll. 290–1). For Milton, tears are fallen: after her dream in Book V, Eve 'silently a gentle tear let fall | From either eye, and wiped them with her hair' (*PL* v. 130–1); and in the closing lines of the poem, both Adam and Eve drop 'natural tears' but 'wipe them soon' (*PL* xii. 645). Christabel, too, learns to weep through falling. In this first stanza, she is 'about to have a tear', but by the penultimate one she is shedding 'large tears that leave the lashes bright!' (l. 316). Her fall propels her into 'a world of sin', but, as in Milton, one of the richest compensations is to be found in these 'gracious signs of sweet remorse'.

The transition is made in a single night. 'Asleep and dreaming fearfully' (l. 293), Christabel has access to experience—not just proleptically, like Eve, but actually, since she is 'Dreaming that alone which is' (l. 295). Coleridge has taken Milton's implications one stage further here, bringing dream true as a literal enactment rather than a narrative anticipation of the fall. (Keats is to do the same, in 'The Eve of St Agnes', of which more later.) As this transition occurs, Coleridge conflates innocence and experience on other than temporal levels. Roles are reversed when, during the night, Geraldine 'seems to slumber still and mild, | As a mother with her child' (ll. 300–1), while Christabel shows all the agitation of a fallen being. But in the morning, Christabel is calmer and quieter, the mirror image, it seems, of her fallen other self:

> Her limbs relax, her countenance
> Grows sad and soft; the smooth thin lids
> Close o'er her eyes; and tears she sheds—
>
> (ll. 313–15)

---

[46] See *PL* ix. 444–72.

In Part II this mirroring process will climax with Bard Bracy's vision of innocence and experience inveterately convolved: the bright green snake coiled around the dove, and the two moving in a single motion:

> Green as the herbs on which it couched,
> Close by the dove's its head it crouched;
> And with the dove it heaves and stirs,
> Swelling its neck as she swells hers!

> (ll. 551–4)

Part I, meanwhile, is complete in itself: a reading of *Paradise Lost* which follows and expands its indeterminate poetic modes.

AWAKENING

'The Eve of St Agnes' takes 'Christabel' as its model but is, if anything, more ambiguous. Coleridge had dealt with dual aspects of one self and one sex. Keats, dividing his focus between Madeline and Porphyro, complicates the fall with two versions of sexuality that are superimposed. He also produces a range of contrapuntal effects—structural, imagistic, narrative—which alert the reader to double implications. W. J. Bate has written of the poem's 'ebb and flow of emerging contrasts and partial resolutions'.[47] No doubt these should be seen as Spenserian also, but one is strongly reminded of the oscillations and conflations in *Paradise Lost*. When examined in this context, specific Miltonic echoes (of which there are a surprising number, in a poem which supposedly marks Keats's momentary abandonment of Milton[48]) have the effect of highlighting ambivalence. The reader is invited, at rhetorical as well as other levels, to make interpretation negatively capable.

Madeline's innocence, like Eve's and Christabel's, is qualified before her 'fall' begins, by the reference to her as one 'Whose heart had brooded, all that wintry day, | On love' (ll. 43–4). The wish-fulfilment on which her fall depends has already started working. As she dances along, 'with vague regardless eyes | Anxious her lips, her breathing quick and short' (ll. 64–5), she seems more eager, and less furtive, than Christabel; but the two figures have in common a degree of sexuality which seems prematurely experienced. Porphyro is equally ambivalent. This emerges, not in psychological observations, but through conflicting literary parallels. Narrative expectations set him up as Romeo, while verbal allusion insists repeatedly that he is Satan. He enters the poem as a Romance hero, coming 'across the moors' with the apparently innocent wish to gaze at his lover and worship her 'all unseen' (l. 80). But as he 'ventures in' to the castle, he transforms it, in his frightened imagination, into a place 'whose chambers held barbarian hordes, | Hyena foemen, and hot-blooded lords' (ll. 85–6). The poetry deals playfully with fancy's gothicizing

---

[47] *John Keats* (Cambridge, Mass., 1964), 442.   [48] Ibid. 438–9.

power, but at the same time the phrase 'mansion foul' (l. 89) takes one to Milton's hell, introducing unmistakable implications. Like Satan, Porphyro carries hell around with him: it is a state of mind.

The reader has, I think, to bear in mind the possibility of an ironic perspective, achieved through the cumulative pressure of multiple allusions, before dismissing as Keat's own the obvious voyeurism of the central scene. If Satanic references are present, and if Jack Stillinger is right in adding to them connections with Richardson's Lovelace,[49] then one is faced with two recognizably Miltonic problems: how moral a significance to give them, and how to restrict the power of the Satanic perspective, once it has started working. If we begin to identify in Porphyro a Satanic attractiveness, does this mean we collude with the trickery he performs? Alternatively, if we do not acknowledge the Satanic perspective, are we missing the poet's own attempt to ironize and so contain his power? The reading I offer is more generous than it perhaps ought to be towards Porphyro: one of the issues this raises is the extent to which, in male accounts of seduction, Miltonic allusion invites a collusive attitude on the part of the reader.

Keats is not interested, to the extent that Coleridge had been, in expanding on Milton's sympathy for tragically fallen compulsion. Porphyro's resemblance to Satan adds drama and poignancy to the moments leading up to Madeline's fall: 'She seemed a splendid angel, newly dressed, | Save wings, for heaven. Porphyro grew faint; | She knelt, so pure a thing, so free from mortal taint' (ll. 223–5). And there is no mistaking the heightened erotic excitement which this Satanic dimension brings:

> Stol'n to this paradise, and so entranced,
> Porphyro gazed upon her empty dress,
> And listened to her breathing, if it chanced
> To wake into a slumbrous tenderness;

> (ll. 244–7)

But the Miltonic allusions do not suggest, as in the case of Geraldine, a sensibility tortured by envy, regret, remorse. Keats's focus is elsewhere, on the erotic impulse itself. One cannot imagine Satan feeling embarrassed or guilty at the thought of sex. (Milton reserves that particular human touch for Raphael and Eve.) But when Porphyro, in his earlier conversation with Angela, first conceives of the stratagem that will allow him to see Madeline naked and alone, he blushes: 'Sudden a thought came like a full-blown rose, | Flushing his brow, and in his pained heart | Made purple riot' (ll. 136–8). Following Milton, Keats makes blushing both the register, within innocence, of experience to come, and the memory, by experience, of innocence that is past. Just as Eve's blush

---

[49] J. Stillinger, 'The Hoodwinking of Madeline: Scepticism in "The Eve of St Agnes"', *Studies in Philology*, 58 (July 1961), 533–55. In addition to Porphyro's resemblance to Lovelace, Stillinger notes parallels with Satan; he points out that Porphyro as 'up to no good' and likens him to a 'peeping Tom and villainous seducer' (pp. 540, 546).

suggested a conflation between her fallen and unfallen selves, so the language of Porphyro's wish erotically anticipates its fulfilment: 'Into her dream he melted, as the rose | Blendeth its odour with the violet, | Solution sweet' (ll. 320–2). Sexuality blurs the borderline between reality and dream, as though thought itself could be transgression.

Geraldine, thoroughly Satanic, had mirrored and heightened Christabel's fall by painfully repeating her own. Porphyro, on the other hand, seems to go through his own transition from quasi-innocence into experience, giving a double focus to the seduction. As Madeline rises 'like a missioned spirit, unaware' (l. 193), then enters her bedroom, 'like ring-dove frayed and fled' (l. 198), we are seeing her through Porphyro's eyes. Her sexuality—passive and victimized—is a male projection. Once in the room, however, a more complicated dual perspective begins to emerge: 'Out went the taper as she hurried in; | Its little smoke, in pallid moonshine, died. | She closed the door, she panted' (ll. 199–201). Her own erotic expectancy reasserts itself, in images which suggest, at one and the same time, fulfilment (the sexual innuendo of 'died' may be intended) and suppressed or frustrated desire:

> But to her heart, her heart was voluble,
> Paining with eloquence her balmy side,
> As though a tongueless nightingale should swell
> Her throat in vain, and die, heart-stifled, in her dell.

(ll. 204–7)

While Madeline kneels at her prayers, 'so free from mortal taint', the window casement—with its 'stains and splendid dyes', and its shielded scutcheon blushing with 'blood of queens and kings' (ll. 212, 215)—reflects an inner taintedness which might be Porphyro's or her own. She undresses with a sort of artless seductiveness: first unclasping her warmed jewels one by one, next loosening her fragrant bodice, and last (though still 'by degrees') letting her rich attire 'creep rustling to her knees' (ll. 229–30). The voyeuristic presence of Porphyro makes this rather more like a strip-tease than it ought to be: perspectives are muddled, so that we do not know whether to see Madeline's innocence or experience as projection.

Miltonic echoes multiply as the seduction is about to occur. Porphyro steals to the bedside 'Noiseless as fear in a wide wilderness' (l. 250)—bringing with him, into 'this paradise', the post-lapsarian world. He tempts Madeline with 'spiced dainties' (l. 269), as Satan in the wilderness had tempted Christ—Keats's imagination, here, returns to *Paradise Regained* rather than *Paradise Lost*[50]—and he whispers in her ear, just as Satan had whispered in Eve's. The song he sings is itself a temptation to transgress, for it suggests to the sleeping Madeline that she might be 'La belle dame sans merci', and have him in thrall. Roles reverse themselves, as in the climax of 'Christabel' Part I, but where Christabel plays an

---

[50] See esp. *Paradise Regained*, ii. 340–67.

active role in the seduction, it is Madeline's unconscious that gives access to her experienced self. Her dream anticipates, and therefore, in a Miltonic sense, *is* her fall. The awakening from it sounds like sexual climax: 'she uttered a soft moan. | He ceased—she panted quick—and suddenly | Her blue affrayed eyes wide open shone' (ll. 294–6). Despite the magic of the moment, full consciousness has about it the air of post-coital tristesse:

> Her eyes were open, but she still beheld,
> Now wide awake, the vision of her sleep—
> There was a painful change, that nigh expelled
> The blisses of her dream so pure and deep.
> At which fair Madeline began to weep,
> And moan forth witless words with many a sigh

> (ll. 298–303)

All the details here, from the sharpness of 'a painful change' down to the weeping and moaning (this latter, particularly, reminding one of Geraldine)—imply not just sexual experience but post-lapsarian consciousness. Yet Madeline is still, in a technical and literal sense, virgin.

Keats's famous comment, 'The imagination may be compared to Adam's dream—he woke and found it truth',[51] has had a misleading effect on readers of 'The Eve of St Agnes'. For the temptation has been to move quickly on, past the complexities of Madeline's disappointed awakening, and into Porphyro's simpler fulfilment, both of Keatsian dictum and of himself. It has therefore not been noticed that the four stanzas dealing with dream and waking (xxxiii–xxxvi) are a careful conflation of two quite separate dream sequences in *Paradise Lost*. The first belongs to Eve, and occurs in Book V, the second to Adam in Book VIII. Milton himself sets up a number of parallels and contrasts between the two, and these prepare the way for Keats's treatment.

'With tresses discomposed, and glowing cheek, | As through unquiet rest', Eve recounts her dream to Adam:

> methought
> Close at mine ear one called me forth to walk
> With gentle voice, I thought it thine; it said,
> Why sleep'st thou Eve? ...
> I rose as at thy call, but found thee not.

> (*PL* v. 10, 35–8, 48)

When she wanders off, looking for Adam, he is replaced by Satan, who stands close to the tree of knowledge—'fair it seemed, | Much fairer to my fancy than by day' (ll. 52–3)—his dewy locks distilling ambrosia. The temptation follows, with its clear verbal anticipations—'He plucked, he tasted' (l. 65); its excitement of the senses—'the pleasant savoury smell | So quickened appetite, that I,

[51] Keats to B. Bailey, 22 Nov. 1817; *Keats Letters*, 37.

ought, | Could not but taste' (ll. 84–6); and its account of the fall itself, envis-
aged by Eve's Satanic imagination as a flight through the heavens. Finally, still
in the dream, we are returned to earth and sleep as a transition into wakefulness:

> wondering at my flight and change
> To this high exaltation; suddenly
> My guide was gone, and I, me thought, sunk down,
> And fell asleep; but O how glad I waked
> To find this but a dream!
>
> (ll. 89–93)

The reassurance offered by Adam, in the theory of dreams he goes on to pro-
pound, is shaky. Dramatic irony darkens his hope 'That what in sleep thou didst
abhor to dream, | Waking thou never wilt consent to do' (ll. 20–1); and in any
case the reader responds to Eve as already, in an important sense, fallen. When
Milton goes on to evoke repentance—'So cheered he his fair spouse, and she
was cheered, | But silently a gentle tear let fall | From either eye, and wiped
them with her hair' (ll. 128–31)—he is anticipating the poem's ending: 'Some
natural tears they dropped, but wiped them soon' (*PL* xii. 645). Whatever his
intention, the effect is to confirm one's sense of an equation between dream and
fall. [52]

Adam has two dreams in quick succession. In the first, an apparition comes, as
Satan did to Eve, seemingly 'of shape divine', and guides him 'over fields and
waters, as in air | Smooth sliding without step', up a woody mountain into Eden
(viii. 295–303). The Satanic parallel persists, as each tree stirs him with 'sudden
appetite | To pluck and eat' (ll. 308–9). But it ends, as he wakes to find 'all real,
as the dream | Had lively shadowed' (ll. 310–11), and discovers his guide to be
in truth 'Presence divine' (l. 314). His second dream comes soon after, still as
part of the same sequence:

> Abstract as in a trance methought I saw,
> Though sleeping, where I lay, and saw the shape
> Still glorious before whom awake I stood,
> Who stooping opened my left side, and took
> From thence a rib,
>
> (viii. 462–4)

Eve is created, in all her perfection, only to disappear like the guide in her own
dream. But when Adam wakes, 'To find her, or for ever to deplore | Her loss'
(ll. 479–80), his earlier experience is repeated: 'behold her, not far off, | Such as
I saw her in my dream' (ll. 481–2). Twice running, he finds reality to be an
extension of dream, the Platonic substance in place of its shadow. This is in
direct contrast with Eve, who, twice running (once within her dream and once

[52] Frye claims that, because she is unfallen, 'Eve's dream can only come from outside her, though
. . . she is troubled to think that it may have proceeded from her own mind. She is right by anticipation'; see 'The Revelation to Eve', 19.

outside it), wakes to find the person she expected replaced by someone else. No matter how emphatically she reassures her husband ('O how glad I waked | To find this but a dream'), he knows, and we know, that Satan's power has begun to encroach on his. The untidy hair and flushed cheek—anticipations of later fallenness (ix. 887 and x. 910)—are telling registers of 'offence and trouble, which [her] mind | Knew never till this irksome night' (v. 34-5).

To summarize Milton's position briefly: Adam's unconscious has access to an ideal, Eve's to a fallen world. Where he rejoices in the freshness of imagination, she is saddened by her awareness of a split between the imagined and the real. Keats plays on these contrasts in the climactic stanzas of his poem, building carefully, first of all, on the parallels between Madeline and Eve, then touching in the momentary likeness of Porphyro and Adam. When Madeline wakes, she finds and does not find the person she expected:

> 'Ah, Porphyro!' said she, 'but even now
> Thy voice was at sweet tremble in mine ear,
> Made tuneable with every sweetest vow,
> And those sad eyes were spiritual and clear.
> How changed thou art! How pallid, chill and drear!
>
> (ll. 307-11)

The remembrance of her dream's intensity leaves her feeling cheated by the actual. Like the unfallen Eve, she achieves experience through dream; and like the fallen Eve she longs for a return to her former state: 'Give me that voice again, my Porphyro, | Those looks immortal, those complainings dear!' (ll. 312-13). Her pleading contains in addition an even later and darker note: 'Oh, leave me not in this eternal woe', she moans, 'For if thou diest, my love, I know not where to go' (ll. 314-15). This has all the plangency of Eve's lament—'Forsake me not thus, Adam'—which is uttered in despair, with an awareness of betrayal and death, as far on as *Paradise Lost* Book X:

> bereave me not,
> Whereon I live, thy gentle looks, thy aid,
> Thy counsel in this uttermost distress,
> My only strength and stay: forlorn of thee,
> Whither shall I betake me, where subsist?
>
> (ll. 918-22)

Keats's imagination produces cross-references and prolepses that are truly Miltonic: Madeline, still technically inexperienced, has by stanza xxxvi undergone, not just feelings of anticlimax, loss, regret, but fears of loneliness, desertion, bereavement.

Porphyro, by contrast, has all the fulfilment attributed to Adam when he wakes to find his dream come true:

> Beyond a mortal man impassioned far
> At these voluptuous accents, he arose,
> Ethereal, flushed, and like a throbbing star
> Seen mid the sapphire heaven's deep repose;
> Into her dream he melted, as the rose
> Blendeth its odour with the violet,
> Solution sweet—
>
> (ll. 316–22)

Not 'into *his* dream', as one might expect from a more sceptical poet, but 'into *her* dream he melted': this is indeed, as John Jones puts it, Keats's dream of love.[53] The moment, for all its macho confidence, is more interesting than that implies. For it is at once deeply affirmative and honestly aware of the fragility which is every dream's cost: 'meantime the frost-wind blows | Like Love's alarum pattering the sharp sleet | Against the window-panes; St Agnes' moon hath set' (ll. 322–4). The abruptness of the last half-line is vital. Within a single stanza, Keats makes reality correspond to dream, then punctures the illusion by coming sharply back to the actual. ''Tis dark', he continues, 'quick pattereth the flaw-blown sleet. | "This is no dream, my bride, my Madeline!"' (ll. 325–6). In Miltonic terms, Eve's experience of reality has in the end displaced Adam's achievement of the ideal. As Walter Jackson Bate puts it, 'a dream—like Innocence—cannot be lived in the world without being violated; and yet, whatever is lost, actual happiness is impossible without an awakening from dream to reality'.[54]

The poem's ending, however, is more ambiguous than Bate's comment will allow, in that it shows the lovers sustaining their dream while they go out into the world. If Keats is being deliberately ironic, then the blandishments Porphyro offers to Madeline, as he persuades her to elope—'Say, may I be for ay thy vassal blest? | Thy beauty's shield, heart-shaped and vermeil dyed?' (ll. 335–6)—are meant to sound like hollow anachronisms from Spenserian romance; and his reassurance that outside is only 'an elfin-storm from fairy land' (l. 343) is supposed to have the air of make-believe.[55] Furthermore, when the lovers make their 'darkling way' downstairs, they transform the castle (as Porphyro had done on entering) into a setting from the *Arabian Nights*: 'there were sleeping dragons all around, | At glaring watch, perhaps, with ready spears' (ll. 353–4). For all its charm, there is something faintly ridiculous in the perpetuation of fantasy which these details imply. They do, however, prepare the way for an affirmation which is not ironic at all: 'And they are gone—aye, ages long ago | These lovers fled away into the storm' (ll. 370–1). As they pass out of the poem's frame, Madeline and Porphyro achieve legendary status. The sudden use of perspect-

---

[53] *John Keats's Dream of Truth* (London, 1969), 239.   [54] *John Keats*, 446.
[55] For a discussion of allusions to Merlin, which make Porphyro both a figure and a victim of enchantment, see K. J. Harvey, 'The Trouble about Merlin: The Theme of Enchantment in "The Eve of St Agnes"', *Keats–Shelley Journal*, 34 (1985), 83–94.

ive—'aye ages long ago' makes them seem immeasurably distant, but at the same time permanent and clear.

They are Adam and Eve, with the earth all before them.[56] But the previous stanza associates them also with Satan as he stands on the threshold of hell. The iron porch, and the porter 'in uneasy sprawl', are not Miltonic; yet there can be no doubt of the verbal echoes as the gate opens to let them through: 'By one, and one, the bolts full easy slide; | The chains lie silent on the footworn stones; | The key turns, and the door upon its hinges groans' (ll. 367–69). Even in its smaller details, Keats's memory has retained the description of hell gate, opened by Sin:

> then in the key-hole turns
> The intricate wards, and every bolt and bar
> Of massy iron or solid rock with ease
> Unfastens: on a sudden open fly
> With impetuous recoil and jarring sound
> The infernal doors, and on their hinges grate
> Harsh thunder,
>
> (*PL* ii. 876–82)

This allusive conflation of paradise and hell is something already encountered, in Milton, Coleridge, and Blake. In each case, what draws Satan and the fallen humans together is a sense of affirmation. As they make their transition from one world into another, they 'evolve their own greatness',[57] to use Coleridge's phrase. The threshold itself, whatever its moral context, becomes a symbol for this growth of inner power.

In 'The Eve of St Agnes', however, the moment of affirmation is short-lived. A punishing realism shatters the stanza and brings the poem to an end, as Angela the old dies 'palsy twitched, with meagre face deform', and the beadsman sleeps for ever 'among his ashes cold' (ll. 376; 378). The Miltonic passage Keats has in mind (and it is marked in his copy of *Paradise Lost*) is Adam's vision in Book XII of the death and woe he has brought into the world:

> all maladies
> Of ghastly spasm, or racking torture, qualms
> Of heart sick agony, all feverous kinds,
> Convulsions, epilepsies, fierce catarrhs,
> Intestine stone and ulcer, colic pangs ...
> Dropsies, and asthmas, and joint-racking rheums.
>
> (ll. 480–4, 488)

Blake also had invoked these lines, but keeping intact an important Miltonic structure: Thel's vision of sickness and mortality was offered *to* her, as it was to Adam, in order to warn her of what the fallen world contained. It was on the basis of this warning, this foreknowledge, that she decided (*un*like Adam) to

---

[56] See the closing lines of *PL*.   [57] *Romantics on Milton*, 245; see also my Ch. 2 and its n. 74.

retreat into the vales of Har. Keats takes more liberties with his source: only the reader is aware of death, which enters the poem after the lovers have gone. Its presence is not a warning to them, causing them to accept or refuse full humanity, but a warning to us not to mistake their optimism too easily for Keats's own. If we are to see the poet as remaining broadly true to the values embodied in a Miltonic structure, then it must partly be at the expense of the lovers themselves. Belinda and Thel are pathetic for their regression, Madeline and Porphyro for the touching naïvety of their hope. They flee away into the storm (instead of back into the vales of Har), oblivious of what the fallen world will bring.[58]

Does Keats intend us to see dream surviving, beyond the poem's frame, as an immunity to the actual? And if so, how does this reflect on his recurrent thinking about reality and art? The perpetuation of the lovers' fantasy world, right up to their departure, suggests an ironic stance, and this in turn implies a higher valuation of the real than of the imagined. But the legendary status they achieve as they cross the threshold is a reminder that their fantasies are symbolically related to the poet's own. One is reminded here of the consolation Pope offers Belinda at the end of *The Rape of the Lock*—a consolation based on the poet's faith in the eternizing properties of his art. It seems, then, that Keats finds himself in a familiar situation: divided between affirming art and mistrusting the escape it implies. One may initially feel tempted to respond to the words 'fled away' as though they betrayed the poet's final stance, but this instinct is checked by what follows. Angela's palsy-stricken death causes one to shrink back, as though from the withering gaze of Apollonius, into the comfort of the lovers' hope, even whilst acknowledging the forlornness of that hope in the face of mortality. It is this tension between opposite impulses, typically Keatsian, that gives the final stanza its open-endedness: no matter how many times one reapproaches the text, both possibilities coexist.[59]

THE REALITY PRINCIPLE

Byron shares with Keats a dualism that runs deeper than the irony and satire which are its formal vehicles. He was, as the narrator of *Don Juan* puts it, 'born

---

[58] In an illuminating article, D. Wiener argues that Porphyro brings Madeline 'out of a limbo-like world of innocence into the world of experience where at least some possibility for growth and fulfilment exists'; see 'The Secularization of the Fortunate Fall in Keats's "The Eve of St Agnes"', *Keats–Shelley Journal*, 29 (1980), 126. The limitations of this argument stem from Wiener's neglect of ironies which play over the text, suggesting that the lovers are constructing their own escapist fictions.

[59] A. K. Mellor, in *English Romantic Irony* (Cambridge, Mass., 1980) writes of Keats's 'delicate hovering between commitment and distrust', and of the poem's 'delicate balancing of romance with disbelief' (pp. 77, 95). T. Rajan, examining 'The Eve of St Agnes' alongside 'Lamia' and 'Isabella', claims that 'What is puzzling about these poems is their emotional indeterminacy, their lack of a clear rhetoric of fiction which will enable us to clarify them as either sentimental or ironic in tone, as either romantic or anti-romantic. Instead they seem to be ironic and sentimental at the same time, to deconstruct and yet to cling to the illusion'; see *Dark Interpreter: The Discourse of Romanticism* (Ithaca, NY, 1980), 101.

for opposition'.[60] The full depth of this dualism emerges when his poetry is at its most vulnerable: straining, that is, towards the idealism of High Romantic Argument, only to collapse upon itself; and in this respect the Juan–Haidee love story is famously, quintessentially, 'Byronic'. The dream of love-as-paradise which is offered in Cantos II–IV is as naïvely hopeful as Porphyro's or Lycius's; but it is also as self-knowingly fragile, and as tragically doomed. We watch Byron in the process of creating it, then we watch it disintegrating, partly through the intensity of hope with which it is invested, and partly through its resistance to the reality principle against which it must be measured, if it is to survive. Byron does not believe, any more than Keats does, that love's privacy and absoluteness are preservable against the encroachments of a public world, or against the passage of time: as Juan and Haidee transfer their relationship from the primitive into the civilized domain, it suffers a sea-change as destructive as that hinted at in the closing stanzas of 'The Eve of St Agnes', or later fully described in the tragic finale of 'Lamia'. More troublingly, Byron feels with Keats an underlying mistrust of love, particularly in its sexual dimension. Whereas in 'Lamia' this mistrust is powerfully registered through Miltonic symbolism (the snake as emblem of treachery, specifically and erotically female), in *Don Juan* it is more subtly diffused through a range of perspectival and narratorial devices. These have their origin in *Paradise Lost*; and their parodic flavour throws into relief Byron's problematic relation to the Edenic ideal.

The love of Juan and Haidee is ironized by its position of belatedness within the poem's narrative sequence. When Juan wakes from his 'damp trance' half way through Canto II, he has already been through an exciting love affair with a married woman, not to mention a dangerous shipwreck, from which he is lucky to have escaped with his life. Haidee, by contrast, is the untouched child of nature, whose existence has so far has been limited by her father's protectiveness. The 'first and passionate love' which 'stands alone,│Like Adam's recollection of his fall' (Canto i, stanza 127), and which has been tasted by Juan, is therefore yet to be known by the unfallen Haidee. This introduces a discrepancy of perspective and experience between the lovers, analogous to that which interests Keats. Throughout the episode, an underlying awareness of Juan's past hovers uneasily in the background of the paradisal theme, qualifying any claims that might be made for equality and absoluteness of love betwen hero and heroine ('But Juan, had he quite forgotten Julia?│And should he have forgotten her so soon?' (ii. 208)). As a result, one reads Cantos II and III much as one reads 'The Eve of St Agnes', noting that, while Juan (like Porphyro) has a relatively simple second taste of paradise, Haidee is like Madeline, losing everything for a dream of love.

An oscillation between 'innocence' and 'experience' is to some extent discernible in the gender alignments discussed above; but as in all the texts which this chapter analyses, there is nothing so simple as binary opposition. Miltonic

[60] Canto xv, st. 22.

devices and topoi, embedded in Byron's narrative, have the effect of cutting across such straightforward divisions, producing ambiguities in several directions at once. Juan, for instance, bringing a touch of libertinism into the paradisal world that Haidee inhabits, clearly ought to resemble Satan/ Lovelace/Porphyro in his seductive appeal and his destructive potential. But Byron offsets this fallen dimension by suggesting his resemblance to the newly created and dreaming Adam: 'as he gazed, his dizzy brain spun fast | And down he sunk, and as he sunk, the sand | Swam round and round, and all his senses passed' (st. 110). The language, lightly parodic, prepares us for Juan's Miltonic awakening from dream to truth: 'And slowly by his swimming eyes was seen | A lovely female face of seventeen' (st. 112). It is as though experience could be altogether undone, and consciousness returned to the Adamic stage at which it first became aware of its sensations and recognitions. This process of erasure or effacement is in keeping with *Don Juan* as a whole, which, in challenging literary and ethical conventions, aims to undercut the expectation that 'our hero' will undergo a programme of moral education along developmental lines—or even that he will develop morally at all. For, as Jerome McGann reminds us, '*Don Juan* is not a poem that develops, it is a poem that is added to. *Don Juan* attacks the organic concept of *development*—a word which never appears, in any form, in the poem.'[61] Byron's use of Miltonic language has a comically incongruous effect, given the stripping away of educational assumptions which it accompanies.[62]

Haidee's 'innocence' is similarly complicated by her likeness to Eve—a likeness which is quickly and confidently suggested, in Byron's focus on the 'clustering hair' which 'nearly reached her heel' (st. 116). Byron goes beyond Milton, however, in suggesting something more than merely 'wanton' in Haidee—a powerful sexual attractiveness, which links her with Satan the tempter, and makes her inherently, rather than incipiently, treacherous:

> Her hair, I said, was auburn, but her eyes
> Were black as death, their lashes the same hue,
> Of downcast length, in whose silk shadow lies
> Deepest attraction, for when to the view
> Forth from its raven fringe the full glance flies,
> Ne'er with such force the swiftest arrow flew.
> Tis as the snake late coiled, who pours his length
> And hurls at once his venom and his strength.
>
> (st. 117)

As in 'Lamia', fear of female sexuality registers mistrust of love: Haidee is seen here, not through the eyes of the sleeping Juan, but by the narrator himself, who clearly anticipates that the desecration of paradise will be an inevitable outcome

---

[61] '*Don Juan' in Context* (Chicago, 1976), 60.

[62] For Shelley's handling of a sentimental education which fails to be truly educative, see my discussion of 'Alastor' in Ch. 7.

of sex. Haidee, through her associations with sin, death, and deadly power, is framed as the cause of this desecration, despite her virginal status.

Further to confuse 'innocent' and 'experienced' perspectives, Byron goes on to contrast Juan's dreamless sleep with the lonely and restless night spent by Haidee, whose tossings and tumblings, startings and stumblings (st. 138) recall Eve's Satanic dream, in *Paradise Lost* Book IV. Just as Eve is given proleptic access to fallen consciousness, so Haidee is put in touch, through nightmare, with Juan's shipwrecked past (here symbolic of his first 'fall'). On waking, she registers the dawn of erotic experience with a 'feverish flush', which dyes her cheek with 'headlong blood, whose race | From heart to cheek is curbed into a blush' (st. 141). Like Eve, Belinda, and Madeline, she is at once innocently overcome by involuntary sexuality and guiltily conscious (as the 'curbing' suggests) of a limit that has been already transgressed. Juan, meanwhile, remains palely and serenely oblivious of the tumultuous experience he has undergone, as of the vicarious suffering he introduces into Haidee's world: 'There like an infant Juan sweetly slept' (st. 143).

Byron, like Keats, supplies a dual focus on love, through alternating points of view: Juan is infantilized by Haidee ('hushed as the babe upon his mother's breast'), while Haidee is etherealized and aestheticized by the awakening Juan: 'her voice was the warble of a bird, | So soft, so sweet, so delicately clear | That finer simpler music ne'er was heard' (st. 148, 151). Here, as in 'The Eve of St Agnes', irreconcilable perspectives ironize each other, implicitly exposing the fictitious basis of love: its projectionist fantasies, its fragile hopes. But Byron goes further than Keats, adding a third view which subjects the idealism of both lovers to open ridicule, much as Clarissa had introduced proportion and good humour into *The Rape of the Lock*. On a dramatic level, this view is represented by Haidee's maid, Zoe, who cooks two breakfasts in a row for the ravenous Juan, and whose homely practical presence deflates the atmosphere of exclusivity, intensity, and unreality surrounding the lovers. On a narrative level, meanwhile, it is represented in the remarks of Byron's jaundiced persona, who punctures the idealistic pretensions of his Miltonic story-line with reminders of a (somewhat sordid) here and now: 'Let us have wine and woman, mirth and laughter, | Sermons and soda water the day after' (st. 178).

The broad truth of Hazlitt's comment on Byron that he 'hallows in order to desecrate'[63] is never more evident than in this episode of *Don Juan*. Yet the comment is inadequate, for it overlooks the two-way process of mock-epic, and opts for bathos as the dominant side of the poetic equation. In practice, Byron's poetry is more equivocal than Hazlitt allows, tending either to be genuinely oscillatory or to suggest opposing impulses that are subtly and carefully

---

[63] According to Hazlitt, Byron has 'prostituted his talents': he 'hallows in order to desecrate, takes a pleasure in defacing the images of beauty his hands have wrought, and raises our hopes and our belief in goodness to Heaven only to dash them to the earth again, and break them in pieces the more effectively from the very height they have fallen'; see *The Spirit of the Age*, ed. E. D. Mackerness (London, 1969), 122.

poised.[64] His Romanticism, thrown into relief by the irony which subjects it to critique, builds up an intense investment in the power of love to create a paradisal world:

> They feared no eyes nor ears on that lone beach,
>> They felt no terrors from the night, they were
> All in all to each other. Though their speech
>> Was broken words, they thought a language there,
> And all the burning tongues the passions teach
>> Found in one sigh the best interpreter
> Of nature's oracle, first love, that all
> Which Eve has left her daughters since her fall.
>
> (st. 189)

For all the 'desecration' to which it is subjected, this paradise is allowed to remain intact, as a *fictional* ideal. The reader who lets irony deflate it altogether will be oblivious to the tragic thread which runs through the Haidee–Juan episode, and which gathers momentum as the lovers' dream of happiness is first prolonged and finally destroyed. The reader, however, who knowingly keeps irony at bay (conscious of its destructive potential, but temporarily suspending disbelief) will be ready to accept as genuine Byron's romantic investment in the sanctity of love, even while observing its distinctly literary flavour:

> And now 'twas done; on the lone shore were plighted
>> Their hearts. The stars, their nuptial torches, shed
> Beauty upon the beautiful they lighted.
>> Ocean their witness, and the cave their bed,
> By their own feelings hallowed and united;
>> Their priest was Solitude, and they were wed.
> And they were happy, for to their young eyes
> Each was an angel, and earth Paradise.
>
> (st. 204)

If Byron's bathos is not intended to dispel romantic idealism, there is none the less a darkening of mood at the end of Canto II, where threatening suggestions begin to introduce themselves into the narrative: suggestions of a possessiveness in Haidee which is frighteningly intense (st. 196–7); of an exclusivity in sentimental attachment, which might be unhealthy (st. 198); of a 'lovely and fearful' absoluteness in women, which turns them into 'tigers' when they are rejected (st. 199); and of an injustice in the treatment of women by men, which perpetuates their emotional and social inequality (st. 200). These suggestions, projected onto Haidee by the experienced consciousness of the nar-

---

[64] In this respect, Byron is the clearest exemplar of romantic irony, as defined by Schlegel. Mellor writes: 'Philosophical irony is ... the necessary prerequisite and counterforce to love and imagination. It criticizes and thus negates one's excessive commitment to the fictions of one's own mind, thereby enabling one to sustain contact with reality' (*English Romantic Irony*, 11).

rator, can scarcely be retracted with the assurance that 'Haidee was Nature's bride and knew not this'.[65] They intrude into the paradisal atmosphere, preparing us for Canto III, where Byron will turn his notes to tragic, and show the inevitable disintegration of love as it moves into the public domain.

Some philosophical musings on women and marriage, with a mischievous digression about Milton's hypocrisy in praising wedded love, open the new canto; then, in imitation of *Paradise Lost* Book IV, Byron focuses on the Satanic figure of Haidee's father, Lambro, whose function will be to enter and destroy the by now 'false' paradise in which Juan and Haidee are living. With a sudden shift of perspective at stanza 15, we are led back into the narrative through Lambro's consciousness: identifying with his homecoming, with the defamiliarization he experiences at being an outsider, and with his alienation and anger, on perceiving that 'home' has been transformed by the young couple into a pleasure-house for the indulgence and exhibition of their feelings. Lambro stands on the margins of a hymeneal scene, as much the envying and excluded observer as Satan. But his *symbolic* function is to expose the falsity and hollowness of an Eden that is already 'lost', rather than to gaze on a purity that is yet to be destroyed. As the bearer of authority, law, and morality, Lambro is indeed closer to Keats's Apollonius than to Milton's arch-fiend. The scene he contemplates bears a resemblance not so much to Adam and Eve 'Imparadised in one another's arms' before the fall (*PL* iv. 506) as to the glowing banquet room in which Lycius and Lamia sustain the final hours of their love, before its baseless fabric collapses under the withering gaze of reason.[66]

Lambro's perspective is vital to Byron's dramatic purpose, in that it provides an external measure of the socialization which has eroded the foundations of Haidee's and Juan's love:

> Meantime the lady and her lover sate
> At wassail in their beauty and their pride.
> An ivory inlaid table spread with state
> Before them, and fair slaves on every side;
>
> (iii. 61)

Their opulence, their dependency, their display of material finery, their public exhibition of intimacy, provide a shocking contrast with the primitivism of Canto II. If Byron 'hallows in order to desecrate', it is here that desecration is most painfully apparent: in the betrayal of private ideals to public values. The moral point behind his satire (at least partially an attack on marriage and high society) would be straightforward, if it were not for the oscillatory narrative method that he chooses to adopt. Having dwelt for some length on the sybaritic indulgence of the lovers, he puts Lambro's perspective carefully to one side, and

[65] For the desecrating power of prognostications made from an experienced perspective, see Ch. 6.

[66] 'Lamia', pt. ii, ll. 170 ff.

re-enters the narrative in Canto IV, adopting the lovers' point of view. This counterpointing of perspectives allows for the maximum tragic sympathy to be extracted from the situation, for the lovers are at this stage stripped of all the public paraphernalia which had surrounded them, and are re-seen in an intimate setting which recalls Canto II: 'they were alone once more; for them to be | Thus was another Eden' (iv. 10).

Byron's narrative now becomes a history of loss: a history as weighted with premonitions as Milton's epic, and equally sensitive to the internal shifts of consciousness by which the presence and pastness of happiness are measured:

> I know not why, but in that hour tonight
>   Even as they gazed, a sudden tremor came
> And swept, as 'twere, across their heart's delight ...
>   And thus some boding flashed through either frame
> And called from Juan's breast a faint low sigh,
> While one new tear arose in Haidee's eye.
>
>   (iv. 21)

Successively projecting onto the lovers an awareness of doom, then retracting it for fear of destroying their illusion, the narrator mediates between innocent and experienced perspectives. His use of Miltonic devices implies that the fall is not an external threat, but an inner tendency. Juan is shaken in his sleep by a nameless 'something'; while Haidee's nightmare, deftly and comically conflating Eve's dream with Adam's, suggests a transitional area between the imagined and the real. In sleep, the face of Haidee's dead lover begins to merge with the features of a father she thinks dead; and she wakes to find some truth in what the dream had 'lively shadowed' (*PL* viii. 311): Lambro stands over her, replacing Juan in her waking consciousness, as disappointingly and reprovingly as Adam replaces Satan for the waking Eve. 'High and inscrutable' (st. 39), his symbolic status is that of the covering cherub who refuses access to happiness—the Great Forbidder, who punishes by inducing a sense of sin. His very presence is sufficient to destroy the dream of love.

'All is Eden or a wilderness' (st. 54). Here, effectively, the narrative of Haidee comes to an end; for, as in 'Lamia', there can be no return to fantasy once the reality principle has triumphed. Paradise has been lost, and the narrative moves swiftly and dramatically towards its inevitable conclusion. The lovers, severed by Lambro, go their separate ways: Juan into the domain of recovery and future relationships; Haidee, first into the madness which marks her refusal to relinquish dream, and then into the death which insulates her from further pain. The choice that Byron makes on her behalf is evidently a protective one ('She was not made | Through years or moons the inner weight to bear'), resembling Thel's flight into the vales of Har. The course chosen for Juan is, by contrast, risk-taking and experiential: if not accepting the value of loss, then at least

having cognizance of a life that continues outside Eden. In the gender alignments with which this episode closes, Byron plays out the central dualism of his
narrative mode. Values which sustain ironic consciousness are here figured as
masculine (acceptance, maturity, continuity, proportion) while in the feminine
is epitomized all that is 'tragic' or 'serious' (absoluteness, imbalance, fear).
Between these different and gendered values, Byron's poetic voice does not itself
make a final choice, but rather, 'a pendulum betwixt a smile and tear',[67] continues to negotiate its tense and oscillating path.

FEMINIST IMPLICATIONS

Milton drew a parallel between Satan and Eve. He stressed that both were
subjected to an arbitrary hierarchical code, and he made this a key factor in the
temptation's success—its effect being to draw Satan and Eve together, in a kind
of alliance. Sandra Gilbert and Susan Gubar have noted this in their chapter on
patriarchal poetry and women readers. 'Despite Eve's apparent passivity and
domesticity,' they point out, 'Milton himself seems to have sketched so many
parallels between her and Satan that it is hard at times for the unwary reader to
distinguish the sinfulness of one from that of the other.'[68] The truth of this
claim can be measured by, among other things, the recurrence in Romantic
poetry of Miltonic habits of parallelism and conflation (most of them probably
the result of careful imitation, as opposed to 'unwary' reading) which have the
same unsettling effect. But Milton's followers go one stage further than he in
destabilizing meaning. The Satanic is psychologized by them as an urge
within the female psyche which must be realized, if stasis is to be left behind.
Authoritarian conclusions about the Fall are thus modified, if not precluded, by
seeing it as a natural stage of human growth. Dream gives women access to a
world that is less imprisoned than the one they normally inhabit, and temptation
comes to them, not just as an external possibility, but in response to a hidden
impulse in themselves. 'Transgression' is their understandable response to
prohibition, and sexuality is completion, not just sin. Maturity of perspective
cannot be reached unless the fall into experience is accomplished, rather than
repressed or shunned.

'Maturity' is, of course, differently defined by each of the writers with whom I
have been concerned in this chapter: for Pope, it is a form of Christian acceptance, accompanying the sense of proportion or 'good humour' which Clarissa
offers as the moral of the poem; for Blake, it is the energy to progress, produced
through the awareness of mutually dependent contrary states; for Coleridge, it is

---

[67] *Childe Harold*, canto iv, st. 109.

[68] *Madwoman in the Attic*, 196. Gilbert's and Gubar's interpretation of *Paradise Lost* lays special
emphasis on the unconscious, both in reading practices (hence their reference to the 'unwary'
reader) and in writing itself. For them, 'all these connections, parallelings and doublings among
Satan, Eve, and Sin are shadowy messages, embedded in the text of *Paradise Lost* rather than
carefully illuminated overt statements'.

the engagement with evil which is both necessary and inevitable, as a stage on the path to redemption; whilst for Keats and Byron it represents that accommodation to reality (in addition or preference to dream) which is vital to the achievement of poetic integrity. For all these writers, though—whatever their differing perspectives—experience is seen as a higher state than innocence; and it is offered, furthermore, as a potential which exists within each individual, before the 'fall' takes place.

The pressure of Miltonic allusions, working on behalf of this experienced perspective, may seem to be in danger, on occasion, of causing the reader to collude with a sexist view of the female gender. This begins to be the case in *The Rape of the Lock*, for instance, when Clarissa makes light of Belinda's 'rape', at the expense of her dignity; and it becomes an even stronger possibility in 'The Eve of St Agnes', where the reader is drawn into a voyeuristic perspective which is only half ironized by Keats himself. The problem seems to be that women are not analysed in these poems entirely on their own merits, but are exploited to symbolize a difficult or transitional area within each poet's aesthetic concerns. The sympathy accorded to them for the social and moral constraints under which they live (*The Rape of the Lock*), and for the inequality they have as a result, when it comes down to sexual experience itself ('Eve of St Agnes', *Don Juan*), may well arise from an accurate observation of the condition of women during the eighteenth century; but it is given a symbolic dimension by male writers who personally identify with the plight of subjection, and who appropriate the 'feminine' as a vehicle for the expression of their own attempts at poetic liberation.

It is likely that any resistance to progression shown by the female figures in their writing registers the lingering reservations and hesitancies which these writers themselves feel, in relation to the emerging (and potentially subversive) faculty of imagination. Their use of the 'feminine' allows them, as it did Milton, to play a complex and ambivalent game: a game of half-releasing, and half-restraining, the subjectivity they need and fear. Eve and her descendants are pressurized by their male creators to accept a movement from innocence to experience, because the ability to progress is bound up with an authorial interest in the emergence of subjectivity. That they should partly resist progression, and that they should encounter regrets once it has been made, is itself indicative of the problematic area they are being asked to negotiate.

For, if Eve is used to represent a Romantic craving for liberty which can only be achieved through transgression, she also symbolizes the difficulties encountered in reconciling imagination with the constraints of the real. Just as the worlds of dream and reality do not coalesce for her, so her descendants feel the unsatisfactoriness of accommodating themselves to an actuality which refuses to live up to their demands. Belinda, understandably, cannot see that the maturity Clarissa offers is any consolation for the loss of Honour, since it is on this concept that her entire social and moral identity is founded. Thel foresees that sexuality is not the happiness she had hoped for (and had been conditioned to hope for, by the Matron Clay) but rather, as Oothoon is later to realize, a route to further oppression. Christabel, once initiated into adult sexuality, can find no means of reconciling it with familial bonds, and is left stranded in a 'world of sin', with no way through to self-fulfilment. Madeline is alienated and bereaved when she encounters experience, but is required by Porphyro to suspend her disbelief and sustain adolescent fantasy beyond its appropriate bounds. Haidee, the most tragic of all these figures, dies rather than resign herself to the loss of love. Each of these women would prefer to regress to the dream-world in which their hopes remained intact rather than face the stunted possibilities which they are granted by their creators.

Far from being liberated into autonomy, then, the women in these texts stand as the symbols of a half-emerging and half-fearful imaginative power. They anticipate the dilemma which will later torment Tennyson, as he looks back on the Romantic aesthetic, from a somewhat more distanced and critical perspective; and they provide a paradigm for his equally ambiguous exploration of the association between poetry and female consciousness.[69] Despite the ambivalence which they continually register, however, and despite the truncated existence that their female figures are allowed, I find myself tempted to claim for all the texts I have been examining a feminist *implication*. 'If Eve is in so many negative ways like Satan the serpentine tempter,' Gilbert and Gubar ask, 'why should she not also be akin to Satan the Romantic outlaw?' 'The connections', they continue, 'between Satan, Romanticism and concealed or incipient feminism are intricate and far-reaching indeed.'[70] Their own concern is, of course, with the pursuit of these connections through the work of specifically female writers, battling against the patriarchal tradition Milton represents. I hope, however, that one thing this chapter may have done is to confirm that the 'incipient feminism' to which they refer is indeed implicit in *Paradise Lost*, and to show also that it is perpetuated in the post-Miltonic writers I have discussed. Surprisingly, then, strategies which have been identified in women writers as 'revisionary' may in fact belong also to the male tradition against which they are seeking to define themselves.

[69] See esp. 'The Lady of Shalott', which makes use of the Fall myth in ways reminiscent of the texts discussed here. Tennyson associates creativity with the embowered consciousness of a woman, which cannot survive being transported from the aesthetic realm to the real world.
[70] *Madwoman in the Attic*, 201, 203.

6

Subjectivity

Two traditions run alongside each other, in post-Miltonic writing: one laments the fallen state, nostalgically yearning to regain or rebuild paradise; the other offers consolation in the face of loss, and celebrates the human qualities that come through falling. For convenience, one might take as an example blank verse, which Edward Young called 'verse unfallen, uncurst'.[1] Broadly speaking, the line of poems stretching from Thomson's *The Seasons* (1726–30) through Cowper's *The Task* (1785) and on into Wordsworth's *Home at Grasmere* (1800) exemplifies nostalgia, the wish to recreate Eden in the natural world, whilst *The Prelude* invests a greater hope in human potential: love and imagination, according to this second tradition, are not residues of the unfallen state, but triumphant by-products of the Fall. It scarcely needs to be pointed out that these two traditions can coexist in a given writer. Blake, for instance, presents Thel's flight back into the Vales of Har as a regressive denial of energy; but in the poem's sequel, *Visions of the Daughters of Albion*, this pattern is reversed. Oothoon takes the step that Thel refused, and plucks the flower that grows in Leutha's vale; but she pays for her adult sexuality by enslavement to the values and fantasies of a male world. Whereas in the stasis of innocence the fallen potential of energy had seemed enough, progression is more complicated in this post-lapsarian state. Sex must be stripped of disguise, in order to provide a route back to eternity, rather than a further stage of the fall into division. Hope can be founded only on the redemptive potential of the human mind, which will ultimately reverse the effects of the Fall. One might sum up by saying that *Thel* privileges experience over innocence, while *Visions* works the other way round; and that the first perspective is that of the insider looking out, the second that of the outsider looking back in.

One should, however, be accustomed to thinking in terms of more subtle and more radical kinds of ambivalence. As well as working in sequence, innocent and experienced perspectives can also be superimposed. This happens most demonstrably across texts, as in the case of *Songs of Innocence* and *Songs of Experience*, where Blake uses a device he learns from Milton's 'L'Allegro' and 'Il Penseroso' of pairing poems that belong to opposite states. The reader's discernment of parallels within contrasts has the effect of breaking down their

[1] See Ch. 1, n. 26.

straightforward division. This is Blake's way of disconcerting his reader—of, as he puts it, cleansing the doors of perception: if we fail to see innocence and experience as mirroring and intersecting, we miss the dialectic on which progression depends. But this dissolving of boundaries can happen also within a single text or a given narrative moment. In Byron's ironic handling of Don Juan's first love, for instance, there is a constant play of equivocation, which unsettles our notions of innocence lost and experience gained. The reader is placed in a position of suspended choice, between different and mutually interactive kinds of pleasure; for, as Jerome McGann puts it,

while Juan and Julia are in the process of experiencing first and passionate love, definitely a gain . . . they are also in the process of experiencing a 'fall' from innocence which, in *Don Juan*'s terms, is a definite 'loss', though not only a loss. . . . The equivocal effect is not simply in the clash of gains and losses but in the clash of the *pleasures* of gains and losses.[2]

Byron himself summarizes the position thus: 'In play, there are two pleasures for your choosing— | The one is winning, and the other losing' (*Don Juan*, xiv. 12); or, alternatively, 'The world is all before me, or behind' (xiv. 9).

Such equivocation can also occur, at a less openly rhetorical level, in the most apparently un-ironic of narratives. In the last stanza of 'The Ancient Mariner', for instance, Coleridge juxtaposes the innocent and experienced perspectives of the wedding guest and the mariner; but he also works toward an awareness of their intersection, in which the reader is significantly implicated:

> He went like one that hath been stunned
> And is of sense forlorn:
> A sadder and a wiser man
> He rose the morrow morn.
>
> (ll. 622–25)

The mariner's is not the only fall that Coleridge is concerned with. For the wedding guest also there is no going back, no possibility of rejoining the marriage feast and picking up his life where he left off. He too is changed utterly by the end of the poem—implicated in the mariner's experience by hearing his story. The presence of that word 'forlorn' resonantly evokes the 'fallen' condition. In the background, one might hear Adam's haunting question, in *Paradise Lost* Book IX:

> How can I live without thee, how forgo
> Thy sweet converse, and love so dearly joined,
> To live again in these wild woods forlorn?
>
> (ll. 908–10)

Adam is not yet fallen when he says these words, but the perspective he offers, and the language he uses, suggest that post-lapsarian consciousness is upon him before he makes his choice. To live in paradise without Eve would be a loss as

---

[2] *'Don Juan' in Context* (Chicago, 1976), 63.

absolute as living in the fallen world—an exercise as futile as Thel's flight back into the vale of Har. As he stands on the threshold between two worlds, he is, in the terms I used earlier, both an insider looking out and an outsider looking back in. The world is all before him, *and* behind.

Coleridge's allusion to the passage is doubly appropriate if one is reading 'The Ancient Mariner' as a fall narrative, in which the wedding guest, too, undergoes a kind of lapse. There is a Miltonic overlapping of perspectives, not just in the contrast between the wedding guest and the mariner, but within the wedding guest himself. Forlorn after hearing the mariner's story, he is like Adam: technically still innocent, but initiated into the fallen world by the act of listening. His sadness and wisdom take on a deeper resonance as part of this larger Miltonic pattern. The framing device Coleridge makes use of, to suggest a connection between the wedding guest and the reader, builds into the poem a directive as to how it should be read. This has the effect, not only of confirming the poet's approval of sadness and wisdom, but of implying a parallel between reading and falling. We too, by the end of the poem, should be in the indeterminate position suggested by that word 'forlorn'.[3] And while this suspension is occurring on a thematic and narrative level, it is present also in the overlapping perspectives suggested by allusive language. Intertextuality puts the reader 'between' texts, creating at the rhetorical level also an illusion of suspended choice.

The impulse to preserve or return to Eden, as though it were unquestionably preferable to being fallen, scarcely ever exists without qualification from a consolatory or celebratory perspective: even the nostalgic blank verse tradition which I identified at the beginning of this discussion turns out to be complicatedly double. Writers attempting to recreate Eden metaphorically—in gardens or in childhood selves—are caught in Milton's own dilemma, of not having access to an unfallen language.[4] Of necessity, then, they project fallen assumptions onto the innocence they attempt to describe. This process is not wholly negative, however, as I shall demonstrate in this chapter. Since fallen distortions are akin to poetic transformations, there is an imaginative 'gain' in letting the projecting mind go to work. The so-called inadequacy of language can thus become a strength, much as the inaccuracy of memory does in Wordsworth's famous simile. 'As one who hangs down-bending from the side | Of a slow-moving boat', he writes, in *The Prelude* Book IV:

> Sees many beauteous sights—weeds, fishes, flowers,
> Grots, pebbles, roots of trees—and fancies more,
> Yet often is perplexed, and cannot part

---

[3] The word resonates through Romantic poetry; cf. Keats's awakening from paradisal dream in 'Ode to a Nightingale': 'Forlorn! The very word is like a bell | To toll me back from thee to my sole self!' (ll. 71–2); and Wordsworth's projection of human pathos onto the sublime: 'Winds thwarting winds, bewildered and forlorn' (*Prelude* vi. 560).

[4] In Fish's reading, Milton entangles the reader in fallen assumptions to a didactic end; see Ch. 2.

> The shadow from the substance, rocks and sky,
> Mountains and clouds, from that which is indeed
> The region, and the things which there abide
> In their true dwelling; now is crossed by gleam
> Of his own image, by a sunbeam now,
> And motions that are sent he knows not whence,
> Impediments that make his task more sweet;
> Such pleasant office have we long pursued
> Incumbent o'er the surface of past time—
> With like success.
>
> (ll. 247-64)

The inability to part substance from shadow is experienced as pleasurable complexity rather than confusion, gain rather than loss: this is the case whether we read the passage as a celebration of subjectivity or as an exploration of the false substitutions (words for things) on which language itself depends. Reflections of the adult Wordsworth, perceived sometimes as gleams of his own image, sometimes as memories of his childhood self, are 'impediments that make his task more sweet'. Ambiguity is valorized as a function of creativity; and the perplexing inextricability of substance and shadow becomes a metaphor for metaphor itself. Just so with the projections from fallen consciousness onto the unfallen state.

Appropriately, Wordsworth refers in the passage quoted above to the lines from *Paradise Lost* which are Burke's most celebrated example of 'judicious obscurity': 'The other shape', Milton calls Death, 'If shape it might be called that shape had none | Distinguishable ... Or substance might be called that shadow seemed, | For each seemed either' (*PL* ii. 666-8, 669-70). The sublimity of this passage consists, for Burke (and for many of his readers, pre-Romantic and Romantic alike) in its 'significant and expressive uncertainty': an oxymoron which empowers linguistic insufficiency, by making it the source of emotional and imaginative pleasure.[5] Since much of the discussion in this chapter will depend on perceiving a close association between indeterminacy and subjectivity, and since the origins of the loss/gain paradigm I shall be exploring are to be found in a theory of the sublime, I shall pause here and give a brief account of the aesthetics of indeterminacy as they emerge from eighteenth-century discussions of Miltonic sublimity. My initial focus will be on passages of criticism and poetry which directly allude to Milton's description of Death; but I shall turn at a later stage to more general definitions of sublime language. My point will be to establish a model for considering the idea of gain-in-loss, which I shall proceed to apply in various ways to the perspectival and temporal games which are played in post-Miltonic poetry.

---

[5] See *Burke Enquiry*, 59.

INDETERMINACY AND THE SUBLIME

As I showed in Chapter 1, the examples of sublimity in Burke's influential treatise are frequently drawn from *Paradise Lost*; and he is responsible for establishing Milton's famous description of Death as a touchstone for sublime language. His analysis rests on the uncertainty of definition with which Milton achieves his effects. 'It is astonishing', he claims, 'with what a gloomy pomp, with what a significant and expressive uncertainty of strokes and colouring Milton has finished the portrait of the king of terrors.' Quoting the passage which begins 'The other shape | If shape it might be called that shape had none | Distinguishable, in member, joint, or limb ...', he comments: 'In this description, all is dark, uncertain, confused, terrible, and sublime to the last degree.'[6] Sublimity is associated with indefiniteness of language because the grandeur of mental conceptions appears to make them uncontainable by verbal forms. Whereas 'A clear idea is ... another name for a little idea',[7] the presence of *un*clear ideas creates an illusion of excess, by suggesting the expansiveness of tenor beyond vehicle. As Burke puts it elsewhere, 'the mind is hurried out of itself by a croud of great and confused images; which affect because they are crouded and confused'.[8] Emotional or intellectual intensity thus correlates with verbal insufficiency: the transcendent signified breaks free of the inadequate signifier, leaving the human mind baffled (and, importantly, *terrified*) by the sense of a power beyond its own conception.[9]

Obscurity of image, and indefiniteness of language, are seen to be effective in intensifying an aesthetic which rests on the sense of terror, because they demonstrate the littleness of the human subject, in the face of unrealizable ideas. (In much the same way, both superstition and religion maintain their hold on the otherwise rational mind, through ideas of greatness and incomprehensibility.) The importance of Burke's critique, for the Romantic reader, is that, although it appears to underwrite superstition by maintaining the obscurity of power, it does observe the role of human subjectivity in constructing ideas of greatness to which the mind allows itself to succumb. Within Burke's analysis of the uncertainty of Milton's language, there is an interest in *what the reader does with this uncertainty*. Burke's followers will take further his analysis of the reader's difficulty in construing meaning, separating it to some extent from the power system in which it operates for Burke, and developing it into a coherent aesthetic.

In Cowper's 'Commentary' on *Paradise Lost* (which, significantly and appropriately, is published as a 'fragment'),[10] Burke's analysis of the sublime is

---

[6] Ibid. [7] Ibid. 63. [8] Ibid. 62.

[9] For the psychology of terror, esp. in Burke's definition of the sublime, see T. Weiskel, *The Romantic Sublime: Studies in the Structure and Psychology of Transcendence* (Baltimore, 1976), 83–106.

[10] As T. McFarland observes, there is a close connection between ideas of sublimity and fragmentariness: 'The sublime ... is the perception of very large fragments, such as mountains, with the accompanying awareness that this largeness implies still larger conceptions that can have no such objectivization and therefore cannot be compared'; see *Romanticism and the Forms of Ruin: Wordsworth, Coleridge, and Modalities of Fragmentation* (Princeton, NJ, 1981), 29.

extended, once again through close analysis of this touchstone passage in Book II. Cowper compares Milton's Death with Spenser's, and claims that there is something 'incomparably more poetical' in 'the ambiguous nature' of the former:

Milton's is in fact an original figure, a Death of his own invention, a kind of intermediate form between matter and spirit, partaking of both, and consisting of neither. The idea of its substance is lost in its tenuity, and yet, contemplated awhile as a shadow, it becomes a substance.[11]

Fascinated by the ambiguity of Milton's language, Cowper slows down (in order to observe) the successive stages of image definition followed by image retraction, whereby an overall effect of obscurity is brought about. Throughout the discussion, his eye is on the achievement of effects through poetic skill rather than on the role of the reader in effortlessly construing meaning; but his description of the poetic process is adaptable to a phenomenological account of the reading process, in which the speculative activity of the reader is foregrounded:

The indistinctness of this phantom form is admirably well-preserved. First the poet calls it a shape, then doubts if it could be properly so called; then a substance; then a shadow; then doubts if it was either; and lastly he will not venture to affirm, that what seemed his head, was such in reality, but being covered with the similitude of a crown, he is rather inclined to think it such. The dimness of this vague and fleeting outline is infinitely more terrible than exact description, because it leaves the imagination at full liberty to see for itself, and to suppose the worst.[12]

Cowper's thematic explanation for this hovering between substance and shadow is at once critically ingenious and predictably ideological in its orientation. He sees a *moral* point in representing Death as 'a being of such doubtful definition', since death will have 'different effects on the fate of the righteous and the wicked. To these it is a real evil, to those only an imaginary one.'[13] It can be seen, then, from the two instances I have examined, how readily appropriable is a model of linguistic indeterminacy to ideological ends: Burke is interested in obscurity as a source of terror, which the mind can to some extent control by aesthetic distancing, but to which it ultimately succumbs, under the oppressive sense of its own littleness. Cowper adapts the Burkean model, so that it reflects his own vividly imaginative grasp of the terrors of damnation. The 'full liberty' which, in Cowper's view, is pleasurably experienced by the mind while it faces the choice between images must in fact come to an end, since it is only the liberty 'to see for itself, and know the worst'.

With this ideological slant to the aesthetic in view, it is interesting to note how frequently the 'Sin and Death' passage from Book II is echoed or quoted, at those moments in Romantic writing when imagination is being celebrated or defined. Coleridge, for instance, in his Shakespeare lectures, pauses in his

[11] *Milton*, ed. Cowper (4 vols., Chichester, 1810), ii. 453.   [12] Ibid. 453–4.
[13] Ibid. 453.

discussion of Romeo to use the 'fine description of Death in Milton' to illustrate what he calls 'an effort of the mind, when it would describe what it cannot satisfy itself with the description of'. This 'effort' (the index of an inadequacy which is built into the structure of the sublime) is aimed towards reconciling opposites and qualifying contradictions, 'leaving a middle state of mind more strictly appropriate to the imagination than any other, when it is, as it were, hovering between images'.[14] Coleridge's 'imagination', directly descended from Locke's 'wit', is given a more emancipated role than Locke could have conceived for it.[15] As soon as the mind is fixed on one image, Coleridge points out, 'it becomes understanding; but while it is unfixed and wavering between them, attaching itself to none, it is imagination'. This activity of 'hovering' and 'wavering' allows the mind to break down cognitive boundaries, and to discover its own subjective power in the refusal of closure:

The grandest efforts of poetry are where the imagination is called forth, not to produce a distinct form, but a strong working of the mind, still offering what is still repelled, and again creating what is again rejected; the result being what the poet wishes to impress, namely the substitution of a sublime feeling of the unimaginable for a mere image.[16]

Coleridge's ideological appropriation of indeterminacy is less heavily accented than Burke's and Cowper's because sublimity has been interiorized, so that in this particular instance there appears to be no submission by human subjectivity to a power or order beyond itself. A 'sublime feeling of the unimaginable' is more liberating to mental activity than Cowper's category of the 'terrible', which allows only so much free play to the mind before belittling it.

In Chapter 13 of *Biographia Literaria*, however, where Milton's description of Death appears again, indeterminacy is clearly manipulated so as to underwrite Coleridge's hierarchy of values. His Miltonic allusion is placed in the middle of the letter which acts as an interruptive mechanism, immediately preceding Coleridge's definition of the primary and secondary imagination.[17] Its presence there is appropriate on two counts: firstly, because it relates to the substance of the letter in which, through the mouthpiece of his invented 'friend', Coleridge discusses the inadequacy of his own philosophical argument; and, secondly, because that so-called inadequacy is an indication of the grandeur and incommunicability of his subject-matter. The complaint made in the letter (that

---

[14] 'Lectures to the London Philosophical Society', lecture 7 (9 Dec. 1811), in *Romantics on Milton*, 200.

[15] 'Wit' was mistrusted by Locke because, in comparing dissimilar things, it risked indiscriminately assimilating objects or qualities: this drew it into close proximity with madness. For the Enlightenment's association of 'wit' or 'fancy' with insanity, see W. Iser, *Laurence Sterne: Tristram Shandy* (Cambridge, 1988), 1–54; and M. Foucault, *The Order of Things: An Archaeology of the Human Sciences* (London, 1970; repr. 1989), 23–4, 49–51.

[16] *Romantics on Milton*, 201.

[17] P. Hamilton is dismissive of readings of *Biographia Literaria* which either emphasize authorial irony or foreground the reader's activity in completing meaning; see *Coleridge's Poetics* (Oxford, 1983), 12–26.

nothing Coleridge has said so far adds up to a logically coherent position) is such as to show the insufficiency of logical argument to the project in hand; and this acts as a preparatory device for introducing the imagination definitions, which themselves are antithetical to logical procedures.

Coleridge makes a comparison between reading *Biographia* and entering a Gothic cathedral by moonlight. He begins by using devices of comic deflation, but these give way to sublime poetic effects. The Miltonic juxtaposition of 'palpable darkness' with 'broad yet visionary lights', and the presence of 'fantastic shapes', add up to an atmosphere of expressive uncertainty, into which Milton's description of Death, made famous by Burke, can be introduced with ease:

In short, what I had supposed substances were thinned away into shadows, while everywhere shadows were deepened into substances:

> If substance might be called that shadow seem'd,
> For each seem'd either![18]

The presence of this Burkean 'touchstone' allows Coleridge to establish the imaginative credentials of his prose style, and to diminish the importance of consecutive reasoning in a context which calls for faith. He validates his method according to the criteria Burke had evolved for discussing Milton's sublimity, making clear on two different levels the importance of linguistic inadequacy (or philosophical imprecision) for imaginative success. His use of judicious obscurity, like Cowper's, is ideological, in that it manipulates the reader into a state of self-mystification: in evolving an idea of what imagination is, faith is seen to triumph over reason.[19]

Like Coleridge, Wordsworth invokes the Miltonic sublime in some of his poetic accounts of imagination. One such account, in *The Prelude* Book VIII, is remarkably close to the passage from *Biographia* discussed above, in its analysis of the unsettling but creative effect which darkness can have on visual impressions. Wordsworth describes how a traveller, entering the Cave of Yordas during the day, 'looks and sees the cavern spread and grow, | Widening itself on all sides' (ll. 715–16) and, as his eye adjusts to the different light, 'sees, or thinks | He sees, erelong, the roof above his head, | Which instantly unsettles and recedes' (ll. 716–17). The lines contain an allusion to the Virgilian trope of uncertainty, 'aut videt, aut vidisse putat', which, as the Norton editors point out, is copied by Milton in *Paradise Lost* Book I;[20] but, more importantly,

---

[18] *Biographia*, i. 301. For a shrewd discussion of this passage, see S. Knapp, *Personification and the Sublime: Milton to Coleridge* (Cambridge, Mass., 1985), ch. 1.

[19] The twofold aim of *Biographia*—to reconcile religion with philosophy, and to reveal that reason is ultimately subordinate to faith—is best summarized in Coleridge's concluding remarks in vol. ii. His claim is to have shown 'that the Scheme of Christianity ... though not discoverable by human Reason, is yet in accordance with it; that link follows link by necessary consequence; that Religion passes out of the ken of Reason only where the eye of Reason has reached its own horizon; and that Faith is then but its continuation' (*Biographia*, ii. 247).

[20] *Prelude*, p. 304, n. 6; the allusion is to *PL* i. 783–4.

Wordsworth goes on to give this uncertainty a sublime dimension, by reference to Milton's Death:

> Substance and shadow, light and darkness, all
> Commingled, making up a canopy
> Of shapes, and forms, and tendencies to shape,
> That shift and vanish, change and interchange
> Like spectres—ferment quiet and sublime.

(viii. 719–23)

A close connection is thus suggested between visual indeterminacy and imaginative potency, which claims its authority from Milton and Burke. Wordsworth has moved further than either Cowper or Coleridge towards a celebration of indeterminacy for its own sake. The subjectivity it demonstrates has become more important than the terror it induces, or the submission it requires.

Shelley, too, invokes Milton's Death as a rhetorical trope for indeterminacy. In 'The Triumph of Life', Death is present as the phantom shape/shadow whose chariot passes by the poet (ll. 85–97), and who is later identified as the shade of Rousseau: a 'grim Feature' whose answers to the poet's metaphysical questionings are wholly resistant to interpretation. At the climax of *Prometheus Unbound*, he reappears. Once again, as in *The Prelude*, the darkness of a cave forms an appropriate setting for revelation, as Panthea and Asia come face to face with the inscrutable shape of Demogorgon: 'I see a mighty Darkness | filling the seat of power', Panthea observes,

> and rays of gloom
> Dart round, as light from the meridian Sun,
> Ungazed upon and shapeless—neither limb
> Nor form—nor outline; yet we feel it is
> A living Spirit.

(II. iv. 2–7)

The Miltonic allusion not only gives Demogorgon his deathliness; it also connects him with ideas of uncertainty and of the inexpressible. Both associations are appropriate, if one is making an allegorical identification between Demogorgon and Necessity. For, according to Shelley's sceptical empiricism, Necessity can explain only what is already known: when the limits of human knowledge are overstepped, 'truth' becomes imageless.[21] So, when Demogorgon speaks, it is as the vehicle of an oracular truth, whose ultimate message is merely a reflex of the human mind's imaginings, and whose enigmatic emptiness suggests the defeat of representation by the grandeur of what is to be represented:

---

[21] See M. H. Abrams, *Natural Supernaturalism: Tradition and Revolution in Romantic Literature* (New York, 1971), 304–5.

> —If the Abysm
> Could vomit forth its secrets:—but a voice
> Is wanting, the deep truth is imageless;

> (ll. 114–116)

Paradoxically, then, Demogorgon stands as an emblem of the success-in-failure of language; in his Miltonic guise, he 'images' the imageless.

The Burkean equation of sublimity with linguistic inadequacy has its parallels everywhere in Romantic theory, even on occasions when Miltonic allusion is not directly involved. Bishop Lowth, for instance, in his *Lectures on the Sacred Poetry of the Hebrews*, gives a careful analysis of the contribution made by bathos to sublime effects:

the human mind is absorbed, overwhelmed as it were in a boundless vortex, and studies in vain for an expedient to extricate itself. But the greatness of the subject may be justly estimated by its difficulty; and while the imagination labours to comprehend what is beyond its powers, this very labour itself, and these intellectual endeavours, sufficiently demonstrate the immensity and sublimity of the object.[22]

A similar analysis is to be found in the note to Wordsworth's 'The Thorn', where there is a 'consciousness of the inadequateness of our own powers, or the deficiencies of language', which accompanies any attempt to 'communicate impassioned feelings'. Wordsworth claims that 'During such efforts there will be a craving in the mind, and as long as it is unsatisfied the Speaker will cling to the same words, or words of the same character'.[23] This unsatisfied craving, synonymous with inadequacy of representation, makes of the passion itself something unreachable or sublime.

Kant's concerns are less explicitly linguistic, but his analysis of sublimity does centre, none the less, on a perception of the inadequacy of nature to represent ideas of greatness and, further, of the inadequacy of imagination to realize the totalizing conceptions of reason. The sublime experience is, in his view, one in which we are 'pushed to the point at which our faculty of imagination breaks down in presenting the concept of a magnitude, and proves unequal to its task'. Far from signalling failure, however, this breakdown offers reassurance. Reason is confirmed in its paramountcy by the proof that it possesses supersensible intuitions, ungraspable by imagination: 'the Subject's very incapacity betrays the consciousness of an unlimited faculty of the same Subject'. Thus, 'the object is received as sublime with a pleasure that is only possible through the mediation of displeasure'.[24] At one point in particular, Kant's critique comes extremely close to a Wordsworthian model. In analysing the 'bewilderment, or sort of perplexity' experienced by the traveller, on first entering St Peter's in Rome, he writes:

---

[22] *Lowth Lectures*, i. 353.   [23] *Wordsworth*, 594.
[24] I. Kant, *The Critique of Judgement*, trans. with analytical indexes, J. C. Meredith (Oxford, 1952; repr. 1978), 101, 108, 109.

here a feeling comes home to him of the inadequacy of his imagination for presenting the idea of a whole within which that imagination attains its maximum, and, in its fruitless efforts to extend this limit, recoils upon itself, but in so doing succumbs to an emotional delight.[25]

As in Burke and Wordsworth, the failure of representation is experienced as a displeasure which is none the less pleasurable: 'emotional delight' is provoked by the traveller's awareness of a disjunction between the totalizing conceptions of which his reason is capable, and the limited sense-apprehensions achieved by imagination. His mind hovers between two alternative ideas, deriving a sense of its own importance from their failure to coalesce. Indeed, this 'failure' is the guarantee that 'a feeling of a supersensible faculty within'[26] has been awakened.

It can be seen that the concept of the sublime occupies a place in Romantic thinking analogous to the idea of God: just as divinity can be celebrated through inexpressibility, so the sublime can be 'defined' by indefiniteness. And just as the humiliation experienced by the human subject in relation to God is a guarantee of reassurance to come, so the bewilderment or perplexity felt in the apprehension of sublimity is replaced by the pleasurable sense of infinite possibilities for the mind. Coleridge quite frequently employs devices of self-defeat, or bafflement, to suggest the infinity of God: for him, the sublime is not so much a separate aesthetic category as a function of the divine. Wordsworth, on the other hand, is at his most Kantian when using notions of the unreachable as substitutes for divinity: in an early fragment, for instance, he describes how the mind retains 'an obscure sense of possible sublimity', aspiring 'with growing faculties' to an ever-receding goal, and strengthened by the consciousness that 'there still│Is something to pursue';[27] and in *The Prelude* he shows how the imagination becomes self-sufficient through its experience of nature's inadequacy, so that disappointment itself is what ensures the replenishment of 'Effort, and expectation and desire,│And something ever more about to be' (vi. 541–2). A formal analogue for this phenomenon of success-in-failure is to be found in the 'fragment', which resembles both the symbol and the sublime, in that it gestures towards unachievable completeness. As a sequence of recent studies have shown, the fragment can be observed as a peculiarly Romantic phenomenon—an offshoot of the cult for the sublime.[28]

The purpose of my lengthy digression has been to provide this chapter with an appropriate theoretical framework, and to show that, when Wordsworth writes in *The Prelude* of his inability to part the shadow from the substance, he is joining an aesthetic debate. By presenting linguistic inadequacy as gain, not

[25] Ibid. 100.   [26] Ibid. 97.

[27] From the fragment known as 'In Storm and Tempest', ll. 15–20; text in J. Wordsworth, *The Music of Humanity* (New York, 1969), 172–3.

[28] See McFarland, *Forms of Ruin*; M. Levinson, *The Romantic Fragment Poem: A Critique of a Form* (Chapel Hill, NC, 1986); and B. Rajan, *The Form of the Unfinished: English Poetics from Spenser to Pound* (Princeton, NJ, 1985).

loss, he foregrounds the role of subjectivity (his own and the reader's) in constructing narrative. Indeterminacy is thus experienced as a pleasurable, and moreover a *creative*, suspension between states, analogous to that described by Burke and Kant. It is comparable to the liminal experience induced in the reader, at the end of 'The Ancient Mariner', by overlapping temporal perspectives; and it resembles what Stephen Knapp has identified as 'an oscillation between difference and identity, or fiction and truth', which is characteristic of Milton's 'moments of imaginative leisure'.[29] As I demonstrated at length in Chapter 2, this model of indeterminacy applies just as easily to the two-way process of allusion as to the innocence/experience divide; and it is frequently the case, in post-Miltonic writing, that thematic and rhetorical levels can be seen to be working in conjunction. The reader becomes involved, on such occasions, in a process very like the one Wordsworth describes in his simile: separating out the text that is echoed from the echoing text is as difficult as attempting to part substance from shadow, or the fallen from the unfallen state.

In the discussion that follows, I intend to examine the ways in which a number of pre-Romantic and Romantic texts both replicate Milton's games with perspective and, through the process of allusion, further multiply the range of interpretative choices available to the reader. My emphasis throughout will be on the heightening of subjectivity which these practices involve, and especially on the importance which is thereby given to the reader in constructing the meaning of the text. Continuing a suggestion made at the end of Chapter 2, I shall be arguing that *Paradise Lost* inevitably frames subjectivity as a 'fallen' product, but frames it in such a way as to affirm the gain-in-loss which experience brings; and that Milton's Romantic readers expand on the latent possibilities of this paradox, along the Burkean and Kantian lines discussed above. This chapter is closely linked to the following one, in that it finds in Milton the origins of a self-consciousness about imaginative activity which is usually seen as 'Romantic'. Whereas here I am concerned with the release and celebration of subjectivity, however, I shall later be examining the strategies whereby it is kept under control, especially by those writers who are wary of its waywardness, its potential irresponsibility, or its autonomy.

PROJECTION AND DESECRATION

Even at its most nostalgic, the paradisal theme gives rise to complicated cross-currents of regression and progression in those writers who address it; and the simplest of post-Miltonic texts can turn out to be constructed around the loss/gain paradox which is implicit in *Paradise Lost*. 'Where ignorance is bliss, | 'Tis folly to be wise', Gray writes in his 'Ode on a Distant Prospect of Eton College'[30]—a message that appears entirely to contradict Coleridge's later valuation of sadness and wisdom. But the neatness of the paradox works to undercut itself.

[29] *Personification and the Sublime*, 48.   [30] See ll. 99–100.

Gray's avoidance of the word 'innocence' has a destabilizing effect: it makes 'ignorance' sound regressive and 'bliss' hollow. The exchanging of wisdom and folly, on the other hand, is nothing more than a superficial inversion, which leaves wisdom's value undisturbed. The impression conveyed is one of ambivalence—the moral absoluteness of epigram, contradicted by a more intuitive set of values. This serves to emphasize a complexity that runs through the poem as a whole: Gray sets out to privilege the innocence of childhood, but spends the majority of his time anticipating the fallen state.

The poem's opening is at first sight straightforwardly nostalgic: Eton, with its 'distant spires', its 'antique towers', its 'watery glades' (ll. 1–2), is invoked as a kind of Eden (the paronamasia can scarcely be accidental), through which the Thames wanders 'His silver-winding way' (l. 10). The poet laments his own lost innocence in the tones of elegy, but suggests that Eden survives, both literally in the place itself, and metaphorically, as a reviving memory. Nostalgia is qualified, meanwhile, by the presence of words that carry moral implications. 'Wander', used of the Thames, contains just a touch of the fallenness implied in its Miltonic parallel; the word 'stray'd' (l. 13), especially in conjunction with 'careless', suggests the proximity of the fallen condition within the oblivious childhood state. When he turns to the schoolboys who inhabit this Eden, three stanzas are given over to their innocent preoccupations, and four to the implications of adulthood, into which they will inevitably fall. But, again, the straightforward privileging of innocence over experience is qualified: firstly, by the intrusion of a moral perspective, which questions the children's activities in words suggestive of self-indulgence—'paths of pleasure' (l. 25), 'idle progeny' (l.28); secondly, by the suggestion that lack of knowledge is a form of constraint. On the level of literal narrative, the 'bold adventurers' who 'disdain | The limits of their little reign' (ll. 35–6) are truants missing lessons; but symbolically they register imaginative impatience to expand beyond the limits of a paradisal world, 'And unknown regions dare descry' (l. 37).

Gray's prognostications take the poem over, projecting knowledge onto ignorance in such a way as to claim further kinship between fallenness and imagination:

> Alas, regardless of their doom,
> The little victims play!
> No sense have they of ills to come,
> Nor care beyond today:
> Yet see how all around 'em wait
> The ministers of human fate,
> And black Misfortune's baleful train!
> Ah, show them where in ambush stand,
> To seize their prey, the murderous band!
> Ah, tell them, they are men!

(ll. 51–60)

The painful consequences of adulthood are further expanded through a disturbing sequence of personifications—Anger, Fear, Shame, Love, Jealousy (ll. 61–70)—which enact the seven ages of man, and project a fallen world as gloomy and comfortless as the one prophesied by Michael in *Paradise Lost* Book X. Here, as in Milton, there is an implication that the world of experience must be encountered, in all its painful actuality, rather than refused. Gray's warning voice is not intended to *halt* the fall, then, but to ensure recognition of what it entails: 'Ah tell them, they are men!' The destructive implications become increasingly evident as we see the poet's projecting imagination at work. A good analogy can be found in Marvell's 'Little T.C. in a Prospect of Flowers', where the young girl's innocence is at once celebrated and threatened by the speaker's erotic fantasies about her future. Projection, in this latter instance, is a form of seduction, just as in Gray's ode it has overtones of desecration. The Satanic parallel is both obvious and appropriate: 'Ah gentle pair', says the arch-fiend, in *Paradise Lost* Book IV, on first seeing Adam and Eve:

> ye little think how nigh
> Your change approaches, when all these delights
> Will vanish and deliver ye to woe,
> More woe, the more your taste is now of joy;

> (ll. 366–9)

Where warnings are concerned, the dividing line between the prophetic and the Satanic is a narrow one. Gray's poetic voice negotiates uneasily between its acceptable resemblance to Michael and its more worrying likeness to Satan. Interrupting himself in the last stanza, the poet attempts to stave off the encroachments of adult vision, thus leaving paradise intact:

> Yet ah! why should they know their fate?
> Since sorrow never comes too late,
> And happiness too swiftly flies.
> Thought would destroy their paradise.
> No more, where ignorance is bliss,
> 'Tis folly to be wise.

> (ll. 95–100)

But it is, of course, too late: the reading process is itself a kind of lapse, and the growth towards sadness and wisdom has already occurred through anticipations of the fall. This last stanza could be read straightforwardly, if it were not for the imaginative power invested in portraying adulthood and the limitation accorded to innocence itself. As it is, we perceive in these final troubling lines both truth and irony. Thought does indeed destroy paradise, but if the child is to move beyond the 'limits of [its] little reign', that is the necessary cost.

PRESERVATION AND COMPENSATION

Successful claims are rarely made, in post-Miltonic poetry, for the retention of paradise in the childhood state. When attempted, they smack of sentimentality or regression. Wordsworth's efforts, for instance, to make of childhood something impregnably fortified against the encroachments of time, are famously troubled. The most extreme example is the embalmed child of *The Prelude* Book VII, who remains immmune to experience despite living in the fallen world. 'Destined to live, | To be, to have been, come, and go, a child | And nothing more', he is unthreatened by the ministers of human fate: 'no partner in the years | Which bear us forward to distress and guilt, | Pain and abasement' (ll. 402–6). In those tell-tale negatives, 'nothing more', 'no partner', one hears a distant echo of Adam, lamenting the separation from Eve which staying in Eden would involve. The choice of perpetual innocence entails the negation of humanity and sharing—or so Wordsworth would appear reluctantly to imply.[31]

Indeed, it would be difficult to read this passage without regarding the impulse to embalm as a (Thel-like) act of denial. Yet it is not possible to claim for Wordsworth a sceptical perspective. 'I think of thee with many fears | For what may be thy lot in future years', he later writes in 'To H.C.'., addressing the six-year-old Hartley Coleridge, who remains as yet unfallen.[32] The poem is a confession of the fear that adulthood brings inevitable loss; and Hartley is a symbol of the primal sympathy that must survive in the poet himself. Following the pattern of the Eton College Ode, Wordsworth at once envies the child his untouched state, and projects onto him the consequences of adulthood. Personification is used, as by Gray himself, to give the world of experience a strange fascination; and the tones of warning or prophecy go hand in hand with an almost Satanic compulsion to desecrate:

> I thought of times when Pain might be thy guest,
> Lord of thy house and hospitality;
> And grief, uneasy Lover! never rest
> But when she sate within the touch of thee.

(ll. 15–18)

Like the sudden interruption, 'No more!', of Gray's last stanza, the exclamations that follow this painful vision are an attempt to protect both child and reader: 'Oh! too industrious folly! | Oh! vain and causeless melancholy!' (ll. 19–20), but as before, the damage has already been done. Consolation is vulnerably and regressively wishful: 'Nature will either end thee quite; | Or, lengthening out thy season of delight, | Preserve for thee, by individual right, | A young Lamb's heart among the full-grown flocks' (ll. 21–4). Presum-

---

[31] I have analysed Wordsworth's literary treatment of children (and esp. Hartley Coleridge, as metaphor of creativity) in Ch. 6 of *Coleridge, Wordsworth, and the Language of Allusion* (Oxford, 1986).

[32] 'To H. C., Six Years Old', ll. 13–14.

ably no irony is intended, but the intensity of Wordsworth's protectiveness creates an effect similar to that of embalming.

A parallel attempt, this time to protect love from temporality, is made by Byron in Canto IV of *Don Juan*:

> Their faces were not made for wrinkles, their
> Pure blood to stagnate, their great hearts to fail.
> The blank grey was not made to blast their hair,
> But like the climes that know nor snow nor hail
> They were all summer.
>
> (st. 9)

Haidee and Juan are 'embalmed', as Hartley Coleridge is, by the wishfulness of their creator—a knowing wishfulness, in this case, since the audience is fully aware of the presence of Lambro, who hovers in the background, ready to destroy their paradise:

> All these were theirs, for they were children still
> And children still they should have ever been.
> They were not made in the real world to fill
> A busy character in the dull scene,
> But like two beings born from out a rill,
> A nymph and her beloved, all unseen
> To pass their lives in fountains and on flowers
> And never know the weight of human hours.
>
> (iv. 15)

The language resonates with pathos, underscoring the futility of its hope with an ironic allusion to Wordsworth's Lucy, who 'seemed a thing that could not feel | The touch of earthly years', and whose death removes her finally from human contact.[33]

If the reader responds with suspicion to these examples of innocence preserved, it is because they seem alien to the experiential bias of Romantic philosophy. Wordsworth in particular is rightly thought of as having no truck with illusion, accommodating himself to 'the very world which is the world | Of all of us, the place in which, in the end | We find our happiness, or not at all' (*Prelude* x. 725–7). His poetry might be seen as repeating the humanist consolation of *Paradise Lost* in a sequence of variations on the loss/gain paradigm. Sometimes, this takes the form of compensation through substitution: in 'Tintern Abbey', for instance, the poet claims to have received 'abundant recompense', in the form of 'other gifts', for the diminution of his animal spirits (l. 87). On other occasions, gain is seen to derive from the acknowledgement of loss, and becomes dependent on it. Both patterns can be observed in the Immortality Ode, where there is a double recompense for the fall into adulthood. 'Years that bring

---

[33] 'A Slumber did my Spirit Seal', ll. 3–4.

the philosophic mind' (l. 189) suggest a mellowing process like that in 'Tintern Abbey'; while moments of childhood trauma can be transformed into sources of adult power. For this latter purpose, the importance of the past is defined in terms quite other than those of childish innocence and exuberance:

> Not for these I raise
> The song of thanks and praise;
> But for those obstinate questionings
> Of sense and outward things,
> Fallings from us, vanishings;
> Blank misgivings of a Creature
> Moving about in worlds not realized,
> High instincts, before which our mortal Nature
> Did tremble like a guilty Thing surprized.

> (ll. 142–50)

The emotions Wordsworth here alludes to—fear, loss, guilt, awareness of mortality—all belong unmistakably to the world of experience, which is projected back onto the past as though deliberately to produce those confusions of 'substance' and 'shadow' which I discussed earlier. The childish episodes themselves are meaningful only according to an adult system of signification, which retrospectively makes them into symbols of initiation into the fallen world; but there is a suggestion that the child himself was aware of their potency, at the time, as epiphanic anticipations.

In *The Prelude*, Wordsworth does not give the child an imaginative life that is sealed off from pain, but constructs a developmental narrative showing the dependence of imagination on sudden shocks of traumatic awareness. The 'spots of time' could indeed be read as spots of experience. Some of them are framed explicitly as transgression narratives, in which the extent of the child's imaginative expansion correlates with the magnitude of his guilt. Crimes against nature, for instance, such as snaring woodcocks, plundering birds' nests, or stealing a boat at night, bring fear of punishment in their wake: the child hears low breathings coming after him, or sees a cliff, rising to pursue him 'with voluntary power instinct', like a punitive father or a vengeful God. The price of experience in such cases is an unsettling of cognitive boundaries: 'a dim and undetermined sense | Of unknown modes of being'.[34] This the child understands as an apprehension of the supernatural, whilst the adult explains it both in psychological terms, as fearful projection, and in aesthetic terms, as a function of the sublime.[35] The events have an immediate afterlife

---

[34] See *Prelude* i. 318–32 (snaring woodcocks); 333–50 (plundering birds' nests); and 372–426 (stealing a boat).

[35] The presence of the word 'undetermined' (l. 419) places Wordsworth's description of the 'unknown modes of being' in the context of an aesthetic debate whose lineage I traced at the beginning of this chapter.

in the child's dreams, which the recuperative gaze of the adult claims as permanent nourishment of the imagination.

Other 'spots of time' involve unaccountable feelings of guilt, not directly
attributed to acts of disobedience, though evidently connected at a deeper psychic level with the unthinkable, the taboo, or the forbidden: such is the episode
in which Wordsworth describes waiting impatiently for the horses to bear him
home from school, shortly before his father dies (xi. 344–88). Here a subliminal
link is made between ignorance of and indifference to the father's dying, which
has been understood by several critics in Oedipal terms.[36] The adult returns
compulsively to the memory of a physical and temporal 'spot', which for him
carries the awesome associations of death, precisely because at the time he was
oblivious to them. Guilt and self-chastisement—the products of complicated
hindsight—are projected back onto an 'innocent' scene, which both invites and
resists their intrusion. Wordsworth is interested by the sense in which such a
scene is unknowingly, even inconsequentially, portentous, according to a system of signification as yet undisclosed.

Another such childhood trauma involves the sighting of a gibbet, where a man
(the murderer of his wife) had been hanged (xi. 278–327). This experience is
fixed in the memory, Wordsworth claims, not primarily through the image of the
mouldered gibbet itself, nor through the uncanny sight of 'a long green ridge of
turf ... | Whose shape was like a grave', but by means of a contrasting and
seemingly irrelevant ingredient of the scene: 'A girl who bore a pitcher on her
head | and seemed with difficult steps to force her way | Against the blowing
wind'. To the fearful child looking round for his 'lost guide' (as Eve does, in the
disturbing Satanic dream which foreshadows her fall),[37] this windblown form is
presumably to be construed as an image of strength and resilience; while to the
backward gaze of the poet it 'prefigures' the later plenitude of imagination.[38]
There emerges an implicit equation between the projections of adult consciousness, which inevitably intrude in the course of developmental narrative, and the
growth of a subjective faculty in the child himself. Thus, in the psychological

---

[36] The best account is by D. Ellis; see *Wordsworth, Freud and the Spots of Time: Interpretation in
'The Prelude'* (Cambridge, 1985), 17–34. The Oedipal implications have been of particular interest
to critics seeking an explanation for the presence of a Shakespearian echo at l. 381, which connects
the 'indisputable shape' of the advancing mist with the 'questionable shape' of the ghost in *Hamlet* I.
iv. 43. See esp. J. Wordsworth, *William Wordsworth: The Borders of Vision* (Oxford, 1982), 63; Ellis,
Wordsworth, Freud, and the Spots of Time 33–4; and J. Bate, *Shakespeare and the English Romantic
Imagination* (Oxford, 1986), 116.

[37] See *PL* v. 91. Milton suggests a disorientation in Eve which is both credibly dreamlike, and
ironically anticipatory of the later loss (of Adam as guide) which causes her fall. Wordsworth
recreates the abrupt, disconnected transitions, and the sense of a pervasive and portentous *unheim-
lich*, which are characteristic of dreams, but which in this context acquire a loaded significance
attributable to their Miltonic resonance.

[38] See *Prelude* xi. 315–27. The girl bears some resemblance to the allegorical figure of 'heavenly
Truth' in Coleridge's 'The Destiny of Nations', who is described 'with gradual steps, winning her
difficult way' (l. 125); see R. Parker, *Coleridge's Meditative Art* (Ithaca, NY, 1975), 116–18. J.
Wordsworth sees additional connections with Martha Ray and Margaret, but stresses the girl's
'haunting dream-like presence', and her 'secret strength' (*Borders of Vision*, 59).

system which the 'spots of time' coherently embody, the child's confrontations with death (whether imagined or real) are seen as encounters with experience, from which the creative process will ultimately gain—'spectacles and sounds' to which the adult mind will 'repair and drink, as at a fountain' (xi. 382, 383–4). They take their place, in the larger narrative of *The Prelude*, as evidence that the fall into experience is the birth of imagination.

Among the many Miltonic aspects of *The Prelude* which Jonathan Wordsworth considers in *The Borders of Vision*, structural allusions to *Paradise Lost* are given special prominence. They are seen as thematically highlighting the poet's claim to have experienced a 'falling off' in his creative powers, first at Cambridge and later on returning from France. Jonathan Wordsworth demonstrates the disingenuousness of this claim by drawing attention to those moments in the narrative when Wordsworth reveals the underlying strength of his faculties, in the face of adversity: 'Imagination slept, | And yet not utterly' (*Prelude* iii. 260–61). Miltonic allusions are, therefore, he demonstrates, the register of resemblances between the poet's life and events in Milton's story— resemblances which the poet himself ultimately disavows.[39] Such a reading does ample justice to *The Prelude* as semi-fictional autobiography, but it overlooks the conceptual link between subjectivity and fallenness, which is Wordsworth's most significant inheritance from *Paradise Lost*. In beginning *The Prelude* as he does—with a double allusion, to the fallen Adam and Eve, as they make their way out of Eden, and to Sin, as she feels the first exhilarating effects of the Fall[40]—Wordsworth signals a connection between post-lapsarian consciousness and creativity. This is amplified, not only in the thematic content of the spots of time, but in the games with perspective which they involve. The *felix culpa* which emerges from *The Prelude* is thus to be understood as something inseparably bound up with experience: in affirming the gain-in-loss of adulthood, it repudiates regression and qualifies lament.

At the centre-point of *The Prelude*'s narrative—prominently placed, and dramatically built up to—is the account of crossing the Alps: an anticlimax, where a climax is both signalled and expected. Wordsworth's handling of this episode usefully highlights the larger structural significance of gain-in-loss, and makes a Kantian connection between the failure of representation and the survival of a supersensible faculty in the mind. According to Kant, 'the sublime, in the strict sense of the word, cannot be contained in any sensuous form', because it 'evidences a faculty of mind transcending every standard of sense'.[41] Wordsworth pursues this argument to its logical conclusion, arranging for Nature to let him down, so as to perpetuate his quest for the unattainable. In its initial impact, the moment of anticlimax is registered as displeasure; but, true to the Kantian pattern of recuperation, the mind derives from this bewilderment or perplexity a reassuring guarantee that it is 'lord and

---

[39] See ibid. ch. 8, esp. 231–46. [40] See my discussion of this double allusion in Ch. 2.
[41] *Critique of Judgement*, 98.

master'; that it is capable of 'Effort and expectation and desire, | And something ever more about to be'.[42]

The unpleasurable frustration of desire thus makes possible the triumph of imagination; and it does so, according to Wordsworth, in such a way that the compensatory second stage of this process is scarcely distinguishable from the perplexed first stage:

> Imagination!—lifting up itself
> Before the eye and progress of my song
> Like an unfathered vapour, here that power,
> In all the might of its endowments, came
> Athwart me. I was lost as in a cloud,
> Halted without a struggle to break through,
> And now, recovering, to my soul I say
> 'I recognise thy glory'
>
>   (*Prelude* vi. 525–32)

Like the childhood spots of time, this passage is constructed around the split between past and present selves: Wordsworth is at pains to emphasize this disjunction by his use of alternating tenses ('I was lost ... And now, recovering'). But a contrary tendency is also to be detected, in his imprecise use of the word 'here', which places the arrival of the 'unfathered vapour' of imagination both in the present as he writes, and in the past ('*came* athwart me') at the geographical point where he was overwhelmed by disappointment.[43] Paul de Man has described the scrambling of temporal perspectives thus:

The moment of active projection into the future (which is also the moment of the loss of self in the intoxication of the instant) lies for the imagination in a past from which it is separated by the experience of a failure. The interpretation is possible only from a standpoint that lies on the far side of this failure, and that has escaped destruction thanks to an effort of consciousness to make sure of itself once again.[44]

Wordsworth's conflation of past and present selves has the effect of collapsing into each other the contrary feelings of anticlimax and recovery, thus underlining the Kantian argument that sublimity is *dependent* on insufficiency.[45] This argument is supported by the function the episode fulfils in relation to Wordsworth's larger narrative scheme: as in the spots of time, his Miltonic handling of double perspective makes the revisited scene into a source, as well as a portent, of imaginative power.

---

[42] *Prelude* xi. 271; vi. 541–2.

[43] G. Hartman perceives 3 distinct stages in Wordsworth's account of loss and recovery, with the address to imagination severing an 'original temporal sequence'; see *Wordsworth's Poetry: 1787–1814* (Cambridge, Mass., 1964; repr. 1987), 44.

[44] *The Rhetoric of Romanticism* (Columbia, NY, 1984), 58.

[45] See *Critique of Judgement*, 100–1.

Alongside the 'spots of time' and the crossing of the Alps one should place Wordsworth's 'Note' on the Immortality Ode, dictated late in life to Isabella Fenwick, and recollecting moments of bewilderment or perplexity experienced in childhood, when the real world appeared to fall away. This note gives a less schematized (though equally Kantian) account of the gain-in-loss which fearful experience entails. The mind, in losing a sense of external reality, becomes conscious of its own subjective state: 'I was often unable to think of external things as having external existence', Wordsworth claims, 'and I communed with all that I saw as something not apart from, but inherent in, my own immaterial nature. Many times while going to school have I grasped at a wall or tree to recall myself from this abyss of idealism to the reality'.[46] Entry into this abyss is felt to be displeasurable at the time, for as Kant puts it, 'the point of excess for the imagination ... is like an abyss in which it fears to lose itself'.[47] But the mind is thereby offered a guarantee of primacy over the external world and, in a recuperative scheme, becomes strengthened by experience.

Since subjectivity is the basis of Wordsworth's imaginative claims, these moments of incertitude are highly valued: looking back, he stresses their dwindling frequency, and laments the subjugation to materiality which adult-hood entails. Shelley, likewise, claims that 'There are some persons who in this respect are always children'. 'Subject', as he puts it, to 'the state called reverie', such people feel 'as if their nature were dissolved into the surrounding universe, or as if the surrounding universe were absorbed into their being'.[48] It is Coleridge, however, who makes a wider and more resonant connection between poetry, subjectivity, and fallenness, when he suggests that 'In all modern poetry in Christendom, there is an underconsciousness of a sinful nature—the mind or subject greater than the object, the reflective character predominant'. He goes on to associate this subjectivity with *Paradise Lost*, whose sublimest passages are 'the revelations of Milton's own mind, producing itself and evolving its own greatness'.[49] That this association was clearly shared by Wordsworth, I hope to have demonstrated: by showing the frequency with which his narrative devices replicate Miltonic games with perspective; by emphasizing the dominance of experience, both as it is projected back onto innocence, and as it is claimed on behalf of adult creativity; and, finally, by pointing to the ways in which Wordsworth's account of the growth of sub-jectivity is framed as a transgression narrative. Thus, the 'Fallings from us, vanishings' which the Immortality Ode locates in childhood are subliminally connected with the Fall itself,[50] just as the 'abyss of idealism' has distant and fearful Satanic overtones.

---

[46] *The Poetical Works of William Wordsworth*, ed. E. De Selincourt (5 vols., Oxford, 1940), iv. 463.
[47] *Critique of Judgement*, 106.   [48] 'On Life' (*Shelley*, 477).
[49] Quoted in full on p. 88.
[50] See 'Ode: Intimations of Immortality', l. 146.

INITIATION

All this is confirmation that, in a Wordsworthian scheme, childhood is valued, not for its happiness or security, but for its troubled apprehensions of loss; not for its innocence, but for its underconsciousness of sin. De Quincey extends this pattern, by magnifying the points of suffering which are the child's initiation into the fallen world. 'The solitude ... which ... appalls or fascinates a child's heart', he writes, 'is but the echo of a far deeper solitude through which already he has passed, and of another solitude, deeper still, through which he *has* to pass: reflex of one solitude—prefiguration of another.'[51] The terms 'echo', 'reflex', and 'prefiguration' suggest that De Quincey links these isolated episodes one to the other, in a typological system of signification whose models are both religious (the Bible and Milton) and secular (Wordsworth's 'spots of time'). He can thus be seen to read his own life-story as a teleology, in which personal suffering at once foreshadows and is identified with the principle of redemption.

In 'Suspiria de Profundis', the death of his sister opens the way into a vast and visionary world. Framing his narrative as a version of the Fall, De Quincey describes how, on the day after her death, he makes his own scheme for seeing her once more. Secretly, he climbs the staircase to her room, reaching her chamber door 'at exactly high noon'. He finds the door locked against him, but since the key has not been removed, the excitement of prohibition is further heightened by temptation. Prolonging the suspense, so that it seems 'an act of stealth | And troubled pleasure' (*Prelude* i. 389–90) he describes entering, and closing the door 'so softly that ... no echo ran along the silent walls'. 'Then turning round', the climax comes, abruptly, 'I sought my sister's face.' In what is a reflex and a prefiguration of the solitude to come, De Quincey's access to her is denied:

The bed had been moved, and the back was now turned. Nothing met my eyes but one large window wide open, through which the sun of midsummer at noonday was showering down torrents of splendour. The weather was dry, the sky was cloudless, the blue depths seemed the express types of infinity; and it was not possible for eye to behold or for heart to conceive any symbols more pathetic of life and the glory of life.[52]

As the child stands on the threshold of the fallen world, having just committed his act of 'transgression', the mighty opposites of death and life come together, in a conflation of loss and gain. Appropriately, in the background, are the lines from *Prelude* Book VI, in which Wordsworth describes his sublime recompense for crossing the Alps. De Quincey's spot of time draws on Wordsworth's for its apocalyptic framework—'Characters of the great apocalypse, | The types and symbols of eternity, | Of first, and last, and midst, and without end' (*Prelude* vi.

---

[51] 'Suspiria de Profundis', in *Confessions of an English Opium Eater and Other Writings*, ed. with introd. G. Lindop (Oxford, 1985), 114.

[52] Ibid. 103.

570–2)—but it also alludes subliminally to the positioning of the Wordsworth passage in a pattern of loss followed by compensation. Elizabeth's death opens a window on vast Piranesi regions of space ('A vault seemed to open in the zenith of the far blue sky, a shaft which ran up forever'), the apprehension of which provokes a comparable expansion in De Quincey's own mind: 'I in spirit rose as if on billows that also ran up the shaft forever'. But, true to a Kantian pattern of sublimation, the awareness of a supersensible faculty linking the mind with God instigates the endlessly frustrated pursuit of an unreachable goal—a Wordsworthian sense of 'something ever more about to be': 'the billows seemed to pursue the throne of God; but *that* also ran before us and fled away continually. The flight and the pursuit seemed to go on for ever and ever.'[53]

In De Quincey's analysis, the preservation of a spot of time such as this one occurs through '*involutes*', which he explains as 'perplexed combinations of *concrete* objects ... compound experiences incapable of being disentangled'.[54] His use of the word 'perplexed' should alert us to the fact that it is not just the objects themselves (bed, window, sunlight streaming in) which are significantly entangled, but the writer's perspective, too. Like 'forlorn', 'perplexed' is a word that conjures up fallenness, and it also describes that state of imaginative uncertainty which constitutes the sublime: Kant, for instance, refers to the 'bewilderment or sort of perplexity', that the visitor experiences on first entering St Peter's in Rome;[55] and when describing the processes of memory, Wordsworth confesses that he 'Often is perplexed, and cannot part | The shadow from the substance'.[56] In the spots of time which unify both *The Prelude* and 'Suspiria de Profundis', perplexity is given an aesthetic function, which is apprehended on three different levels: in the objects themselves, which combine mysteriously to produce emotion; in the overlapping of past and present, which occurs within the memory; and in the intersection of innocence and experience which is symbolized by the incidents themselves, as initiations into the fallen world.[57]

Wordsworth claims that he feels himself to be 'two consciousnesses—conscious of myself | And of some other being' (*Prelude* ii. 32–3), and it may well be with this in mind that De Quincey provides his own model of typological reading. 'Though the child's feelings are spoken of', he writes, 'it is not the child who speaks. I decipher what the child only felt in cipher.' He goes on to emphasize that this disjunction between past and present selves is a necessary

---

[53] Ibid. 106.   [54] Ibid. 103.   [55] *Critique of Judgement*, 100.

[56] Kantian perplexity thus underwrites the Burkean obscurity which Wordsworth invokes in his quotation from *Paradise Lost*; see *Prelude* iv. 254–5, discussed and quoted in full at the beginning of this chapter.

[57] For the applicability of De Quincey's definition of involutes to Wordsworthian 'spots of time', see J. Wordsworth, *Borders of Vision*, 61–2. In his discussion of the 'Waiting for Horses' episode, J. Wordsworth stresses that the poet is 'disentangling his compound memory, showing us how his improbable involutes have gained their power'. My own emphasis would be on a deliberate entanglement of past and present (innocent and experienced) perspectives, which is artfully presented by the poet as involuntary.

function of the signifying process: 'I the child had the feelings, I the man decipher them. In the child lay the handwriting mysterious to *him*, in me the interpretation and the comment.'[58] Thus, the binary system which is at first implied turns out to be a system of interdependency. De Quincey shares with Wordsworth his interest in the intersection of contraries: as the simile in *Prelude* Book V has shown, substance and shadow, past and present, child and adult are all divisions which tend to be dissolved by remembering, writing, and reading. Each of these activities implies a position sufficiently distanced for the mind to belong neither to one state nor to the other, but to take up a role that mediates between both. The remainder of this chapter will be concerned with that mediatory position.

RECOGNITION

In breaking down the binary scheme of Blake's contraries, it is tempting to turn to the notion of a 'higher innocence', which mediates between them both. The word 'higher' might be used to distinguish this state from naïvety, ignorance, and stasis; whilst the word 'innocence' might signify a redemptive possibility beyond the fallen world. This so-called higher innocence might be seen as the third term, or 'progression', that is produced from the clash of contraries. It could be thought of in political terms, as the state finally to be achieved when the Fall is reversed and the Eternals reunited. But it could also be seen as the visionary potential in fallen man—what Milton referred to as the paradise within. 'If the doors of perception were cleansed, everything would appear to man as it is—infinite', Blake writes in *The Marriage of Heaven and Hell* (pl. 14, ll. 80–1). To achieve this cleansing does not imply a regression to innocence itself, but a progression to the third or higher state.

The mediatory position which I wish to discuss, however, is closer to 'higher experience' than to 'higher innocence', since what the latter term fails to take into account is the extent to which this third or mediatory function is dependent on both the other two. It can occur in the process of writing itself, where contraries are arranged in juxtaposition or conflation, and it can take place, too, in the readerly activity of perceiving likeness in difference—of mediating between contraries. Without Blake's reminders to us of the ways we are implicated in a fallen perspective, we should lose hold of one part of the dialectic on which 'progression' depends. The activities both of writing and of reading thus involve a recognition of fallenness which can be seen (like the wedding guest's listening to the Mariner's story) as themselves a repetition of the Fall.

Blake alerts us to this in the Bard's song at the beginning of *Songs of Innocence*: 'And I made a rural pen, | And I stained the waters clear' (ll. 17–18). The implication is that writing inevitably involves some degree of desecration. For Blake, the act of staining is associated with the practical business of producing

[58] 'Suspiria de Profundis', 113.

coloured engravings; but it is also, and paradoxically, linked to the artists's redemptive purpose: that of 'cleansing' the doors of perception. Instead of lamenting the trap into which the artist inevitably falls—staining when he intends to cleanse—Blake is in fact affirming experience as the route to redemption. This pattern repeats itself in 'London': 'I wander through each chartered street', Blake begins, 'Near where the chartered Thames does flow' (ll. 1–2). The fallen perspective touched in (as by Gray) by that word 'wander', goes on darkening in the next two lines: 'And mark in every face I meet | Marks of weakness, marks of woe' (ll. 3–4). The echoic language takes us back to Book IX of *Paradise Lost*, and to the climactic moment of Eve's fall: 'Earth felt the wound, and nature from her seat | Sighing through all her works gave *signs of woe*, | That all was lost' (ll. 782–4). In Blake, though, the 'marks of woe' are not just 'given' by the faces of passers by, but projected onto them by the poet. That verb 'remark' allows him the dual role of interpreter reporting and engraver re-inscribing. We must conclude that he is as responsible for the mind-forged manacles he perceives as those in whom he perceives them. Only by acknowledging this can he hope to expand perception.[59]

The implicated status of the artist is taken further in *Urizen*, a poem which, as I showed in Chapter 4, presents all modes of creation as versions of the Fall. Entering the poem at the point where Los, personification of creative energy, is separated off from Urizen (who stands for intellect's tyrannical power), we can see that this act of division gives Urizen a chaotic formlessness: 'Los smitten with astonishment, | Frightened at the hurtling bones | And at the surging, sulphureous | Perturbed Immortal, mad-raging' (pl. 8, ll. 154–7). The wound of separation cannot heal until Urizen takes organic form, and it is only through Los's creative powers that form can be realized: 'And Los formed nets and gins | And threw the nets round about. | He watched in shuddering fear | The dark changes and bound every change | With rivets of iron and brass' (ll. 160–4). In attempting to curtail Urizen's repressive and tyrannical power, Los is forced into adopting the very strategies he opposes. Binding Urizen, he becomes that tyrant's mirror image, thus completing one further stage of the fall into division. His double-bind mirrors that of the artist: creative energy must of necessity take a form, but all form is inevitably a limiting, or enclosing, of energy.

One might take as a further analogy Shelley's 'Ozymandias', which tells of a tyrant apparently overthrown by forces beyond him—other civilizations, the passage of time—but in fact enjoying perpetual dominion: For his 'frown, | And wrinkled lip, and sneer of cold command' (ll. 4–5) are memorialized by the artist who mocked them. They 'Tell that its sculptor well those passions read | *Which yet survive*, stamped on these lifeless things' (ll. 6–7). Tyranny is ironically perpetuated, first by the sculptor who gives it form, next by the traveller who lives

[59] Numerous commentators have pointed to the ironies discussed here, but I am indebted esp. to E. Larrissy, who points to a consistent underlying ambivalence in Blake's treatment of outline as both limiting and necessary; see *William Blake* (Oxford, 1985).

to tell his story, and last by the poet himself, who writes of his meeting with the 'traveller from an antique land' (l. 1). The framing device serves to heighten irony—implying a deliberate parallel between sculptor and poet.

But there is a redemptive possibility, which lies with the reader. 'Higher experience', to return to the term I used earlier, is not in fact the third in a sequence of states, except in so far as narrative presents it in linear terms. It is, rather, the role played in the reading process by mediation between contraries. This process is both more sophisticated and more tainted by experience, than the 'higher innocence' which I earlier defined. That it bears a significant resemblance to Romantic irony can be demonstrated by turning back to the contrast between childhood and adulthood, as defined by the most apparently nostalgic of writers, Charles Lamb. In 'My First Play', Lamb describes the difference between going to the theatre aged six, when 'it was all enchantment and a dream', and going back again ten years later, 'a rationalist'. 'In that interval', he writes, 'what had I not lost! ... At the first period I knew nothing, understood nothing, discriminated nothing. I felt all, loved all, wondered all.' And in the second period, 'The same things were there materially; but the emblem, the reference, was gone!' This transition from innocence into experience is described as a fall into materiality, reminiscent of Wordsworth's message in the Fenwick note to the Immortality Ode:

The green curtain was no longer a veil, drawn between two worlds, the unfolding of which was to bring back past ages, to present a royal ghost—but a certain quantity of green baize, which was to separate the audience for a given time from certain of their fellow-men who were to come forward and pretend those parts. The lights—the orchestra lights—came up a clumsy machinery. The first ring, and the second ring, was now but a trick of the prompter's bell—which had been, like the note of a cuckoo, a phantom of a voice, no hand seen or guessed at which ministered to its warning.

'The actors were men and women painted', Lamb concludes abruptly: 'I thought that the fault was in them; but it was in myself.'[60]

On the surface this is straightforward enough—a lament for the scepticism which comes with adulthood, making illusion no longer possible. But it seems probable that Lamb's intention is to guide the reader towards the more sophisticated position adopted elsewhere. He writes in a letter to Wordsworth of the mind's capacity 'knowingly [to] pass a fiction on herself':[61] a process which is referred to by Coleridge as 'that willing suspension of disbelief for the moment which constitutes poetic faith'.[62] It should be noticed that the emphasis falls on the mind's active and conscious contribution to illusion: knowingly passing a fiction upon oneself, and willingly suspending disbelief, are thus sharply

[60] *Elia and the Last Essays of Elia*, ed. with introd. J. Bate (Oxford 1987), 114.

[61] Lamb makes this observation in a comment on 'The Old Cumberland Beggar': 'The mind knowingly passes a fiction on herself, first substituting her own feelings for the Beggar's, and, in the same breath detecting the fallacy, will not part with the wish'; see *Lamb Letters*, i. 265.

[62] *Biographia*, ii. 6.

distinguished from credulity. In his essay 'On the Artificial Comedy of the Last Century', Lamb clarifies the distinction, by demonstrating the pact, or 'sub-insinuation', that exists between actors and their audience.[63] When attention is drawn by someone on stage—if not verbally, then through gesture—to the play as a play, it can proceed with a full indulgence toward fictionality. 'This secret correspondance with the company before the curtain', Lamb claims, 'has an extremely happy effect ... in the more highly artificial comedy of Congreve or of Sheridan ... where the absolute sense of reality ... is not required, or would rather interfere to diminish your pleasure.'[64] What he values here, then, is not the child's ingenuous submission to illusion but the self-consciousness which allows fiction to be acknowledged and enjoyed.

When he argues that, by contrast, self-consciousness is 'the bane and death of tragedy', Lamb makes a generic distinction which presupposes that tragedy requires the audience's credulity, whereas comedy involves the willing suspension of disbelief. It is none the less possible to see a consistent thread of Romantic irony, linking the 'Comedy' essay with the 'Essay on The Tragedies of Shakspeare'. Describing his first experience of seeing a tragedy performed, Lamb claims that 'it seemed to embody and realize conceptions which had hitherto assumed no distinct shape.' 'But', he goes on,

dearly do we pay all our life after for this juvenile pleasure, this sense of distinctness. When the novelty is past, we find to our cost that instead of realizing an idea, we have only materialized and brought down a fine vision to the standard of flesh and blood. We have let go a dream, in quest of an unattainable substance.[65]

A Kantian interpretation would align this passage with Lamb's account of first seeing Milton's handwriting, quoted in Chapter 1.[66] The fall into materiality, presented as loss, is also a kind of gain. 'What we see upon a stage is body and bodily action', Lamb asserts. 'What we are conscious of in reading is almost exclusively the mind, and its movements.'[67] But if, as he claims, *Lear* is genuinely unactable, then seeing it performed must offer reassurance of the primacy of mind over matter. Like the anticlimax which Wordsworth arranges at the centre of *The Prelude*, it allows for the perpetuation of the imaginative quest, precisely because of the fact of disappointment. What Lamb calls the 'unattainable substance' is Wordsworth's 'something evermore about to be'.

Lamb's comments on comedy and on tragedy have this in common: both of them draw attention to the role played by adult scepticism in enhancing, rather than reducing, the world of imagination. Scepticism necessarily involves an absolute sense of loss: writing of *The Tempest*, Lamb says that 'The Garden of Eden, with our first parents in it, is not more impossible to be shewn on a stage,

[63] *Lamb as Critic*, ed. R. Park (London, 1980), 48.
[64] 'On some of the Old Actors', ibid. 60.
[65] 'On the Tragedies of Shakespeare, considered with reference to their Fitness for Stage Representation', ibid. 86.
[66] See p. 61.   [67] 'On the Tragedies of Shakespeare', 98.

than the Enchanted Isle, with its no less interesting and innocent first settlers'.[68] But of course this loss is productive, in intensifying the mind/matter dualism on which all claims for imagination depend. In other words, if each performance of *The Tempest* is for the audience a repetition of the loss of Eden, the awareness of disappointment is a gaining of something higher. Both the mind's capacity to pass a fiction on itself and its ability to detect the inadequacy of representation are products of fallenness.

A more resonant term than 'higher experience' is needed adequately to describe the state which is achieved by the wedding guest in 'The Ancient Mariner', as he becomes a sadder and a wiser man; by the narrators of *The Prelude* and 'Suspiria de Profundis' as they project spots of experience onto the past; and by the reader who learns to negotiate between overlapping perspectives, in Blake and Lamb. The term should imply the humanness of experience, without the entrapment of Blake's fallen world; and the method should suggest the sophistication of a double perspective, rather than the linearity of progression towards a higher state. The best description I can give is one in which the reader acknowledges the trap of fallenness, responds to the invitation to fall, and stands back sufficiently to watch the process as it happens. I pointed in Chapter 2 to the duck-rabbit as a model of indeterminacy; and one might return to that here, with a new emphasis on the eye that is observing. Wittgenstein was interested, not just in the theoretical possibility of coexistence between images, but in the observer's awareness of 'the dawn of an aspect', as one image gave way to the other.[69] The moment of arrest, in which the mind watches itself in transition, is what I am attempting to define.

The problem with the various terms I have been using is that they suggest no escape, either from the linearity of narrative or from a binary moral scheme. This is so with the catch-all phrase, 'higher experience' and the clumsy attempt to describe superimposed perspectives—as, for instance, when I referred to Adam as both the 'insider looking out' and the 'outsider looking back in'. But then, as any reader of Sterne will know, all attempts to describe moments of arrest are caught in the trap of sequential language; indeed, all descriptions are narratives, in that they try to recover what is already past. In the absence of a critical term that is subtle enough to suggest, and also to enact, a double perspective, the study of allusion is the nearest one can get to watching it at work. It should be remembered, however, that the processes of recognition and interpretation which allusion invites from the reader can be explained only in sequential terms. Allusion is, indeed, a perpetual reminder of the tendency to explain progression as a story—to 'people' the gap between present and past. Even the duck-rabbit enacts a mini-narrative—the 'dawn of an aspect' Wittgenstein calls it, creating as his protagonist the mind in transition.

In *Minima Moralia*, Adorno writes that 'no one who is happy can know that he

---

[68] Ibid. 100.
[69] *Philosophical Investigations*, trans. G. E. M. Anscombe (Oxford, 1958; repr. 1963), 194.

is so. To see happiness, he would have to pass out of it: to be as if already born. He who says he is happy lies, and in invoking happiness, sins against it. He alone keeps faith who says: I was happy.'[70] This can be taken on three different levels, in the context of what I have been exploring in this chapter. It can be interpreted as an account of the growth of consciousness that comes with falling, and which constitutes subjectivity as a process of mediation betwen past and present: Byron's 'The world is all before me, or behind'. It can be used to describe the 'dawn of an aspect' that is observable in allusion and interpretation; and it can be read, finally, as a confession of the inescapable narrative which consciousness makes of itself. 'The only relation of consciousness to happiness is gratitude', Adorno concludes, 'in which lies its incomparable dignity.'[71]

[70] *Minima Moralia: Reflections from Damaged Life*, trans. E. F. N. Jephcott (London, 1974), 112. I am grateful to Ying Chang for this parallel.
[71] Ibid.

7

Imagination

Enlightenment and Romantic theories of imagination rely as heavily as do earlier formulations on the parallel between human and divine creativity. God is the great original, in Whose image man is made. Acts of imagination are repetitions, and therefore imitations, of His Creation.[1] The hierarchical structure this implies can, however, be dissolved (at least in theory), since, by imitating God, man might hope to equal Him, go one better than Him, or merge into Him. Indeed, the potential for rivalry is built into the act of imitation: to the imitator this offers the excitement of aspiration, but from a higher moral perspective it looks like presumption. One might take as an analogy from *Paradise Lost* Satan's estimate of his own powers, which appears compellingly imaginative from one point of view and impotently rebellious from the other.

Because the imagination is seen as a divine faculty, it is natural that the relationship between self and authority in a literary context should be conceived in quasi-religious terms. This is particularly the case where Milton is concerned, because (as I demonstrated in Chapter 1) the subject-matter and style of *Paradise Lost* invite comparison between the author who seeks to justify God's ways to man and the God whose ways are being justified. The 'inimitableness' of Milton's genius must therefore be understood in terms of the nature of his subject-matter, and of the divine authority to which he thus lays claim. By tackling the great religious themes of the temptation, the Fall, and man's redemption through Christ, he does something his classical forebears could not do. (As Hayley puts it, 'he fixed on a subject so different from those of Homer and Virgil, that he may be said to have accomplished a revolution in poetry'.) And in rewriting the epic tradition by adapting it to a Christian theme, he also manages to 'classicize' Genesis—to appropriate God's Word for his own imaginative ends.

Furthermore, if Milton has access to divine authority—if, as he claims, *Paradise Lost* was indeed dictated to him by God—then the process of imitating, echoing, or in some way reworking Milton's text is to be seen as analogous to quoting the Bible. Miltonic allusion is thus more than a way of gaining poetic credibility; it is also, because of the subject-matter of *Paradise Lost*, a means of claiming quasi-scriptural authority. The quasi-divinity of Milton's status makes him doubly interesting, but it also makes for complexities in the rela-

[1] For a wide-ranging survey, see J. Engell, *The Creative Imagination: Enlightenment to Romanticism* (Cambridge, Mass., 1981).

tionships his successors have with him. The aim behind all poetic imitation is to earn the right to a place in the canon by using earlier models in new ways; and there is an inevitable process of competition in all redefinitions of a given genre. This we see in Milton's Christianized transformation of epic. He claims that he is not 'sedulous by nature to indite | Wars, hitherto the only argument | Heroic deemed' (*PL* ix. 27–9), and he goes on to declare that 'higher argument | Remains, sufficient of itself to raise' the name of heroism (ll. 42–3). He dismisses Arthurian epic as 'long and tedious', and firmly establishes that the Fall of Man is a subject 'not less but more heroic than the wrath | Of stern Achilles' (ll. 14–15). If Milton must go one better than Homer and Virgil, those who come after him must in their turn challenge his claims. Wordsworth, for instance, can only take his place in the long line of epic poets by redefining what is suitable as a subject for epic poetry. *Paradise Lost* is therefore firmly discarded ('Jehovah, with his thunder, and the choir | Of shouting angels, and the empyreal thrones— | I pass them unalarmed')[2] and his own imaginative scheme put in its place.

So long as the relationship with a precursor remains on a purely poetic level, the poet's attitude towards this potential for competition is relatively straightforward: there is nothing particularly dangerous about one-upmanship where mere mortals are concerned. With *Paradise Lost*, though, the implications are more complicated: if the poem invites competition, it is inevitably a dangerous competition, because of the scriptural authority that is involved. At their most extreme, Romantic allusions can therefore smack of rivalry with God, or signal a daring repudiation of Christian orthodoxy. In the passage just cited, for instance, the process of going one better than Milton depends on seeing imagination as a subject that is more, not less, heroic than the Fall of Man: Wordsworth challenges, not just Milton as the greatest English poet, but Milton as the representative of Christian tradition. He does so, confidently and consciously, because this helps him to define his secular ends; whereas other writers, such as Coleridge or De Quincey, find themselves in a more problematic and potentially guilt-inducing situation by virtue of their different religious views.

The widespread habit of deifying Milton is demonstrated, therefore, not only in critical observations such as Coleridge's—'Milton is Prescience; he stands ab extra';[3] but also in the frequency with which allusions to *Paradise Lost* are put in a warning context, given a Satanic dimension, or seen as a bid for the usurpation of divine power. We are not dealing, these allusions tell us, merely with a daunting precursor, but with the authority of a sacred text. It is no accident, either, that definitions or discussions of imagination frequently coincide with Miltonic allusion. The possibility of rivalling Milton, which, as we have seen, is built into the very act of imitation, has all the dangerous associations which

---

[2] 'Prospectus' to *The Recluse*, ll. 21–3; text in J. Wordsworth, *William Wordsworth: The Borders of Vision* (Oxford, 1982), 388–90.

[3] *Table Talk*, i. 125 (9 May 1830).

accrue also to the autonomous imagination, in its unsettling of hierarchy and its questioning of religious absolutes. So long as God's (or Milton's) supremacy remains unchallenged, the imagination can be kept in its place, as an echo or repetition of divine creativity. But as soon as faith is unsettled, or the hierarchy begins to be dissolved, imagination starts to claim its own, autonomous power. It follows that, in the transition from Augustanism to Romanticism, we can trace an increasing emphasis on originality and imaginative autonomy, which is partly the product and partly the articulation of political and religious restlessness. The confidence with which writers of this period identify themselves with a Satanic perspective is proportionate, not just to their political radicalism, but to their readiness to experiment with religious authority: in this respect, as I demonstrated in Chapter 4, religion and politics are inseparable.

Thus, at one extreme, Miltonic allusion can be used to give voice to something more than poetic one-upmanship—to a kind of spiritual presumption, which at times takes on the status of transgression. One has only to read the poetry of Gray and Collins to see that, from a very early stage, there is an implicit connection between imitating Milton and disobeying God. One obvious way of interpreting the contrast between their poetry and the lines from Wordsworth's 'Prospectus', quoted above, is to see in it a confirmation of Bloom's distinction between weak Augustanism and strong Romanticism. Strong poets, Bloom argues, can only emerge into adulthood by waging war on their Oedipal father, Milton, whose massive poetic prowess would otherwise inhibit them from achieving an independent poetic voice. This they do by means of a series of rhetorical manœuvres or 'revisionary ratios'.[4] It is central to his scheme that Romantic poets should be seen as independent, while earlier poets are weak and passively subservient. Collins, then, is as unlike Wordsworth as a poet could be: instead of defeating his precursor by issuing a challenge to his supremacy (regaining or redefining 'paradise'), he might be seen as accepting defeat—willing upon himself the weakness which makes him perpetually adolescent.

What this analysis fails to take into account is the sea-change in attitudes to imitation and originality which I was concerned to illustrate in Chapter 1. Augustan writing, as observed from a post-Romantic perspective, contains an abnormal amount of imitation, classical as well as Miltonic, which mistakenly tends to be thought of as diminishing with the onset of Romanticism—*Lyrical Ballads* in 1798 being taken to mark a watershed in attitudes to poetic language. It is to be remembered that the notion of poetic 'originality' did not fully emerge until Young wrote his *Conjectures on Original Composition*, and that the dismissal of eighteenth-century writers (*pace* Bloom) as weakly and passively imitative is therefore a Romantic anachronism. Moving into the beginnings of Romanticism, there is an altering estimate of the imagination, which affects attitudes to the process of imitating, rather than diminishing the habit itself. The Romantics did not imitate or allude any less than their eighteenth-century

[4] H. Bloom, *A Map of Misreading* (Oxford, 1975).

forebears. They were just as dependent on poetic models, and just as ready to use them—even the *Lyrical Ballads* are allusive[5]—but they had a new incentive to transform what they borrowed into something of their own.

Returning to the shortcomings of Bloom's system, the term 'anxiety of influence' narrows down a problem which is complicated and diffuse. Instead of seeing the relationship between Milton and his successors as the struggle for purely poetic power within a patriarchal family, one should observe that Milton provides the focus for those larger, more important shifts of attitude which were taking place during the eighteenth century, and which formed the subject of my first chapter: attitudes towards politics, towards imitation and originality, towards sublimity and divinity, and above all towards the imagination itself. If it is useful to draw a distinction between Augustan and Romantic uses of Milton, one might do worse than to see Collins's modesty as representative of his time, but to give it the credit for being a poetic strategy. Thus, in eighteenth-century imitations, the emphasis is on a cautious restraining of the potential for creative transgression, whilst in Romantic allusions it is on the fearful appropriation of power. One might see the whole phenomenon, not in terms of an anxiety of influence, but in terms of an anxiety of imagination.

But Romantic writers do not invert what in *Paradise Lost* is a stable moral scheme. Instead, they throw into relief the ambivalence which Milton himself discloses. Whilst in general terms the historical development I have outlined can be allowed to stand, I would suggest that to identify caution as 'Augustan' and presumption as 'Romantic' is an oversimplification, where claims for the imagination are concerned. Instead, I shall make a distinction between individual writers, which in some cases will involve qualifying a straightforward historical progression. There are those who finally bow to Miltonic authority, in allowing a divinely ordained hierarchy to reassert itself in the face of a presumptuous or 'Satanic' imagination, and those who are less inhibited in the challenges they make, choosing to experiment with a balance of divine and human power. This distinction is intended neither to divide 'strong' from 'weak' poets nor to separate Romantic writers from their forebears, but to show a continuity of tradition, within which there are a range of responses and strategies. The deferential and submissive tactics adopted by Collins and Gray are shared by Coleridge, and to a certain extent by De Quincey also, because their religious beliefs predispose them to a cautious (even fearful) attitude to the autonomous imagination. Humanists such as Wordsworth and Keats, or atheists such as Shelley, are bolder in their appropriation and adaptation of Milton's terms, though they too are preoccupied with the controlling of power.

Wherever Miltonic (and especially Satanic) allusion reappears, one should be alert to the potential duality of meaning it conveys. Miltonic reference acts as an invitation to transgress, by exciting sympathy for Satanic impulses, but it also

[5] See M. Jacobus, *Tradition and Experiment in Wordsworth's 'Lyrical Ballads', 1798* (Oxford, 1976).

creates an admonitory supertext, by showing the antisocial effects of liberation. For some writers, the challenge imagination poses to divinity can receive little or no sanction, so long as it fails to construct a moral system that adequately replaces Christianity. Of this we are pointedly reminded by the message of *Frankenstein*, which takes to a cautionary extreme Romanticism's checking of its own (incipiently anarchic) power. We can, as readers, understand the curiosity which lies behind Frankenstein's experiments sufficiently to be drawn into his creative aspiration, but we are invited to question his wisdom in appropriating divinity. Our sympathy is turned round at the moment when he rejects his creation. Imaginative compulsion of this order seems in Mary Shelley's view to involve a wholly irresponsible relinquishing of moral obligations, personal and social ties: the tragic fall of the monster, and the trail of devastation he leaves behind him, are directly attributable to his creator's original act of usurpation, made doubly culpable by his inability to sympathize with the being he has created.

Everywhere one looks, in Romantic literature, one finds the simultaneous celebration and curtailment of imaginative power. The moral and ideological implications of this doubleness are not always so overtly signalled as in the pages of *Frankenstein*, but I shall be arguing in the course of this chapter that they are discernible none the less. The importance of Miltonic allusion, in the context of this wider ambivalence, is to suggest an authority which is at once deferred to and displaced. Bloom's theory of influence takes authority to be a family affair—a matter of the psychic relations between ephebe and precursor. But I shall demonstrate that competition with Milton is a synecdoche for rivalry with God, rather than (as Bloom would have it) rivalry with God being symbolic of anxiety towards Milton.

The structure of this chapter is intended to reflect the tenor of my disagreement with Bloom, by gradually widening its focus from the psychological to the social. I shall begin by looking at cases where Milton is consciously or allusively invoked, in order to assist the writers concerned (Collins, Gray, Coleridge, Wordsworth) in the process of defining poetic status and identity. Here my concern will be with the simultaneous expansion and curtailment of imaginative power that is observable in the tension between ambition and deference. I shall then proceed to cases where Miltonic allusions and paradigms can assist the reader in understanding the place of self in a wider social or religious context. Here my concern will be to read duality, equivocation, and irony as indicators of the divided role which is accorded to the imagination, by De Quincey, Shelley, and Keats. Whether one is examining these writers in their struggle for poetic power or in their concern with the responsibility of the imagination, there is observable, I shall argue, both a liberation of the ego and a repudiation of its excesses. Romanticism could be said to create its own critique—building into its celebrations of poetic power the acknowledgement of a dangerous potential in the transforming mind.

HUMILITY AND SUBMISSION

When Young, in a moment of anxious optimism, exclaims, 'What glory to come near, what glory to reach, what glory (presumptuous thought!) to surpass, our predecessors!'[6] he is giving voice to every eighteenth-century poet's hope of rivalling Milton. And he is doing so in a characteristically eighteenth-century way, by building the acknowledgement of presumption into what is otherwise an ambitious claim. The tonal effect is very nearly mock-deferential—suggesting, in Bloomian terms, a defence, or 'trope'. But this should not distract us from the genuine submissiveness that is implied. The point is that here, as elsewhere, deference to a higher authority plays an important part in the defining of self. Just as eighteenth-century poets sought, in their own writing, the balance of originality and imitation which Milton himself achieved, so, when imitating him, they invoked his genius as a check on their wish to surpass. It was through the acknowledgement of inferiority that they achieved their poetic voice.

Collins, for instance, in his 'Ode on the Poetical Character' (1746), follows George Herbert's practice of writing poetry that moves towards silence—willingly submitting, in this way, to an authority higher than his own. The ode turns on an analogy between God's and man's creative powers, and on the potential rivalry between them, which ends by being no rivalry at all. Collins arranges the expansion and final eclipse of his poetic self by giving Milton a mediatory role: the author of *Paradise Lost* comes as near as is humanly possible to divinity, and it is to him—rather than, as in Herbert, to God—that the voice of the poet finally gives way.

Rewriting Milton's account of the Creation so that it includes the weaving of Fancy's girdle, Collins at once establishes the divine origins of poetry and confirms the analogy between the creative powers of God and man. The primacy of God is, of course, implied in most Miltonic allusions; but here it is also subtly questioned by some of the more surprising ingredients in Collins's Creation myth. He describes the divine creative fiat, for instance, in terms of the clothing metaphors already used of Fancy. This has the ambiguous effect of making God seem ancillary to poetic creation:

> The band, as fairy legends say,
> Was wove on that creating day
> When He, who called with thought to birth
> Yon *tented* sky, this laughing earth,
> And *dressed* with springs and forests tall,
> And poured the main *engirting* all.[7]

---

[6] Young, *Conjectures*, 23.
[7] ll. 23–8; my italics. For an excellent critical discussion of Collins's literary relationship with Milton, see P. Sherwin, *Precious Bane: Collins and the Miltonic Legacy* (Austin, Tex., 1977).

Fancy, furthermore, is seen both as an attribute of God and as the 'lone enthusiast' who woos Him. Significantly personified as a woman,[8] she sits retired with Him on his sapphire throne, and has powers equal to His. When, 'from out the veiling cloud' she 'Breathe[s] her magic notes aloud' (ll. 37–8), she is at once *likened* to the emerging sun, and imagined as its source or creator. This double effect is achieved by the use of personification—'And thou, thou rich-haired youth of morn, | And all thy subject life was born!' (ll. 39–40)—which can be read either in apposition, as a simile, or in sequence, as a dependent event. Language is used persistently by Collins, in this way, to obscure the relation between cause and effect, analogy and source.

The allegory as a whole anticipates Blake's *Urizen*, both in the weaving metaphor itself (which Blake uses twice—first for Science and then for Religion[9]) and in the suggestion of multiple creations, all occurring simultaneously. Just as, in *Urizen*, the 'vast spine' forms *of itself* 'upon the winds', and just as the net of religion twists its own chords, and knots its own meshes, so here the woof of poetry appears to grow of its own volition—'The dangerous passions kept aloof, | Far from the sainted growing woof' (ll. 41–2)—witnessed by Wonder, Truth, and Mind, all of them at once attributes of God and His creations. This claiming of priority, or at least parity, for the poetic imagination leads Collins to ask the warning question implied at the end of Stanza 1:

> Where is the bard, whose soul can now
> Its high presuming hopes avow?
> Where he who thinks, with rapture blind,
> This hallowed work for him designed?
>
> (ll. 51–4)

The implication of that 'now' is clear enough: to claim poetic genius is (audaciously) to claim godlike powers. And, as the linguistic confusions between analogy and source suggest, to claim god-like powers is, in its turn, to conceive the possibility of rivalling them.

Collins answers his own rhetorical question in the final stanza by suggesting that Milton alone is worthy of these 'high presuming hopes', this 'rapture blind'. He does this allusively: by leading the reader towards a spot supposedly frequented by Milton, and then refusing access to the inner sanctum. The 'cliff, to heaven up-piled' (l. 55) has Parnassian overtones—pointing forward to the stairs mounted so painfully by the dreamer in 'The Fall of Hyperion'.[10] At the same time, it is resonant with Miltonic associations: 'Of rude access, of prospect wild, | Where, tangled round the jealous steep, | Strange shades o'erbrow the valleys deep' (ll. 56–8). As line 62 confirms, Collins is recalling the difficult approach to Paradise, seen through the eyes of Satan, in *Paradise Lost* Book IV, as 'the champain head | Of a steep wilderness, whose hairy sides | With thicket overgrown, grotesque and wild, | Access denied' (ll. 134–7). Roger Lonsdale's

---

[8] See Ch. 5, nn. 30, 32.   [9] pl. 19, ll. 325–31; pl. 25, ll. 462–9.   [10] ll. 124–36.

note draws attention to the sense Collins has of 'Milton's, as it were, pre-lapsarian imagination'. 'In his imaginative recreation of Eden in *Paradise Lost*', he comments, 'Milton imitated God's creative powers ... both literally and metaphorically. Milton's poem about Eden reveals an imaginative power as difficult of access and imitation as was Eden itself.'[11]

This is true enough; but it misses the admonitory implications of the Satanic perspective. What Collins has achieved by this stage in the poem is a complex layering effect, whereby one form of rivalry is seen in relation to another. Stanza 1 deals with the competition between poets for the girdle of Fancy; Stanza 2 with the more audacious rivalry of Fancy with God; and now Stanza 3 turns, as Lonsdale suggests, to the poet's own sense of competition with Milton. As Collins leads us up the steep ascent towards paradise, he makes us see through Satan's eyes so as to tempt us with, and warn us against, the presumption of hoping to compete. On one level, the ambition involved is poetic; and the central concern is with the poet's own wish to be seen in a Miltonic rather than an Augustan tradition. But on another level, Milton becomes conflated with God, and the 'fancied glades' are literally paradise, as well as metaphorically a place of poetic power. Hence the Satanic allusions, and hence, too, the sense of this sanctified and holy spot as something threatened by violation. Collins sets out, thus, to preserve paradise from the encroachments of Satan, and *Paradise Lost* from those of its readers and would-be rivals: 'In vain—such bliss to one alone | Of all the sons of soul was known' (ll. 72–3), he writes, making it clear that Milton, and no one else, deserves the right of entry to this holy place. The poet silences himself, and all others, in the face of Milton, because the author of *Paradise Lost* comes nearer to divinity than any poet, before or since. In this way, defeat functions as a device for preserving intact the highest possible status that can be accorded to poetic imagination.

In 'The Progress of Poesy' (1751–4), Gray agrees with Collins about Milton's status, but feels it more evidently as a threat. Adopting the warning voice which is so typical of this period, he suggests that post-Miltonic poets would be wise to steer the middle course, rather than follow their greatest precursor in his soaring flights of imagination. Built into his definition of poetic self, then, there is the same complex tension between the acknowledgement of inferiority and the wish to compete. Gray's need is to define an Augustan tradition to which he can comfortably and modestly belong. He does this by declaring his allegiance to Dryden, rather than to Milton himself. Where Collins had seen his own ambitions as presumptuous, Gray projects Satanic aspirations onto the author of *Paradise Lost*:

> Nor second he, that rode sublime
> Upon the seraph-wings of Ecstasy,
> The secrets of the abyss to spy.[12]

---

[11] See R. Lonsdale's n. to ll. 55–61 (*Gray, Collins, Goldsmith*, 433).
[12] 'The Progress of Poesy: A Pindaric Ode', ll. 95–7.

Lonsdale cites the invocation to Urania, in *Paradise Lost* Book VII—'Up led by thee | Into the Heaven of Heavens I have presumed | An earthly guest, and drawn empyreal air' (ll. 12–14) as a possible source for this passage. He also points to a number of eighteenth-century imitations: Isaac Watts, for instance, in 'The Adventurous Muse':

> There Milton dwells: The mortal sung
> Themes not presumed by mortal tongue ...
> Behold his muse set out t'explore
> The unapparent deep where waves of chaos roar,
> And realms of night unknown before.[13]

But though in their general import these passages are relevant, they fail to pin-point the Satanic reference which is particularly telling. Gray does in fact have in mind one of the most famous and quoted moments in *Paradise Lost*, when Satan, for whom the gates of hell have just been opened, looks round and sees 'the secrets of the hoary deep, a dark | Illimitable ocean without bound' (ii. 891–2). To portray Milton's imagination in these Satanic terms is to under-line the parallels between divine creativity, poetic ambition, and diabolic hubris which are in any case conveyed in the pairings of *Paradise Lost*.[14]

The moral purpose, to take a Miltonic model, of lines such as 'Into the Heaven of Heavens I have presumed' (*PL* vii. 13) is to keep ambition in check; but one of their effects is to suggest a sympathy in Milton himself with Satan's presumption. Milton himself seems to have been unabashed by the diabolic aspect of creativity: Sin, 'with terrors and with clamours compassed round' (*PL* ii. 862), has affinities with the poet, who is echoically described 'in darkness and with dangers compassed round' (*PL* vii. 27). Gray repeats the Miltonic pattern, confirming a moral ambivalence in his attitude to creative power. Hubristic implications are allowed to develop, but not so as to cancel out the analogy between the poetic and the divine:

> He passed the flaming bounds of place and time:
> The living throne, the sapphire-blaze,
> Where angels tremble while they gaze,
> He saw; but blasted with excess of light,
> Closed his eyes in endless night.

(ll. 98–102)

Icarus's flight too near the sun can be discerned in the background of Milton's sublime journey through the heavens, suggesting an admonitory implication. At the same time, the Homeric and Virgilian allusions work the other way, to imply a visionary power which is the subject of authorial approval.[15] The ambivalence deepens if one assumes that Milton's being 'blasted with excess of light' is both a

---

[13] Quoted by Lonsdale, n. to ll. 95–100 (*Gray, Collins, Goldsmith*, 173).   [14] See Ch. 2.
[15] See Lonsdale's note (*Gray, Collins, Goldsmith*, 174).

punishment for his hubris and a sign of his wish to compete. A reference to Homer himself is implied in the tribute-paying quotation from the Odyssey: blindness thus becomes a symbol of poetic status, handed down from poet to poet—a confirmation of Milton's classical lineage, and of his imitative power.

In this way it is to the classics, rather than to Milton, that Gray finally defers. Dryden, invoked as the greatest classical writer of his age and the sublimest user of the Pindaric ode, emerges as a more sensible role model than Milton himself:

> Behold, where Dryden's less presumptuous car
> Wide o'er the fields of glory, bear
> Two coursers of ethereal race,
> With necks in thunder clothed, and long-resounding pace.

> (ll. 103–6)

His 'thoughts that breathe and words that burn' (l. 110) are given unqualified approval; and his adoption of the middle course prepares the way, by impli-cation, for Gray himself, who manages to claim kinship with his precursors while at the same time acknowledging that competition with them would be futile. The audacity of his question 'What daring spirit | Wakes thee now?' (l. 112) gives way to a stance of modesty, from which more ambiguous claims are then made:

> Yet shall he mount and keep his distant way
> Beyond the limits of a vulgar fate,
> Beneath the good how far—but far above the Great.

> (ll. 121–3)

The layerings of allusive language have the effect of bewildering the reader: we do not know whether to identify the writers mentioned earlier with the labels used here or to treat this final epigrammatic assertion in more general terms. If the spatial metaphors are consistent, Milton must be above Gray in his nearness to the sun, and therefore 'good' according to this final schema. But has not the poem also suggested in him a greatness that is not entirely good? These final lines sustain the moral ambivalence of the poem as a whole. They leave the reader in some discomfort—not knowing whether to see Milton as good or great, and unsure as to whether the poet himself is being ambitious or unassuming. And so, through one of the most complex of 'transumptive' manœuvres, Gray finds his poetic voice. What both he and Collins demonstrate is that their final submission to higher authority is not the defeat of individual talent by canonized text, but rather the finding of self through imagining its limits. A voice in both poems warns against the expansion of human creativity beyond its proper bounds; and, as we see in 'Kubla Khan', it is a voice which goes on sounding.

ADMONITION

Coleridge exploits the Pindaric ode used by Collins and Gray, and is presumably aware of it as an appropriate medium: he, too, is both celebrating the power of human creativity and checking its excesses. Like Collins, he centres on the analogy between the divine creative fiat (the 'infinite I AM') and the imagination (its 'finite repetition'), seeing the potential for competition as latent in the analogy itself. And, like Collins again, he suggests the struggle for creative power within a sequence of allusions to *Paradise Lost*, making Milton an instance of imagination that is at once rivalrous and unrivalled. But whereas, in both the 'Ode on the Poetical Character' and 'The Progress of Poesy', Milton is explicitly invoked, in 'Kubla Khan' he is present entirely through allusion. The poem deals, at an overt level, with the affinity between Kubla, creator of the paradisal world of Xanadu, and the poet, striving to imitate (and possibly to outdo) that creation. The reader may extrapolate from this either or both of the equations: Kubla = God, Kubla = Milton: to do so is to arrive at a reading of the poem which is essentially allegorical, and which must refuse therefore to accept the myth of inexplicability offered by Coleridge himself.

As a result of (among others) K. M. Wheeler's study, *The Creative Mind in Coleridge's Poetry*, we no longer take it for granted that 'Kubla Khan' is the product of an opium dream, that its transcription was interrupted, or that the poem is incomplete.[16] The concept of Romantic irony has eroded our credulity, leaving us with a Shandyan narrator, a fictional Person from Porlock, a finished product which artfully resists closure by declaring itself as a 'fragment'. All this is very much to the point in establishing that the poem is allusive and allegorical, rather than impenetrable and unwilled. It is, moreover, a basis for claiming that the Preface is not so much an account of the poem's origins as a myth of origins parallel to the poem itself.

Coleridge's claim to have composed 'Kubla Khan' while he was unconscious is a claim to have a direct transcription of God's word. It is analogous to Adam's account of waking, to find 'all real, as the dream | Had lively shadowed' (*PL* viii, 310–11), or to Milton's assertion, that God dictated *Paradise Lost*. If this is translated into the terms of *Biographia Literaria*, it is like claiming that the distinction between the primary and the secondary imagination can be dissolved. According to the Chapter 13 definition, the primary is a 'repetition in the finite mind, of the eternal act of creation in the infinite I AM': that is, a creative act both analogous and subordinate to God's. The secondary, described as 'an echo of the former', must therefore be both dependent on the primary and a diminished version of it. Furthermore, whereas the primary is involuntary, the secondary coexists with the conscious will. Everything conspires in Coleridge's prose to suggest a hierarchical system, with writing one step behind imagining,

[16] pp. 17–41; cf. M. Levinson, *The Romantic Fragment Poem: A Critique of a Form* (Chapel Hill, NC, 1986), 97–114; and L. Brisman, *Romantic Origins* (Ithaca, NY, 1978), 21–54.

and imagining one step behind God. The quotation from *Paradise Lost* Book VII, used as one of the epigraphs to Chapter 13, confirms the idea of a ladder leading upwards, from discursive to intuitive reason.[17]

It is this hierarchy which the Preface to 'Kubla Khan' attempts to undermine. By suggesting that composition can be performed in an unconscious state, Coleridge temporarily closes the gap between primary and secondary imagination. When he describes having 'continued in a profound sleep, at least of the external senses', during which 'he could not have composed less than from two to three hundred lines', he is establishing the involuntary nature of poetic genius, and the transcendent nature of what is dreamt. '[I]f that indeed can be called composition', he continues, 'in which all the images rose up before him as *things*, with a parallel production of the correspondent expressions, without any sensation or consciousness of effort.'[18] In the dreaming state, then, words and things coalesce—as they did in paradise, and would do again, if language evolved towards perfection. For, as David Hartley puts it in *Observations on Man*: 'Was human life perfect, our happiness in it would be properly represented by that accurate knowledge of things which a truly philosophical language would give us'. This language, Hartley goes on, 'would as much exceed any of the present languages as a paradisiacal state does the mixture of happiness and misery, which has been our portion ever since the fall. ... It is no improbable supposition that the language given by God to Adam and Eve, before the fall, was of this kind.'[19]

In the numerous comments on language scattered throughout his letters and notebooks, one finds Coleridge again and again 'endeavouring' as he puts it, 'to destroy the old antithesis of *Words* and *Things*'[20]—seeking to abolish the arbitrary relation of signified and signifier. His purpose is not to describe how language actually functions, but to suggest how it might work in an ideal world.[21] We can choose to read the statements as millenarian cravings; but we can also observe that, for Coleridge, there is in the imagination itself a coalescence of word and thing which survives the Fall. His famous definition of symbol in *The Statesman's Manual* makes this clear: 'that reconciling and mediatory power', the imagination, 'gives birth', as he puts it, 'to a system of symbols,

---

[17] For a reading of the *Biographia* definitions in the context of English empiricism and English poetic tradition (incl. Milton), see J. Wordsworth, '"The Infinite I AM": Coleridge and the Ascent of Being', in R. Gravil, L. Newlyn, and N. Roe (eds.), *Coleridge's Imagination: Essays in Memory of Pete Laver* (Cambridge, 1985), 22–52. For an alternative account, which places Coleridge in the context of German thought, see T. McFarland, *Originality and Imagination* (Baltimore, 1985), 90–200.

[18] *CPW*, i. 296.

[19] *Observations on Man, His Fame, His Duty, and His Expectations* (2 vols., London, 1749), reissued with notes by H. Pistorius (3 vols., London, 1791), i. 320, 315–16.

[20] See e.g. Coleridge's letter to Godwin, 22 Sept. 1800: 'Are not words &c parts & germinations of the Plant? And what is the Law of their Growth?—In something of this order I would endeavor to destroy the old antithesis of *Words* and *Things*, elevating, as it were, words into Things, & living Things too' (*Coleridge Letters*, i. 625).

[21] See J. C. McKusick, *Coleridge's Philosophy of Language* (New Haven, Conn., 1986).

harmonious in themselves, and *consubstantial with the truths, of which they are the conductors*'.[22]

When words become symbolic in the highest possible sense, a paradisal world is revealed. In this paradise, things are not just *read* as God's word, they are of the same substance with it. But this symbolic mode of vision cannot be sustained. Wordsworth, in *The Prelude*, describes the process whereby images become 'Exposed, and lifeless as a written book' (viii. 727); and Blake, in *Urizen*, shows the hardening of Los's spiritual energy into the materiality of form.[23] It is Charles Lamb, though, who offers the most appropriate comment on 'Kubla Khan'. 'Coleridge is printing Xtabel by Ld. Byron's recommendation to Murray', Lamb writes to Wordsworth, in a letter of April 1816, 'with what he calls a vision Kubla Khan.' '[W]hich said vision', he goes on,

he repeats so enchantingly that it irradiates & brings heaven & Elysian bowers into my parlour while he sings or says it, but there is an observation Never tell thy dreams, and I am almost afraid that Kubla Khan is an owl that wont bear day light, I fear lest it should be discovered by the lantern of typography and clear reducting to letters, to be no better than nonsense or no sense.[24]

We should be alert to the Romantic irony revealed in this passage: the mystique of 'Kubla Khan' is heightened, not diminished, by the threat of anticlimax, which proves the untranslatability of dreams. The waking world's intrusion into the heavenly dream-world of imagination is, after all, the only means of registering the value of what has been lost: Keats is later to realize the full implications of this pattern.[25]

The Preface to 'Kubla Khan', like Lamb's comment, is a myth of gain-in-loss. It describes the attaining of symbolic vision, and its falling away, as an expression of the anxiety that words can never truly match up to imaginings; that the 'soulless image' replaces the 'living thought',[26] or that the telling destroys the dream. Coleridge's investment, in describing 'Kubla Khan' as incomplete, is therefore twofold: he succeeds in expressing nostalgia for the unfallen state, and in pointing toward 'the tomorrow [that] is yet to come',[27] when language will once again be paradisal. But he also claims the poem itself as a product of true symbolic vision. What the interruption from the Person from Porlock suggests is that, once lost, this vision cannot be restored. Rather than fall back on post-lapsarian language, to complete the poem, Coleridge preserves what he has already written as a 'fragment' of higher truth.

Past interpretations of the poem have tended to make a choice between seeing Kubla as human and allegorizing him as God. But neither reading is sufficient

---

[22] *The Statesman's Manual*; *Collected Coleridge*, vi, *Lay Sermons*, ed. R. J. White (London, 1972), 29.

[23] *Urizen*, pl. 8, ll. 154–65.   [24] To Wordsworth, 26 Apr. 1816 (*Lamb Letters*, iii. 215).

[25] See his 'Ode to a Nightingale', and my discussion, p. 252 below.

[26] See Wordsworth's anticlimactic sighting of Mont Blanc (*Prelude* vi. 454–5).

[27] 'Preface' to 'Kubla Khan' (*CPW*, i. 297).

on its own: Coleridge sustains the ambiguity throughout, allowing his allusive language to pull in different directions. This process is helped along by the Preface, which has the effect of dividing the poem in two: lines 1–36 are taken to be an account of the dream, and lines 36–54 suggest the poet's attempt to recover his lost vision. We see the poem in terms of gap between primary and secondary imagination, whilst reading it also as an allegory of the poet's rivalry with God. The two levels work in parallel, producing oscillations and coalescences of meaning.

Coleridge's nearness to his source, in the opening lines, suggests that one should keep hold of a literal interpretation, seeing Kubla as an Eastern potentate, and his pleasure-dome as an indulgence. But the first two lines also recall the absoluteness of God's original decree: 'And God said, Let there be light: and there was light.'[28] God's thoughts are His acts; no division exists, in the divine mind, between word and thing. Just so, the pleasure-dome appears as though by magic at Kubla's command. There is, furthermore, an ambiguity in the dependent clause, 'where Alph the sacred river ran', which suggests that the river, the caverns measureless to man, and even the sunless sea, are all Kubla's creations. This has the effect of tempting the reader into seeing him as God, even if, on second thoughts, one may wish to adopt the alternative grammatical meaning.

Ambiguities proliferate, as we register that Kubla is not fully in charge of his creation. Like Blake's Urizen, he attempts to contain energy, by measuring and bounding: 'So twice five miles of fertile ground | With walls and towers were girdled round' (ll. 6–7), and like Urizen he fails. The scenery of Stanza 1, with its serpentine rills and its incense-bearing trees, evokes the ordered world of the picturesque. Beneath it, in Stanza 2, is the anarchic world of the sublime. The split between them is emphasized by the break between stanzas, and by the more frequent use of exclamation in Part II. The 'deep romantic chasm' becomes associated, in this way, with uncontainable energy, and so with forces that are more evidently a threat: 'And mid this tumult Kubla heard from far | Ancestral voices prophesying war!' (ll. 29–30). This line might be taken as final confirmation of Kubla's limited (and therefore human) powers, were it not for the Miltonic allusion which pulls in a different direction. The 'dark | Illimitable ocean' in *Paradise Lost* Book II (ll. 891–2) is a place where eldest Night and Chaos, ancestors of Nature, 'hold | Eternal anarchy, amidst the noise | Of endless wars' (ll. 895–7). In Milton's thinking, this passage tells us, there were qualities which preceded the Creation. Coleridge draws on this ambiguity in creating his own: Kubla can be threatened, by ancestral voices prophesying war, without losing his status as God.

But if Kubla *is* God, he is also Milton.[29] The allusions to *Paradise Lost* Book IV

---

[28] Gen. 1: 3.
[29] *Paradise Lost* is just one of the poem's many literary antecedents to have been subtly examined by J. Beer; see 'The Languages of "Kubla Khan"', in Gravil, Newlyn, and Roe (eds.), *Coleridge's Imagination*, 218–62.

make a clear connection between Eden and Xanadu. 'In this pleasant soil', Milton writes, 'His far more pleasant garden God ordained' (l. 215); and the lines that follow provide one of Coleridge's cues: 'Out of *the fertile ground* he caused to grow | All trees of noblest kind' (ll. 215–16). In Milton's Paradise a fresh fountain rises, watering the garden with 'many a rill' (l. 229), and the brooks flow 'With *mazy error* under pendant shades' (l. 239), carrying the same suggestion of fallen potential as do 'sinuous rills'. Rich trees weep 'odorous gums and balm' (l. 248), like the incense-bearing trees of Xanadu; and there is a contrast between places where 'the morning sun first warmly smote | The open field, and where the unpierced shade | Embrowned the noontide bowers' (ll. 244–6), which points forward to the light/dark, domestic/savage contrasts present throughout 'Kubla Khan'. Even the sexuality of Coleridge's 'romantic chasm' has a Miltonic origin: when Satan approaches Eden, he has to climb the rural mound 'whose hairy sides | With thicket overgrown, grotesque and wild, | Access denied' (ll. 135–7). It is partly through its associations with the female sexual anatomy that this landscape conveys prohibition and the threat of violation.

As in Collins, these Miltonic echoes work both literally and metaphorically, to produce parallel meanings: in narrative terms, Kubla creates a real paradise, thus echoing God; whilst in poetic terms Coleridge re-describes Eden, so repeating Milton. A suggestion of rivalry on the poet's part is latent in this pattern of analogy and conflation, but its full implications are delayed until Stanza 3. The invocation of the Abyssinian maid, and the abrupt shift from third to first person, split the coda off from the main body of the poem, emphasizing the gap between two stages of composition and two levels of creative power. Whether we see these levels in terms of God and the poet, Milton and the poet, or the primary and secondary imagination, the ambition to bridge them has similar implications. Coleridge's use of the conditional tense, together with his yearning tone, suggest fear of failure; but working against this is the more revealing fear of success. 'Beware! Beware!' is the cry that greets his achievement of divine status. The cost of poetic genius, he implies, is alienation from the rest of the human race.

Two further warnings are implied (one in the poem itself, and one in the Preface) by means of Miltonic allusion. Firstly, the Abyssinian maid who is the poet's muse, and who signals his way back into the paradisal world, may in fact be misleading him. 'Mount Abora' is Coleridge's correction of the Crewe manuscript, which read 'Mount Amara': a reference, as Beer and others have pointed out, not to the true paradise, but to one of its numerous pale imitations, described by Milton in *Paradise Lost* Book IV.[30] Secondly, to return to the Preface, we have seen that dream is associated for Coleridge with prophecy, and that in the dreaming state words and things coalesce; but dream also has its

---

[30] Ibid. 241–3; further admonitory implications, deriving from Cowper and others, are discussed in ibid. 243 ff.

Satanic associations—as Adam intuits (and Eve discovers) in *Paradise Lost* Book V:

> Oft in [Reason's] absence mimic fancy wakes
> To imitate her; but misjoining shapes,
> Wild work produces oft, and most in dreams,
> Ill matching words and deeds long past or late.

(ll. 110–13)

This diabolic alternative to Coleridge's prophetic claims is present tacitly in the Preface and more openly in the poem itself. The dual status of the poet-dreamer is emphasized in his 'flashing eyes and floating hair', which signal Satanic frenzy and imaginative genius at one and the same time.

In the light of its ambivalence toward poetic power, 'Kubla Khan' takes on stronger and stronger affinities with the odes of Collins and Gray. Just as they defined their poetic selves by letting rivalry give way to imitation, so Coleridge builds defeat into his achievement of prophetic voice. Recovering Paradise is not possible, the poem's ending shows us, without the acknowledgement that success might be either hubristic or illusory. This awareness functions as a curb on poetic ambition, even as it excites the urge to compete. Thus the hierarchy suggested in *Biographia* stays as it is, with God at the top and the secondary imagination two steps behind, no matter how convincingly the poem has suggested a usurpation of power. Coleridge maintains the tradition of proscribing limits on imagination, whilst making for it the highest possible claims.

BALANCE OF POWER

As my remarks on literary authority at the beginning of this chapter implied, a distinction may be made between those writers like Coleridge, whose religious beliefs predispose them to caution, and those like Wordsworth, whose semi-atheism allows them to take more risks with the imagination. In his 'Prospectus' to *The Recluse*, for instance, Wordsworth does not seem particularly anxious about displacing Milton, and with him the whole of Christian tradition: 'Jehovah, with his thunder, and the quire | Of shouting angels, and the empyreal thrones— | I pass them unalarmed' (ll. 21–3). Using Milton's own methods of one-upmanship, he sees the mind of man as 'the haunt and the main region of his song'—a fitting replacement for the story of man's fall and redemption through Christ. There is a Satanic audacity in his claims which Coleridge would have found unthinkable, and indeed it is on this very issue— the balance of power between deity and humanity—that these two poets most noticeably divide.

Coleridge subjugates everything to religion: even *Biographia Literaria* makes its claims for the imagination by showing the powerlessness of philosophy in the face of religious belief: 'We begin with the I KNOW MYSELF, in order to end with the absolute I AM; we proceed from the self in order to lose and find all self in GOD.'[31] Disguised as a work of philosophy, so as all the more powerfully to affirm the status of faith, *Biographia* leads its reader up the garden path for twelve densely argued and illustrated chapters, then neatly pulls the ground from under our feet with the 'spoof' letter of Chapter 13. This allows the deferral of a truly *philosophical* definition of the imagination, and Coleridge chooses instead to make an affirmation through tautology. 'The living power and prime agent of all human perception' is a 'repetition in the finite mind of the eternal act of creation in the Infinite I AM'. The famous conclusion to Chapter 13 is thus a demonstration, as its Miltonic epigraph had promised, of the primacy of intuitive, rather than discursive, reason.[32]

In *The Prelude*, on the other hand, Wordsworth's relation to divinity is sceptical, and his experimentation with Milton more daring than anything Coleridge could envisage. The glad preamble opens with his claiming of fallen consciousness as a fitting subject: the world is all before him, as it was for Adam and Eve when they left Paradise; but he has no need as they did of providence: 'Should the guide I chuse | Be nothing better than a wandering cloud | I cannot miss my way' (i. 17–19). The conflation of Sin and Death with Adam and Eve, present in the assertion 'I cannot miss my way', shows Wordsworth's awareness of the Satanic associations which will inevitably accrue to his claims for the imagination. There is, then, as Coleridge would put it, 'an underconsciousness of a sinful nature', which will be significantly amplified as the poem proceeds. This is not primarily an expression of Wordsworth's fear of displacing Milton or doing without God; it points, rather, to his Miltonic apprehension of the Fall as the birth of imagination.

It is in keeping with his confidence as a 'revisionary' poet, to use Bloom's term, that Wordsworth should incorporate into *The Prelude*'s two most important definitions of the imagination an attitude towards Milton which is at once deferential and transumptive. In the Simplon Pass episode in Book VI, he offers the sublimity of the gorge as a recompense for the anticlimax of crossing the Alps. His language, apocalyptic in its associations, mounts towards a Miltonic conclusion:

> Tumult and peace, the darkness and the light,
> Were all like workings of one mind, the features
> Of the same face, blossoms upon one tree,
> Characters of the great apocalypse,
> The types and symbols of eternity,
> Of first, and last, and midst, and without end.

(ll. 567–72)

The God of *Paradise Lost* is clearly invoked in this echo of the Morning Hymn: 'Him First, Him last, Him midst and without end' (*PL* v. 165); and if the description were Coleridge's, there would be no doubt as to the stability of the divine reference. Quoting the same Miltonic passage in 'The Destiny of Nations',

[31] *Biographia*, i. 283.   [32] See my Ch. 6 and its n. 20.

Coleridge makes divinity perceivable through the symbols of natural landscape, which he sees as 'one mighty alphabet for infant minds':

> Him First, Him Last to view,
> Through meaner powers and secondary things
> Effulgent, as through clouds that veil his blaze.

(ll. 15–17)

But Wordsworth's language contains a revision of both Milton and Coleridge, by removing the important word 'Him' which, with its capital letter, inescapably invokes God. The face which animates the Simplon Pass is at once *like* God and not explicitly identified *as* Him. We could see a process here that is analogous to the one in 'The Pedlar', whereby the child traces in the 'fixed and steady lineaments' of the cave 'an ebbing and a flowing mind, | Expression ever varying' (ll. 56–7). The mind might belong to God, or it might alternatively be a mental projection of the perceiver himself: Wordsworth characteristically refuses to spell out which of two alternatives he finally opts for, suggesting the mind's analogy to godhead without implying the complete eclipse of divinity by human power.

This pattern recurs in *The Prelude*'s climactic episode, the climbing of Snowdon, where Milton once again presides over the defining of imagination. The foothills of Snowdon, half-personified as giant forms, their 'dusky backs upheaved' (l. 45), are verbally connected with the mountains in *Paradise Lost* Book VII, which 'appear emergent, and their broad bare backs upheave | Into the clouds' (ll. 285–7). The passage Wordsworth is invoking is Milton's account of the Creation, so that by implication the poet becomes God-like at the moment when the light falls like a flash upon the turf: his imagination, in other words, *creates* the scene that is before him. Just as the real sea is 'usurped upon, as far as sight could reach' by the mist (l. 51), so the poetic imagination transforms the external world—and, by extension, we might see a sort of usurpation of divine power in the Miltonic allusion. Wordsworth keeps all these levels operating simultaneously within the description itself, then offers an explicit equation in his subsequent gloss:

> A meditation rose in me that night
> Upon the lonely mountain when the scene
> Had passed away, and it appeared to me
> The perfect image of a mighty mind,
> Of one that feeds upon infinity,
> That is exalted by an under-presence,
> The sense of God, or whatsoe'er is dim
> Or vast in its own being

(ll. 66–73)

Importantly, it is not God as such who is being invoked, but the *sense* of God. And yet, as in the Simplon Pass episode, there is no replacement of divinity by the human, but a careful conflation in which two possibilities coexist. If one opts for the sense of God at the expense of inner vastness, or reads the inner vastness as though it had altogether dispensed with God, one misses the tentative hedging of bets on which all Wordsworth's claims for the imagination depend.

DUALITY

De Quincey's use of Miltonic allusion is important, not so much for what it tells us about his conscious defining of creative identity in relation to the author of *Paradise Lost*, as for what it reveals more indirectly about his estimate of the imagination's status, in relation to divinity itself. The synecdochal relation between Milton and God is less overtly acknowledged in his writing than in that of Collins and Gray, Coleridge and Wordsworth; but I shall none the less assume its unspoken figural presence in his use of Miltonic language. My focus, accordingly, will move from the ego psychology of conscious invocations and allusions to the power politics of Miltonic paradigms. These will be used to show that the problematic status De Quincey accorded to the imagination is somewhat similar to Coleridge's, in the religious caution with which it views the expansion of self beyond its proper bounds.

De Quincey displays a profound anxiety when it comes to defining the origin and status of imagination. Even the choice of title for his major work, *Confessions of an English Opium Eater*, suggests an important ambivalence: 'Confessions' have overtly moral associations, in that they are connected with sin—they imply a laying bare of guilt, an 'obtruding on our notice [of] moral scars and ulcers'.[33] But they also raise competing generic expectations, by fitting into a tradition of apologia and self-justification. They require a tone of confiding honesty in order to draw the reader into sympathy, and establish his or her trust. This doubleness of narrative mode reflects a doubleness of attitude, for De Quincey sees his opium-eating as an act of transgression—'To taste but once from the tree of knowledge', he says, in 'Coleridge and Opium-Eating', 'is fatal to the subsequent power of abstinence';[34] but he is none the less defensively eager to establish that the succumbing to opium is not a moral lapse. In one of the 1856 revisions, for instance, he asks himself the question how it was, and through what steps, that he became an opium eater:

Was it gradually, tentatively, mistrustingly, as one goes down a shelving beach into a deepening sea, and with a knowledge from the first of the dangers lying on that path; half-courting those dangers, in fact, whilst seeming to defy them? Or was it, secondly, in pure ignorance of such dangers, under the misleadings of mercenary fraud?

[33] *Confessions of an English Opium Eater*, ed. A. Hayter (Harmondsworth, Middx., 1971), 29.
[34] Ibid. 129.

Having set up these two opposite interpretations, which we might connect back with the two available readings of the Miltonic fall, he is eager to establish a third, which avoids transgressional implications altogether:

Thirdly, and lastly, was it (Yes, by passionate anticipation, I answer, before the question is finished)—was it on a sudden overmastering impulse derived from bodily anguish? Loudly I repeat *Yes*; loudly and indignantly—as in answer to a wilful calumny.[35]

The over-protestation gives him away, but De Quincey's intention is clear enough: establishing the medical grounds for his addiction is a means of removing opium from the reductiveness of normal moral assumptions: it is his way of establishing a purely aesthetic category to which imagination can belong. None the less, his narrative persists in oscillating uneasily between affirmation and admonition: dreaming itself is seen as both prophetic and Satanic; while Miltonic allusions place the imagination first in heaven or paradise, then in hell or the fallen world.

Take, for instance, his account of the first opium incident in his life, which transforms the squalor of a druggist's shop in Oxford Street into 'the Paradise of opium eaters' (p. 37), and presents the drug-dealer himself as the 'unconscious minister of celestial pleasures': an 'immortal druggist, sent down to earth on a special mission to myself' (p. 38). This 'beatific vision' is offered as confirmation of opium's heavenly origins, but also of the elect status of De Quincey himself. Its implications are glossed in the playful reworking of *Paradise Lost* Book XI which De Quincey includes in 'Coleridge and Opium-Eating'. 'You remember', he writes, with whimsical assurance,

that laudanum must have already existed in Eden—nay, that it was used medicinally by an archangel; for, after Michael had purged 'with euphrasy and rue' the eyes of Adam, lest he should be unequal to the mere *sight* of the great visions about to unfold their draperies before him, next he fortifies his fleshly spirits against the *affliction* of these visions, of which visions the first was death. And how? 'He from the well of life three drops instilled.' What was their operation?

> So deep the power of these ingredients pierced,
> Even to the inmost seat of mental sight,
> That Adam, now enforced to close his eyes,
> Sank down and all his spirits became entranced
> But him the gentle angel by the hand
> Soon raised....

Having, as it were, established the credentials of opium by reference to this sacred text—'the second of these lines it is which betrays the presence of laudanum', he suggests pedantically—he goes on to claim that 'It is in the faculty of mental vision, it is in the increased power of dealing with the shadowy and the dark, that the characteristic virtue of opium lies.'[36]

---

[35] Ibid. 139–140.   [36] Ibid. 129–30.

By the shadowy and the dark, De Quincey presumably means both literal darkness and the world of mortality which Michael reveals to Adam. Opium is thus put in the ambiguous position of heightening the perception of suffering and fortifying the mind against pain. Elsewhere, it is invoked as the tool for 'a healthy restoration to that state which the mind would naturally recover, upon the removal of any deep-seated irritation of pain that had disturbed and quarrelled with the impulses of a heart originally just and good'.[37] It offers the 'keys to Paradise',[38] and it makes the opium eater feel 'that the diviner part of his nature is paramount; that is, the moral affections are in a state of cloudless serenity; and over all is the great light of the majestic intellect'.[39]

But there is a more disturbing side to De Quincey's affirmations: his notes turn to tragic in Part II, and the pleasures of opium are balanced more equally than he himself supposes by its pains. The Satanic associations in his phrase 'the abyss of divine enjoyment' darken into nightmare as he describes some of his later excesses: 'I seemed every night to descend, not metaphorically, but literally to descend, into chasms and sunless abysses, depths below depths, from which it seemed hopeless that I could ever reascend.'[40] We are reminded of the 'unfathomable hell within', which, in the nightmare world of Coleridge's 'The Pains of Sleep', replaces the 'Paradise within' of a redemptive imagination. De Quincey's dreams are similarly haunted by hellish images: 'the perplexities of my steps in London came back and haunted my sleep, with the feeling of perplexities moral or intellectual, that brought confusion to the reason, or anguish and remorse to the conscience'.[41] But worse than this moral confusion, more poignant than this fear of being, like Milton's devils, 'in wandering mazes lost', there is the appalling knowledge of separation:

clasped hands, and heart-breaking partings, and then—everlasting farewells! and with a sigh, such as the caves of hell sighed when the incestuous mother uttered the abhorred name of death, the sound was reverberated—everlasting farewells! and again, and yet again reverberated—everlasting farewells![42]

The design of *Confessions* as whole depends on a conjunction of those mighty antagonists, pleasure and pain. But it also plays on the drawing together of imaginative worlds—the paradise within of beatific vision, and the unfathomable hell within of suffering. As De Quincey looks back, in the final lines of the book, on the dreams which he has almost but not entirely relinquished, these two separate worlds are acknowledged to be one: 'my sleep is still tumultuous', he writes, 'and like the gates of Paradise to our first parents when looking back

---

[37] Ibid. 74. De Quincey here suggests a reversal of the effects of the Fall, much along the lines proposed by Hartley, when he discusses philosophical language; see n. 19 above.
[38] Ibid. 83.   [39] Ibid. 75.
[40] Ibid. 103. The language, suggestively indicating De Quincey's sense of fellowship with Coleridge, is reminiscent of 'Kubla Khan'.
[41] Ibid. 81. See Ch. 1, n. 12, for the Romantics' association of London with hell.
[42] Ibid. 113.

from afar, it is still (in the tremendous line of Milton)—"With dreadful faces throng'd and fiery arms"'.[43] We have here a conflation of opposites which is implicit in Milton's own language. The world of dreams, guarded by the covering cherub who is at once Satanic and angelic, is given the dual status of an inaccessible Eden and a thankfully removed hell. Implicit in that final tremendous line is the voice heard by Collins and Coleridge, which warns of the consequences of attempting re-entry.

IRONY

One tends to associate Shelley with unqualified imperatives, of the kind that resonate through 'A Defence of Poetry': 'A man, to be greatly good, must imagine intensely and comprehensively'; 'The great instrument of moral good is the imagination'; 'Poetry strengthens that faculty which is the organ of the moral nature of man, in the same manner as exercise strengthens a limb'.[44] At first sight, then, he appears to be Romanticism's most confident spokesman for the moral imagination. But even Shelley is wary of the penalties which imagination can incur, if circumstances cause it to become misdirected, over-idealistic, or irresponsible. From a position that is antithetical to Coleridge's and De Quincey's, in that it refuses affiliations with religion, he too is therefore concerned with the controlling of power.

His misgivings are especially discernible in his allusive language, which is used pervasively as an ironic device. Miltonic allusion in particular has a pointedly self-critical function. In envisaging imagination as a transforming power, and in closely connecting it with freedom of the will, Shelley makes it appear analogous to the defiant self-sufficiency of Satan, whose claim that 'The mind is its own place and in itself | Can make a heaven of hell, a hell of heaven' (*PL* i. 254–5) makes a powerful appeal to Romantic idealism, as Byron's heroes frequently remind us.[45] In noticing that some of Shelley's most fervently revolutionary utterances have their origin here, one might associate him with the revisionary extreme of Romanticism, and suppose that he borrows this Satanic voice without implying immorality. In 'Julian and Maddalo', for instance, Julian makes his revolutionary appeal against the 'mind-forged manacles' of religion in a language shot through with Satanic associations:

> we might be all
> We dream of, happy, high, majestical.
> Where is the love, beauty and truth we seek
> But in our mind? And if we were not weak
> Should we be less in deed than in desire?
>
> (ll. 172–6)

[43] Ibid. 116.   [44] *Shelley*, 487–8.

[45] Manfred and Lucifer both evolve their belief in the freedom of the individual mind and will on the basis of this Satanic claim; see J. McGann, *'Don Juan' in Context* (Chicago, 1976), 23–50.

But, as I shall show, the voice of idealism is not always approved by Shelley. Here, for instance, it is subtly undermined, firstly by the presence of an answering voice (Maddalo) whose jaundiced fatalism brings it down to earth: 'You talk Utopia' (l. 179), and secondly by the admonitory content of the narrative itself. Satanic allusion functions as a register of Shelley's ambivalence towards the power of mind: it allows him to play out as a kind of internal temptation the possibility of an extreme of self-sufficiency which he acknowledges to be inherently flawed. This internal temptation is fully developed in the poem's formal structure, and in the wider moral issues which it explores.

Shelley implies neither whole-hearted revision of Milton's views nor submission to them. He exploits the moral paradigms created by *Paradise Lost* to examine the responsibility mankind bears for its own good and evil, in a universe that is not governed by God. Sharing with Coleridge the belief that 'the sensual and the proud rebel in vain | Slaves by their own compulsion',[46] he sees Satan as the most powerful literary exemplar of this problem. In 'Julian and Maddalo', three species of Satanism draw attention to moral deficiencies in the imagination—Maddalo's being the crudest:

it is his weakness to be proud: he derives, from a comparison of his own extraordinary mind with the dwarfish intellects that surround him, an intense apprehension of the nothingness of human life.... His ambition preys upon itself, for want of objects which it can consider worthy of exertion.[47]

Maddalo is used to voice the appalling possibility that a Godless life is meaningless: that, if the comforting notions of destiny and providence are stripped away, one is left with nothing. He remains locked in despair: proudly refusing the grandeur of human possibility, seeing no purpose for an existence which ends only in death. He can find no adequate replacement for the God he doubts; and his Satanism is a form of moral cowardice.

Julian's rhetoric, by contrast, recalls Lucifer's rallying call to the fallen angels in *Paradise Lost* Book I, and suggests the temptation of audacious self-sufficiency:

> We are assured
> Much may be conquered, much may be endured
> Of what degrades and crushes us. We know
> That we have power over ourselves to do
> And suffer—what, we know not till we try;
> But something nobler than to live and die—
>
> (ll. 182–87)

His is the boundless energy of the idealist, who sees all things as subject to the power of his will, including the suffering and madness which for others are proof of the purposelessness of existence: 'This is not destiny', he claims, 'but

---

[46] 'France: An Ode', ll. 85–6.   [47] *Shelley*, 113.

man's own wilful ill' (ll. 210–11). His position is subtly undermined by dramatic ironies which are partly imported from *Paradise Lost* itself, and partly inherent in the narrative Shelley is writing. For just as Satan is mocked by the
providential scheme which his own defiance plays a part in fulfilling, so Julian
will be forced to acknowledge that there are degrees of suffering which no
amount of willpower can explain away.

This is suggested to him by his encounter with the maniac, who embodies a
third species of Satanism. His is the voice of extreme suffering, which goes
through many moods: anguish, at the pain of rejection; regret, mingled with a
sense of injury and injustice; rage, at the thought that something beyond him is
responsible for his torment; and finally despair. This is the Satan who burns in
the 'full hell | Within' (ll. 351–2), a hell of his own making. His appeal to the
imagination rests in the extremities of feeling that he proves it possible for the
mind to experience and endure; and he becomes heroic, as do Satan or Manfred,[48] at moments when defiance allows him to assert the strength of inner self:

> Believe that I am ever still the same
> In creed as in resolve, and what may tame
> My heart, would leave the understanding free
> Or all would sink in this keen agony—
>
> (ll. 358–61)

Shelley appears to be offering solipsism and madness as possible outcomes for
an over-idealistic frame of mind; but he also exploits his dialogic method, to set
up competing explanations for the problem of suffering. Both Julian and Maddalo attempt to accommodate the madman's predicament to their own moral
perspective, while the narrative itself resists deciding whether or not suffering is
self-induced. There is, however, a suggestion that excessive sensitivity exac-
erbates pain: the maniac describes himself as 'a nerve o'er which do creep | The
else unfelt oppressions of this earth' (ll. 449–50); but his capacity to perceive and
feel is insufficient, in Shelley's view, unless accompanied by the ability to leave
self behind, by empathizing with another.

Shelley makes the health of imagination dependent on love. Self must
endeavour to purge itself of selfness, through the quest for an ideal other: 'a soul
within our soul that describes a circle around its proper Paradise which pain and
sorrow and evil dare not overleap'.[49] This quest is however vulnerable, problematic, and flawed. Shelley believes, with Hazlitt, that sympathy is a reliable
safeguard of imaginative power, but he does not appear to share Hazlitt's confidence that true sympathy comes naturally—even to imaginative beings, such as
the poet in 'Alastor'. Nor does he always have faith in the triumph of love over
environment, as 'Julian and Maddalo' has shown. There is, furthermore, in
Shelley's view, only a thin dividing line between genuine sympathy and egotistical self-projection, since love is defined as the capacity to 'see within our

[48] See McGann, *'Don Juan' in Context*, 36–7.   [49] 'On Love' (*Shelley*, 474).

intellectual nature a miniature as it were of our entire self, yet deprived of all that we condemn or despise'.[50] Unless love involves a genuine 'going out of our own nature', the mind is likely to become 'its own circumference and centre'—self-defeating, in its quest for an ideal 'miniature' of itself, because failing to realize the otherness of the loved being.[51] The poet's admonitory implications are subtly self-ironizing: constancy to an ideal object turns all too easily into self-worship, since the ideal is in any case a projection.[52] Only by empathy, or loss of self, can the alternative traps of solipsism and imaginative deadness be avoided.

The Preface to 'Alastor' centres on the mind's capacity to create these traps. Shelley begins by presenting a summary of the poem's narrative, as a moral fable showing how 'an imagination enflamed and purified by familiarity with all that is excellent and majestic' can miss out on love. His poet-hero degenerates into 'self-centred seclusion', as the inevitable consequence of an over-active imagination. Waking suddenly to the need for 'an intelligence similar to itself', he searches for the 'prototype' of his vision of perfection in the ideal, not in the actual, world;[53] and his quest for self-fulfilment spirals narcissistically, downward and inward. Shelley goes on to expound two kinds of admonitory implication: one for those whose extreme espousal of imagination is potentially dangerous or irresponsible; and one for those who repudiate visionary potential altogether. These 'meaner spirits' are reminded that deficiency of imagination could lead to the 'inanimate cold world' of lovelessness described by Coleridge in 'Dejection'. Shelley thus conveys a full sense of the potential that imagination contains, so long as it is responsible to the human community of which it is part. A charge is implicitly levelled at the poet of 'Alastor', who is guilty of refusing social and emotional bondings in the real world.

The poem itself has been read as a rebuke directed at the Wordsworthian imagination which, in its retreat into solitude, betrays the human community and, in its espousal of 'natural piety', neglects the value of love.[54] This rebuke may well be present as part of what Shelley is here doing, but only as part. His larger aim is to examine the disproportionate emphasis which poetry gives to what is removed, distanced, or abstracted, to the detriment of the actual and the realizable; and in so far as he has an identifiable target, it is the tendencies of Romanticism towards abstraction and sublimation. These are tendencies that

---

[50] Ibid. 473.

[51] Wordsworth is figured by Shelley as the antitype of love, in that 'He had a mind which was somehow | At once circumference and centre' ('Peter Bell the Third', pt. iv, ll. 294–5).

[52] See Coleridge's 'Constancy to an Ideal Object', esp. the closing lines, which ironize love as self-projection.

[53] Correcting a common misunderstanding of 'Alastor', E. K. Gibson writes that 'we certainly would not expect a philosopher of [Shelley's] surpassing powers to make the blunder of expecting to find the prototype, the original of his vision, in the realm of the physical'; see '"Alastor": A Reinterpretation', in *Shelley*, 549.

[54] See M. Butler, *Romantics, Rebels and Reactionaries: English Literature and its Background, 1760–1830* (Oxford, 1981), 140–1.

Shelley is quite aware of contributing to himself; and the critique he offers is all the stronger for its self-ironizing implications.

This experiential and humanist emphasis in 'Alastor' comes fully to light through an examination of its Miltonic paradigms, used to expose what Shelley sees as the deficiencies and dangers of High Romanticism.[55] The poem's narrative is constructed along developmental lines, as though its intention is to trace the growth of a poet's mind; and since one is led to expect a 'fall' into experience, one reads the early part of the poem as an account of the hero's preparation for this event. The successive branches of 'doubtful knowledge' he pursues are seen as adolescent surrogates for experience, which can only temporarily satisfy an innate hunger in the growing mind; but they also symbolize regressive tendencies in Romanticism itself. His journey to undiscovered lands conjures the exotic appeal of travel literature; his living among savage men recalls the primitivist ideal; and his visit to the noble ruins of civilization evokes the fashionable glamour of the past.[56] An implicit critique of Romanticism is sustained throughout, in the association of each phase with what is ideal, imagined, or past, rather than with what is human, actual and present. Shelley's critical position is in this respect remarkably similar to Byron's, as we see in the comic deflation of lines 120–39, where oblivious idealism is juxtaposed with erotic actuality in a manner worthy of *Don Juan*.[57]

The hero's 'fall' into sexual experience ought to take place at the point where his dissatisfaction with the infinite signals the ending of adolescence, the maturing of Romanticism, and the accommodation of imagination to reality. But the narrative suggests a 'sentimental education' in which no such development can take place; for the hero refuses to move from the inner world to the outer. Like Adam, he has a dream in which the perfect being appears before him—perfect in that she unites all his highest aspirations while also fulfilling his sexual needs. Unlike Adam, however, he does not awake to find 'all true, as the dream had lively shadowed'; nor does he, like Madeline, face a real lover whom he must somehow accommodate to his projected ideal. In the 'cold white light of morning', he confronts the features of a post-coital landscape which bear witness to the emptiness of fantasy, not the completion of sex. At this moment of anti-climax, which in Keatsian terms ought to bring with it a wholesome 'sense of real things' followed by the courageous passage into maturity, the hero makes a

[55] McGann writes that 'in the High Romantic theory of Imagination, everything posited of God as creative principle was merely transferred to the creative activity of men. The essential categories of thought remained unaltered, however' (*'Don Juan' in Context*, 148).

[56] ll. 50–128. There are strong verbal reminiscences of Coleridge's 'The Foster Mother's Tale' at ll. 60 and 77, which suggest that Shelley is looking at Rousseau's primitivism through the filter of first-generation Romanticism; there also appears to be a reference to Shelley's vegetarianism at ll. 100–1.

[57] The youthful romantic poet is busy 'poring on memorials | Of the world's youth', while the Arab maiden brings him food, tends his steps, and watches his nightly sleep, then returns 'wildered, and wan, and panting' to her lonely bed (ll. 129–39). Cf. the early stages of the Haidee/Juan interlude, discussed in Ch. 6.

mistake which condemns him to remain unfruitfully embalmed in his imagination; for, instead of continuing to look for the actualization of his dream in reality, he searches for its 'prototype' in the ideal realm. Lamenting the disappearance of his dream-woman in language that is heavily laden with Miltonic absolutes—'Lost, lost, for ever lost, | In the wide pathless desart of dim sleep, | That beautiful shape'[58]—he transforms sleep itself into a 'mysterious paradise', and elevates the worlds of dream, imagination, even death, over reality.

Shelley presents, as his hero's central tragic predicament, this Thel-like inability to make the transition from innocence to experience—this refusal to relinquish the safety of the imaginative realm, in order to engage with the actual; and in this sense 'Alastor' joins those other studies of sexuality with which I was concerned in Chapter 5, as a poem which half releases and half curbs imaginative potential. In its critique of poetry, meanwhile, the remainder of the text focuses on poetic modes and figurations which suggest the retreat and self-immolation of the mind. Shelley's allusiveness points to general patterns of Romantic symbolism, within which specific examples function as a mapping of the topical onto the generic: the hero's dangerous voyage on stormy seas (ll. 307ff.) contains pointed references to 'The Ancient Mariner' and 'Peter Bell', but can be understood more generally as a Romantic metaphor of mental exploration. His entry into the forest glade (ll. 420–68) symbolizes an embowered retreat from social demands;[59] and his projection of procreative fantasies onto the trees (ll. 469–92) enacts a (Wordsworthian?) substitution of Nature for sexuality.[60] Finally, in the climactic ascent of lines 544ff., towards the 'one silent nook' which is the hero's resting place, Shelley offers sublimity itself as a repudiation of the real and the human.[61]

Shelley is interested by the *substitutive* function of metaphor, using it to expose the dangers of refusal, or self-embalmment, which are inherent in High Romanticism. Just as, in 'Julian and Maddalo', Satanic allusion registers an implicit caution towards the imagination which is reminiscent of some Enlightenment writers, so, in 'Alastor', Miltonic paradigms are used to suggest a mistrust of imaginative activity when it involves a thwarting or denial of experience. If this is a difficult poem to place, that is because it allows the coexistence of two kinds of discourse, which contradict each other. Shelley's Romantic irony is not so overt as Byron's, but 'Alastor' is none the less a poem which fulfils the

[58] Shelley appears to be recalling Samson's lament for his lost sight: 'Oh dark, dark, dark, amid the blaze of noon, | Irrevocably dark, total eclipse | Without all hope of day!' (ll. 80–1).

[59] This retreat might be thought of in terms of the paradigm offered by Coleridge's 'Conversation poems', where domestic retirement is given a paradisal association.

[60] See e.g. 'Nutting'; which might be contrasted with Shelley's complaint, in 'Peter Bell the Third', that Wordsworth was 'a kind of moral eunuch', who only dared to touch 'The hem of Nature's shift', and 'never dared uplift | the closest, all-concealing tunic' (pt. iv, ll. 314–17).

[61] Here the hero dies, and it becomes clear that each genus of poetic symbol that Shelley has used represents a stage in the poet's life. See Gibson's argument (*Shelley*, 559–69).

Schlegelian dictum that 'the work of art must reveal the presence of an authorial consciousness that is simultaneously affirming and mocking its own creation'.[62]

EQUIVOCATION

Keats offers a suitable end-point for this chapter because, in his ambivalent attitude to divinity, to Milton, and to imaginative power, he encompasses the full range of positions which I have examined in other writers, making his distinct-ive contribution through a counterpointing of different voices whose argument remains unresolved. He is Romanticism's most equivocal exponent of the creative imagination; and this gives him a strong claim to being a representa-tive voice: a voice, that is, which successfully mediates between the optimism of High Romantic argument and the realism of ironic critique. Moreover, in his poetic method, as in his accounts of creativity, he provides evidence of the open-endedness which I have been seeking to locate in Milton, and seeking, moreover, to define as Romanticism's most important inheritance from *Paradise Lost*.

Keats is more subtly and confidently 'revisionary' in his relation to *Paradise Lost* than his own accounts imply. The sense of defeat which he records when abandoning 'Hyperion' is that of a poet who has been attempting to rival the acknowledged master of epic, by writing in the same medium. This isolated submission to authority is instrumental in defining poetic self, since it contains a powerful expression of the difference which Keats senses between his own imagination and Milton's: 'Life to him would be death to me.'[63] Articulation of this difference is perhaps at its clearest when Keats defines 'negative capability': the capacity to remain 'in uncertainties, Mysteries, doubts, without any irritable reaching after fact and reason'.[64] This Shakespearian quality he contrasts explicitly with the 'Wordsworthian or egotistical sublime';[65] but, by extension, we can see it as opposite also to the sacred sublime, embodied in Milton's poetry. The latter Keats found daunting in its religious and moral absoluteness, seeing his own poetic temperament, by contrast, as flexible and unenthralled.

Keats's use of Milton is, however, more complex than this implies—not just because Milton's poetry is less categorical and absolute than the myth of Milton, but because some aspects of Keats draw him towards the moral scheme he appears to be repudiating. His poetic quest is indeed divided against itself: what he calls the 'camelion poet' in him searches for an aesthetic category which exists independently of moral absolutes, and he defines this variously, in his

---

[62] A. K. Mellor, *English Romantic Irony* (Cambridge, Mass., 1980), 17. I am here in disagreement with T. Clark, who argues that 'the total contradiction between Shelley's theory and practice implied by the ironist kind of reading is difficult to accept'; see *Embodying Revolution: The Figure of the Poet in Shelley* (Oxford, 1989), 7.

[63] To G. and G. Keats, 24 Sept. 1819 (*Keats Letters*, 325).

[64] To G. and T. Keats, Dec. 1817 (ibid. 43).

[65] To R. Woodhouse, 27 Oct. 1818 (ibid. 157).

poetry and in his letters, as 'imagination', 'dream', 'beauty', 'the poetical character', and 'gusto'. The 'virtuous philosopher' in him is, however, convinced (and this conviction increases with the passage of time) that 'there is no worthy pursuit but the idea of doing some good for the world',[66] that the poet should be 'a sage, | A humanist, physician to all men';[67] and that, if poetry is to have this beneficial function, it must take account of suffering and experience. His writing oscillates, therefore, between 'an exquisite sense of the luxurious' and 'a love for Philosophy'.[68] The patterns of duality and ambivalence which, as a result, run all the way through his poetry are demonstrations of negative capability, in that they show us a poet who refuses to settle for closure. But they are also proof that the 'camelion poet' must depend on the 'virtuous philosopher' for self-definition. What appears to be an outright refusal of Miltonic morality may in some respects be considered as a careful expansion of ambiguities inherent in Milton's own imagination. Keats's revisions of *Paradise Lost* show us a poet who is able at once to displace and to defer to authority, who can play ambiguous games with divinity, and who caricatures Milton as the poet of absolutes, whilst plundering his text for the indeterminacies which are themselves redolent of 'negative capability'.

In his 'Letter to John Hamilton Reynolds', Keats writes of an imagination which, when brought 'Beyond its proper bound, yet still confined, | Lost in a sort of purgatory blind, | Cannot refer to any standard law | Of either earth or heaven' (ll. 79–82). His suggestion that there might be a 'proper bound' for creative power is vestigially cautionary, in that it invokes Satanic presumption, and there is even a tone of lament in his notion that the 'lost' imagination functions amorally, in a world removed from both earthly imperatives and divine sanctions. Here, as elsewhere, in attempting to define an aesthetic category which exists separately from morality, Keats must begin by invoking the 'standard laws' he questions. His concept of the aesthetic depends on a pleasurable response to moral indeterminacy; but this indeterminacy can only be perceived by way of the polar opposites it mediates between. Negative capability is thus the willing refusal of closure, which can occur only if the effects of closure are perceived. Similarly with the 'poetical character', which 'has as much delight in conceiving an Iago as an Imogen': its levelling sympathy, its enjoyment of 'light and shade ... foul or fair, high or low, rich or poor' can only be effective through a response to the opposites it juxtaposes, and the gradations it blurs:

What shocks the virtuous philosop[h]er, delights the camelion Poet. It does no harm from its relish of the dark side of things, any more than from its taste for the bright one; because they both end in speculation.[69]

---

[66] To J. Taylor, 24 Apr. 1818 (ibid. 88).   [67] 'The Fall of Hyperion', ll. 189–90.
[68] To J. Taylor, 24 Apr. 1818 (*Keats Letters*, 88). For an impressive handling of oscillatory and ambivalent tendencies in Keats's poetry and letters, see Mellor, *English Romantic Irony*, 77–108.
[69] *Keats Letters*, 157.

The intellectual enjoyment of indeterminacy is Keats's formula, as it is also Lamb's, for defeating the oppressive certainties of reason, morality, and religion. Poetry must, however, in Keats's view, negotiate its independence from moral categories by speculative distance, and not by thoughtless escapism. The fantasy worlds he creates for the indulgence of an amoral imagination are exposed, therefore, as false paradises—fragile, impermanent, and subject to encroachments from outside—even as they are celebrated for their liberating potential. The happy dreamscape of 'Sleep and Poetry', for instance, is punctured by 'a sense of real things' which necessarily recalls the dreamer to his conscious self, even whilst 'like a muddy stream' it seems to 'bear along his soul to nothingness' (ll. 153–9). The 'fairy lands forlorn' of 'Ode to a Nightingale' are no sooner glimpsed than they disappear, leaving the poet—half-dreaming, half awake—to draw his own anticlimactic conclusions: 'the fancy cannot cheat so well | As she is famed to do, deceiving elf' (ll. 73–4). Madeline's fantasy of Porphyro, in 'The Eve of St Agnes', is more glamorous than the real thing, while for Porphyro dream is a higher plane of reality, attainable only through oblivion. As I showed in Chapter 5, the couple sustain their mismatching love by escaping the flawed and temporal world in which they need to live, if they are to progress beyond illusion. In 'Lamia', on the other hand, the balance tips the other way. Lycius awakes to the full consciousness of self-deception, but only at the cost of love: 'Do not all charms fly | At the mere touch of cold philosophy?' (ll. 229–30). The deathly world of abstraction is shown winning out over imagination, as though there were no negotiable balance between reality and fictive play.

And yet balance is precisely what Keats seeks, in presenting these oscillating extremes. His overall position, consolidated through approaching and reapproaching the same problem, is deeply experiential. To be seduced by the idyllic pastoral scene depicted on the Grecian urn, without acknowledging the loss of humanity which this entails, is as much a refusal of experience as Thel's flight back into the vales of Har. The urn tempts with its simple aesthetic answers—'beauty is truth, truth beauty, that is all | Ye know on earth, and all ye need to know' (ll. 49–50)—answers which, at one level, Keats himself believes and propounds. But the fragility of its wish-fulfilment is thrown into relief by the poet's own admission: 'Cold pastoral!' (l. 45). Reluctantly, it has to be conceded that the paradisal world of art is not enough—or, rather, that art must somehow include a perception of suffering if it is to avoid being static and regressive.

Progression, as in *Thel* and 'Christabel', can come about only through the embracing of experience, which Keats sees both as a necessary aspect of human education and as the inevitable product of passing time. The Chamber of Maiden-Thought may initially intoxicate with its 'light' and 'atmosphere', causing the poet to 'see nothing but pleasant wonders'; but this soon gives way to sensations which sharpen one's 'vision into the heart and nature of Man ...

convincing one's nerves that the world is full of Misery and Heratbreak [*sic*] Pain. Sickness and oppression'.[70] The ideal education (human and poetic) must involve an enhancing of this insight into the human condition: 'Do you not see how necessary a World of Pains and troubles is to school an Intelligence and make it a soul?'[71] Keats therefore boldly substitutes 'the holiness of the heart's affections' for the props of Christianity—'Not merely is the Heart a hornbook, It is the Minds Bible, it is the Minds experience, it is the teat from which the Mind or intelligence sucks its identity'—thereby constructing his own personal faith, which is a cross between humanism and deism: 'As various as the Lives of Men are—so various become their souls, and thus does God make individual beings. Souls, Identical Souls of the sparks of his own essence.' Experience is his replacement for redemption through Christ, offering a direct, rather than vicarious, path to human fulfilment:

This appears to me a faint sketch of a system of Salvation which does not affront our reason and humanity—I am convinced that many difficulties which christians labour under would vanish before it—[72]

In his championing of experience, Keats both challenges and echoes Milton. Perhaps not surprisingly, the passage of *Paradise Lost* which comes to have a particular resonance for him, and to which he returns again and again, is Michael's prophecy of the heartbreak, pain, sickness, and oppression which Adam and Eve must face as the consequence of their fall. In Chapter 5, I showed how Keats's allusions to this passage significantly slant the ending of 'The Eve of St Agnes', signalling a world of suffering and mortality which the lovers vulnerably refuse. 'Hyperion' shows the alternative to this refusal, and suggests that by embracing suffering, as a necessary aspect of experience, divine status can be achieved:

> Knowledge enormous makes a God of me.
> Names, deeds, grey legends, dire events, rebellions,
> Majesties, sovran voices, agonies,
> Creations and destroyings, all at once
> Pour into the wide hollows of my brain,
> And deify me, as if some blithe wine
> Or bright elixir peerless I had drunk,
> And so become immortal.
>
> (iii. 113–20)

Keats's language, in describing the transformation of Apollo, offers a conflation which should by now be familiar, since it has been observed in Pope, in Blake, and in De Quincey. Satan, tempting Eve with the possibility of divine status, is suggestively connected with Michael, who purges Adam's eye with euphrasy

[70] To J. H. Reynolds, 3 May 1818 (ibid. 95).
[71] To G. and G. Keats, 14 Feb.–3 May, 1819 (ibid. 250).
[72] Ibid.

and rue in order to give him access to prophetic vision: 'So deep the power of those ingredients pierced, | Even to the inmost seat of mental sight | That Adam now enforced to close his eyes, | Sunk down and all his spirits became entranced' (xi. 417–20). The forbidden fruit of the tree of knowledge is thus incorporated into Keats's personal system of salvation—a scheme which does not 'offend our reason and humanity' by refusing the value of experience, but rather sees knowledge as the route to a responsible imagination.

This message is further emphasized in 'The Fall of Hyperion', where Milton once again presides over a scene of poetic enlightenment. Here the part of Adam is played by the bewildered poet-dreamer, who, in his difficult ascent towards greatness, finds himself in the presence of Moneta (half-muse, half-sphinx), from whom he is to receive the insight necessary for progression: '"High Prophetess", said I, "purge off, | Benign, if so it please thee, my mind's film"' (ll. 145–6). Unlike Michael, however, Moneta delays the purging of vision until the full implications of her message have been absorbed. The poet-dreamer must first be warned against presumption—'"None can usurp this height," returned that shade, | "But those to whom the miseries of the world | Are misery, and will not let them rest"' (ll. 147–9). He must, furthermore, be reminded of the complacency which embalms his imagination:

> All else who find a haven in the world,
> Where they may thoughtless sleep away their days,
> If by a chance into this fane they come,
> Rot on the pavement where thou rottedst half'
>
> (ll. 150–54)

Only then can he be granted the privileged sight of Moneta's face—'Not pined by human sorrows, but bright-blanched | By an immortal sickness which kills not' (ll. 257–8)—and, through sharing her knowledge of transience and desolation, achieve the divine status earlier accorded to Apollo: 'Whereon there grew | A power within me of enormous ken | To see as a god sees' (ll. 302–4).

In this triumphant apotheosis, Keats succeeds in reversing the admonitory expectations which are normally raised by imagination's rivalry with God. Instead of warning that sorrow and pain are the price to be paid for Satanic presumption, he suggests that, without a true perception of suffering, the imagination will remain paradisally embalmed. The poet-dreamer's access of divinity is to be trusted, rather than discounted as presumptuous, because he has now earned his right to greatness. In the same way, by implication, the anxiety Keats had felt towards Milton can be dispelled, and the ambitious poetic project of 'Hyperion' reapproached, because its theme has now been successfully redefined.[73]

For Keats, then, as for De Quincey, the perception of transience and pain is

[73] See H. Bloom, 'Keats and the Anxieties of Poetic Tradition', in *The Ringers in the Tower: Studies in Romantic Tradition* (Chicago, 1981), 131–42.

redemptive. Moneta, like Our Lady of Sorrows, bears some resemblance to Christ, but only in the sense that she is the symbol of magnified and transcendent suffering which none the less can be understood in human terms. Her function is neither sacrificial nor vicarious, since she is essentially a witness and participant in sorrow, rather than a victim. Keats succeeds in rejecting those aspects of Christian dogma he finds most offensive to 'reason and humanity', whilst absorbing a central Christian paradigm into his own revisionary myth. Milton presides over this transformation, not, finally, as the 'covering cherub' who refuses him access to Paradise, but as the voice of authority who allows him to see the limitations of an amoral imagination.

8

Milton

In writing *Milton*, Blake undertook a task that extended far beyond the struggle for individual creative identity with a strong precursor or a sacred text. In addition to offering, as Joseph Wittreich has argued, an answer to 'all those ... biographers, critics, and editors who falsified both Milton and his poetry, blocking from view the spiritual form of the poet',[1] Blake's prophecy is also an attempt to undo mistaken notions of divinity, of politics, of sexuality, and of imagination which can be seen, if not to have their origin in *Paradise Lost*, then at least to be underwritten by some of its theological implications. Indeed, these two aspects of the poem are closely interconnected: acknowledging the powerful cultural symbol which Milton has become, Blake holds the reception of *Paradise Lost*, as much as its author, responsible for ideas which, in his view, maintain a stranglehold on the dominant ideology of his day, and urgently need to be reconsidered.

In the same way that priesthood begins in 'choosing forms of worship from poetic tales' and, through systematized abstraction, causes men to forget that 'all deities reside in the human breast',[2] Blake sees that a 'Church' of Milton has gradually obscured his 'spiritual form'[3] and has caused his poetry to ossify into doctrine or law, with damaging repercussions for the notion of divinity which it enshrines. He seeks to reverse this process of abstraction by exposing some of the most obvious ways in which Milton might be thought to have invited the misappropriations and misunderstandings of his eighteenth-century readers. This is done so as to clear a path for the true poet, who supposedly understood divinity along Blakean lines: the Milton who, according to Blake's own account, appeared to him in a dream and warned him not to be misled by *Paradise Lost*.[4]

The 'revisionary' procedures Blake adopts are thus envisaged as restorative on a large scale and towards a grandly redemptive end, rather than as corrective at a local level, and for the purposes of individual self-definition. Joseph Wittreich has seen the combativeness of such procedures in terms of the tra-

---

[1] *Angel of Apocalypse: Blake's Idea of Milton* (Madison, Wis., 1975), 232.
[2] *MHH*, pl. 11, l. 15.
[3] See D. Riede's observation that 'Paul can become the "Church Paul" and Milton can become the "Church Milton" if their fierce writings are not encountered by fierce readers'; 'Blake's *Milton*: On Membership of Church Paul', in M. Nyquist and M. W. Ferguson (eds.), *Re-Membering Milton: Essays on the Texts and Traditions* (New York, 1988), 258.
[4] 'I saw Milton in imagination and he told me to be aware of being misled by his *Paradise Lost*' (*Romantics on Milton*, 96).

dition of prophecy to which *Milton* belongs, arguing that they fulfil 'the prophetic dictum that the precursor, even if mistaken, is not an oppressor but a
liberator'.[5] In Wittreich's view, 'the first obligation of the prophet is to explicate
the vision that serves as a gateway to his own; and explication involves correction, sometimes of the visionary himself, but more often of the body of commentary that has perverted his vision'.[6] He suggests that the beneficent and
fruitful antagonism which Blake reveals towards Milton is in keeping with
Milton's own rewriting of the Bible: every prophet establishes himself as one in
a 'chain composed of many links',[7] and all revise each other. Further, he argues
that the prophet takes up a position of antagonism towards his audience, too, as
part of the redemptive process: multifarious allusiveness is used to educate the
reader through harassment, along the lines established by Stanley Fish.[8] In
making 'the vigilance of the reader' a necessary criterion for true understanding,[9] Blake, in Wittreich's view, asserts his continuity with the 'line of vision' to
which he, Milton, and the Old Testament prophets all belong.

    As a corrective to the psychological and individualist approach of Harold
Bloom, Wittreich's generic placing of prophecy is salutary. It reminds us of the
broader implications which are involved in revisionary practices, as well as of
the more general literary tendencies which they typify. But, as David Riede has
more recently argued, Wittreich does not go far enough in envisaging the kinds
of vigilance which Blake in particular demands from the reader, and he tends
also (partly in his reaction against Bloom) to underestimate the extent of the
revisionary processes involved in all acts of interpretation. Riede proposes an
alternative, Barthesian approach: Blake, he argues, sets out to replace the
'divinely authoritative voice of *Paradise Lost*' with 'a contentious heteroglossia'
in which multiple voices (notably those of Milton, Blake, and St Paul) compete
with each other and with 'the myriad voices of the living Judeo-Christian
tradition'.[10] Blake's aim, according to this interpretation, is to correct the
reading process itself, so that it no longer involves passive submission to
authority: he encourages a combative reading practice in his readers which will
prevent them from being 'misled' by the encumbering doctrines which *Paradise
Lost* appears to embody; and this educational process is such as to prepare them,
as well as Milton himself, for reconceiving divinity along Blakean lines. In
Riede's interpretation, Blake's *Milton* becomes an exemplar of what Barthes
calls 'the 'writerly' text (that is, an experimental text, in which the reader is
acknowledged as primary creator of meaning); while *Paradise Lost* itself remains
the typical embodiment of a 'readerly' text, in which the reader is required to
submit to the authority of the author.[11]

    [5] *Angel of Apocalypse*, 221.   [6] *Milton and the Line of Vision* (Madison, Wis., 1975), p. xvi.
    [7] Ibid. p. xiv.   [8] Ibid. 106.
    [9] J. Wittreich, 'Opening the Seals: Blake's Epics and the Milton Tradition', in S. Curran and J.
Wittreich (eds.), *Blake's Sublime Allegory: Essays on 'The Four Zoas', 'Milton' and 'Jerusalem'*
(Madison, Wis., 1973), 38.
    [10] 'On Membership of Church Paul', 259.   [11] Ibid. 275–6.

In the discussion that follows, I shall be presenting an argument that is similar in some important respects to David Riede's; but I hope to pay more attention than he does, firstly, to Blake's active undoing of the effects of Milton's canonization and, secondly, to the function (revisionary or otherwise) of Miltonic allusions themselves. In respect of the first of these, my approach will be dependent on Wittreich's view that correction of the precursor is importantly bound up with correction of 'the body of knowledge' which has 'perverted' the original vision of the precursor, or which blocks the precursor from view.[12] In respect of the second, I shall be sustaining the argument offered throughout this book, namely, that the allusive practices adopted by Milton's followers are importantly continuous with his own; and that if Blake's practices are to be seen as 'revisionary', it is in the sense that they revise an authoritarian reading of Milton which is itself the product of his canonization. Furthermore, in discussing the relation between 'univocal' and 'multivocal' methods of narration, I shall be pointing to strategies which *Milton* shares with the texts discussed in Chapter 4, in all of which contending narratives or narrative expectations are used, not just to challenge divine authority, but to unsettle the stability of the author, by foregrounding the reader's role in constituting 'truth'. Blake's strategies will thus be shown to belong to a more broadly based tradition than Riede's interpretation implies.

Finally, since it is my contention that *Paradise Lost* is considerably less controlled by its 'divinely authoritative voice' than Reide, Bloom, or Wittreich have allowed, I shall be emphasizing the continuity between Blake's own narrative strategies and those elements in Milton's technique which work against or undermine the epic voice of his narrator. If Barthes's terms are as useful here as Reide suggests, then I would argue that *Paradise Lost* is not the monolithic 'readerly' text which Riede makes it but is, rather, a writerly text with a readerly superstructure; and that Blake's prophecy is typically Romantic in its demonstration of how easily this latter can be stripped away. I would further suggest that, in stressing the radicalism of Blake's experimentation with the 'writerly' mode, Riede joins in a general conspiracy (headed by Stanley Fish, and outlined in Chapter 2) to make Milton himself more Urizenic than he is. Such an approach, I shall conclude, underestimates both the experimentalism of *Paradise Lost* and Blake's capacity to notice its implications.

DECANONIZATION

The Preface to *Milton* announces the first stage in Blake's programme for rewriting the reception of *Paradise Lost*. Placing himself at the centre of the 'imitation versus originality' debate, which I discussed in some detail in Chapter 1, Blake refuses to adopt the traditional eighteenth-century attitude of awe towards Milton, either as paragon of neo-classicism or as exemplar of

[12] *Milton and the Line of Vision*, p. xvi.

sublime originality. It had become something of a critical cliché to wonder at the paradox of his being both: witness Hayley's remarks, in 'Conjectures on the Origin of Paradise Lost', that 'he was a poet of nature's creation, but one who added to all her endowments every advantage that study could acquire' and that 'no poet who revered the ancients with such affectionate enthusiasm, has copied them so little'.[13] To which Blake offers the pugnacious reply that Milton not only failed to go far enough, in his own repudiation of classical models, but that his plundering from the classics, and his popularization of them within the framework of the Christian story, had been responsible for sustaining their importance far longer than they merited in their own right. 'The stolen and perverted writings of Homer and Ovid, of Plato and Cicero' which, in Blake's view, 'all men ought to contemn' had, as a result of Milton's influence, been 'set up by artifice against the sublime of the Bible'; and this false elevation would only be realized with the coming of a new age, when 'all would be set right', and 'the daughters of Memory' would become 'the daughters of inspiration'.[14] Although the debt is not here acknowledged, Blake places himself alongside Bishop Lowth in heralding the sublimity and naturalness of Hebrew poetry; one of the unstated implications of the Preface is that the prophetic mode Blake himself adopts is inspired and original—as Milton's might also have been, but for its epic intrusions.

In claiming that the classicist in Milton won out over the Hebrew prophet, Blake seeks to remove one side of the originality/imitation paradox which had so successfully placed Milton's genius on a pedestal. This allows him to begin the process, which his prophecy will extend, of bringing Milton down to earth and so of humanizing the creative imagination, which has become sublimated largely as a result of Milton's influence. (Here Blake would agree with Shelley in perceiving the dangers of abstraction and over-idealization.) On a more specific level, his remark that Milton's imagination was 'curbed by the general malady & infection from the silly Greek and Latin slaves of the sword'[15] is also intended to signal a deep dissatisfaction with the war-mongering values which are purveyed by classical models of heroism and which, in his view, Milton's Christian epic serves only to legitimize and perpetuate, despite its avowal of quite opposite aims. As David Fuller points out, Milton's 'redefinition of heroism as entirely concerned with mental attitudes' is compromised by, for example, 'his presentation of Christ's supreme merit in terms of military greatness in Book VI of *Paradise Lost*'.[16]

Confronting the social repercussions of *Paradise Lost* as a matter of urgent concern, Blake places art at the centre of politics, and makes the poet answerable to the community at large. In thus refusing to allow the aesthetic to become hived

---

[13] *Hayley Life*, 246, 274.

[14] 'Preface' to *Milton*, ll. 6–7; for comparable observations, see *Coleridge Letters*, ii. 865–6.

[15] Hayley, on the other hand, approved of Milton for taking a stand against war, and contrasted him favourably with his classical forebears; see Ch. 1, n. 108.

[16] *Blake's Heroic Argument* (New York, 1988), 163.

off, as a category separate from the moral and the political, he restores to Milton himself his lost or forgotten social responsibilities, and offers an implicit general rebuke of the escapist or élitist imagination. This in its turn provides him with a secure platform from which to make his own alternative plea to the revolutionary impulse in his readers: 'Rouse up, O young men of the new age! Set your foreheads against the ignorant hirelings! For we have hirelings in the camp, the court and the university, who would, if they could, for ever depress mental and prolong corporeal war' ('Preface', pl. 1, ll. 10–13). Reminding painters, sculptors and architects that they too are the unacknowledged legislators of mankind, Blake appeals to them to resist colluding with the commercial mechanisms which ensure that a high price is set on imitative trash, at the expense of genuine originality: 'Suffer not the fashionable fools to depress your powers by the prices they pretend to give for contemptible works or the expensive advertising boasts that they make of such works; believe Christ & his apostles that there is a class of men whose whole delight is in destroying' ('Preface', pl. 1, 13–18). The material constraints which Blake takes into account give an air of practicality to the revolutionary proposals he is making, and supply his millenarian message with immediacy and force: 'We do not want either Greek or Roman models, if we are but just & true to our own imaginations, those worlds of eternity in which we shall live for ever—in Jesus our Lord' ('Preface', pl. 1, 18–20). This message will provide the central thread of Blake's prophecy, as he attempts to make Milton 'just and true to his own imagination', by releasing the prophetic potential of *Paradise Lost* from the epic mode in which it is confined.

HUMANIZATION

Blake seeks in his prophecy not only to expose the deficiencies of institutionalized religion but to replace the hypostasized God of the Church with 'The eternal great Humanity Divine' (bk. i, pl. 2, l. 8) which, in his view, dwells in every individual. He accuses the author of *Paradise Lost* of misrepresenting divinity as an abstraction from the human condition, and so of contributing to the evolution of religion as a system capable of enslaving mankind: he therefore confronts Milton with the necessity of reconciling divinity with humanity, so that the effects of oppression may be undone and mankind (here conceived as the sleeping Albion) awakened to its latent potential. He also perceives that there is in Milton's characterization of God a paradoxical movement away from abstraction into those unacceptable human foibles—anger, vengefulness, caprice—which, as I demonstrated in Chapter 4, make Him vulnerable to attack from questioning readers, and which provide a role model and justification for earthly tyranny. Blake seeks to reverse the damaging effects of Milton's self-division by making him face up to the implications of his hypocrisy, and perceive that the law-giving God he has elevated is as faulty as the Satan he has demeaned. He leaves unaltered the most famous and quoted line of *Paradise*

Lost, 'To Justify the Ways of God to Men', making it the subtitle of his own poem as an implicit rebuke to Milton for his failure in this respect.

As a character in Blake's poem, 'Milton' becomes a synecdoche for 'Milton's God': an apt rhetorical trope, not only because it allows Blake to correct the self-divisions of dramatic character and metaphysical concept at one and the same time, but also because it accurately reflects the synecdochal relation between Milton-as-author and God, which had been turned into a critical cliché by the eighteenth century's reception of *Paradise Lost*. Blake's confrontation with Milton points to some damaging repercussions of the confusion (which I have shown to be habitual) between the author of *Paradise Lost* and his removed, abstracted God. He sets out to reverse the process of deification which began with Milton's self-construction (in, for instance, the 'Ode on Christ's Nativity') and which continued through the eighteenth century, as biographers determinedly transformed him into a paragon of puritan virtue, while commentators, in Wittreich's words, 'directed their efforts toward surreptitiously snaring the poet in their own net of orthodoxy'.[17]

Specifically, Blake addresses the deficiencies of Hayley's *Life of Milton*, a book which (like *Paradise Lost)* is divided against itself, in that it makes powerful claims for Milton the radical which are eclipsed by its restraining misrepresentation of Milton the man. Wittreich is in some respects right to hail this *Life* as a novel and daring Romantic text: in boldly defending Milton's 'genuine patriotism' (p. 65), and in praising the 'devotion to public good' which comes through in his republican tracts, it revives an aspect of Milton which the eighteenth century had suppressed, and offers a political perspective which Blake can approve. Furthermore, in its discussion of Milton's 'confident vigour of mind', his 'intense and inextinguishable fire of imagination' (p. 73), it seems to accord with Blake's valuation of (Satanic) energy. And yet, in his earnest desire to correct Johnson's detraction of Milton the man, Hayley falls back on all the old clichés of Puritan perfection: the 'steadiness and unconquerable integrity' of Milton's character (p. 8), the 'refined and hallowed probity' of his decisions (p. 23), the 'mildness and affability' of his manner (p. 203). He handles with sympathy Milton's marital problems, emphasizing the purity and benevolence of his views on divorce (p. 78), and the 'forgiveness and beneficence' with which he treated his wife and her parents (p. 93). Most worryingly of all, in view of Blake's pro-feminist sympathies, he takes Milton's side in describing the relationship between 'a blind and desolate father' and his 'disobedient daughters', pointing to 'the anguish he endured for their filial ingratitude, and the base deceptions, with which they continually tormented him' (p. 200).

From Blake's perspective, it can be seen that Hayley's whitewashing of

---

[17] *Angel of Apocalypse*, 71.

Milton's character colludes in the dehumanization of imagination of which *Paradise Lost* is itself guilty: only by reconciling Milton's readers to the faults of their deified hero can the true Milton—his spiritual form—be retrieved. *Paradise Lost* is thus rewritten as an alternative, revisionary 'Life of Milton', tracing the 'fortunate fall' of its author, who learns in the course of Blake's narrative to acknowledge his human failings, in particular those which relate to his maltreatment of women. By facing up to the exiled Satan as part of his own identity, Milton is enabled to cast off 'selfhood' (abstracted being) altogether:

> I will go down to self-annihilation & eternal death,
> Lest the Last Judgement come & find me unannihilate,
> And I be seized & given into the hands of my own selfhood ...
> What do I here before the Judgement? Without my emanation?
> With the daughters of memory & not with the daughters of inspiration?
> I in my selfhood am that Satan; I am that evil one,
> He is my spectre! In my obedience to loose him from my hells
> To claim my hells, my furnaces. I go to eternal death.
>
> (bk. i, pl. 14, ll. 22–4, 28–32)

The statement 'I in my selfhood am that Satan' is first in a sequence of recognitions which will allow redemption to take place. In tracing the fall of Milton 'from grace into humanity',[18] Blake asks Milton to celebrate his human condition in all its frailty, since, as Mark Bracher puts it, 'Only through suffering and perishing can the multiplicity and individuality of existence occur at all; and only through suffering and ultimately through perishing can an individual achieve its authentic essential identity.'[19]

Redemption is made possible by the 'Bard's song', which rouses Milton from his slumbers. In its prominent position before the narrative proper, it draws attention to the status of Blake's own prophetic poetry as the awakener of repressed truths; and the language introducing it—'Say first: what mov'd Milton ... To go into the deep her to redeem and himself perish? | What cause at length moved Milton to this unexampled deed?' (bk. i, pl. 2, ll. 16–21)—makes a clear analogy between the 'fall' of Milton into humanity and the transgression of Adam and Eve in *Paradise Lost*: 'say first what cause | Moved our grand parents in that happy state ... to fall off | From their creator .... Who first seduced them to that foul revolt? | The infernal serpent' (*PL* i. 28–34). The implied equation between Blake as awakener and Satan as seducer has important implications which, as David Riede has pointed out, are not far from those of *The Marriage of Heaven and Hell*:

---

[18] Ibid. 144. Cf. N. Frye's useful summary of Blake's position: 'The final revelation of Christianity is not that Jesus is God but that "God is Jesus"'; *Fearful Symmetry: A Study of William Blake* (Princeton, NJ, 1947), 53.

[19] *Being Form'd: Thinking Through Blake's Milton* (New York, 1985), 2.

From the start Blake's theme is that passive obedient acceptance of restraint by a mysterious Providence is inimical to imaginative vision and prophetic utterance. ... the true bard in Milton is in Milton's sense 'Satanic', but in Blake's he represents the 'true poet'.[20]

In the terms which I have elsewhere adopted in this book, we might see Blake as the rescuer of the 'subtext' of *Paradise Lost* from its constraining 'supertext'. By awakening Milton's imagination to its own latent fallenness, he draws attention to the extent to which Milton reads the transgression of Adam and Eve as a 'fortunate fall' which not only heralds the redemption but is, in some broader humanist sense, itself redemptive.

PERSPECTIVISM

Blake presents the redemptive process as a transformation occurring in several dimensions simultaneously—within the spirit of Milton, who by taking mortality upon himself is saved from abstraction; within the poet Blake, who becomes the vessel for Milton's reincarnate spirit; within the reader of Blake's prophecy, who is awakened from torpor into vision; and within the sleeping Albion, who is prepared by Milton the Awakener for the 'great harvest and vintage of all the nations' (bk. ii, pl. 43). As a moment of epiphany, the descent of Milton can be temporally and physically located at the point where his spirit enters the tarsus of Blake's left foot, when the lark-song is heard and the scent of wild thyme fills the garden at Felpham.[21] But it expands to take up most of the narrative, and is multi-layered, both in its mythical associations and in its symbolic implications.

Blake uses the Miltonic device of bifocal allusion to draw the reader's attention to important ambiguities in Milton's descent, and to their twofold interpretation. Relinquishing his safe position as one of the elect in heaven, and journeying to the abyss (our world of generation), the hero is most evidently paralleled with the Son in *Paradise Lost*: his willingness to undergo 'Eternal Death', even in the face of incredulity and opposition, resembles Christ's offer to redeem mankind by taking human form—to suffer and be crucified, so as to ensure eternal life. This Christian parallel is used by Blake to highlight the insufficiency of Milton's God, whose abstraction from humanity is dramatically emblematized in His separation from the Son. By having Milton voluntarily make the transition from invulnerability to frailty, he conflates the two 'persons' of Father and Son, so undoing division and pointing the way forward to 'Humanity Divine'. This correction by Blake of his precursor implies a prefer-

---

[20] 'On Membership of Church Paul', 268; Riede gives a careful and subtle reading of the Miltonic allusions to which I refer.
[21] See bk. ii, pls. 35–6.

ence for *Paradise Regained* over *Paradise Lost*: as Wittreich suggests, the later poem retracted the earlier one's 'terrifying theology', 'revealing Milton to be a broader and wiser man than was ordinarily thought'.[22] Blake expands on the humanity of Christ, as revealed in *Paradise Regained* (see especially the final lines, with their homely emphasis on his return to his mother's house),[23] so as to remind Milton of where his imaginative strength really resides.

But Milton's journey through the abyss has Satanic as well as Christian associations: here, as on so many occasions, Blake carefully amplifies the parallels between opposites which proliferate in *Paradise Lost*, and so demonstrates that 'in equivocal worlds, Up and Down are equivocal'.[24] The Milton who is pictured in eternity, 'pondering the intricate mazes of Providence | Unhappy tho' in heav'n' (bk. i, pl. 2, l. 17), resembles the fallen angels in hell, 'in wandering mazes lost' (*PL* ii. 561), and recalls Satan's declaration that 'To reign is worth ambition though in hell: | Better to reign in hell, than serve in heaven' (*PL* i. 262–3). But these diabolic associations are counteracted by ones that move in an opposite direction; for in the same breath, as he volunteers to redeem his sixfold emanation (bk. i, pl. 2, l. 17), Milton is likened to Christ. This doubling of allusion playfully parodies Milton's own parallel between Christ's mission to redeem, and Satan's to tempt, mankind.[25] Similarly, in Book I, Plate 14, Milton's entry into fallen sexuality is envisaged as a painful incarnation. In one direction, this passage alludes to Christ's taking of human form; in the other, it recalls Satan's Ovidian metamorphoses, first into a toad and finally into a snake—metamorphoses which Milton himself presents as semi-blasphemous parodies of Christ's incarnation. Again, in Book I, Plate 15, Milton's entry into mortality (a redemptive reversal of the Fall-as-Creation in *Urizen*) strongly recalls the expulsion of Mulciber, who 'Dropped from the zenith like a falling star' in *Paradise Lost* Book I (l. 745). At the same time, as Riede has plausibly argued, it suggests a connection with Christ's appearance before St Paul, on the road to Damascus,[26] thus generically defining itself as the climax of a conversion narrative:

> But as a wintry globe descends precipitant through Beulah bursting
> With thunders loud and terrible, so Milton's shadow fell,
> Precipitant loud-thundering into the sea of time & space.
> Then first I saw him in the zenith as a falling-star,
> Descending perpendicular, swift as the swallow or swift;
> And on my left foot, falling on the tarsus, entered there;
>
> (bk. i, pl. 15, ll. 44–9)

[22] *Angel of Apocalypse*, 144.
[23] 'He unobserved | Home to his mother's house private returned' (*Paradise Regained*, iv. 638–9).
[24] 'Notes on the Illustrations to Dante', in *The Complete Writings of William Blake*, ed. G. Keynes (London, 1966), 785.
[25] See N. Frye, *The Return to Eden: Five Essays on Milton's Epics* (Toronto, 1966), 55 f.
[26] 'On Membership of Church Paul', 261.

The point of likening Milton to Satan as well as to Christ is, of course, to provide an ironic prolepsis (itself Miltonic) of his later reunification with the Satanic principle he has exiled. The author of *Paradise Lost* is thus reminded, through verbal interconnections he has himself devised, that the 'contraries of the human soul' need each other. He is led toward the acknowledgement of his own repressed sympathy with Satan, and so toward the marriage of heaven and hell which will occur when he finally confronts Satan as himself. In approximating Milton to Satan in this way, Blake makes use of the journey through the abyss which had become a traditional eighteenth-century topos in describing Milton's sublime imaginative questing.[27] The Satanic resonances of this motif indicate a readiness in pre-Romantic readers to make connections between poetry and transgression, which Blake willingly exploits in reminding his precursor of the fallenness of his imagination.

Milton's duality, as Christ/Satan, also provides Blake with an allusive device for multiplying the confusions, mis-identifications, and belated recognitions of his narrative, which will ultimately become unravelled when the design of his prophecy lies open to view. He can alert the reader to the limitations of his or her moral perspective, by exposing the 'aspect blindness' of those who witness Milton's journey;[28] yet at the same time, he can avoid the reductive clarity of a Miltonic overview, since there is no epic narrator to underline the signification of events as they unfold, and no character within the poem who is truly omniscient. Thus, Enitharmon and Los see Milton's descent only as a Satanic threat: 'Surely to unloose my bond | Is this man come. Satan shall be unloosed upon Albion' (bk. i, pl. 18, ll. 32–3). Their partial vision indicates unreadiness for receiving the whole truth, which would involve integrating the divided Satan and Christ, according to the allusive practices which disclose Blake's prophetic plan. However, true to the dramatic ironies Blake is borrowing from *Paradise Lost*, it is precisely their partial vision which allows the fall-as-redemption to take place. For, in failing to understand that Milton's mission is redemptive, the Eternals oppose it; and in the process they both strengthen his heroic status and underline his affinities with Christ.

Even after they have woken up to the nature of Milton's mission, the Eternals fail to see the role which their oppositional actions have played in assisting his fortunate fall: 'they lamented that they had in wrath & fury & fire | Driven Milton into the Ulro; for now they knew too late | That it was Milton the Awakener' (bk. i, pl. 21, ll. 31–3). Their blindness is doubly ironic in the light of the poem's final outcome, for it is as a result of hearing their lamentations that the sons and daughters of Ololon 'descend also, & ... give | [them]selves to death in Ulro among the transgressors' (bk. i, pl. 21, ll. 45–6); and it is this descent which will ultimately allow Milton to be reintegrated with the female principle, so achieving the humanity which is his redemption. The Eternals

---

[27] Cf. e.g. Gray's 'Progress of Poesy', ll. 95–7.
[28] Wittgenstein's phrase for those able to see only one aspect of the 'duck-rabbit'; see Ch. 2.

thus become unwilling and unwitting participants in redemptive events they cannot understand. Their oppositional actions resemble the purblindness which characterizes Milton's protagonists (Adam and Eve, who bring about their own Fall, despite warnings and because of temptations; but more obviously Satan, whose engineering of tragic events is itself stage-managed by Providence). Blake thus succeeds in turning *Paradise Lost* on its head, by making the eternal perspective appear 'flawed' and the human perspective appear 'redeemed'. The resistance of the Eternals becomes symbolic of the limitations inherent in any tragic or disapproving reading of the Fall—any attempt to refuse humanity—and Blake uses it both to expose Milton's theology and to anticipate the reader's resistance to his meaning. (This meaning will ultimately be shown to triumph, not despite but because of the obscurity which gives it prophetic status.)

The confrontation between Urizen and Milton which takes place in Book I, Plate 19 is crucial, both as an action which symbolically interprets the unfolding story and as a meta-comment on the functional obscurity of Blake's narrative method. Urizen is here pictured (unexpectedly) as a type of John the Baptist, taking water from the river Jordan and pouring the 'icy fluid' over Milton's brain 'with his broad cold palm' (l. 9). Milton, in his turn, is presented in terms which surprise and perplex the reader: as a version of the Jehovah of Genesis, taking red clay and 'moulding it with care | Between his palms' (ll. 10–11), and rebuilding Urizen 'as with new clay, a human form' (ll. 13–14). This extraordinarily arresting image depends for its effect on the perspectivism Blake is disclosing, in his reversal of expected roles. The reader must pause to unravel overlapping viewpoints in order to observe that Urizen, in obstructing Milton's emergence as redeemer, sees him as (and turns him into) an image of himself as the Old Testament God; whilst Milton, in resisting Urizen's retardation, sees him as (and turns him into) the biblical figure who both prefigures and heralds Christ.

These two figures, locked in silent strife, 'one giving life, the other giving death' (l. 29), construct each other as reflexes of themselves; and in the complex *Gestalt* which their perspectives yield, Blake allows us to see some of the important senses in which life and death are interchangeable, according to his own redemptive scheme: Milton, in discarding the Old Testament idea of God, replaces Urizenic death with life-giving energy, just as Christ, in exchanging heaven for earth, accepts mortality in order to give eternal life. We can read the embattled interlocking of Urizen/Milton as a comment on the relationship between Old and New Testament ideas of divinity (and the hermeneutic practices which conflate or oppose them), while also seeing the choice which Blake is guiding both the reader and the author of *Paradise Lost* towards, in his *amalgamation* of Jehovah as giver of human life and Christ as its sacrificial summation. The characteristics of Blake's bifocal simile are analogous to Milton's own, in that they depend simultaneously on 'lurking antagonism' and 'assimilation';[29] furthermore, this simile follows the 'duck-rabbit' pattern in building the reader's subjectivity into the *Gestalt*, as a further layer of perspectivism.

DECONSTRUCTION

The arrival of Milton the Awakener in Albion is intended to prophesy the Second Coming of Christ, and Blake exploits the sacrificial and redemptive ingredients of the Christian story to underline the millenarian message and purpose of his prophecy. The incomprehension of Milton's fellow Eternals, in the face of his decision to descend to eternal death, does double duty: as a reference to the unreadiness of mankind to be saved, and as a rebuke to Milton's theology for its complacent resistance to change:

> And Milton said, 'I go to eternal death!' Eternity shuddered,
> For he took the outside course, among the graves of the dead
> A mournful shade. Eternity shuddered at the image of eternal death.
>
> (bk. i, pl. 14, ll. 33–5)

In presenting his descent as an occurrence which is misunderstood and under-valued by those who witness it, Blake uses a central ingredient of the Scriptures, mankind's blindness to the status of the Saviour: this alerts his readers to their own resistance to the Second Coming, to their own perplexity in the face of Blake's redemptive purpose, and to the transformation of their own fallen perceptions which is needed to make true vision possible. But, as I have shown, he also exploits one of the central devices of *Paradise Lost*—its repeated use of dramatic irony—in order to parody and repudiate Milton's providential plan. Blake draws the reader, through identification with the multiple narratives in his prophecy, into mistaken or partial recognitions of the 'truth', just as Milton does; but at the same time he attempts to empty his prophecy of the law-giving univocal truth which is embodied in Milton's epic voice, with its warning interventions, and its summary belittling of human perspective. The incomprehension of the Eternals becomes a metaphor for the resistance and perplexity of the reader in the face of Blake's idea of redemption; and if this resistance and perplexity persist, they do so because the reader is demonstrably habituated to the epic voice of *Paradise Lost*, and has come to expect the clarification of a providential overview, delivered from on high.

The parodic ingredients of Blake's narrative mode draw attention to the deficiencies of *Paradise Lost*, as he sees them; but they also allow him to educate his reader along lines that are distinctly reminiscent of Miltonic method; and there is a danger, as Riede reminds us, that, in creating his own revisionary version of the providential plan, Blake will merely perpetuate in the reader a

[29] See my discussion of Milton's similes in Ch. 2.

passive willingness to submit to the authority of an alternative 'truth'.[30] In unravelling his narrative so as to redefine redemption in his own terms, Blake is careful, therefore, to avoid what he sees as Milton's abstracting tendencies, and to this end he uses what Bracher has called a 'disjunctive style'. Unsettling our notions of linear time with abrupt narrative transitions, overlapping perspectives, and delays or lapses in the narrative thread, he challenges the reader's consciousness and, by showing 'the immanence of the transcendental in the phenomenal', overcomes 'the idea of a God beyond the skies or of a Being beyond individual Beings'.[31]

Central to Blake's dethroning of God as authority is his deconstruction of the author as God. Discarding the perspective of an omniscient narrator, he gives his poet-persona a changing role, which both reflects and provides a model for the education of his reader. At the outset of the narrative, he is a bewildered human, waiting to receive as univocal 'truth' what he later learns to understand as complex and multiform. At various points in the course of the poem (for instance, as the moment when he perceives Milton's descent as the fall of Mulciber) we become aware that his vision is as partial as that of the Eternals, even though it is less resistant to prophetic implications. But it is only when united with Los that he becomes capable of understanding the prophecy which he is himself speaking. In making himself, at this late point in the narrative, the vehicle of another's voice, Blake offers a subtle parody of Milton's claim to have transcribed the whole of *Paradise Lost* by dictation from God: whereas Milton's epic narrator is in charge from the outset, speaking the words of 'a God beyond the skies', the poet-persona of *Milton* is inserted into the narrative as the belated interpreter of a prophecy he has hitherto been unable to comprehend.

Alone of the Eternals, Los is capable of prophetic insight, and it is he who comes nearest to embodying the epic voice of Milton's narrator, by emerging as the interpreter of Blake's underlying prophetic design, and by translating its obscurities for the other characters involved. Even Los, however, is denied Miltonic omniscience: as we have seen, his actions early in the narrative are as purblind as those of the other Eternals, and he is driven to desperation before recalling 'an old Prophecy in Eden recorded' that Milton should 'set free | Orc from his chain of jealousy' (bk. i, pl. 20, l. 56). This belated memory occurs simultaneously with the entry of Milton into Blake's foot, and prepares the way for Blake's recognition, both of himself as prophet, and of Milton as redeemer. The delaying of this recognition is a reminder that the poet himself has limited vision, and is as yet unconscious of his role as vessel for the fallen/redeemed Milton:

> But Milton entering my left foot, I saw in the nether
> Regions of imagination, also all men on earth

---

[30] 'On Membership of Church Paul', 273–4.
[31] *Being Form'd*, 7, 9; interestingly, Bracher sees the poem's abrupt transitions and stylistic changes as forcing the reader to remain 'in an extreme state of negative capability' (p. 8).

> And all in heaven saw in the nether regions of imagination,
> In Ulro beneath Beulah, the vast breach of Milton's descent.
> But I knew not that it was Milton, for man cannot know
> What passes in his members till periods of space & time
> Reveal the secrets of Eternity;

> (bk. i, pl. 21, ll. 4–10)

At this point, Milton's notion of truth as a divinely coherent message, dictated by an omniscient 'being beyond the skies', is thoroughly deconstructed. Blake succeeds in showing not only that the vehicles of prophetic truth (Los/Blake) are flawed in their interpretative capacity but that their flaws are precisely constitutive of the 'truth' as it is perceived. This is the point underlined by the perspectivism of his narrative method, and by the symbolic significance of making Milton descend to earth in the first place.

FEMINIZATION

When Los enters into Blake's soul, and they become one man, he is able (through Los's voice) to proclaim Milton's arrival and his own transformation as the coming of the Millennium:

> This mighty one is come from Eden: he is of the Elect
> Who died from earth & he is returned before the Judgement. This thing
> Was never known; that one of the holy dead should willingly return.
> Then patient wait a little while, till the last vintage is over,

> (bk. i, pl. 23, ll. 56–9)

Having brought his prophecy to its turning-point, Blake is ready to orchestrate the events which will clarify its redemptive purpose. In the sequence of confrontations, reunifications, and purgations which occur in rapid succession during Book II, the female principle is given a central role; and it is crucial to Blake's message that this should be so: he wishes to rebuke Milton for the neglect he showed towards his wives and daughters (and so to undo the damage which Hayley's defence of his actions may have caused); but he also wishes to reveal to Milton that, while his imagination remains resistant to the feminine, his humanity will be incomplete. This rebuke is self-evidently necessary, in Blake's view, since the Milton of *Paradise Lost* is guilty of at once elevating the female principle (Urania as holy inspiration, the muse who helps him transcend earthly concerns) and vilifying woman (Eve as seductive temptress, the cause of man's fall). His double standard in this respect exactly mirrors his hypocrisy in elevating God and demeaning Satan: Blake's project is in both cases to reunite perspectives that have become separated, and so to restore humanity to Milton's vision.

Book II opens, therefore, with an evocation of the 'feminine' imagination:

Beulah, 'a pleasant lovely shadow | Where no dispute can come' (bk. ii, pl. 30, ll. 2–3), into which the sons and daughters of Ololon descend. This is 'a place where contrarieties are equally true' (l. 1)—where the univocal is replaced by the equivocal, the absolute by the relative, martial glory by moony receptivity or 'mild and pleasant rest'. It is at only one remove, in Blake's cosmology, from the Eden of visionary imagination; and in the terms I have elsewhere adopted from Keats, we might read it as the 'negative capability' of Milton, which Blake seeks to rescue from the restraining hold of masculine/authoritarian 'truth'. (In much the same way, in *The Marriage of Heaven and Hell*, he had set out to loosen the hold which Milton's reason had exerted over his repressed 'energy' or 'desire'.) Blake restarts his prophecy from this place so as to recount events from a female perspective, thus purging Milton of his hostility towards the feminine. He replaces the epic voice of the narrator in *Paradise Lost* with a divine voice which is stripped of misogynist prejudice, and which retains no vestiges of the blinkered ideas about sexuality and sex that (in Blake's view, as in DiSalvo's) hamper Milton's bourgeois ideal of familial love.[32] This voice tells fallen humanity of Milton's mission to redeem his emanation (bk. ii, pl. 33), and of the ending of jealousy which such liberation will allow. The narrative follows Ololon's descent to seek Milton in the Ulro, and recounts how this action opens a thoroughfare from eternity to the world of vegetation (bk. ii, pl. 35). Blake's allusive language suggests that a parody is intended, here, of the causeway built by Sin and Death in *Paradise Lost* Book X, to allow free passage from hell to earth: he replaces Milton's monstrous representation of hermaphroditic sexuality (Sin) with the flawed but benevolent Ololon, and undoes the malign associations of Milton's Death. As a result, his thoroughfare, by contrast with Milton's, becomes a positive symbol: a guarantee of the free passage of the Eternals into mortality, and so of the redemptive potential of earthly beings.

Unlike Milton, who envisages creative potential primarily in terms of ascent—'Into the heaven of heavens I have presumed' (*PL* vii. 13)—Blake's idea of poetic creativity is bound up with this vividly realized possibility of a two-way passage between the eternal and the temporal.[33] To correct Milton's tendency towards abstraction, he replaces the upward mobility of Raphael's ladder of creation with something that more closely resembles Jacob's ladder, on which angels both ascend and descend. More dramatically still, in the opening address of his prophecy, he discards Milton's invocation to Urania (a removed and mythologized female principle) with what Bracher has called 'a physiological description of the poetic act, completely confounding the traditional view of poetry as a sublime and elevated endeavour': 'Come into my hand | By your mild

---

[32] See J. DiSalvo, *War of Titans: Blake's Critique of Milton and the Politics of Religion* (Pittsburgh, Pa., 1983), 311 f.

[33] Coleridge follows Milton in figuring imagination as a subliming process, an 'ascent of being'; as does Wordsworth, by making his ascent of Snowdon the culminating episode of *The Prelude*. Cf. also the difficult ascent of the poet/dreamer in Keats's 'The Fall of Hyperion' and Shelley's (parodic) treatment of sublime mountain-climbing in 'Alastor'.

power descending down the nerves of my right arm | From out the portals of my brain' (bk. i, pl. 2, ll. 5–7).[34]

Milton had prayed to a muse who dwelt on high, and whose aid he called on in attempting to imagine the unfallen state. By contrast, the muse of *Milton* appears to Blake in his garden at Felpham: a fallen place, in which he is troubled by earthly concerns, and particularly by the sickness of his wife (bk. ii, pl. 36). His revision of Milton's conception of creativity is simultaneously a revision of Milton's conception of the feminine; and Ololon's fall into human form is a bringing down to earth of both. As an event, it both parallels and resembles Milton's earlier incarnation, in being presented as a reversal of the Urizenic fall into creation. Blake underlines its symbolic status by making it a moment of imaginative epiphany and sensual delight, heralded by the scent of wild thyme, and by the flight of a lark. It is thus a celebration of physicality and temporality (like the revisionary address to the daughters of Beulah with which his prophecy had opened), and at the same time a palpable moment of access to the eternal perspective from which Milton has fallen. Eliot (who recalls this passage when he writes *Four Quartets*) would call it 'the point of intersection of the timeless | With time'.[35]

Ololon appears in physical form, as a twelve-year-old virgin, who speaks to Blake of her quest to find Milton: 'Him I seek, terrified at my act | In great Eternity, which thou knowest. I come him to seek' (bk. ii, pl. 37, ll. 2–3). The emergence of her articulate female voice coincides with Blake's recognition that Milton's shadow, the 'Covering Cherub' or restrainer of spiritual form, is either unable to hear her words or indifferent to them, depending on how the syntax is read: 'Mild was the voice, but more distinct than any earthly | That Milton's shadow heard' (bk. ii, pl. 37, ll. 5–6). At this pivotal moment in the narrative, Blake brings into focus the nature of his quarrel with Hayley over the details of Milton's life. Implicitly rebuking Milton for his neglect of both wife and daughters, he contrasts the indifference of Milton's shadow with the anxieties he more humanely feels for his own wife, in her sick fatigue (bk. ii, pl. 36). More importantly, however, he here reveals an intuition similar to Wollstonecraft's: that the 'sublimity' of Milton, as defined by Burke and others, is both cause and effect of his poetry's indifference to the feminine; indeed, that the compelling combination of 'majesty and beauty' for which *Paradise Lost* is famous[36] is nothing more nor less than a repudiation of femininity, since it depends on gender alignments which underwrite woman's subjection to man. 'Condensing all his fibres | Into a strength impregnable of majesty and beauty infinite | I saw

---

[34] *Being Form'd*, 11.

[35] 'The Dry Salvages', ll. 201–2. Eliot recalls Blake at l. 130 of 'East Coker', where he creates an epiphany from 'The wild thyme unseen and the wild strawberry'.

[36] Blake's use of the phrase 'majesty and beauty' recalls Burke's collocation of the sublime and the beautiful; but he may also be parodying Hayley's habit of persistently referring to Milton in mechanical doublets: 'generous and devout' (*Hayley Life*, 13); 'tenderness and enthusiasm' (ibid. 17); 'austerity and moroseness' (ibid. 20), etc.

he was the Covering Cherub' (bk. ii, pl. 37, ll. 6–8), Blake writes, identifying in Milton's sublime indifference all that is morally repugnant in his vision—all that is antithetical to the divine humanity which Blake wishes to celebrate, equally in women and men:

> I beheld Milton with astonishment, & in him beheld
> The monstrous churches of Beulah, the gods of Ulro dark—
> Twelve monstrous dishumanised terrors, synagogues of Satan,
>
> (bk. ii, pl. 37, ll. 15–17)

Satan is now identified, not in Milton's terms, as the 'evil' which opposes 'good', but in Blake's terms, as the 'evil' which Milton's faulty definition of 'good' brings monstrously into being. He is one and the same with the law-giving, Urizenic God of *Paradise Lost*, and their joint power can only be defeated by redefining divinity as human potential, liberated firstly from the institutionalized oppression of the Church and secondly from the mind-forged manacles of Reason, both in their different ways responsible for perpetuating the sexual hierarchy which Blake wishes to undo. This recognition of the 'Covering Cherub' prepares the way for the culminating scene of Blake's prophecy—a Last Judgement, in which the Urizenic Milton will confront Satan as a version of himself and, by identifying the evils for which he is responsible, will cast off his 'selfhood'. In its daring play with biblical expectations, and in its confrontation and mirroring of the Creator and his Creation, this Last Judgement scene recalls *Caleb Williams* and *Frankenstein*. But it outdoes both of them in its surreal stage effects and the solemn apocalyptic grandeur of its mood.

Appropriately, Milton descends to his Last Judgement in the Puritan garb familiar to his eighteenth-century readers: 'Clothed in black; severe and silent he descended' (bk. ii, pl. 38, l. 8). In this guise (itself a cherubic covering) he stands in the dock as both judge and criminal: passing judgement on himself, by confronting what he has created. He learns to acknowledge that, as the restrainer of Satanic energy, he is responsible for 'self-righteousness | In all its hypocritic turpitude' (bk. ii, pl. 38, ll. 43–4)—responsible, that is, for the warping of divine humanity into its Urizenic forms. Only by refusing to act as 'Covering Cherub', by exploring 'these wonders of Satan's holiness' (l. 45) in 'all its selfish natural virtue' (l. 47), is it possible for him to 'put off | In self-annihilation all that is not of God alone' (ll. 47–8). This purgation of self, this casting off by Milton of his 'spectre', forms the climax of Blake's prophecy; and here the voice of Blake's 'eternal great Humanity Divine' can be heard within Milton, passing judgement on the law-giving God which he has created, and learning to name this creation 'Satan':

> Such are the laws of Eternity, that each shall mutually
> Annihilate himself for other's good, as I for thee.
> Thy purpose & the purpose of thy priests & of thy churches
> Is to impress on men the fear of death; to teach

Trembling & fear, terror, constriction, abject selfishness.
Mine is to teach men to despise death, & to go on
In fearless majesty annihilating self, laughing to scorn
Thy laws & terrors, shaking down thy Synagogues as webs.

(ll. 35–42)

In a magnificent expansion of Milton's conflationary methods, the law-giving
Jehovah and the exiled Satan of *Paradise Lost* converge, mirror, amalgamate,
and finally cancel each other out.[37] Milton is purged of one side of his hypocrisy; and, preparing for self-renewal, Albion begins to awaken from his sleep
(bk. ii, pl. 39).

Milton now returns to his earlier struggle with Urizen, who continues to
block his progress towards self-purgation and who separates him from his
emanation. This second stage of the 'Last Judgement' symbolizes his confrontation with the rationality which still maintains its hold on both him and the
cultural assumptions he has helped to form. Blake's critique of Milton is here
impressionistically sweeping: he draws into a single category 'This Newtonian
phantasm | This Voltaire & Rousseau, this Hume & Gibbon & Bolingbroke'
(bk. ii, pl. 40, ll. 11–12), not because he holds Milton literally responsible for
their disparate (though similarly pernicious) visions, but because he has made
Milton's Urizenic God symbolic of the monstrous products of Enlightenment
thinking which he wishes to repudiate *en masse*. At the point where it becomes
possible 'to cast off rational demonstration by faith in the Saviour' (bk. ii, pl. 41,
l. 3) and 'to cast off Bacon, Locke & Newton from Albion's covering' (l. 5), the
immortal spirit of Milton emerges.[38]

The liberation of Ololon from the constraints of Milton's Urizenic God is
presented as the discarding of her 'sexual garments' which hide her 'human
lineaments' from view. This process of self-purgation is dependent on Milton's
own, because it is his religious hypocrisy which has imposed limits on her
humanity, and his excessive rationality which has caused her subjection to him,
as well as his neglect of her. Purgation is presented, therefore, as subsequent to
Milton's self-judgement, though logically both events are happening at one and
the same time. At Plate 42 this process is completed, with the annihilation of
Ololon's evil part (Milton's appropriation of the feminine, as symbol of sexual
temptation), which flees 'into the depths | Of Milton's shadow' (bk. ii, pl. 42,
ll. 5–6), allowing the redeemed Ololon to descend, like the New Jerusalem of
Revelation, 'In clouds of blood, in streams of gore, with dreadful thunder-
ings | Into the fires of intellect that rejoiced in Felpham's vale' (ll. 8–9). 'One
man Jesus the Saviour' emerges, folded in the clouds of Ololon 'as a garment
dipped in blood', and walks forth into Albion (ll. 11–12, 19–20); then, as Blake
returns from his visionary to his mortal state, 'the great harvest and vintage of

---

[37] This is Blake's version of the dethronement of Jupiter in *Prometheus Unbound*, which Shelley
presents in terms of internal transformation rather than violent overthrow.
[38] For Blake's consistent repudiation of natural religion, see Frye, *Fearful Symmetry*, 44.

the nations' begins (pl. 43). The reunion of Milton and his emanation thus provides both a model for human potential and, in Blake's optimistic vision, the beginnings of redemption itself.

CONCLUSION

In the final plates of *Milton*, Blake provides a programme of revolution for the human mind which (like Shelley's *Prometheus Unbound*) avoids the repetition-compulsion of history, with its endless cycles of tyranny and rebellion. As Wittreich has said, 'Milton's redemption involves his assuming the role of Awakener—a role that commits the poet to bursting through cyclical patterns in order to achieve Apocalypse'.[39] By deconstructing what he sees as Milton's binary moral scheme, and by demonstrating that the law-giving Jehovah is one and the same with the exiled and vilified Satan, Blake allows a redemptive principle to emerge which need be identified with neither one nor other of these 'negations', but rather with the integration of opposites that are complementary:

> There is a negation, & there is a contrary:
> The negation must be destroyed to redeem the contraries.
> The negation is the spectre, the reasoning power in man.
> This is a false body, an incrustation over my immortal
> Spirit, a selfhood which must be put off & annihilated alway.
>
> (bk. ii, pl. 40, ll. 32–6)

Genuine revolution is here defined, not as the casting out of one term by its opposite (necessarily a cyclical process, as Blake himself demonstrates in the 'Argument' to *The Marriage of Heaven and Hell*), but as the acknowledgement of the system of difference which constitutes both terms in their relation to each other.

Blake's engagement with the reader, in *Milton*, involves at every level a carrying through, or putting into practice, of this insight: he deploys all the dividing/unifying strategies of his mature prophetic style—a style which, as McGann reminds us, 'is precisely designed to foster ambivalent perspectives—to "tease us out of thought"'[40] by the perception of similarities and differences in perpetual oscillation. And he deploys them, here, to a particular 'redemptive' end. The poem's bipartite structure reflects the separation of male and female principles, which must be integrated if redemption is to take place; and its handling of temporal and eternal perspectives suggests a point of intersection in the 'eternal great Humanity Divine'. Its method of characterization depends on the mirroring and amalgamation of moral polarities; and its narrative mode at once divides and mediates between opposing points of view. In its practices of two-

---

[39] *Angel of Apocalypse*, 239.

[40] 'The Aim of Blake's Prophecies', in Curran and Wittreich (eds.), *Blake's Sublime Allegory*, 13, 16.

faced allusion, bifocal simile, and internal cross-reference, the poem constantly encourages the reader to play an active part in the redemptive process, by anticipating the future coalescence of contraries wherever similarities are unexpectedly disclosed.

Blake deploys these strategies in a poem whose explicit intention is to *correct* Milton, to revise all that is wrong-headed in *Paradise Lost*, and to replace Milton's false image of God with Blake's true one. And yet, in the act of deploying them, Blake imitates, replicates, or amplifies all those characteristics of *Paradise Lost* which I examined in my second chapter—characteristics which reveal what Geoffrey Hartman has called a 'spirit of accommodation' in Milton himself, that allows 'two different, even contradictory ideas to coexist'.[41] Blake's prophecy is indeed the supreme example of a paradox which this book has been concerned to uncover: namely, that those who exposed the closure of Milton's imagination in their critical observations were involved in revealing a quite different Milton—open-ended, ambiguous, indeterminate—when it came to the practice of rewriting his poems. 'Rewriting' is therefore a useful pun, since it suggests both revisionary intent and continuity of practice.

I refer to *Milton* as 'the supreme example' of this finding because I wish to make special claims for it, as a poem which crosses the boundary between 'criticism' and 'creation' more evidently, more self-consciously, and more sustainedly than any other text I have examined, or, indeed, than any isolated act of Miltonic allusion. (One must, I think, concede that most allusions embedded in poems are in some sense acts of 'criticism', as well as the more general point that criticism is a 'creative' act.) Crossing this boundary as he does, in both correcting Milton and making *Milton*, Blake is in an ideal position to observe the paradox which I have just expounded: that is, the contradiction between 'Milton' as he is consciously received, constructed, and appropriated, and Milton as he emerges, line by line, simile by metaphor, in the act of alluding to or imitating his work. I shall conclude by suggesting not only that Blake observes and makes use of this disjunction but that it is crucial (to both the meaning and the dramatic unfolding of his prophecy) that the reader should perceive it, too. For, as this chapter has shown, what Blake causes to happen in the course of his poem is the replacement of one Milton by the other. He demotes the Milton who is a synecdoche for God, in order to allow the emergence of a 'human' Milton; and in so doing he deconstructs the machinery of critical reception which has caused the indeterminate Milton to become hidden, and Milton the 'Great Forbidder' to become deified and ossified, along Urizenic lines.

In suggesting a role for Milton's 'spirit of accommodation' in the unfolding of Blake's prophecy, I have offered a reading of the poem which is in some senses compatible with Wittreich's observation that, as he wrote the poem, 'Blake became less and less intent on rebuking Milton, and simultaneously, much more cognizant of the visionary dimensions of Milton's art'.[42] But

[41] Ibid. 40.   [42] *Angel of Apocalypse*, 43.

whereas Wittreich's claim is based on the evolving significance of Blake's illustrations, and suggests his increasing empathy with Milton as an unconscious and spontaneous act, my own is based on poetic practices that can be observed to have a more consciously ironic function. I have suggested that the reader is baffled by Miltonic indeterminacies into an acknowledgement of where the 'true' Milton really resides; and that these indeterminacies play both a metaphoric role, in creatively uncovering the 'true' Milton, and a dramatic role, in suggesting a process which occurs during and through the acts of reading and writing.

Thus, as I have shown, Blake's parodic treatment of the Eternals implies a knowing awareness of the built-in resistances his prophetic message will encounter, as the reader is forced to adjust received ideas. But meanwhile, in his self-ironization, his playing down of the prophetic role of his persona, Blake suggests an important sense in which the poem is a learning process for him as well. His use of Miltonic indeterminacies is thus both evidence of and commentary on the emergence of the open-ended Milton. If the act of writing does indeed make possible the act of recovering Milton from the critical myth which obscures him, Blake observes this to be the case, and builds it into his poem as a metaphorical dramatization of the endeavour he is engaged upon. In this way, the 'creative' process is acknowledged by him to be playing a part in his conscious 'critical' practices.

Stanley Fish, one of this century's strongest perpetuators of the Urizenic Milton, has said of *Paradise Lost* that 'it is an instruction manual to its readers in how to read it';[43] but the same could be more tellingly said of *Milton*, which offers a creative/critical model of the reading process leading to quite different conclusions. I give it the final word in this book because it provides a summation of several ingredients in the critical endeavour on which I have myself been engaged. The first and most evident of these is that it offers, in Milton's descent, a metaphorical dethronement of the author as Great Forbidder: this allows for the emergence of a desublimated notion of the creative process, and for a more liberal reading of Milton's engagement with his audience. As I suggested at the beginning of this chapter, we can define this more 'liberal' relationship in Barthesian terms: Blake removes what Barthes would call the 'readerly' superstructure of *Paradise Lost*, allowing its experimental or 'writerly' aspect to emerge more fully.

Blake's *Milton* also corresponds to my own interpretative procedures in that it reads the Fall as 'fortunate' for the humanization it makes possible. In so doing, it expands the latent implications of what I have referred to as the 'subtext' of *Paradise Lost*, making a connection between transgression and imagination which is analogous to all the Romantic texts discussed in Chapters 6 and 7. Furthermore, in presenting Beulah as the model for a feminized Miltonic imagination, Blake allows the patriarchal ingredients of Milton's writing to seem less important than his association of creativity with the feminine. Defined

---

[43] *Surprised by Sin: The Reader in 'Paradise Lost'* (Berkeley, Calif., 1976), 162.

as the place 'where contrarieties are equally true', Beulah becomes, indeed, a metaphor of the ideal or 'Shakespearian' imagination as Keats would have defined it: that is, an imagination divested of its authoritarian need for closure, and capable of resting content with mysteries and doubts. In this way, Blake's *Milton* does self-consciously and critically what other Romantic texts do through their creative practices of allusion, and what I have myself attempted to do, throughout this book: it succeeds in rescuing from the constraints of Milton's epic narrator the 'negative capability' which is latent within the multivocal narrative of *Paradise Lost*.

Select Bibliography

ABRAMS, M. H., *Natural Supernaturalism: Tradition and Revolution in Romantic Literature* (New York, 1971).

—— *The Mirror and the Lamp: Romantic Theory and the Critical Tradition* (Oxford, 1953; repr. 1976).

ADDISON, J., *The Spectator*, ed. with introd. and notes, D. F. Bond (5 vols., Oxford, 1965).

ADORNO, T., *Minima Moralia: Reflections from Damaged Life*, trans. E. F. N. Jephcott (London, 1974).

BALDICK, C., *In Frankenstein's Shadow: Myth, Monstrosity, and Nineteenth-Century Writing* (Oxford, 1987).

BARTHES, R., *Selected Writings*, ed. with introd. S. Sontag (London, 1982).

BASLER, R., *Sex, Symbolism, and Psychology in Literature* (New Brunswick, NJ, 1948).

BATE, J., *Shakespeare and the English Romantic Imagination* (Oxford, 1986).

BATE, W. J., *John Keats* (Cambridge, Mass., 1964).

—— *The Burden of the Past and The English Poet* (London, 1971).

BAYLEY, J., 'Intimacies of Implication' (review of J. Hollander, *The Figure of Echo*), *The Times Literary Supplement*, 7 May 1982.

BEER, G., 'Richardson, Milton and the Status of Evil', *Review of English Studies*, n.s. 19 (1968), 261–70.

BELSEY, C., *John Milton: Language, Gender, Power* (Oxford, 1988).

BENNETT, J. S., *Reviving Liberty: Radical Christian Humanism in Milton's Great Poems* (Cambridge, Mass., 1989).

BIRCH, T. (ed.), *A Complete Collection of the Historical, Political and Miscellaneous Works of John Milton* (London, 1738).

BLAIR, H., *Lectures on Rhetoric and Belles Lettres* (2 vols., London, 1783).

BLAKE, W., *The Complete Writings of William Blake*, ed. G. Keynes (London, 1966).

—— *Blake: The Complete Poems*, ed. W. H. Stevenson, text by D. V. Erdman (London, 1971).

BLESSINGTON, F. C., *'Paradise Lost' and the Classical Epic* (Boston, 1979).

BLOOM, H., *The Visionary Company* (New York, 1961).

—— *Blake's Apocalypse: A Study in Poetic Argument* (Ithaca, NY, 1970).

—— *The Ringers in the Tower: Studies in Romantic Tradition* (Chicago, 1971).

—— *The Anxiety of Influence: A Theory of Poetry* (Oxford, 1973).

—— *A Map of Misreading* (Oxford, 1975).

—— *Poetry and Repression: Revisionism from Blake to Stevens* (New Haven, Conn., 1976).

BLOOM, H., *Ruin the Sacred Truths: Poetry and Belief from the Bible to the Present* (Cambridge, Mass., 1987).

BRACHER, M., *Being Form'd: Thinking through Blake's Milton* (New York, 1985).

BRISMAN, L., *Milton's Poetry of Choice and its Romantic Heirs* (Ithaca, NY, 1973).

——*Romantic Origins* (Ithaca, NY, 1978).

BROMWICH, D., *Hazlitt: The Mind of a Critic* (Oxford, 1983).

BROWER, R. A., *Alexander Pope: The Poetry of Allusion* (Oxford, 1959).

BURKE, E., *A Philosophical Enquiry into the Origin of our Ideas of the Sublime and Beautiful*, ed. with introd. and notes J. T. Boulton (Oxford, 1958; repr. 1990).

——*Reflections on the Revolution in France*, ed. with introd. C. C. O'Brien (Harmondsworth, Middx., 1968; repr. 1986).

BURNS, R., *The Letters of Robert Burns*, ed. G. Ross Roy (2 vols., Oxford, 1985).

BUTLER, M., *Romantics, Rebels and Reactionaries: English Literature and its Background, 1760–1830* (Oxford, 1981).

——(ed.), *Burke, Paine, Godwin, and the Revolution Controversy* (Cambridge, 1984).

BYRON, Lord, *The Complete Poetical Works*, ed. J. McGann (6 vols., Oxford, 1980–91).

CHANDLER, J. K., 'Romantic Allusiveness', *Critical Inquiry*, 8 (1981–2), 461–87.

CLARK, T., *Embodying Revolution: the Figure of the Poet in Shelley* (Oxford, 1989).

COLERIDGE, S. T., *The Complete Poetical Works of Samuel Taylor Coleridge*, ed. E. H. Coleridge (2 vols., Oxford, 1912).

——*The Collected Letters of Samuel Taylor Coleridge*, ed. E. L. Griggs (6 vols., Oxford, 1956–71).

——*The Notebooks of Samuel Taylor Coleridge*, ed. K. Coburn (4 vols., New York, 1957–61).

——*The Collected Works of Samuel Taylor Coleridge*, gen. ed. K. Coburn (Princeton, NJ, 1971–).

——*Poems*, selected and ed. J. Beer (London, 1974).

COLLINS, W., *The Poems of Thomas Gray, William Collins, and Oliver Goldsmith*, ed. R. Lonsdale (London, 1969).

COWPER, W. (ed.), *Milton* (4 vols., Chichester, 1810).

——*Correspondence of Cowper*, ed. T. Wright (4 vols., London, 1904).

CULLER, J., *The Pursuit of Signs: Semiotics, Literature, Deconstruction* (London, 1981).

CURRAN, S., and WITTREICH, J. (eds.), *Blake's Sublime Allegory: Essays on 'The Four Zoas', 'Milton' and 'Jerusalem'* (Madison, Wis., 1973).

DARBISHIRE, H. (ed.), *The Early Lives of Milton* (London, 1932).

DE MAN, P., *The Rhetoric of Romanticism* (Columbia, NY, 1984).

DE QUINCEY, T., *Confessions of an English Opium Eater*, ed. A. Hayter (Harmondsworth, Middx., 1971).

——*De Quincey as Critic*, ed. J. E. Jordan (London, 1973).

——*Confessions of an English Opium Eater and Other Writings*, ed. with introd.

G. Lindop (Oxford, 1985).

DiSALVO, J., *War of Titans: Blake's Critique of Milton and the Politics of Religion* (Pittsburgh, Pa., 1983).

DOODY, M. A., *The Daring Muse: Augustan Poetry Reconsidered* (Cambridge, 1985).

DOUGLAS, J., Revd, *Milton no Plagiary: or a Detection of the Forgeries Contained in Lauder's Essay on the Imitations of the Moderns in Paradise Lost* (2nd edn., London, 1756).

DuROCHER, R. J., *Milton and Ovid* (Ithaca, NY, 1985).

ECO, U., *The Role of the Reader: Explorations in the Semiotics of Texts* (London, 1979).

ELLIS, D., *Wordsworth, Freud and the Spots of Time: Interpretation in 'The Prelude'* (Cambridge, 1985).

EMPSON, W., *Milton's God* (Cambridge, 1961; repr. 1980).

ENGELL, J., *The Creative Imagination: Enlightenment to Romanticism* (Cambridge, Mass., 1981).

ERDMAN, D. V., *Blake: Prophet Against Empire* (Princeton, NJ; 3rd edn., 1977).

ESSICK, D., *William Blake and The Language of Adam* (Oxford, 1989).

EVEREST, K., *Coleridge's Secret Ministry: The Context of the Conversation Poems, 1795–1798* (Brighton, 1979).

FAIRER, D., *Pope's Imagination* (Manchester, 1984).

FALCONER, C., *An Essay upon Milton's Imitations of the Ancients in his Paradise Lost, with some observations on the Paradise Regain'd* (London, 1741).

FISH, S. E., *Surprised by Sin: The Reader in 'Paradise Lost'* (Berkeley, Calif., 1967).

——*Is There a Text in this Class?* (Cambridge, Mass., 1980).

——'Interpreting the *Variorum*', in D. Lodge (ed.), *Modern Criticism and Theory: A Reader* (London, 1988).

FERRY, A. D., *Milton and the Miltonic Dryden* (Cambridge, Mass., 1968).

FOUCAULT, M., 'What Is an Author?' in D. Lodge (ed.), *Modern Criticism and Theory: A Reader* (London, 1988).

——*The Order of Things: An Archaeology of the Human Sciences* (London, 1970; repr. 1989).

FREUND, E., *The Return of the Reader: Reader Response Criticism* (London, 1987).

FRUMAN, N., *Coleridge, the Damaged Archangel* (New York, 1971).

FRYE, N., *Fearful Symmetry: A Study of William Blake* (Princeton, NJ, 1947).

——*Anatomy of Criticism: Four Essays* (Princeton, NJ, 1957; repr. Harmondsworth, Middx., 1990).

——*The Return of Eden: Five Essays on Milton's Epics* (Toronto, 1966).

FULLER, D., *Blake's Heroic Argument* (New York, 1988).

GILBERT, S., and GUBAR, S., *The Madwoman in the Attic: The Woman Writer and the Nineteenth-Century Literary Imagination* (New Haven, Conn., 1979).

GLEN, H., *Vision and Disenchantment: Blake's 'Songs' and Wordsworth's 'Lyrical Ballads'* (Cambridge, 1983).

GODWIN, W., *Enquiry Concerning Political Justice*, ed. I. Kramnick (Harmondsworth, Middx., 1976).

——*Caleb Williams*, ed. D. McCracken (Oxford, 1970).

GOLDSMITH, O., *The Poems of Thomas Gray, William Collins, and Oliver Goldsmith*, ed. R. Lonsdale (London, 1969).

GOOD, J. W., *Studies in the Milton Tradition* (Urbana, Ill., 1915).

GRAVIL, R., and LEFEBURE, M. (eds.), *The Coleridge Connection: Essays for Thomas McFarland* (Basingstoke, 1990).

——, NEWLYN, L., and ROE, N. (eds.), *Coleridge's Imagination: Essays in Memory of Pete Laver* (Cambridge, 1985).

GRAY, T., *The Poems of Thomas Gray, William Collins, and Oliver Goldsmith*, ed. R. Lonsdale (London, 1969).

GREENE, T., *The Descent from Heaven: A Study in Epic Continuity* (New Haven, Conn., 1963).

GRIFFIN, D., *Regaining Paradise: Milton and the Eighteenth Century* (Cambridge, 1986).

GROSSMAN, M., *'Authors to Themselves': Milton and the Revelation of History* (Cambridge, 1987).

HAGSTRUM, J. H., *The Romantic Body: Love and Sexuality in Keats, Wordsworth, and Blake* (Knoxville, Tenn., 1985).

HAMILTON, P., *Coleridge's Poetics* (Oxford, 1983).

——*Wordsworth* (Brighton, 1986).

HARDING, D. P., *The Club of Hercules: Studies in the Classical Background of 'Paradise Lost'* (Urbana, Ill., 1962).

HARTMAN, G. H., *Wordsworth's Poetry: 1787–1814* (Cambridge, Mass., 1964; repr. 1987).

——'Adam on the Grass with Balsamum', *English Literary History*, 36 (1969), 168–92.

——*Beyond Formalism: Literary Essays, 1958–1970* (New Haven, Conn., 1970).

HARVEY, K. J., 'The Trouble about Merlin: The Theme of Enchantment in "The Eve of St Agnes"' *Keats–Shelley Journal*, 34 (1985), 83–94.

HAVENS, R. D., *The Influence of Milton on English Poetry* (Cambridge, Mass., 1922).

HAYLEY, W., *An Essay on Epic Poetry (1782) by William Hayley*; fac. reprod., with introd. by M. C. Williamson, SSJ (Gainesville, Fla., 1968).

——*The Life of Milton* (2nd edn., 1796); fac. reprod., with introd. by J. A. Wittreich, Jr. (Gainesville, Fla., 1970).

HAZLITT, W., *Selected Writings*, ed. with introd. R. Blythe (Harmondsworth, Middx., 1970).

——*The Spirit of the Age*, ed. E. D. Mackerness (London, 1969).

HILL, C., *Puritanism and Revolution* (Harmondsworth, Middx., 1958).

——*Antichrist in Seventeenth-Century England* (Oxford, 1971).

—— *The World Turned Upside Down: Radical Ideas during the English Revolution* (Harmondsworth, Middx., 1972; repr. 1984).

——*Milton and the English Revolution* (London, 1977).

HOGG, J., *The Private Memoirs and Confessions of a Justified Sinner*, ed. with introd. J. Carey (London, 1969).

HOGLE, J. E., *Shelley's Process: Radical Transference and the Development of his Major Works* (New York, 1988).

HOLLANDER, J., *The Figure of Echo: A Mode of Allusion in Milton and After* (Berkeley, Calif., 1981).

HOLUB, R. C., *Reception Theory: A Critical Introduction* (London, 1984).

HUGHES, M., *Ten Perspectives on Milton* (New Haven, Conn., 1964).

ISER, W., *The Act of Reading: A Theory of Aesthetic Response* (London, 1978).

——*Laurence Sterne: Tristram Shandy* (Cambridge, 1988).

JACOBUS, M., *Tradition and Experiment in Wordsworth's 'Lyrical Ballads', 1798* (Oxford, 1976).

——*Romanticism, Writing, and Sexual Difference: Essays on 'The Prelude'* (Oxford, 1989).

JARVIS, R., *Wordsworth, Milton and the Theory of Poetic Relations* (Basingstoke, 1991).

JAUSS, H. R., *Toward an Aesthetic of Reception*, trans. T. Bahti, introd. P. de Man (Minnesota, Minn., 1982).

JOHNSON, S., *Lives of the English Poets*, ed. G. B. Hill (3 vols., Oxford, 1905).

——*Yale Edition of the Works of Samuel Johnson* (16 vols., New Haven, Conn., 1958–80); xvi, *Rasselas and Other Tales*, ed. G. J. Kolb (1980).

JONES, J., *John Keats's Dream of Truth* (London, 1969).

JORDAN, J. E. (ed.), *De Quincey as Critic* (London, 1973).

KANT, I., *The Critique of Judgement*, trans. with analytical indexes, J. C. Meredith (Oxford, 1952; repr. 1978).

KEATS, J., *The Poems of John Keats*, ed. M. Allott (London, 1970).

——*Letters of John Keats*, a selection, ed. R. Gittings (Oxford, 1970).

KNAPP, S., *Personification and the Sublime: Milton to Coleridge* (Cambridge, Mass., 1985).

KNIGHT, R. P., *An Analytical Inquiry into the Principles of Taste* (London, 1805).

LAMB, C., *The Letters of Charles and Mary Lamb*, ed. E. W. Marrs, Jr. (3 vols., Ithaca, NY, 1975).

——*Lamb as Critic*, ed. R. Park (London, 1980).

——*Elia and the Last Essays of Elia*, ed. with introd. J. Bate (Oxford, 1987).

LANDY, M., 'Kinship and the Role of Women in *Paradise Lost*', *Milton Studies*, 4 (1972), 3–18.

LARRISSY, E., *William Blake* (Oxford, 1985).

LAUDER, Revd W., *An Essay on Milton's Use and Imitation of the Moderns, in his Paradise Lost* (London, 1749).

LAUDER, REVD W., *King Charles I Vindicated from the Charge of Plagiarism brought against him by Milton, and Milton himself convicted of Forgery* (London, 1754).

LEVINSON, M., *The Romantic Fragment Poem: A Critique of a Form* (Chapel Hill, NC, 1986).

LEWALSKI, B. K., 'Milton on Women—Yet Once More', *Milton Studies*, 6 (1974), 3–20.

——*'Paradise Lost' and the Rhetoric of Literary Forms* (Princeton, NJ, 1985).

LEWIS, C. S., *A Preface to 'Paradise Lost'* (Oxford, 1942; repr. 1979).

LIPKING, L. (ed.), *High Romantic Argument: Essays for M. H. Abrams* (Ithaca, NY, 1981).

LOCKE, J., *An Essay Concerning Human Understanding*, ed. with introd. P. H. Nidditch (Oxford, 1975).

LODGE, D. (ed.), *Modern Criticism and Theory: A Reader* (London, 1988).

LOWTH, Bishop, *Lectures on the Sacred Poetry of the Hebrews* (2 vols., London, 1787).

McCOLLEY, D. K., *Milton's Eve* (Urbana, Ill., 1983).

McFARLAND, T., *Romanticism and the Forms of Ruin: Wordsworth, Coleridge, and Modalities of Fragmentation* (Princeton, NJ, 1981).

——*Originality and Imagination* (Baltimore, 1985).

McGANN, J., *Fiery Dust: Byron's Poetic Development* (Chicago, 1968).

——*'Don Juan' in Context* (Chicago, 1976).

——*The Romantic Ideology: A Critical Investigation* (Chicago, 1983).

McKUSICK, J. C., *Coleridge's Philosophy of Language* (New Haven, Conn., 1986).

McNIECE, G., *Shelley and the Revolutionary Idea* (Cambridge, Mass., 1969).

MARTZ, L. L. (ed.), *Milton: A Collection of Critical Essays* (Englewood Cliffs, NJ, 1966).

MATURIN, C., *Melmoth the Wanderer*, ed. with introd. A. Hayter (Harmondsworth, Middx., 1977).

MELLOR, A. K., *English Romantic Irony* (Cambridge, Mass., 1980).

——*Mary Shelley: Her Life, Her Fiction, Her Monsters* (New York, 1988).

——(ed.), *Romanticism and Feminism* (Bloomington, Ind., 1988).

MILLER, D., BRACHER, M., and AULT, D. (eds.), *Critical Paths: Blake and the Argument of Method* (Durham, 1987).

MILTON, J., *The Complete Prose Works of John Milton*, gen. ed. D. Wolfe (8 vols. in 10, New Haven, Conn., 1953–82).

——*Complete Shorter Poems*, ed. J. Carey (London, 1968).

——*Paradise Lost*, ed. A. Fowler (London, 1968).

MOLLENKOTT, V. R., 'Milton's Technique of Multiple Choice', *Milton Studies*, 6 (1974), 101–11.

MOORE, L. E., *Beautiful Sublime: The Making of 'Paradise Lost', 1701–1734* (Stanford, Calif., 1990).

NELSON, J., *The Sublime Puritan: Milton and the Victorians* (Madison, Wis., 1963).

NEVE, P., *Cursory Remarks on some of the Ancient English Poets, particularly Milton* (London, 1789).

NEWLYN, L., '"In City Pent": Echo and Allusion in Wordsworth, Coleridge and Lamb, 1797–1801', *Review of English Studies*, n.s. 32 (Nov. 1981), 408–28.

——*Coleridge, Wordsworth, and the Language of Allusion* (Oxford, 1986).

——'For the Fallen', review article in *The Times Literary Supplement*, 8 Aug. 1986.

NEWTON, T. (ed.), *Paradise Lost* (2 vols., London, 1749).

NYQUIST, M., and FERGUSON, M. W. (eds.), *Re-Membering Milton: Essays on the Texts and Traditions* (New York, 1988).

PAINE, T., *The Thomas Paine Reader*, ed. M. Foot and I. Kramnick (Harmondsworth, Middx., 1987).

PALEY, M. D., *Energy and the Imagination: A Study of the Development of Blake's Thought* (Oxford, 1970).

PAULSON, R., *Representations of Revolution (1789–1820)* (New Haven, Conn., 1983).

PERRI, C., 'On Alluding', *Poetics*, 7 (1978), 289–307.

PETER, J., *A Critique of 'Paradise Lost'* (Columbia, NY, 1960).

PIPER, H. W., *The Active Universe: Pantheism and the Concept of Imagination in the English Romantic Poets* (London, 1962).

POPE, A., *The Twickenham Edition of the Poems of Alexander Pope*, gen. ed. J. Butt (11 vols., London, 1961–9).

——*The Poems of Alexander Pope*, a 1–vol. edn. of the *Twickenham Pope*, ed. J. Butt (Bungay, Suffolk, 1963; repr. 1980).

——*Correspondence of Pope*, ed. G. Sherburn (5 vols., Oxford, 1956).

PRICKETT, S., *Words and The Word: Language, Poetics and Biblical Interpretation* (Cambridge, 1986).

PUNTER, D., *The Romantic Unconscious: A Study in Narcissism and Patriarchy* (New York, 1989).

RAJAN, B., *'Paradise Lost' and the Seventeenth-Century Reader* (London, 1947).

——(ed.), *'Paradise Lost': A Tercentenary Tribute* (Toronto, 1969).

——*The Form of the Unfinished: English Poetics from Spenser to Pound* (Princeton, NJ, 1985).

RAJAN, T., *Dark Interpreter: The Discourse of Romanticism* (Ithaca, NY, 1980).

RICHARDSON, J., *Explanatory Notes and Remarks on Milton's Paradise Lost* (London, 1734).

RICKS, C., *Milton's Grand Style* (Oxford, 1963; repr. 1983).

——'Allusion: The Poet as Heir', in R. F. Brissenden and J. C. Eade (eds.), *Studies in the Eighteenth Century*, iii (Canberra, 1976), 209–40.

ROE, N., *Wordsworth and Coleridge: the Radical Years* (Oxford, 1988).

ROSTON, M., *Prophet and Poet: The Bible and the Growth of Romanticism* (London, 1965).

RUOFF, G. W., *Wordsworth and Coleridge: the Making of the Major Lyrics, 1802–1804* (New Brunswick, NJ, 1989).

RZEPKA, C. J., *The Self as Mind: Vision and Identity in Wordsworth, Coleridge and Keats* (Cambridge, Mass., 1986).

SACKS, S., (ed.), *On Metaphor* (Chicago, 1979).

SAGE, V. (ed.), *The Gothick Novel* (Basingstoke, 1990).

SCHULZ, M., *Paradise Preserved: Recreations of Eden in Eighteenth- and Nineteenth-Century England* (Cambridge, 1985).

SHARROCK, R., 'Godwin on Milton's Satan', *Notes and Queries*, n.s. 9 (Dec. 1962), 463–5.

SHAWCROSS, J. (ed.), *Milton 1732–1801: The Critical Heritage* (London, 1969).

SHELLEY, M., *Frankenstein* (London, 1976).

——*The Mary Shelley Reader*, ed. B. Bennett and C. E. Robinson (Oxford, 1990).

SHELLEY, P. B., *Shelley's Prose, or, The Trumpet of a Prophecy*, ed. with introd. and notes, D. L. Clark (Albuquerque, N. Mex., 1954; corrected edn., 1966).

——*Shelley's Poetry and Prose*, selected and ed. D. H. Reiman and S. B. Powers (New York, 1977).

SHERWIN, P., *Precious Bane: Collins and the Miltonic Legacy* (Austin, Tex., 1977).

SHOAF, R. A., *Milton, Poet of Duality: A Study of Semiosis in the Poetry and the Prose* (New Haven, Conn., 1985).

SISKIN, C., *The Historicity of Romantic Discourse* (New York, 1988).

SMITH, O., *The Politics of Language, 1791–1819* (Oxford, 1984).

SPATZ, J., 'The Mystery of Eros: Sexual Initiation in Coleridge's "Christabel"', *PMLA* 90/1 (Jan. 1975), 107–16.

SPERRY, S., 'Keats, Milton and the Fall of Hyperion', *PMLA* 77/1 (1962), 77–84.

STEIN, E., *Wordsworth's Art of Allusion* (University Park, Pa., 1988).

STEVENS, P., *Imagination and the Presence of Shakespeare in 'Paradise Lost'* (Madison, Wis., 1985).

STILLINGER, J., 'The Hoodwinking of Madeline: Scepticism in "The Eve of St Agnes"', *Studies in Philology*, 58 (July 1961), 533–55.

THOMSON, J., *'The Seasons' and 'The Castle of Indolence'*, ed. J. Sambrook (Oxford, 1972).

THORPE, J., *Milton Criticism: Selections from Four Centuries* (London, 1951).

TILLYARD, E. M. W., *Studies in Milton* (London, 1951; repr. 1973).

TYSDAHL, B. J., *William Godwin as Novelist* (London, 1981).

VOGLER, T., *Preludes to Vision: The Epic Venture in Blake, Wordsworth, Keats and Hart Crane* (Berkeley, Calif., 1971).

WALDOCK, A. J. A., *'Paradise Lost' and its Critics* (Cambridge, 1947).

WALKER, J. (ed.), *Milton and the Idea of Woman* (Urbana, Ill., 1988).

WASSERMAN, E., 'The Limits of Allusion in *The Rape of the Lock*', *Journal of English and German Philology*, 65 (1966), 425–44.

——*Shelley: A Critical Reading* (Baltimore, 1971).

WATSON, J. R. (ed.), *Pre-Romanticism in English Poetry of the Eighteenth Century* (Basingstoke, 1989).

WEBB, T., *Shelley: A Voice not Understood* (Manchester, 1977).

WEBBER, J. M., 'The Politics of Poetry: Feminism and *Paradise Lost*', *Milton Studies*, 14 (1980), 3–24.

WEISKEL, T., *The Romantic Sublime: Studies in the Structure and Psychology of Transcendence* (Baltimore, 1976).

WHEELER, K. M., *The Creative Mind in Coleridge's Poetry* (London, 1981).

WIENER, D., 'The Secularization of the Fortunate Fall in Keats's "The Eve of St Agnes"', *Keats–Shelley Journal*, 29 (1980), 120–30.

WILLIAMSON, G., 'Milton the Anti-Romantic', *Modern Philology*, 60 (1962), 13–21.

WITTGENSTEIN, L., *Philosophical Investigations*, trans. G. E. M. Anscombe (Oxford, 1958; repr. 1963).

WITTREICH, J. A., Jr., 'The "Satanism" of Blake and Shelley Reconsidered', *Studies in Philology*, 65 (1968), 816–33.

——(ed.), *The Romantics on Milton: Formal Essays and Critical Asides* (Cleveland, 1970).

——*Angel of Apocalypse: Blake's Idea of Milton* (Madison, Wis., 1975).

——(ed.), *Milton and the Line of Vision* (Madison, Wis., 1975).

——*Visionary Poetics: Milton's Tradition and his Legacy* (San Marino, Calif., 1979).

——*Feminist Milton* (Ithaca, NY, 1987).

WOLLSTONECRAFT, M., *The Works of Mary Wollstonecraft*, ed. J. Todd and M. Butler (7 vols., London, 1989).

WORDEN, B., 'Milton's Republicanism and the Tyranny of Heaven' in G. Bock, Q. Skinner, and M. Viroli (eds.), *Machiavelli and Republicanism* (Cambridge, 1990).

WORDSWORTH, J. (ed.), *Bicentenary Wordsworth Studies in Memory of John Alban Finch* (Ithaca, NY, 1970).

——William Wordsworth: The Borders of Vision (Oxford, 1982).

WORDSWORTH, W., *The Poetical Works of William Wordsworth*, ed. E. De Selincourt (5 vols., Oxford, 1940).

——*The Letters of William and Dorothy Wordsworth*, ed. E. De Selincourt: *The Early Years, 1787–1805*, rev. C. L. Shaver (Oxford, 1967); *The Middle Years, 1806–11*, rev. M. Moorman and A. C. Hill (Oxford, 1970).

——*The Prose Works of William Wordsworth*, ed. W. J. B. Owen and J. W. Smyser (3 vols., Oxford, 1974).

——*The Prelude, 1799, 1805, 1850*, ed. J. Wordsworth, M. H. Abrams, and S. Gill (New York, 1979).

——*The Borderers*, ed. R. Osborn (Ithaca, NY, 1982).

——*William Wordsworth*, selected and ed. S. Gill (Oxford, 1984).

WORTON, M., and STILL, J. (eds.), *Intertextuality: Theories and Practices* (Manchester, 1990).

WYLIE, I., *Young Coleridge and the Philosophers of Nature* (Oxford, 1989).

YOUNG, E., *Conjectures on Original Composition in a Letter to the Author of Sir Charles Grandison* (London, 1759).

Index